Unlikely Dissenters

UNIVERSITY PRESS OF FLORIDA

Florida A&M University, Tallahassee
Florida Atlantic University, Boca Raton
Florida Gulf Coast University, Ft. Myers
Florida International University, Miami
Florida State University, Tallahassee
New College of Florida, Sarasota
University of Central Florida, Orlando
University of Florida, Gainesville
University of North Florida, Jacksonville
University of South Florida, Tampa
University of West Florida, Pensacola

Unlikely Dissenters

White Southern Women in
the Fight for Racial Justice, 1920–1970

ANNE STEFANI

University Press of Florida
Gainesville · Tallahassee · Tampa · Boca Raton
Pensacola · Orlando · Miami · Jacksonville · Ft. Myers · Sarasota

Copyright 2015 by Anne Stefani
All rights reserved
Printed in the United States of America on acid-free paper

This book may be available in an electronic edition.

22 21 20 19 18 17   6 5 4 3 2 1

First cloth printing, 2015
First paperback printing, 2017

Library of Congress Cataloging-in-Publication Data
Stefani, Anne, author.
Unlikely dissenters : white southern women in the fight for racial justice, 1920–1970 / Anne Stefani.
pages cm
Includes bibliographical references and index.
ISBN 978-0-8130-6076-7 (cloth)
ISBN 978-0-8130-5465-0 (pbk.)
1. Women, White—Political activity—Southern States—History—20th century. 2. Women civil rights workers—Southern States—History—20th century. 3. Women—Southern States—History—20th century. 4. Southern States—Social life and customs. 5. Women political activists—Southern States—History—20th century. 6. African Americans—Civil rights—Southern States—History—20th century. I. Title.
F220.A1S74 2015
320.08207509'04—dc23
2015004617

The University Press of Florida is the scholarly publishing agency for the State University System of Florida, comprising Florida A&M University, Florida Atlantic University, Florida Gulf Coast University, Florida International University, Florida State University, New College of Florida, University of Central Florida, University of Florida, University of North Florida, University of South Florida, and University of West Florida.

University Press of Florida
15 Northwest 15th Street
Gainesville, FL 32611-2079
http://upress.ufl.edu

Contents

List of Figures vii

Acknowledgments ix

List of Abbreviations xiii

Introduction 1

1. Profiles: Two Generations, One Identity 12
2. Before *Brown*: Southern Lady Activism 57
3. After *Brown*, Part One: The Tactics of Respectability 97
4. After *Brown*, Part Two: Open Confrontation 134
5. The 1960s Movement: Modern Abolitionists 179
6. A Peculiar Brand of Feminism 217

   Conclusion 251

   Appendix: Selected Biographical Sketches 255

   Notes 267

   Bibliography 307

   Index 323

Figures

Figures follow page 166.

1. Dorothy Rogers Tilly, n.d.
2. Juliette Hampton Morgan, circa 1935
3. Lillian E. Smith, 1944
4. Margaret Long, 1950
5. Nan Pendergrast, "Thrower for Congress" tea, 1956
6. Women's Emergency Committee to Open Our Schools members, 1963
7. Anne Braden and Ella Baker, n.d.
8. Anne Braden, SCEF office, n.d.
9. Frances Freeborn Pauley, Fisk University Race Relations Seminar, 1961
10. Joan C. Browning, Fisk University Race Relations Seminar, 1962
11. Margaret Burr Leonard, Freedom Rider, 1961
12. Joan Trumpauer Mulholland, Freedom Rider, 1961
13. Joan C. Browning, 1962
14. Dorothy Dawson Burlage, n.d.
15. Constance Curry, 1973
16. Sara Mitchell Parsons and Angela Davis, 1977
17. Casey Hayden, 1988
18. Mary E. King, 2013
19. Margaret Burr Leonard, 2008
20. Joan C. Browning and Joan Trumpauer Mulholland, 2011
21. Four friends commemorating the 1960s struggle (Patricia A. Jarvis, Joan C. Browning, Faye Powell, and Cinda Kinsey), 2012
22. Nan Pendergrast, circa 2010
23. Virginia Foster Durr and her four daughters, 1993

Acknowledgments

The present book would never have existed without the work, help, and support of a myriad of people I have met since I embarked on this research project and even earlier. Although I cannot thank them all by name, I want to express my gratitude to every one of them.

First on the list are the many librarians and archivists who always welcomed and helped me in every possible way to facilitate my work. It has been a true pleasure to do research in the conditions they created for me. The adventure started a very long time ago at the Hargrett Rare Book and Manuscript Library of the University of Georgia; the Manuscript, Archives, and Rare Book Library (MARBL) of Emory University; and the Southern Historical Collection at the Louis Round Wilson Special Collections Library of the University of North Carolina (UNC) at Chapel Hill, when I first conducted research on Lillian Smith and white southern liberalism. It was at UNC I met the American scholars who introduced me to the fascinating field of southern studies. I thank Fred Hobson, John Shelton Reed, and Joel Williamson for generously sharing their scholarly expertise with the student I was then—my very first inspiration being Michel Bandry, who became a colleague and friend. After finishing my Ph.D. and working for several years on other related subjects, I returned to my original favorite concern, white southern womanhood, which took me to the Schlesinger Library at the Radcliffe Institute for Advanced Studies; to the Wisconsin Historical Society at Madison; to MARBL at Emory University again; to the King Library and Archives at the Martin Luther King, Jr. Center for Nonviolent Social Change; to the Archives and Special Collections, Woodruff Library, at Atlanta University Center; to the Special Collections Department at Georgia State University; and to the Caroliniana Library Archives at the University of South Carolina. Wherever I went, the people I met provided invaluable advice and assistance, before, during, and after my stays. Without their help I would not have been able to complete this research. They were all the more precious to me since, living in France, I could not visit archives and libraries as often as I wanted to. I am also grateful to two archivists I never met, but who helped from a distance, Laura Caldwell Anderson, of the Birmingham Civil Rights Institute, who provided contact information for people I wanted to interview, and Stephen Gateley, of the Scarritt-Bennett Center, who kindly found and gave me a missing piece of biographical information I could not obtain from France.

My gratitude then goes to the women I had the opportunity to interview, and to others I could not meet but who kindly agreed to spend time and energy completing a questionnaire, or corresponding with me by mail. I treasure these personal contributions as the greatest strength of the book. Here I must thank Joan C. Browning, Dorothy Dawson Burlage, Connie Curry, Doris A. Derby, Virginia "Tilla" Durr, Margaret Rose Gladney, Casey Hayden, Patricia Jarvis-Sulgit, Jeannette King (and Rev. Ed King who put me in contact with her), Mary E. King, Margaret Burr Leonard, Sheila Michaels, Joan Trumpauer Mulholland, Nan Pendergrast, Faye Powell, Patricia Sullivan, Sue Thrasher, and Eileen Walbert. My deepest appreciation goes to Connie Curry and Joan Browning. Connie, Joan—I feel so fortunate to have become acquainted with you. It is such a privilege to have shared your memories and the spirit of the 1960s movement. Connie, thanks ever so much for welcoming me so generously to Atlanta after I first contacted you, and for introducing me to other civil rights movement veterans, including Joan. Joan, I will never find the right words to thank you for what you did for me: you turned what had started as conventional research work into an exhilarating human adventure.

It was especially important for me to find illustrations reflecting the richness and variety of my subject—my core sample comprising approximately thirty women. I wanted the public to discover as many faces as possible of these extraordinary women. Although it unfortunately proved impossible to collect all the pictures I sought, the ones I did manage to gather testify to the thread of continuity between the two generations, running from the 1920s to the early twenty-first century. Here again, I owe much to a great number of people. I want to thank first the women who provided photos of themselves, Joan Browning, Dorothy Burlage, Connie Curry, Virginia "Tilla" Durr—who provided a wonderful picture of herself with her mother and her three sisters—Casey Hayden, Patricia Jarvis-Sulgit, Mary King, Cinda Kinsey, Margaret Leonard, Joan Mulholland, Nan Pendergrast, and Fay Powell. I also thank the known photographers of some photos who kindly granted permission to publish them: Eric Etheridge, Noah Friedman-Rudovsky, Michael Gaylord James, Carl McGrath, Autumn Shelton, and Penny Weaver. As far as the older generation is concerned, I am indebted to the women's relatives and friends, and, once more, to scholars, librarians, and archivists, who tracked down pictures for me: my gratitude goes to Laura Thrower Harris, Cliff Lyon, Perry Mitchell, Eason Jordan, Mark Pendergrast (and his parents, Nan and Britt, whom I was able to reach through him), and Margaret A. Rostker. I also thank Cate Fosl, Patrick O'Donnell, Mary Stanton, Craig Amason (of the Lillian Smith Center), Charles J. Barber (of the Hargrett Rare Book and Manuscript Library at the University of Georgia), Stephanie Bayless (of the Butler Center for Arkansas Studies), Anne Causey (of the Small Special Collections Library at the University of Virginia), Elizabeth Chase and Sara J. Logue (of MARBL at Emory University), Kate Collins (of the Rubenstein Library at Duke University), Deborah S. Davis (of Valdosta State University Archives and Special Collections), Sean Garrett (of the University of Georgia Press), Christopher Harter (of the Amistad Research Center), Marcia Leitch (virtual assistant), Lisa Marine and Simone Munson (of the Wisconsin Historical Society), Meredith McDonough (of the Alabama Department of Archives and History), Laura Peimer and Ellen Shea (of the Schlesinger Library at Radcliffe Institute), and Susan Williams (of the Highlander Research and Education Center). I am finally indebted to Patrick Besse and Isabelle Bonjean for their technical support with illustrations. Patrick and Isabelle, you performed miracles! I could never have processed these photographs on time without your precious assistance.

On my various research trips to the United States, American colleagues and friends were so helpful and hospitable they made me feel like I was almost on vacation. My last stay in Atlanta was fantastic. I must especially thank here Susan Ashley and Matthew Roudané, who warmly welcomed me to their wonderful home, drove me around Atlanta, and made me feel so comfortable it was hard to leave in the end; Michelle Brattain, who helped with the thorny issue of long-term accommodation; Katherine Hankins and John Ford and his family, who invited me to their houses for memorable dinners; and Lauren McIvor Johnson and her family, who hosted me for a wonderful weekend in Kentucky. I also want to thank Patricia Sullivan for spending time with me in Columbia, South Carolina, discussing my research in such a stimulating way. Thank you, Pat, for your invaluable advice, and for your ongoing support to this day.

I am also indebted to many people on my side of the Atlantic. I am grateful to my research center at the University of Toulouse-Jean Jaurès, the CAS (Cultures Anglo-Saxonnes), for funding my research trip to Atlanta in 2010. A few people stand out among all those who helped. Two friends put their expertise to the service of the long writing process. Both carefully read the first and the revised versions of the manuscript. Nathalie Dessens provided precious advice on the contents while Sheryl Rahal edited the text. I am obliged to you, Nathalie and Sheryl, for your patience, your availability, and your unflinching support. You believed in me when I did not. I am ever grateful for this. Several native English speakers contributed to polishing my writing or improving the manuscript at various stages of the publication process. Thanks to Ken Aslakson, Joan Browning (again . . .), Wendy Harding, and Sharon Iverson.

Finally, I want to dedicate this book to the people I love. I thank Olivier, my longtime partner, for sharing all the joys and pains related to the writing of this book, as well as my parents and brother for their unconditional support. I also thank all the members of Olivier's family, with a very special thought for Pierre, who would have been so happy to hold this volume in his hands.

Abbreviations

AFSC	American Friends Service Committee
ASWPL	Association of Southern Women for the Prevention of Lynching
CHR	Council on Human Relations
CIC	Commission on Interracial Cooperation
CIO	Congress of Industrial Relations
CORE	Congress of Racial Equality
FOC	Fellowship of the Concerned
HOPE	Help Our Public Education
HUAC	House Un-American Activities Committee
LUAC	Louisiana Joint Legislative Committee on Un-American Activities
LWV	League of Women Voters
MFDP	Mississippi Freedom Democratic Party
NAACP	National Association for the Advancement of Colored People
NACW	National Association of Colored Women
NAG	Nonviolent Action Group
NCAHUAC	National Committee to Abolish the House Un-American Activities Committee
NCAPT	National Committee to Abolish the Poll Tax
NCJW	National Council of Jewish Women
NCNW	National Council of Negro Women

NOW	National Organization for Women
NSA	National Student Association
PAW	Panel of American Women
PCCR	President's Committee on Civil Rights
SCEF	Southern Conference Educational Fund
SCHW	Southern Conference for Human Welfare
SCLC	Southern Christian Leadership Conference
SDS	Students for a Democratic Society
SISS	Senate Internal Security Subcommittee
SNCC	Student Nonviolent Coordinating Committee
SOS	Save Our Schools
SRC	Southern Regional Council
SSOC	Southern Student Organizing Committee
UCW	United Church Women
VCPS	Virginia Committee for Public Schools
WEC	Women's Emergency Committee to Open Our Schools
YWCA	Young Women's Christian Association

Introduction

In 1962, Sandra "Casey" Hayden, a white staff member of the Student Nonviolent Coordinating Committee (SNCC), attended the trial of Freedom Riders in Albany, Georgia. She was with her husband, Tom Hayden. During the trial, Charles Sherrod, a SNCC black leader, entered the courtroom and sat in the white section to challenge the segregationist etiquette. After the police dragged Sherrod out of the room, Casey and her husband moved to sit in the "colored" section of the courtroom. They resisted as the police asked them to move back to their side, and Casey recalls, "I hooked my legs under the bench so that they had to pry me out sideways." The police were not the least impressed by her race and gender, although, she adds, "Ever the young lady, I wore white gloves."[1] The apparent incongruity in Casey Hayden's testimony tells much about the subject of the research presented here.

This work focuses on a very special brand of white southerners, the minority of white women who lived in a white supremacist society but rejected the segregationist system and contributed to its demise from the 1920s to the 1960s. These women lived in different times and places, but they can be considered together as a specific group of the white southern population during the segregation era. Their collective identity was primarily conditioned by their race and gender because it was shaped by the white supremacist doctrine placing white women at the core of regional identity. As members of the white southern community, they belonged to the "oppressor" group. Yet as women in a conservative, patriarchal society, they could also be considered "victims," which made their condition unique. This study analyzes how the women concerned coped with this paradox. It argues that their double identity as both "oppressors" and "victims" forced them to confront their native culture against their will by developing a unique form of racial activism and breaking free from white supremacist culture. Their paradoxical status was reinforced by the fact that, being white women, they were not likely to become racial dissenters, the ideal of the "southern lady" prevailing in the regional culture throughout the segregation era. Part of their uniqueness resided in their dissenting from southern norms with manners, just as Casey Hayden did in the Albany courtroom as late as 1962. These women rebelled against their native culture while conforming to southern standards of respectability. Many were, in fact, reluctant dissenters insofar as they were deeply attached to the South and suffered from antagonizing it. Their rejection of white supremacy went along with a constant inner struggle between their personal values and their sense of community, between an urge to act according to principle and at the same time a need to be understood and accepted by other white southerners. However, in choosing to dissent by committing their adult lives to the struggle against racism, they emancipated themselves as white southerners and, ultimately, as women.

White southern women have interested scholars for decades, but there is, to this day, no comprehensive monograph covering the subject of white southern antiracist women activists between the 1920s and the 1960s. In 1970, Anne Firor Scott's groundbreaking study, *The Southern Lady: From Pedestal to Politics, 1830–1930*, examined the fate of middle- and upper-class white women in the South from the slavery era to the early twentieth century, testing the ideal of white southern womanhood against the reality of southern society. In 1979, Jacquelyn Dowd Hall's *Revolt against Chivalry: Jessie Daniel Ames and the Association of Southern Women for the Prevention of Lynching* further probed the issue of white southern womanhood by analyzing in depth the interconnection of race and gender in segregationist society as crystallized by lynching and white women's organized fight against it in the South of the 1930s. A number of scholars have explored the issue of southern womanhood since the publication of these pioneering works. In the wake of the civil rights movement and of the women's liberation movement, analysts and commentators first proceeded to re-place women in American history, while deepening the definition of women's identity. Different subgroups soon emerged from the reflection on American women's experience, bringing to light a variety of factors in the shaping of female identity. Region and race stand out as paramount among them. Like Scott and Hall before them, most scholars of the 1980s identified the fundamental difference between black and white southern women created by slavery, and focused their research accordingly on one or the other of the two groups.² From the 1990s on, however, while the interconnectedness of race, gender, and class became central to interpretive analysis, historians went on to examine black and white women in a new light, emphasizing not only the interaction between them but also their interaction with men of both racial groups. The importance of class in the shaping of all identities and relations also drew increasing attention. The evolution of Anne Scott's and Jacquelyn Hall's works reflects this epistemological turn. In an article published in 1990 in the *Journal of Southern History*, Scott admitted to having denounced the invisibility of women in American historiography in the mid-1980s while ignoring the experience and role of black women in her own work. Similarly, in 1993 Hall published a revised edition of *Revolt against Chivalry*, regretting in the preface not having paid sufficient attention to black women.³ The rise of race studies and gender studies after 1990 testifies to the new emphasis scholars have placed on the concepts of interconnectedness and interaction, affecting both the historiography of women and that of the civil rights movement. In the past two decades, historians have revisited the civil rights movement by analyzing the combination of factors at work in its development. The place of women in the struggle for racial equality has become a major research topic.⁴ The works published since the mid-1990s, whether dealing with white women, black women, or both, systematically take into account the factors of race, gender, and class in their interpretations. More specifically, they analyze black and white women's experiences in relation to each other, crossing perspectives, and pointing out the converging and diverging elements of the two groups within the same historical framework. Such is the case, for instance, of Glenda Gilmore's *Gender and Jim Crow: Women and the Politics of White Supremacy in North Carolina, 1896–1920* (1996), of Belinda Robnett's *How Long? How Long? African American Women in the Struggle for Civil Rights* (1997), of Lynne Olson's *Freedom's Daughters: The Unsung Heroines of the Civil Rights Movement* (2001), of Joan Marie Johnson's *Southern Ladies, New Women: Race, Region, and Clubwomen in South Carolina, 1890–1930* (2004), of Christina Greene's *Our Separate Ways: Women and the Black Freedom Movement in Durham, North Carolina* (2005), and of Shannon Frystak's *Our Minds on Freedom: Women and the Struggle for Black Equality in Louisiana, 1924–1967* (2009).

A number of books published in the last decade deal specifically with white southern women reformers during the segregation and/or civil rights eras, which is the subject of this research. One of them, *Throwing Off the Cloak of Privilege* (2004), a collection of essays edited by Gail Murray, illuminates the richness and variety of white female racial activism in the segregated South by examining a number of emblematic individuals and groups. Biographies and monographs have also placed a few of these women in perspective in the struggle against segregation. Some authors have focused on individuals; others have limited their studies to local groups, or to specific states or cities.[5] The present study builds on the recent scholarship by providing a comprehensive view of this peculiar brand of women who struggled for racial equality in their native region from the 1920s to the late 1960s. It brings to light in one volume the distinctive features that characterized a small but significant number of white women raised in the South who rejected white supremacy without rejecting their southern identity at a time when southern politicians and opinion leaders presented segregation as the "southern way of life." It weaves together a multiplicity of converging trajectories, evidencing the existence of a clearly identifiable subgroup in southern segregated society. It analyzes the evolution of these women's collective identity between 1920 and 1970, showing in particular how they redefined their place and role in white supremacist society through their racial activism. Given the interconnection of race and gender in their experience as white women, the analysis hinges primarily on their interaction with black women, black men, and white men.

The study covers five decades, from the end of World War I to the late 1960s. The period under examination is split into two parts, the first half extending from the 1920s to the mid-1950s, the second covering the modern civil rights movement from the mid-1950s to the late 1960s. The U.S. Supreme Court decision in the *Brown v. Board of Education* case, which in 1954 declared school segregation unconstitutional and in 1955 ordered the states to desegregate their school systems "with all deliberate speed," is a landmark in the history of the South. It is also a pivotal moment in the history of white southern women reformers. The decade between the *Brown* decision and the Voting Rights Act of 1965 is actually a key period regarding the present subject inasmuch as it brought together two generations of women sharing a significant number of cultural characteristics, who were all deeply disturbed by segregation, but differed in their approaches to the issue. The present work demonstrates how the 1960s—that is, the last part of the period covered here—marked the culmination of decades of behind-the-scenes activism involving thousands of anonymous white southern women, led by a few more visible, but hardly recognized "leaders."

The women who constitute the main sample of the study—approximately thirty cases—and the thousands of others who were members of women's organizations active during the period under study can be divided into two generations, the term "generation" being used here in a broad sense. The women in the older generation were born at the beginning of the segregation era, between the late nineteenth century and World War I. They reached full maturity during the Great Depression and were still active when the desegregation crisis started in the late 1950s. These women had to adjust throughout their lives to the evolution of southern society from segregation to desegregation. The younger generation was born closer to World War II (mostly in the late 1930s and early 1940s). Its representatives came of age in the 1950s and early 1960s, in the midst of the crisis, and joined the civil rights movement straightaway. A few individuals do not fit into these two broad generational categories, either because they were born in between or because they were born into one generation but were closer to the other in their approach to segregation. These cases can be considered as bridging the two groups.

The concept of a "long civil rights movement"—expanding the boundaries of the civil rights movement beyond the classic 1954–68 periodization—proved an especially useful analytical tool for this research. Jacquelyn Dowd Hall, author of an important essay on the subject in 2005, had already paved the way in 1979 for this new interpretive approach with her study of Jessie Daniel Ames and her Association of Southern Women for the Prevention of Lynching.[6] The concept provides historians with a broader perspective and with the opportunity to include in the civil rights movement new individuals and groups whose contribution had not been recognized so far. Several scholars have brought to light the crucial role of pre-*Brown* organizations in preparing the ground for the modern civil rights movement.[7] The older generation profiled in this book fits into this frame. While Hall and many contemporary historians trace the roots of the "long civil rights movement" back to the 1930s—when the New Deal favored the growth of liberal and radical movements—I take the 1920s as a starting point, for it was in that decade that white southern women reformers first engaged in biracial cooperation. Moreover, although some women remained active in the struggle for social justice well into the late twentieth century, thus confirming the relevance of enlarging the scope of the civil rights movement through the 1970s, this study does not extend beyond 1970, its subject being limited to the legally segregated South that officially died in the mid-1960s. Thus it is not so much the time frame of the long civil rights movement as the idea of a "more expansive story," as Hall puts it, that serves the present research.[8] Such a conceptual tool helps illuminate the connection between the two generations studied here. It provides an encompassing frame as well as a valuable argumentative thread between the pre-*Brown* and the post-*Brown* eras. Because the two generations seem so different in kind, one can only highlight elements of continuity between them by adopting a longer view and a broader perspective. In her essay, Hall also expands the classic historiographical narrative by applying the paradigms of race, class, and gender to her analysis, thus following the latest epistemological trends. While the three paradigms are relevant to my subject, this research shows that, in the case of white southern women reformers of the long civil rights era, race, gender, and region were more determining than class in the shaping of their identity.

The South on which the research is grounded is the historic South, comprising the ex–slave states that reasserted their regional identity after the abolition of slavery by enacting segregation laws at the turn of the twentieth century. Although the women considered here lived in a great variety of places across the region, from border to Deep South states, from rural to urban areas, and belonged to various social backgrounds, their identities were all shaped by the same white supremacist culture. Thus the South constituting the framework of this book should be primarily understood in cultural terms, even if the social and political aspects of segregation are an obvious part of the whole picture. Although the reality of segregation varied from one southern place to another and various degrees of racial oppression existed across the region, the women examined here learned the same white supremacist lessons buttressing segregation, or the "southern way of life," which determined their life experiences. They obviously had very different trajectories owing to the periods and contexts in which they were born. Yet as white women in the segregated South, they shared the same cultural background.

The analysis first concentrates on the main common characteristics singling white women out as a distinctive component of southern society during the segregation era. The most fundamental feature was that, despite their differences, they all had to deal with the ideal of the "southern lady" that prevailed in southern society and culture throughout the era. Another characteristic they shared without exception was the major influence of religion on their lives and outlooks. Religion was a central element of their education and played a key role in their realization, at some point in their lives, of the discrepancy between the values they had learned to uphold in their youth and the reality of segregation. For most of them, this realization led to a break with family and community, with some form of estrangement from their native environment.

After identifying the common factors conditioning these women's collective identity, the book examines their evolution throughout the segregation and desegregation eras. Starting from heavily paternalistic efforts at biracial cooperation in the 1920s, white women reformers became increasingly radical in their stance on segregation up to the *Brown* decision. After 1954, the two generations joined their efforts and influenced each other in open support of desegregation, the younger adopting an uncompromising, confrontational stance. The analysis shows that, whatever degree of radicalism they might have displayed, the two generations found in racial activism the means to liberate themselves from the constraints southern culture had imposed on them. The older generation built extensive female networks on which the next could rely for support in the 1950s and 1960s. Thus white female racial reformers gradually asserted themselves as a special brand of activists within their communities, acquiring a definite authority and influence during the desegregation crisis. If decades of network-building and solidarity in racial activism played a key role in the collective emancipation of white southern women, this experience can also be credited with providing them with the means to emancipate themselves as individuals. Because race and gender were so inextricably linked in the definition of their place and role in southern society, the white women who rejected racial norms were bound to subvert gender norms in the process. They did so to various degrees, the older generation remaining deeply attached to the ideal of the southern lady. Whatever the degree of conformity to the ideal that characterized them, however, the white women who struggled for racial justice throughout the segregation era submitted to prevailing social and gender norms only on the surface. Even those of the earlier generation who cultivated manners and respectability undermined the norms of white southern womanhood through their racial activities. As for the members of the younger generation, many of them developed an acute gender awareness during their involvement in the modern civil rights movement, and later became feminists while remaining highly sensitive to the articulation of race and gender in social relationships. As southern women, they continued to distinguish themselves from other American women. If their struggle against southern racism led them to emancipation from gender conformity, it also placed them at odds with the most radical trend of second-wave feminism since white women integrationists had long downplayed the question of their own gender oppression, deeming racism a more urgent issue. Thus the history of southern racial activism left its mark on the identity of white southern women, even after their personal emancipation.

The starting point of the research, a few years ago, was the reading of various autobiographies, memoirs, and biographies of white southern women, born and raised in the segregated South, who had participated in the long struggle against segregation between the 1920s and the 1960s. A first set of memoirs, written in the thick of the desegregation crisis, belonged to a larger group of autobiographical narratives written by male and female white southerners struggling with racial guilt in the midst of the desegregation crisis. Female authors strikingly distinguished themselves from their male counterparts by their scathing critique of white supremacy and of their native culture, presenting themselves as victims of a sick society. Only one of them, Lillian Smith, explicitly theorized about the interconnection of race, sex, and gender in segregationist culture and on the unique condition of white women in this culture, of which she was the incarnation. In the late twentieth and early twenty-first centuries, a second wave of white southern women recounted their personal experiences in the civil rights movement. This time, however, most of them associated their racial activism with their personal emancipation from southern patriarchy. In addition to autobiographical writings, several biographies have traced the peculiar racial activism of prominent white southern women during the segregation era. The activists profiled in the various works published so far constituted the initial sample of my study, suggesting the existence of great numbers of anonymous women sharing characteristics with them. Their personal papers, located in a large variety of universities and research centers, while providing further insight into their own experiences, revealed the presence of many lesser-known women presenting similar profiles across the South. These women had also dissented from white supremacy, participated in the same movements, belonged to the same organizations, and shared the same values and goals. In addition to personal papers, the records of the main organizations involved in racial and social reform between 1920 and 1970 testified to women's active role in the long civil rights movement. Several women could be added to the original sample because they had been members and/or officers of these organizations, and had left evidence of their activities. The archives also contained less extensive documentation on other women whose experiences strikingly resembled those of the core cases. The final sample, representing the two generations, all ex–slave states except Maryland, and the major organizations relevant to my subject, provided solid material for a qualitative study. Ultimately, given the extent of the female networks the protagonists belonged to, involving thousands of anonymous, grassroots members devoted to the same causes, one can legitimately assume that the conclusions of the research apply to great numbers of women whose names will never be remembered, but whose actions should be acknowledged.

The study of correspondence was fundamental in the reconstruction and interpretation of the women's experiences, revealing many similarities as well as a great wealth of nuances. It also shed light on the way they established links and created networks across the region. An important thread of the research consisted in exploring the women's intimate perception of their female identity in the context of their time and place, which could only be done by examining private correspondence and, in some cases, personal diaries. The most fruitful method of analysis consisted in confronting private correspondence with the women's public stance—as expressed in articles, essays, pamphlets, and autobiographical writings published during and after the period under examination. This confrontation revealed that, although white southern women did not make their female condition a public issue until the mid-1960s, they were acutely aware of it and struggled with it in private. This ultimately revealed the complexity of the women's situation in relation to the context in which they lived. It illuminated their internal struggles and shed light on the fundamental contradictions they had to cope with—notably the fact of being oppressors and victims, loyal southerners and dissenters at the same time.

Autobiographical narratives also helped much in interpreting the connection between the women's racial activism and their personal emancipation. These works constitute key documents from a historian's perspective. They are all the more crucial to the subject of this book as it attempts to define a collective identity for a particular group of southern women. The concept of identity being closely connected to that of personal consciousness, the autobiographical writings of these women can inform readers much more than factual accounts of their activities. As the historian Kathryn Nasstrom reflects, "the strength of autobiography is to detail how people come to activism and to register the impact of the [civil rights] movement on personal development. Autobiography shares with other individual narratives, such as oral history and biography, the ability to probe identity and consciousness."[9] Many of the activists concerned here participated in oral history programs developed since the 1970s. Oral history interviews complemented the autobiographical material and the private correspondence of already identified activists, while others yet provided new testimonies confirming the findings of the core research. Finally, several veterans of the 1960s movement, and a few representatives of the older generation, still alive and eager to share their experience, provided precious direct testimony as well as historical material on the civil rights struggle in which they participated. I used personal interviews and a written questionnaire in part to buttress the information I had collected from published works and archival material, but mostly to probe deeper into the subjective experience of the women who responded. This qualitative approach allowed me to confirm the commonalities previously observed, while qualifying and deepening my interpretation, especially as to the issue of gender emancipation.

The book is organized along two lines: it follows the overall chronology of events from the first decades of the twentieth century to the late 1960s, with the 1950s as a pivot, which allows taking into account the specificities of the two generations, but it also hinges thematically on the common characteristics that bind these women as a distinctive, significant group in the history of the segregated South. The first chapter examines the particular status of white women in the segregationist South and their common identity. Based on autobiographical writings and personal interviews, it focuses more particularly on their subjective perception of themselves and of their relationship to their native region. Chapters 2 through 5 analyze the various forms of racial activism the two generations engaged in between the 1920s and the 1960s. They study the evolution of white southern women reformers' collective identity by analyzing the dialectical link between their emancipation from southern racial norms and gender norms. Finally, the last chapter demonstrates the persistence of a unique white southern female identity at the end of the period covered, in spite of their participation in the national social movements of their time, including second-wave feminism.

1

Profiles

Two Generations, One Identity

Throughout the segregation era in the United States, the pervasiveness of the white supremacist doctrine and the repression of all forms of dissent created the impression that the "southern way of life" was there forever, as was the concept of white southern womanhood, supposedly its major raison d'être. Appearances were misleading, though, since from the 1920s to the 1960s, a significant minority of white women undermined the system from within in a quiet but steady way. The two broad generations that overlapped over these four decades were obviously very different. The women living in this period were born in different times and places. The oldest were raised in a world that was in many respects alien to the youngest, a world in which women could not vote, in which no world wars had ever occurred, nor had any Bolshevik revolution or Great Depression. Some became social or political activists, some did not; some married and had children, some did not; some were outspoken in their views, some were not. They distinguished themselves by a great variety of opinions and attitudes between the 1920s and the 1960s, from the most moderate to the most radical. The members of what I have labeled the "older generation"—that is, the women born between the late nineteenth century and the early 1920s—clearly belonged to the white elite of their time. Those who constitute the "younger generation," born in the 1930s and 1940s, were of more diverse socioeconomic backgrounds.

Despite these differences, the individuals profiled in this book were bound by a fundamental feature: they all grew up in the segregated South. The two generations thus went through the same educational process. Being raised in the segregationist South, they all learned the lessons of white supremacy, based not only on racism but also on specific gender norms applying neither to African American women nor to white American women of other regions. Between the early twentieth century and the 1960s, white southern women's education consisted in learning racism as well as the prescriptions of white southern womanhood. Those who became involved in the long civil rights movement, however, formed a unique subgroup. They distinguished themselves by questioning their education upon reaching adulthood and by deliberately unlearning the lessons of white supremacy.

It is no easy task for the historian to reconstruct the inner experience of individuals in a given context if those individuals do not relate it themselves. The task can prove close to impossible when the subjects of the research are not recognized public figures. The white women who became involved in the fight for racial justice in the South, however, were members of organizations whose activities are well documented. Moreover, a significant number of them have left a sufficient amount of written material—in the form of administrative records and correspondence—for us to assess their status and their role in society. As for the key impact of southern education on the evolution of all these women, essential to understand the unique character of their position, it can be grasped best through a number of direct testimonies by the women themselves. Several of them published autobiographical works in which they deliberately identified the roots of their actions in their southern childhood. Some, like Lillian Smith, Anne Braden, Sarah Patton Boyle, and Katharine Du Pre Lumpkin, did so at the very beginning or in the midst of the desegregation crisis, between the late 1940s and the early 1960s. Others, such as Virginia Durr, Sara Mitchell Parsons, Dorothy Dawson Burlage, Joan Browning, Sue Thrasher, and Connie Curry, waited for the end of the civil rights movement to reflect upon their experiences from a distance.[1]

The authors of these autobiographies and memoirs wrote out of various motives, but one can identify two major impulses behind their writing. The first was to overcome the trauma of repudiating their native culture while remaining deeply attached to it. The second was to expiate the sins of the white southern community as a whole, by identifying their personal, individual experience with that of all whites in the South, and, in many respects, with that of all white women born in the region. Far from presenting their story as unique, they made it clear that it was the story of all whites born and raised in the South. Their writing was a personal cathartic gesture and a militant act meant to expose the hidden damage of segregation on the members of the white community that had imposed it, and to prove by their example that the situation could be changed. As such, these works can be used as a privileged source to examine the key factors of white southern childhood that were common to and impacted the lives of all the women examined here, whatever their differences. In addition to published autobiographical narratives, personal interviews provide illuminating information about the subjective experience of these women during and after the segregation era. These sources shed light on the way segregation and their struggle against it shaped their identities as white southern women reformers.

Learning Segregation

Between the late nineteenth century and the passage of the federal Civil Rights Act in 1964, which prohibited segregation in all public places across the United States, segregation was not simply the law in the southern states. It was a way of life and an ideology based on the concept of white supremacy. The rigid legal system established at the turn of the twentieth century could not have been totally effective had not the population been psychologically conditioned to enforce it. This process was achieved through the work of two major institutions that shaped the daily lives of children in local communities across the region, the church and the school. The lessons of white supremacy were taught in the classroom, at church, and in Sunday school, in such a way that the so-called southern way of life was inculcated, even in the children who were raised in "liberal" families—that is, families that did not endorse the doctrine of white supremacy—in segregated institutions. This applied to all social classes, in urban as well as rural areas.[2] Joan Browning remembers growing up in a rural Georgia community where her "schools, church, friends, neighbors—except for one family who lived at the very edge of the school attendance district—and all social institutions were all white." As she puts it, "Segregation simply was an unquestioned way of life."[3] Schools were segregated by law, and most Protestant denominations, which represented almost 90 percent of all white southerners, practiced segregation in their churches.[4] Many ministers used the Bible to justify segregation, just as they had done in the nineteenth century to justify the enslavement of black people. "One platitude spoken from the pulpit was 'race mixing is against nature,'" notes Dorothy Burlage.[5]

It was not so much the teaching itself as the conditions and setting in which it occurred that made their way into the children's hearts and minds. Some pastors did not openly advocate white supremacy but ignored the issue of racism altogether. Yet however universal the message might be, white children learned it in all-white schools and all-white churches; as Sara Parsons sums up: "I had a typical, happy southern childhood. I enjoyed school and was an average student. I had friends, played outside (but never with any black children), went to church, and saw relatives." They were never placed in direct contact with black children except occasionally with the children of black domestic servants, which made them unaware of the very existence of black people as part of the larger community. Parsons notes about her teenage years that she "had no idea where—or even whether—black girls and boys went to high school in Atlanta."[6] White children were thus taught the values of Christianity at church and of democracy at school in an exclusively white environment, and were presumably led to associate these values with whiteness. As Anne Braden recalls, "The Bible said all men were brothers, and the pictures on the Sunday school walls showed Jesus surrounded by children of all colors, the black and the yellow along with the white—all sitting in a circle together." Yet she goes on to reflect, "Long before I could put it into words even in my own mind, I sensed that this did not square with the relations I saw practiced and which I practiced myself in the world around me. I knew some Negro children. But we did not sit in a circle together. We did not sit anywhere together."[7] Among the white women who have written about their childhood experiences, Lillian Smith provides a highly personal analysis that meshes with all others' accounts:

> From the day I was born, I began to learn my lessons. I was put in a rigid frame too intricate, too twisting to describe here so briefly, but I learned to conform to its slide-rule measurements. I learned it is possible to be a Christian and a white southerner simultaneously; to be a gentlewoman and an arrogant callous creature in the same moment; to pray at night and ride a Jim Crow car the next morning and to feel comfortable in doing both. I learned to believe in freedom, to glow when the word *democracy* was used, and to practice slavery from morning to night.[8]

The role of church and school in the shaping of segregationist minds thus stands out as essential, but it was supplemented by another solid institution in southern society: the family.

Although one can always find exceptions such as Constance Curry and Frances Pauley, who grew up in the South but whose parents did not conform to segregationist practices, most white children learned the subtleties of white supremacy from their parents at home—and more specifically from their mothers and grandmothers. As traditional gender roles remained the rule in southern society throughout the segregation era, women were in charge of children's education, and as such, they were given the task of transmitting the tenets of white supremacy to the young generations of white southerners. Hence Lillian Smith's comment: "The mother who taught me what I know of tenderness and love and compassion, taught me also the bleak rituals of keeping Negroes in their 'place.'"[9] Indeed, segregation laws established a status of inferiority for African Americans that could not have gone unquestioned had not these laws been sustained by manners or common behavior. Racial etiquette reasserted blacks' assumed inferiority as an everyday justification of unequal treatment.

Segregationist rules of behavior were not made explicit before adolescence, probably because they mainly applied to social life and did not concern young children. One of the first lessons consisted in adopting a new way of relating to black people. Courtesy titles, white girls discovered, should be reserved for whites. Sarah Boyle remembers being told so on her twelfth birthday: "The current cook, the farm hand, and all the colored children (hired at 50 cents a day during rush seasons to weed and plant) were ordered to stop calling me Patty and call me 'Miss Patty'—for I was never called Sarah. Worse, I was instructed to insist that they do." Dorothy Burlage's account sounds strikingly similar: "I learned to be polite and respectful to all my elders, regardless of color. But while I was to speak to white adults as 'Mr.' or 'Mrs.,' I was taught to address black men and women by their first names." Similar scenes are reported by all the women who describe their childhood in detail.[10]

Along with the code, white youths learned racial prejudice. All the women insist in their accounts on the process of indoctrination that invariably turned white children into segregationists. "My stereotype of the 'typical Nigra' grew as a result of a type of indoctrination which was, I think, eighty per cent pure implication, unvocalized and unconscious, on the part of my elders," writes

Boyle.[11] She devotes a whole chapter to the theme, which she explicitly titles "Product of the Code." So, by the end of childhood, southern whites shared the stereotypical view of blacks as intellectually inferior, lazy, unreliable, or unable to control their instincts. The girls were also warned against the sexual aggressiveness of black males, which supposedly constituted a permanent danger to them. Racial prejudice had come to permeate southern culture as a direct consequence of the institutionalization of segregation. Historians have shown that the suppression of all forms of exchange or communication between whites and blacks entailed a profound estrangement of the two communities. This development was worsened by the ideological conditioning that accompanied the establishment of segregation laws and practices. The restoration of white supremacy went along, and to a certain extent depended on, a systematic use of racist stereotypes that justified the official subordination of blacks in the New South. At the turn of the twentieth century, the black and white worlds were cut off from each other when the ideology of white supremacy effectively imposed a stereotypical image of blacks that prevented any real interracial relationship.[12]

Several white women who wrote about their gradual emancipation from their racist education stressed the unreal character of their initially prejudiced perceptions of blacks. To Virginia Durr, "the whole idea of segregation was based on the idea that blacks were diseased—usually venereal disease was what people suspected blacks of having. You couldn't drink from the same water fountain or use the same bathroom because they were diseased. You couldn't sit by them on the bus because they smelled bad. You couldn't eat with them in the drugstore or restaurant because they were offensive, smelled bad, and were diseased." Sarah Patton Boyle similarly recollects, "I was instructed not to visit our cooks in their rooms as I 'might catch diseases.' . . . There was some grumbling and much soft laughter over the body odors of our cooks, but it occurred to none on us that this could be remedied by letting them bathe in the forbidden bathroom."[13] Such prejudices were used to justify the physical separation of blacks and whites in society. Several women who ultimately came to combat racism in a militant way illustrated the depth of their initial racism by describing their inability to pronounce the word "Negro" correctly—the term was then commonly used to designate African Americans in a nonoffensive way. For instance, when in 1961 Sara Mitchell Parsons ran as an integrationist candidate for a position on Atlanta's board of education, she first spoke at a rally in a black Baptist church. After the meeting was over, Lonnie King, a black civil rights activist who supported her, took her aside to warn her: "You don't pronounce Negro the way it should be pronounced. Say KNEE-GROW. Keep practicing until you get it perfect." "Like virtually all southern whites," she comments, "I had grown up pronouncing the word more like 'nei-gra.'" Sarah Boyle suffered from the same disability. In 1950, she decided to unlearn her prejudices by taking actual lessons from a local black newspaper editor who agreed to reeducate her. He kept correcting her as the lessons went by, but she was not a good student. She only managed to pronounce "knee-grow" after two years, but she later discovered that "*still* I had the word only half right." As she corrected a fellow white liberal, "pointing out to her that she did not throw the accent on the 'grow,'" the other woman "hotly replied that I made nothing of the 'Knee.'" "Horrified," writes Boyle, "I realized that I had indeed been saying 'Ni*grow*,' and that this doubtless tortured sensitive ears as much as my fellow liberal's version, '*Knee*gra.'" Anne Braden experienced the same difficulties when she began interacting with the black community. "I [even] had a hard time pronouncing the word 'Negro,'" she admitted. "I suspect I said 'Nigra' because you had a feeling you were speaking in a very affected sort of way when you said 'Negro.'" Even a woman raised in a racially liberal family such as Frances Pauley needed reeducation. The black woman who first corrected her pronunciation in the 1950s, Sadie Mays, became her friend.[14]

White southerners learned to apprehend black people as types rather than individual human beings by resorting to a whole range of constructed images, but whatever nuances they could make in their use of imagery, their main approach to blacks was based on a fundamental dichotomy. As late as 1984, the historian Joel Williamson asserted that "in the mind of Southern whites for something over six generations, there has been a tendency to look at black people in essentially two ways. Blacks are either children and loved, or beasts and hated." Williamson pessimistically implied that little progress had been made since the abolition of segregation, which could perhaps be argued, but his statement directly echoed Boyle's autobiography, published in 1962. She had drawn then a strikingly similar conclusion from her personal experience. As she recalled an episode from her childhood when she had dug a "cave" in the yard to hide from eventual German invaders during World War I, she wrote, "Looking back, I see how well defined already was my typically

Southern split image of Negroes. 'Bad Nigras' were beastlike, dangerous, repulsive beyond the lowest reaches of white men, even of Germans. But these bad ones didn't include any Negroes I knew. They were all good, and with them alone I shared the secret of my cave."[15] Thus the major characteristic of whites' racial views, be they benevolent or hostile, was an ingrained belief in black inferiority, which expressed itself in various forms, from paternalism to extreme violence. In addition, Boyle's testimony reveals that the supposed badness of certain blacks was invariably contradicted by the reality of everyday life where no "bad Nigras" existed, thus bringing to light the role of indoctrination in the perpetuation of racism.

The main representation of blacks in the segregation era was a twentieth-century version of the Sambo figure inherited from the antebellum era. Hence Boyle's comment: "My thoughts became saturated with the assumption that Negroes belonged to a lower order of man than we. Loving them—after my father's fashion at first, and then after my mother's—I quickly learned not to judge them by our standards, but by a segregated, separate standard." Later in her life, she was shaken into the realization of her own racism when she expressed support and encouragement in a highly paternalistic way to the first black man to register at the University of Virginia in 1950. Local blacks' negative reactions to her gesture revealed to her the extent of her prejudices. "I was in a white prison," she analyzed, "I knew nothing of that outside world, the Negro's thoughts, knew only that I was acting in a spirit which they seemed not to recognize." Not only had segregation separated blacks and whites physically, but it had excluded blacks from whites' perception of the world.

The doctrine of white supremacy indeed redefined the regional identity as all-white by obliterating blacks from the whole picture. In the first stages of her "reeducation" process, Boyle noticed her instructor's "Yankee accent" and asked him if he was from the North, to which he replied: "Oh, no, I'm a Southerner." Such an answer came as a shock to the white woman, who had never in her life associated blacks with southern identity. "A Southerner!" she thought. "Never had I heard a Negro thus designated. Southerners were white. Sellers was a Southern Negro, not a Southerner."[16] It appears from Boyle's reaction that white southerners merely could not apprehend the South in its entirety. They could not conceive of a black South, although they lived next to it. Frances Pauley explains that even years after her joining reform-oriented interracial organizations, the reality of black people's lives remained alien to her. She recollects, "I had been on the board of the Atlanta Urban League. I had been on different committees with blacks in different health organizations. But I hadn't really known black people. All I knew was the cook and the yardman and what they told me. I didn't know much about poor black people; I didn't really know the problems." So she made up her mind to learn and realized that the only way to do so was to go to predominantly black areas such as Atlanta University. Similarly, commenting on her first visits to Louisville's black business district in the late 1940s, Anne Braden remarked, "I don't know what any of those black people [during that time] thought of me because I was like a bull in a china shop. I didn't have any experience with black people at all."[17]

Thus the natural end-result of segregation proved to be total misunderstanding of blacks by whites and a systematic mistrust of whites on the part of blacks. This was what Boyle found out when she struggled to understand how her attitude toward the black student she had so warmly welcomed to the University of Virginia could have been offensive. Nobody among her "liberal" friends could account for Gregory Swanson's and local blacks' initial anger at her condescending overtures. She concluded that "southern white liberals do not necessarily know any more about the Negro whose side they are on than do the segregationists who oppose him. The people I consulted had no colored friends in the sense that they had white friends. Some had acquaintances among educated Negroes who they called friends, but in no case that I know of was there the kind of intimacy which results in uninhibited exchanges of personal confidence." When Pauley became head of the Georgia Council on Human Relations in 1961, her job consisted in creating bridges between the two races by organizing interracial groups across the state. She worked in close collaboration with Vernon Jordan, a black National Association for the Advancement of Colored People (NAACP) leader. They would go together to places where he would talk blacks into meeting with whites and she would talk whites into meeting with blacks. Mistrust of whites was so pervasive among blacks that she would never have been able to reach them on her own. "It's hard to get that confidence from blacks," she explained. "They try you, and I don't blame them!"[18]

Misunderstanding often proved to be total alienation, and in many cases mistrust turned into resentment and anger at whites, even when the latter meant well. Indeed, even at the height of the civil rights movement, when a small but significant minority of whites joined blacks in a spirit of brotherhood, the gap was so wide between the two communities that the most dedicated activists could experience pessimism even as they fought for change. In 1958, Anne Braden recognized misunderstanding and mistrust as the main obstacles to the victory over racism. Since blacks and whites did not know each other, she argued, whites could only fear blacks, and blacks could only resent whites for racial oppression. She remembered hearing a black NAACP leader address a majority-black audience after the lynching of Emmett Till. She reported the woman as saying, "They will not stop us by murder and killing." Braden went on to comment, "She did not identify the 'they,' but I knew she was not speaking only of the men who murdered Emmett Till. She talked for an hour and not once did she mention any white person in the South as her friend or her ally in what she saw as a fight for survival. When she spoke of 'they,' she meant all of us cursed with white skin."[19]

Thus, whatever their racial views and attitudes, white women were originally the prisoners of prejudices inherited from the culture of segregation, as they had been cut off from the reality of the black world. As members of the white community, they shared with all whites a stereotyped view of blacks as a mass of innately different, somewhat inferior beings living in an abstract world.

Prejudice, however, was in no way synonymous with hatred on the part of whites. As a large majority of the women concerned were of middle- to upper-class background, their families prided themselves on being part of an enlightened elite who had inherited the tradition of noblesse oblige established by slaveholding ancestors. The result was a subtle blend of racism and paternalism transmitted from generation to generation throughout the segregation era. The absence of racial hatred made the indoctrination much smoother and easier to accept. The children were happy as they grew up under the guidance of loving and benevolent adults, and they developed a good, Christian conscience, as did Sarah Boyle: "My 'paternalistic' relationship to Negroes gave me the release of unobstructed, uncostly love, and provided me with easily found ways of proving myself gentle, high-principled and kind."[20] Although blacks should be kept in their place owing to their "inferior nature," Anne Braden recollects that "the point was to treat them kindly, not only because this was of course right according to Biblical teaching but also because if you treat a Negro with kindness he is also good to you—somewhat in the way a pet dog is good to the master who is good to him."[21] Years later, once engaged in the struggle for racial equality, the women would struggle on an everyday basis to unlearn these prejudices. In doing so, however, they would also have to face another set of norms learned since childhood, the prescriptions of white southern womanhood.

Learning Ladyhood

Although the identity of white southern women cannot be reduced to that of the middle and upper classes, the fact is that the definition of southern white womanhood imposed by the white elite at the turn of the twentieth century was so central in the maintenance of white supremacy that it affected all white women of all classes and pervaded society as a whole.[22] The evolution of white women's condition after Reconstruction was directly linked to the spread of the "Lost Cause" and "Old South" myths, which as late as 1961 made Virginia Durr complain, "I think the rest of the country is really taken in by the 'myth' of the Old South and the beautiful women and white pillared mansions and faithful Negro slaves."[23] Thus the redefinition of white southern womanhood after Reconstruction was part and parcel of the reshaping of southern identity in direct opposition to national standards. From the 1890s on, the United Confederate Veterans (1889) and the United Daughters of the Confederacy (1894) organized celebrations to the glory of Confederate soldiers, in which white women, elevated to the rank of saints, were presented as living proof that the soldiers had not fought in vain. The identification of white womanhood with the Lost Cause was a way to cement the new social and racial order that was being imposed at that time through black disfranchisement and the establishment of segregation. The white woman and the Confederate soldier became two reassuring figures of loyalty and orthodoxy for the masses of southerners at a time of transition and uncertainty.[24]

The girls who participated in the celebrations did not interpret them in this way at the time, but, reflecting on them later, they confirmed the impact that the white supremacist ideology had had on the construction of their identity as white women. Virginia Durr, who was raised in Birmingham, Alabama, recalled the Confederate celebrations held in the 1910s. As she puts it in her autobiography, "all the nice girls from the age of about twelve to twenty" were dressed up as pages to parade with the old veterans. "We would ride in the parade and the politicians would make speeches about pure white Southern womanhood—and I believed it. I was pure white Southern womanhood and Southern men had died for me and the Confederate flag was flying just to save me. I got to thinking I was pretty hot stuff, to have the war fought for me."[25] Katharine Du Pre Lumpkin was equally impressed. "What child would not love it, when everywhere was unbounded enthusiasm and her own family in the thick of everything?" she observed about the Confederate reunion of 1903 in Columbia, South Carolina. The parade was a source of amazement and excitement to the young girl, who looked for her sister among the carriages "graced by their owners and by 'beautiful young ladies.'"[26] Like many other young women of her generation, Elizabeth Lumpkin, Katharine's sister, was often invited to speak in homage to the veterans. According to Gaines Foster, "A ritual presentation of virgins to veterans . . . assured the soldiers that the women of the South loved them despite their defeat and thereby indirectly affirmed their manhood." The message could not be more explicit when Lumpkin addressed the veterans once by asking, "how can I find words to give you greeting when every pulsing heart beat says: I love you—you grand old men who guarded with your lives the virgin whiteness of our Georgia?"[27] Such words reveal that between the Civil War and the late 1960s, the concept of white womanhood was a complex combination of racial and sexual images used by white supremacists to maintain the racial and social order in the region. The myths of the Old South and the Lost Cause constituted the framework in which white womanhood was redefined, the central figure of the "southern lady" becoming its incarnation. This cultural development had lasting consequences for southern society in general, and for white women in particular. The latter found themselves at the confluence of contradictory forces involving race, sex, gender, and, to a lesser extent, class. As a result, they had to cope with norms that placed them in a paradoxical position of "oppressors" and "victims," objects and subjects at the same time.

The education of the women examined here was twofold. In addition to learning segregationist rules, they learned how to be "southern ladies," that is, how to conform to a complex combination of racial and gender expectations of behavior. Such an education was more normative than others because of the confluence of white supremacy and patriarchy in the set of rules to be assimilated. More than education, it was a conditioning process, which led Sarah Boyle to observe, "When my training period was over, I was as close to a typical Southern lady as anyone ever is to a typical anything."[28] Such a process unfolded from childhood through the end of adolescence, when the girl could happily turn into a belle if she was pretty. Then she could hope to find a husband, which officially entitled her to the status of lady.[29]

The primary "quality" of a belle or lady was her lack of interest in all things intellectual and her downplaying of her own intellectual qualities. These traits were closely associated with an emphasis on beauty and attractiveness, or "charm," a key word in the education of girls. Whereas Lillian Smith theorized about the condition of white southern women as early as the 1940s from the vantage point of her personal experience, Virginia Durr reflected later in life upon the issue, as she gradually became aware of it, but both women point out this "quality" as a fundamental trait of the typical southern lady. To Smith's bitter statement that "culturally stunted by a region that still pays nice rewards to simple-mindedness in females, they had no defense against blandishment," Durr answers that "to be smart was . . . considered fatal, as it would scare the men away, and the best recipe for 'southern charm' seemed to be beauty, lovely clothes, stupidity, and also enthusiasm, to have lots of pep and to be admiring and make the men feel good."[30]

Higher education was not deemed essential, but by the early twentieth century it had become an acceptable option for women of the white middle and upper classes, insofar as it did not steer them away from the "natural" course of their life, which was to become "good" wives. To many parents of the white elite, a few years in college seemed to offer good opportunities for their daughters to find a husband, which remained the priority. "Evidently," says Durr, "to be stupid, dull, pretty and plump was a good way to get a husband and keep one."[31] Almost all the women of the first generation examined here experienced some form of higher education, but did not necessarily go on to complete their graduate studies.[32] Yet even if some engaged in professional careers after college, the main function of higher education for women was not meant to be professional training but achieving the transition between adolescence and married life. Such a conception became common at the end of the nineteenth century and remained prevalent for decades.[33]

Several autobiographical narratives reveal that searching for a husband was considered serious business by the white elite. The search began in high school, and went on in college if the first attempts were not successful. This could be a source of stress and anxiety if the girls did not conform to the feminine ideal of the time. Anne Braden, for instance, recalls, "I figured out that I didn't have a lot of boyfriends because I was too smart so I'd better hide the fact that I had brains. I don't think I put it in those words but almost. That was the prevailing notion: that the way you would get boys to like you was to make them think they were absolutely brilliant no matter how stupid they might sound. So I began that play-acting thing. I never was the belle of the ball but I was in that crowd." Braden makes it clear that she conformed to the general rule, and adds that "most of the people I knew went to college to enjoy the dances, join a sorority, and catch a man."[34] This is confirmed by other accounts. "My great fear," remembers Durr, "was that I wouldn't be popular. . . . Attracting men and being attractive to men and getting a nice beau and the best marriage that we could was our only ambition and our only future, our only career. So naturally the boys were in total command of the situation." Such a statement could be dismissed as an exaggeration on the part of the author were it not confirmed by the description of the circumstances in which Virginia finally married Cliff Durr. She recalls, "My mother and father were sitting on the front porch after dark one night in 1925. I was twenty-one years old and the family had about given up on me. I had had some proposals, which I hadn't accepted, but I hadn't had very many serious love affairs. They decided I was an old maid." Her brother explicitly reproached her with being too critical of everybody. Her father asked her who she was "looking for." Her mother explained that Virginia did not want to marry someone she did not love. Finally, Virginia told them she had noticed a handsome boy in church. They invited him the next Sunday. Virginia and Cliff Durr were married on Easter Monday, 1926.[35] Durr's experience does not seem to be unique. Jessie Daniel Ames evoked her own in the very same words. "In the South," she wrote, "an unmarried woman is an unwanted woman [and] marriage even to a 'gatepost' . . . is the only estate to which a woman should aspire. . . . Missing it, all is lost."[36] So marriage was undoubtedly the major goal white middle- and upper-class parents had for their daughters in the first half of the twentieth century, even when they sent them to college.

The southern lady was first defined as a wife, and her primary virtue was submissiveness. Just like the notion of black inferiority, the subordination of white women to white men was not a thing to be discussed. It was taken for granted. Durr could observe this in her sister, Josephine, who married future U.S. Supreme Court justice Hugo Black in 1921. She recalled that Black loved his wife more than anything else and was entirely devoted to her, but that "she was Mrs. Hugo Black. He expected her to subordinate herself to his life and his ambitions. It never occurred to him otherwise." Josephine was indeed the supreme incarnation of the southern lady to her sister, who described her as "beautiful and sweet and charming."[37]

Besides being a wife, the lady was also a mother, like the Victorian lady in the nineteenth century. This role took on a crucial dimension in southern culture because of the ideology of white supremacy. Indeed, owing to their reproductive capacity, white women were closely identified with the notion of integrity of the white race. Not only was their purity to be preserved, but they were also considered the guardians and transmitters of the culture. As mothers and educators, they had the major responsibility of making sure that white children would learn the lessons of white supremacy and become good southerners. White women were in charge of education in the home and in the community at large. This endowed them with an unquestionable moral authority, which they were to use to their advantage throughout the desegregation crisis from 1954 on. In the first half of the twentieth century, however, motherhood limited white women's freedom by confining them to the domestic sphere. It also precluded any reference in words or behavior that might connect them with sexuality. White women were taught to repress all sexual instincts, as all women had been in Victorian society. In the case of southerners, however, sexual taboos were reinforced by the culture of white supremacy, which opposed the sacred chastity of white women to the lasciviousness of black women. As a result, the former were maintained as long as possible in a state of total ignorance with respect to sexuality. They learned about sex upon marrying because they were expected to have children as soon as possible. The notion of sexual pleasure remained taboo for life. Many women could be said to be sexually crippled by their education and the sexual norms of their time. This was definitely the case of Jessie Daniel Ames, whose marriage to an army surgeon in 1905 immediately turned into a disaster, as "their sexual relationship was shrouded in fear, embarrassment, and jealousy."[38] She attributed this failure to her education, as she remembered, "I was not a fully developed woman.... I had not been allowed to grow up." Not surprisingly, she had become convinced that sexual desire was natural in men, but that it was not necessarily part of women's nature. She explained that "a woman may be and in my day usually was a passive agent in this matter of conceiving a child. No man can beget a child except at a time when he is wide awake and in the throes of very strong passion. A woman can conceive in her sleep."[39] She remained trapped in her body all her life.

The pervasive image of white women as wives and mothers effectively buttressed the idea that they should be confined to the domestic sphere. Even after ratification of the Nineteenth Amendment, women were commonly defined as unfit for active participation in public life. Of the eleven former Confederate States, only Texas, Arkansas, Kentucky, and Tennessee actually voted in favor of ratification in 1919 and 1920, and for years afterward, southern women were deterred from exercising their newly won right to vote.[40] Although the woman's suffrage movement did not attract as many women in the South as it did in the rest of the country—owing to the reinforcement of patriarchy that went along with the restoration of white supremacy at the turn of the twentieth century—some did try to resist the pressure by claiming their right to participate in political life. In doing so, they violated southern etiquette and lost their status as ladies. The cult of southern womanhood demanded conformity to the rules. So, the southern lady could also be defined negatively by pointing out the inappropriate behavior of dissenters. Durr narrates how a suffrage leader in Birmingham was presented as a "fast woman," that is, an impure one, who did not deserve respect or protection anymore. "That was a terrible sin," says Durr. "You were supposed to be 'chased and chaste.' You were supposed to be totally pure and terribly attractive to men but not give them an inch. If you did, you would be banished, packed off to New Jersey."[41] In equating participation in politics with the violation of a major taboo—the white woman's chastity—Birmingham community leaders made it clear that the southern lady was expected to stay within the boundaries of the home.[42]

The women of the older generation absorbed the tenets of white supremacy from early childhood and learned in particular how to conform to the ideal of womanhood that their parents, teachers, ministers, and political leaders had placed at the core of southern culture in the late nineteenth century. These norms tended to lose their strength as southern society modernized, but change was slower in the South than in the rest of the nation because the preservation of white supremacy required a strict maintenance of the status quo in all spheres of life. Consequently, the prescriptions of ladyhood also affected the women of the following generations, although in a more indirect way.

Several testimonies reveal that, whatever their social background or the degree of liberalism characterizing their education, the white women born around World War II became aware of the lady ideal at an early stage of their development. This is especially true of those born into traditional upper-class families, such as Dorothy Dawson Burlage, born in 1937, who remembers: "My perception was that southern women were like certain gemstones: polished to be pleasing in appearance, but not brilliant. Women, particularly those of my kind of background, were socialized for this role from the time we were young." To the question, "Were you educated to conform to the ideal of the 'Southern lady,'" Faye Powell (born in 1940) answers: "Yes, but it didn't take. Southern girls of that day were expected to be polite, well-mannered, socially graceful, self-effacing, non-confrontational, not too competitive, and always show deference to authorities, i.e., men." To the same question, Margaret Burr Leonard (born in 1942) responds: "Yes. I was supposed to skip the racism and go straight to perfection, that is, wear the gloves and the hat, speak softly and grammatically, respect adults (especially men) and read enough to be interesting." She says that southern culture shaped her identity as a woman in the sense that she "was supposed to be beautiful, charming, nice, brave, religious, honorable and patriotic." Interestingly, Leonard adds: "But we never called ourselves, or anybody, southern ladies. We never used that expression except in jokes," thus confirming the lasting influence and the concomitant decline of southern gender norms at midcentury.[43]

Some women, like Joan Browning (born in 1942), were definitely aware of the lady model but were educated into rejecting it. In any case, whatever their choices and attitudes toward the ideal in their adult lives, white southern women could not fully escape its influence and more often than not contributed to its perpetuation. Some of the younger generation even point out the fundamental ambivalence of their mothers' status regarding the issue. Margaret Leonard, for instance, whose own mother, Margaret Long, supported the civil rights movement as a writer and journalist, observes that if her mother did not conform to the ideal, being divorced and working for a living, her daughters, Margaret Leonard and her sister, were expected to be ladies, and they "tried." Dorothy Burlage expresses the same sense of contradiction.

"I had been raised with the expectation that I would be a southern lady—well mannered, never involved in political discussion or controversy, with all opinions and personal matters kept private, and dependent on men," she writes, but she goes on to comment: "The fact that my mother had a job was of course inconsistent with her southern model, and in that sense she displayed an alternative to what she taught me." As for Virginia Durr's daughter (born in 1939), she observes: "Like my mother, I was rotten in my ability to conform to this ideal but I DID try."[44]

Ultimately, whether they belonged to the older or the younger generation, the women profiled here could not escape the influence of the various myths that shaped southern identity in the post-Reconstruction era, including the ideal of the southern lady. As the various testimonies at hand show, the evolution of southern society and culture after the Civil War and Reconstruction determined the ideal of white southern womanhood in a very specific way, superimposing white supremacist dogma on traditional Victorian norms. Whatever their social origins, virtually all white women learned the code of ladyhood as they learned the segregationist etiquette, the two being inextricably linked.

White Women, Black Women, Black Men

While the establishment of segregation at the turn of the twentieth century created a new racial order, it significantly altered sexual and gender roles in southern society. This development not only modified white women's relationship to white men, but it also deeply affected their relationship to black men and women. As a result, the experiences of white women, black women, and black men became connected in many ways, having a significant impact on their attitudes to each other throughout the segregation and desegregation eras.

The position of white women in southern society since the slavery era cannot be dissociated from that of black women in the sense that white men's treatment of the latter directly influenced their treatment of the former. Several historians have studied at length the weight of antebellum culture on race and gender relations long after the abolition of slavery. The slavery system had separated white and black women in many ways, the most devastating one being the raping of slave women by planters. Slavery thus turned white women into chaste, sacred creatures and placed them on a pedestal while it transformed black women into objects of pleasure and contempt. Lillian Smith reflects that these two opposite processes actually fueled each other in a "race-sex-sin spiral" as white men felt a growing sense of guilt over being attracted to black women. "The more trails the white man made to back-yard cabins," she writes, "the higher he raised his white wife on her pedestal when he returned to the big house. The higher the pedestal, the less he enjoyed her whom he had put there, for statues after all are only nice things to look at." Smith's view had a definite psychoanalytical twist, since she discussed at length the role of unconscious sexual impulses in social and race relations. Like Wilbur Cash, her contemporary, she placed the notion of white male guilt at the core of her reflection on white women.[45] After the restoration of white supremacy in the late nineteenth century, the fundamental opposition between black and white women continued to influence cultural representations and the relationships between the two. The reconstruction of southern identity in the late nineteenth century thus went along with a reconstruction of gendered identities that only exacerbated these antagonistic representations.[46]

Needless to say the title of "lady" was reserved for whites. If most white women workers were implicitly denied the status of lady owing to their class, black women of all classes were denied it because of their race.[47] These discriminatory norms were imprinted onto the minds of all women from youth, and they were expected to respect them whatever their views. Interestingly, the minority of white women who rebelled against segregationist culture in the twentieth century took pains to subvert the etiquette by using the term "lady" to designate black women. Such was the case, for instance, of Virginia Durr, when she recollected the wife of Montgomery's NAACP leader E. D. Nixon: she described her as "the sweetest, prettiest thing you ever saw, just a lovely woman." And she added, "If you ever want to meet a real Southern lady, meet Mrs. Nixon." This seemingly casual remark could have gone unnoticed to the reader of Durr's autobiography had she not included a particular anecdote a couple of hundred pages earlier. In the first part of the book, she reported her mother correcting her after she had said that a lady was there to see her. "You can't say, 'A lady's here'; you have to say, 'A woman's here,'" her mother had instructed her. Evidently, Durr's subsequent remark about Arlette Nixon then takes on an altogether different dimension. In the same vein, Anne Braden notes in her memoir that her mother corrected her once: "You never call colored people ladies, Anne Gambrell.... You say colored woman and white lady—never a colored lady."[48]

The reinforcement of old stereotypes emphasized the idea that black women were sexually uninhibited and impure, while providing a good reason to perpetuate the sexual abuse of black women. Moreover, whereas depicting black women as Jezebels constituted a form of sexual discrimination, segregationist culture emphasized a difference in class that, unlike sexually connoted stereotypes, corresponded to a social reality. Black and white women were more than symbolically opposed, and their relationship was all the more problematic since black women were subordinated to white women in southern society, so that the latter's education consisted of acquiring a subtle combination of social and racial prejudices they applied on reaching adulthood. The best illustration of this fact was the relationship between middle- or upper-class white women and their domestic servants.[49] When Sarah Patton Boyle was first married, in the thick of the Great Depression, she could not afford a full-time household servant but, as she puts it in her autobiography, "Foregoing a maid entirely was one sacrifice to poverty which I didn't propose to make." It took her more than a decade to realize that she had participated in the social and economic exploitation of the young women she had employed. She recollects, "My requirements were that the girl know her place, do her work quickly, and show appreciation of the opportunity I was offering by making a real effort to learn what nice people expected of their maids. Then she could get a better job later, using me as reference. Unconscious of exploitation, I felt rather magnanimous."[50] As Boyle's example shows, all white women were not necessarily mean or authoritarian with their black servants, but they were in a de facto position of superiority, which, combined with the usual set of prejudices they nourished regarding black women, was most likely to entail deep resentment on the part of the latter. Besides, as black women were forced to neglect their own homes and could not care for their own children, they naturally blamed their mistresses for their predicament, creating permanent tensions between employer and employee. White women may or may not have been aware of their status as oppressors, but they most of the time perceived their relationship with their servants as antagonistic.[51]

The separation of black and white women in these two categories—be it at the symbolic or concrete level—had lasting consequences on their relationships, as the two groups tended to resent each other for the respective characteristics that shaped their identities. Lynne Olson cites the writer Marita Golden saying, "We have been defined as symbolic and actual opposites. The white woman weak/the black woman strong, the white woman undersexed/the black woman oversexed, the white woman the symbol of sexual desire/the black woman neutered. And this mumbo jumbo of imprisoning, corrupting imagery still rages in our heads and in our hearts, and makes it all the more difficult to throw a life or love line to one another."[52]

Finally, black and white women's relationship was even more complicated by another key element of southern society and culture in the first half of the twentieth century, the figure of the black mammy.[53] White women found themselves caught in an ambiguous relationship with black nurses in two ways, first as children and later as mothers. As the mammy was in charge of the white children from their birth, she became a second mother to them, and they developed a very affectionate relationship that tended to exclude the white mother altogether. This deeply undermined white women's sense of motherhood as they had to share their children's love with black nurses. In her autobiography, Lillian Smith analyzes in depth the psychological, social, and cultural implications of this distinctive trait of the segregationist system. "In my home," she writes, "our nurse lived in the back yard beyond Mother's flower garden in a small cabin whose interior walls were papered with newspapers. Much of my young life was spent there." She remembers more particularly the time when another child was born in the family, drawing her parents' attention away from her. Feeling rejected, Lillian stopped eating for a time until Aunt Chloe, the black nurse, took her to her cabin. After several failed attempts at feeding her, the nurse finally took some food, chewed it first in her mouth, and then gave it to the child, who ate it instantly. "Soon I was prospering on this fine psychological diet," Smith comments, "gaining in weight and security as the weeks went by." The author stresses the blend of physical and psychological intimacy that, according to her, linked the mammy to the white child. She goes on to add, "I was once more the center of somebody's universe. What did it matter that this universe encompassed only one room in a little back-yard cabin? It filled my need and I loved her." In this example, the mammy literally took the place of the mother and won the child's love as a result of it. Smith shows that the incident not only created a unique, lasting bond between the black woman and herself but also widened the distance between the black and white women who cared for the same child. The writer considered it so symptomatic of the unhealthy effects of segregation on human relations that she included a fictionalized version of it in her novel *Strange Fruit* (1944).[54]

It is clear then that segregationist culture pitted black and white women against each other not only by imprisoning them in antagonistic stereotypes but by separating them socially and physically. This dichotomy created by white supremacy is essential not only to understand the overall attitudes of black and white women during the segregation era but also to grasp the ambivalent nature of their relationship in the social reform movements of the interwar years and in the civil rights movement that unfolded after World War II, a relationship characterized by a constant back-and-forth movement between closeness and distance.

If the relations between white and black women were complex, to say the least, those between white women and black men remained almost impossible for decades. Indeed, from the end of Reconstruction on, the fates of white women and black men were bound by the legacy of lynching, which became an efficient instrument of control in the hands of white supremacists. Lynching came to crystallize gender and racial oppression as it conveniently deprived black men of the status they had gained during Reconstruction while subordinating white women to the protection of white men. The consequences of this phenomenon were far-reaching. For decades afterward, black men could not interact with white women on an equal basis without running the risk of being killed by white men. This obviously created extreme sexual tensions between them as the women were virtually endowed with a power of life and death over the men. Ultimately, with the development of the civil rights movement, sex between white women and black men became a symbol of liberation from white male oppression, and this came to distort their mutual relationship in a new way.

The spread of lynching in the late nineteenth century coincided with the celebration of the Lost Cause. This was the time when the fates of white women and black men became inextricably linked.[55] Lynching proved particularly efficient in bringing the black man back under control, but it did much more than that in depriving him of his masculinity and ultimately of his human integrity. Lillian Smith stressed the deep sexual forces at work in a lynching: "The lynched Negro becomes not an object that must die but a receptacle for every man's forbidden feelings. Sex and hate, cohabiting in the darkness of minds too long, pour out their progeny of cruelty on anything that can serve as a symbol of an unnamed relationship that in his heart each man wants to befoul." Lynchings often ended up in actual castration of their victims, but even when they did not, they invariably achieved castration at a symbolic level. According to Smith, "That, sometimes, the lynchers do cut off genitals of the lynched and divide them into bits to be distributed to participants as souvenirs is no more than a coda to this composition of hate and guilt and sex and fear, created by our way of life."[56] The consequences of such mutilations affected whole generations of African American men long after lynching had virtually disappeared from southern life.[57]

As for white women, lynching and the discourse used to legitimize it placed them in a tangle of contradictions. The function of lynching as a means to assert white supremacy and to keep black men under control is obvious. Its implications concerning white women are more difficult to assess, but many scholars have shown that lynching also maintained white women under the control of white men at a time when the latter's position of power became uncertain.[58] White women found themselves in an ambiguous position in relation to white and black men. On the one hand, they were responsible for lynchings since these lynchings were committed in their name. On the other, most of them did not directly participate in these crimes, and they were maintained in a passive position by white men's discourse that presented them as the victims or potential victims of black men.[59] In the prevailing collective imagery of the New South, white women became vulnerable creatures permanently threatened by oversexed black men. Lynching became an act of chivalry in the defense of white womanhood. Virtually all white girls of the middle and upper class were educated into fearing the black man as the devil incarnate, and believed in the rape myth on entering adulthood.

Moreover, class prejudice on the part of the white elite contributed to the perpetuation of lynching for decades, for the whites benefited from mob violence while not taking direct responsibility for it. Lynching was recognized as an act of savagery, but its legitimacy was hardly ever questioned. As a result, young white "ladies" remained indifferent to lynching, even approved of it in theory, as long as they were not directly confronted with it, or as long as nobody forced them to face the reality of it. Sara Alderman Murphy, for instance, who was born in the early 1920s in Tennessee, reports how her mother took her outside of their house one night, so she could see what was happening in the distance. The county courthouse had been set on fire by a mob who thought a black man accused of rape was in it. The girl could guess what was going on, but she nevertheless was kept at a safe distance. The mother wanted her to be aware of lynching as a fact of southern life, but she did not condemn it as evil, which was a way of maintaining fear in the girl's mind. Murphy comments, "my mother and my church instilled in me a strong belief that all people are connected as human beings, but neither she nor the church questioned the Jim Crow realities of our society." As for Virginia Durr, she confessed, "I knew there were lynchings but like so much else in my life, I simply did not think about them. I pushed them out of my mind."[60]

The crime of lynching steadily declined over the first half of the twentieth century, but all the white women and black men who lived in the South during the segregation era remained under its influence. The close association of the myth of the black rapist with that of the southern lady proved a particularly efficient means not only to control black men but also to regulate white women's behavior, buttressing white supremacy and patriarchy at the same time.[61] The myth remained alive until the 1970s and imposed restrictions on white women's behavior, preventing them from interacting with black men. For instance, Margaret Rose Gladney, born in 1945 to a white upper-middle-class family, recalls her early teaching experience in Memphis in 1968. The student body being 97 percent black at the school where she had applied for a position, her father had warned her not to invite any students into her apartment because she "could be raped." By ignoring the warning and joining African Americans in the struggle for equality, the young woman simultaneously challenged the racial and gender norms she had been expected to respect from youth.[62]

White supremacy thus made it impossible for black men and white women to relate since any contact between them conjured up the ultimate sexual taboo of miscegenation. Sarah Boyle learned it at her own expense when she naively offered her friendship to Gregory Swanson, the black man who registered at the University of Virginia in 1950 after a court had asserted his right to do so. After an encouraging exchange of letters between them, he suddenly changed in his attitude and rejected her without explanation. As she realized later, one passage from her last letter had been highly suggestive whereas she had not meant it to be so. It read as follows: "I wish there were some way we could know each other personally. I want us to very much. But I don't quite see how it can be done. It would be humiliating to us both to be clandestine about it, and would be unwise to be open about it. For us there can be no middle road between those two, for there's no privacy where I live." These words sound extraordinarily naive on the part of a forty-four-year-old woman, but, on the other hand, they also reflect the stark reality of segregation. When she later commented on this episode, Boyle wrote that, like all white southern women of her class—and arguably of all classes—she had not been educated into thinking of black men as men. As she put it, there were two ways of apprehending black men, either as dangerous beasts or as harmless dumb creatures. Accordingly, there were "two distinct schools in handling the Southern interracial sex problem." She described her own experience as follows:

> One [school] consists in warnings against "the bestial natures of Negroes." This school makes white girls super-sex-conscious and continually on their guard against doing or saying anything to "inflame the primitive imagination" when dealing with Negro men. The other school employs an opposite method. Ignoring entirely the simple scientific fact that Negro men are members of the opposite sex, it encourages white girls to regard them rather as one does male dumb animals. The latter method was used with me.

As a result she must have approached Swanson in a way he deemed inappropriate owing to her race and sex, but, first and foremost, he undoubtedly felt that her attitude was highly dangerous to him. She only realized much later that she had put him at risk by getting too close to him. Swanson certainly made sure to create a safe distance between Boyle and himself because he was taught by his elders, like all young black men, "that to take white women in their arms, be they ever so willing, is virtually certain death."[63]

Virginia Durr was probably not as unaware of sexual taboos as Boyle, as she had been educated in the opposite school, according to which black men were "dangerously oversexed." Unlike Boyle too, she became an integrationist activist at an early time in her life and challenged authorities and norms whenever she could. Yet, like Boyle, she remembered that she did not fully grasp the problems inherent in personal interaction between white women and black men until they were pointed out to her by a black activist whom she came to know well. E. D. Nixon was the head of the NAACP in Montgomery, Alabama, where Virginia and Cliff Durr lived from 1951 on. Nixon brought Cliff, a lawyer sympathetic to the black cause, cases and engaged in friendly relations with the couple. In her autobiography, Virginia relates a revealing incident. She had always addressed the black man as Mr. Nixon, but one day, on seeing him at the post office, she held out her hand and said, "Hello Ed," to which he did not react. After she had come back to her husband's office, Nixon arrived and informed her he needed to discuss something with her. As she waited in surprise, he said, "Look, don't you ever call me Ed again. If I called you Virginia, I'd be lynched." He explained to her that under segregation rules, a black man and a white woman could not interact on an equal basis. "Now when I can call you Virginia, you can call me Ed. And I'll shake your hand in public when it's safe. You ought to have better sense than to come up to a black man in the public post office and say 'Hello, Ed' and put out your hand." With hindsight, she reflected, "It wasn't that he was mad at me. It was that I was putting him in danger. He didn't think they were going to do anything to *me*, but he thought they might do something to him." And indeed, the risks were real for black men.[64]

The issue was so crucially rooted in segregationist culture that it became a stake in the fight for equality. Actually, as white women and black men were physically and psychologically kept apart by fear of retaliation, some black men challenged the etiquette as a form of militancy. This was the case of Ralph Abernathy, with whom Durr became friends. Contrasting Abernathy's behavior with Martin Luther King Jr.'s "dignity and reserve," she recalled, "Abernathy was different. Every time he'd see me in a public place, he'd come up and kiss me. He knew as well as I did that that was absolutely taboo, but I was an old lady by then, and that was his way of showing that he liked me." The fact that Durr was old did not change the subversive character of Abernathy's attitude, and she knew it. "He was an old Southern politician—he kissed all the ladies, both black and white. Underneath that clownish manner, he is a very brave man." As Durr points out, such an attitude was not insignificant, considering that King told the American public on television during the same period that black men had been "robbed of their manhood."[65]

If one adds that the civil rights movement radicalized in the 1960s under the influence of a new generation of black activists, it is easy to understand that physical contact with white women could become for black men a conspicuous way of challenging white supremacy. The issue became all the more sensitive since the members of the new generation represented by the Student Nonviolent Coordinating Committee (SNCC) not only challenged the racial order but also sought to overthrow all the traditional social norms deemed oppressive, including sexual taboos. In this context, the young white women who joined the movement in the early 1960s stood as constant reminders of the ultimate taboo of interracial sex, but their very presence and dedication to the black cause also offered the immediate opportunity to violate this taboo. Commenting on the interracial relationships that occurred during the 1960s civil rights movement, Lynne Olson observes that white female volunteers "insisted that being part of the 'beloved community' meant being free to love whomever they chose, regardless of what society had to say about the choice." According to another historian, Mary Aickin Rothschild, having sex with black men "was a way to 'prove' their 'commitment' to black and white equality." As for black men, they were bound to nourish ambivalent feelings toward white women, who represented both an object of desire and a symbol of oppression. Thus one of them told psychiatrist Alvin Poussaint: "Whenever I'm around one of these white girls, I don't know whether I feel like kissing her or punching her in the mouth!" It was perfectly understandable that after decades of oppression, black males should "come to view sexual intimacy with white girls as a weapon of revenge against white society."[66] Moreover, relationships between black men and white women could cause resentment among black women, as their own relations with white women were also unfavorably conditioned by the legacy of white supremacy. The potentially liberating character of interracial sex between white women and black men, however, ended up actually occurring only occasionally. Indeed, for the most part, relations between white women and black men within the modern civil rights movement were still thwarted by fear and insecurity. Personal relations remained conditioned throughout the movement by the intertwined forces of race, sex, and gender lying at the core of southern culture, and the main goal of these male and female activists consisted in overcoming the barriers created by segregation.[67]

Thus the generation of white women who came of age during the desegregation crisis—that is, between the late 1950s and the mid-1960s—although distinctively marked by the economic and social changes brought about by World War II, shared with the previous generation the burdensome legacy of southern history. Whether one considers the early period of reform activism between the two world wars or the post–World War II era, the common bond between all white southern women seems to have been the impossibility for them to relate in a natural, unambiguous way to black men and women. What actually distinguished white southern women from other white American women from the slavery era to the 1960s was the interconnection of Victorian gender norms and white supremacy in the shaping of their identity. As they became ever more committed to racial equality between the 1920s and the 1960s, the women challenged these norms and broke free from their initial indoctrination.

Unlearning Racism

The typical trajectory of the women studied in this volume, after reaching adulthood, consisted in first breaking a racial taboo, realizing the essential morality of such an act, and then struggling to reeducate themselves by forgetting their childhood lessons. They were thus bound to reject their native culture at one point or another in their adult lives. Such a rejection could occur on reaching adulthood or at an already mature age, it could be sudden or could take years, but in all cases the women were ultimately turned into dissenters in their native communities after going through the same pattern of events, the same stages of psychological awakening, and, for most of them, the same traumas.

In describing at length the effect of education on their young minds, the authors of memoirs present themselves as victims of their culture. Their writing is an act of personal expiation but also a gesture of emancipation, as they find extenuating circumstances for their original racism. Racial guilt is a pervasive feeling residing deep in the conscience of all the whites who joined the struggle against segregation at mid-twentieth century. It is the major factor accounting for the disproportionately high number of memoirs and other life narratives published by white southerners between the 1940s and today, narratives that Fred Hobson has described as "racial conversion narratives," in an analogy with the Puritan conversion narrative of the seventeenth and early eighteenth centuries. Just as the Puritan finds redemption through confessing his or her sin in writing, white southerners, "all products of and willing participants in a harsh, segregated society, confess racial wrongdoings and are 'converted,' in varying degrees, from racism to something approaching racial enlightenment."[68] Guilt affected all the women studied here, whatever their differences in age or social background. It is obviously not present in the recollections of early childhood, but it is nevertheless identified in all memoirs and interviews as an inherent feature of white identity. "I knew something was wrong," writes Braden, "but for years I did not understand what it was."[69] Indeed, as the memoirs show, the realization at some point that segregation was not the ideal way of life that adults claimed it was, and that it was harmful to blacks and whites, triggered a feeling of guilt that marked the beginning of a long process of unlearning and led ultimately to the rejection of childhood lessons.

The process went through several stages between childhood and adulthood—and in some cases even mature age. Most women recalled key moments in their spiritual development that can be split into two kinds, traumatic episodes and epiphanies. Traumatic episodes most often occurred early in life and represented turning points at which the children were shocked by the adults' attitude and started to question their legitimacy. Katharine Lumpkin, who was the direct descendant of slaveholders, witnessed a scene that changed her outlook enough for her to relate it in detail in her autobiography. Her family, a prominent Georgia family, was living in South Carolina in an old country house reminiscent of plantation society. One morning, she came into the house and found her father thrashing the black cook. She was hurt as she saw the pain on the woman's face and heard her screaming. "I could see her writhing under the blows of a descending stick wielded by the white master of the house. I could see her face distorted with fear and agony and his with stern rage." Later that day, on inquiring about the reasons for the thrashing, she was answered that the cook had been "'impudent' to her mistress." She was then overcome with a mixed feeling of sympathy for the black woman, on the one hand, which made her question the legitimacy of the punishment, and loyalty to her parents, on the other. "I knew 'impudence' was intolerable," she comments. "In this sense I had no qualms about what I had witnessed. But in another sense I did have, and this disturbed me." This incident opened Lumpkin's eyes to the unjust reality of segregation, as she concludes: "The inevitable had happened, and what is bound to come to a Southern child chanced to come to me this way. Thereafter, I was fully aware of myself as a white, and of Negroes as Negroes. Thenceforth, I began to be self-conscious about the many signs and symbols of my race position that had been battering against my consciousness since virtual infancy."[70] In other words, she suddenly realized that her white skin indirectly turned her into an oppressor of black people.

For Anne Braden, that realization occurred in two stages. The first shock came to her when a male friend of hers told her in the heat of a discussion, "We have to have a good lynching every once in a while to keep the nigger in his place." She was stunned to discover hatred where she had not expected it: "Words of murder from one of the gentlest people I ever knew." The second incident occurred after she had finished college and was working as a reporter for a local newspaper in Birmingham, Alabama. She covered the city courthouse. One morning, she was having breakfast in a cafeteria with a friend, who asked her if she had news, to which she answered, "No . . . everything quiet. Nothing but a colored murder." She realized the horror of what she was saying while saying it, because she could sense the reaction of the black waitress who was serving them at the same moment, but it was too late. In a variant of the scene that Lumpkin had experienced, Braden suddenly discovered that she was as guilty of racism as her male friend: "But all of a sudden—like a shaft of morning sunlight over that breakfast table—the truth dawned on me. I had meant what I had said; I had meant it just as surely as the man who had talked to me about lynching had meant what he said." She was a potential murderer just like any other white southerner. As she put it, "I was part of this white world that considered a Negro life not worth bothering about. If I did not oppose it, I was part of it—and I was responsible for its sins."[71]

Like Braden, several women of the older generation trace back their awakening to a sudden confrontation with the horror of lynching. Adolphine Fletcher Terry, who had been raised in Little Rock, Arkansas, under the influence of southern ideology, recalled arguing with a fellow student soon after entering Vassar College in 1898. In the heat of the discussion, she naturally repeated the saying she had assimilated as moral evidence, "If a black man assaulted a white woman he should be lynched on the spot." Not only could she not conceive of lynching without associating it with the rape of a white woman, but she thought the practice legitimate and obviously did not apprehend it as murder. It took a northern student's shocked reaction, "For the sake of taking revenge on one poor black wretch, would you destroy the very foundations of law and order in your community?," to make her realize the flaw in her outlook. "I knew she was right," she later wrote in her autobiography. "It gave me an entirely different look, an adult look, at the situation we faced here in the South."[72] This example shows that on reaching adulthood, white women naturally adopted the rhetoric of protection and even encouraged lynching. Terry did not get rid of her prejudice overnight, since when a lynching occurred in Little Rock in 1927, she did not feel concerned by the event. She was not directly involved in it, and like all women of her race and class, she had been conditioned into thinking that although they were sometimes necessary for the preservation of order and justice in society, lynchings were committed by unworthy whites and should not be encouraged. This early episode, however, constituted a first step in her personal transformation from racist to integrationist.[73]

As for Thelma Stevens, who grew up in Mississippi, she was unexpectedly confronted with brutal reality at the age of nineteen. She was then a high school teacher in Mississippi, and was asked by a group of students to go with them on a bus trip. They did not tell her where they were going, but they needed to be accompanied by an adult. It turned out that what they wanted to see was a spectacle lynching. Stevens tells, "And suddenly the bus turned down into the hillside. And there were hundreds, literally hundreds, of people on the hillside. And there was a man hanging from a limb. And men standing all around him with guns in their hands, shooting at him." It was an intense trauma to the young teacher, whereas the girls were apparently too excited by the event, which was organized as a show, to realize the horror of it. The lynching constituted a turning point in Stevens's life, as she decided, "if the Lord would let me live long enough, that I would do something to bring a little bit of relief from fear and a little human dignity to black people in Mississippi."[74] She later became a leader for the Woman's Division of the Board of Missions of the Methodist Church, and as such participated in the struggle for desegregation until 1968.

Another form of trauma concerned all the women who had been first taken care of by black nurses—that is, most of them since it was common for middle- and upper-class families to hire black servants—and who were in contact with black children in the first years of their lives. The black nurse, or mammy, was a staple figure in the experience of non-working-class white southerners who grew up during the segregation era, since, as Smith informs us, "It was customary in the South, if a family possessed a moderate income, to have a colored nurse for the children."[75] The loving nurse, identified as a second mother, features in most fiction and nonfiction narratives set within the framework of segregation. As the authors reveal in a great diversity of styles, from the most subjectively emotional to the most analytical, the nurse's status was a highly ambivalent one, because it crystallized all the contradictions inherent in segregationist culture. She was family and not family at the same time. As she was in care of the children from their birth, a privileged intimate relationship developed between her and them. Whereas the white mother stood for moral authority and rules, the black nurse represented unmitigated love and warmth. "Memories of Negro nurses for most of us are devoid of unpleasant associations," writes Boyle. The children often found comfort from their nurse after being scolded by their parents. Yet, as a black woman, the nurse was never considered part of the family, even if she lived within the white household, and this reality became painfully apparent to the white child when the lessons in segregationist etiquette began. The bond that had tied the white child to the nurse was systematically severed as the child grew up, leaving him or her with a sense of loss that was hard to overcome. Smith argues that "however they dealt with it, nearly all men—and women—of the dominant class in the South suffered not only the usual painful experiences of growing up in America but this special southern trauma in which segregation not only divided the races but divided the white child's heart."[76]

To Virginia Durr, the trauma included losing her beloved nurse and her black playmates on the same day. She remembers her seventh birthday as a fateful turning point in her life. Until that year, it had been the habit to celebrate Virginia's birthday by having a barbecue with the black children in the backyard. This time, however, she was told the black children could not participate. After she had a temper tantrum, a compromise was agreed upon. There would be a barbecue in the backyard in the morning with the black children, and an all-white party in the front yard in the afternoon. The barbecue was marred when Virginia's cousin insulted Sarah, the black nurse's daughter, by declaring, "I'm not going to eat any chicken that your black hand has touched, you little nigger." By the end of the day, Virginia had gone into a rage, been punished by the white adults, and found comfort in the lap of her offended nurse, who left the next morning, never to return. "That was a terrible trauma in my life," she concludes.[77] Her feelings then must have been quite akin to those of Lillian Smith, who learned her lessons well. "I knew by the time I was twelve ... that my old nurse who had cared for me through long months of illness, who had given me refuge when a little sister took my place as the baby of the family, who soothed, fed me, delighted me with her stories and games, let me fall asleep on her deep warm breast, was not worthy of the passionate love I felt for her but must be given instead a half-smiled-at affection similar to that which one feels for one's dog."[78] Such experiences were not isolated cases, and they were bound to happen due to the way segregationist society functioned. Virtually all white southerners remembered having lived two lives, an integrated one in early childhood and a segregated one after being separated against their will from the blacks who had surrounded them in their first years.[79]

Whereas the traumas of childhood opened cracks in the cement of segregationist education, but were soon buried deep with the unfolding of adolescence, epiphanies, which occurred later, marked the real start of a conscious process of unlearning. Such moments were the catalysts that set white women on the path of rejecting white supremacy. In virtually all cases, the women were made to realize, by a black person, not only that segregation rules were not moral as they had been taught, but that violating them was no sin. At the age of nineteen, in 1915, Katharine Lumpkin went to a student Young Women's Christian Association (YWCA) conference in North Carolina. The YWCA was more advanced on race at the time than other associations, but it had separate branches for black and white women. That summer, a leader of the conference, who was a southerner, asked the group if they would listen to a black speaker whom she presented as "Miss Arthur," thus ignoring the rule that precluded the use of courtesy titles for blacks and thus implying that she treated the woman as an equal. The white students accepted after a night of confusion and great apprehension. "We were like a little company of Eves, who, not from being tempted—surely, we did not long to eat the fruit which up to now had been called forbidden—but by sheer force of unsought circumstance found ourselves called upon to pluck from the Tree of Life the apple that would open our eyes to see what was good and evil." As Lumpkin put it, the confusion was caused by the fact that they were asked to commit an act that was deemed wrong by the standards of their segregationist education, but that was deemed right by the standards of their YWCA leader. Lumpkin was afraid, but she ran the risk. And she discovered that the black woman was as well-mannered, as articulate, and as dignified as any white woman in her position would be. "If I closed my eyes," she told herself, "would I know whether she was white or Negro?" She realized at the same time that interacting with blacks as equals was not the sin she had been warned against all her life, and she adds, "In any event, when it was over, I found the heavens had not fallen, nor the earth parted asunder to swallow us up in this unheard of transgression." She had always been forbidden to cross the color line, but here she was: "I had done it, and nothing, not the slightest thing had happened."[80]

For the white southern women who later became integrationists, such as Lumpkin, the first step in unlearning their segregationist education took the form of interracial contact. Several remember being transformed after violating the ultimate taboo of eating with a black person. Lumpkin did so a few years after her first transgression, which spared her the shock of violating southern etiquette.[81] Braden experienced it in her third year of college (she was also nineteen). She had been invited by a southern white friend to have lunch with a black student in New York City, where her friend was studying. Feeling uncomfortable at first, she soon realized that she had completely forgotten about color after a while. "It was a tremendous revelation," she recalls. "It may sound like a small thing when it is told, but it was a turning point in my life. All the cramping walls of a lifetime seemed to come tumbling down in that moment. Some heavy shackles seemed to have fallen from my feet."[82] The same feeling of liberation was felt by Sarah Boyle when she learned that for the first time in its history, the University of Virginia, where her husband taught, would have to admit a black student in the fall of 1950. She writes, "I felt lighter. Although I hadn't known it, my chest had been in a plaster cast and now was sawed free. I could breathe!" Boyle also sensed the same reversal of standards that Lumpkin had when she had agreed to violate southern rules. "As this heresy broke free from my center, I felt myself growing tall. From my new height, I saw how small and cheap, mechanical and far from the basic works of the Creator, are many of the laws, customs, and beliefs of the South."[83] Virginia Durr did not have such moral pangs the first time she had lunch with a black student, although the incident was important enough to be remembered. She explains she was forced to do so by the head of Wellesley College in Boston in 1922. She actually had to choose between abiding by the school's rules or leaving. Her main motive for her first opposition to it was fear of her father's reaction if he learned that she had violated the southern code. She finally decided to stay, assuming that her father would never know about it. Even though the act was not such an intense experience for Durr as it had been for others, it was nevertheless a step in her personal transformation. It "may not have been crucial at the time, but it was the origin of a doubt. It hurt my faith, my solid conviction of what I had been raised to believe."[84]

The younger generation had similar experiences. Connie Bradford, the daughter of a prominent conservative family, used the word "epiphany" to describe her first encounter with black people at a Congress of Racial Equality (CORE) meeting in late 1961, while she was a student at Newcomb College in New Orleans. "I shook their hands and talked to them. My head was turned around real instantaneously," she recalled. The historian Shannon Frystak adds: "Bradford immediately joined the movement and never looked back, even at the cost of her relationship with her family." Rebecca Owen, born in 1940 in Virginia, joined the Methodist Youth Fellowship (MYF) at adolescence, and attended her first interracial gathering, the Purdue National Conference, in 1955. She notes, "I was not able to escape the feeling that there should be some relationship between what I heard in my larger church and the segregation I knew in my community. I returned home deeply puzzled and talked with my MYF leader and other persons whom I respected." Sue Thrasher went to her first interracial event in 1961 at Vanderbilt University in Nashville, Tennessee. The event was sponsored by the Methodist Student Movement. Her real awakening occurred soon after she had come back to Jackson, Tennessee, where she was studying. She drove past a black student she had met in Nashville, who was picketing Woolworth's downtown store. She only then grasped the deep implications of segregation for black people, and what it meant to fight against it. "There was so much dignity and courage in his act," she writes, "but I also recognized the danger of what he was doing. There was something about that moment that made me stop and think." The sight of the picketing black student revealed to her the evil she had not been able to see before. As a result, "I was growing ashamed of the South. Having been taught about the Fatherhood of God and the brotherhood of man, I couldn't see why anyone should have to picket in order to eat at a lunch counter."[85]

Religion was indeed the major force that brought the women first to question the legitimacy of their childhood lessons, and then to act in accordance with their principles. All of them, with no exception, stress the omnipresence of religious lessons in their youth, be it at home or in the community.

According to Constance Curry, of the younger generation, the central place of religion in their lives constituted the major common denominator between old and young white southern antiracist women.[86] A significant number of racial dissenters were Catholics and Jews. The large majority, however, were Protestants. Some historians have stressed the determining influence of the Protestant tradition on southern women reformers. The individuals profiled here corroborate this idea.[87] Lillian Smith reminds us that "we cannot understand the church's role as a teacher of southern children without realizing the strength of religion in the lives of everybody, rich and poor." Sue Thrasher declares, "the church was one the most important institutions in my life." Frances Pauley echoes her by remembering, "I was very religious. I was trying to live what I thought was a Christian life." Joan Browning describes her story as a "spiritual journey," "from Daddy's all-white Shiloh Methodist Church in south Georgia and Mother's Mt. Zion Baptist Church in west Georgia to Albany's all-black Shiloh and Mt. Zion Baptist Churches, where I was welcomed as a Freedom Rider."[88] Many women were the daughters of Protestant ministers. Such was the case of Sarah Boyle, Virginia Durr, Edith Dabbs, Lucy Mason, Dorothy Tilly for the older generation, of Sheila McCurdy, Mary King, and Jane Stembridge for the younger. When they were not, their education was nevertheless punctuated by Bible readings at home and in Sunday school. The result was that they developed deeply religious conceptions of life and society, which determined their later commitment to the civil rights movement. It is indeed quite clear that their Protestant faith drew them close to the southern black liberation movement, which had its roots in black religion.[89] Sheila McCurdy actually uses the word "conversion" to relate how she was driven to the black movement in 1963 on hearing Martin Luther King Jr. preach. She writes, "As I heard his prophetic words, I knew that my life would never be the same again. When I reflect on that evening, I realize that it was a conversion experience, a time in which I experienced the liberating spirit of the God of Exodus in a new way."[90] Obviously, McCurdy was not converted out of nothing. She had been prepared for this moment by her former religious development since childhood.

Religion determined the women's future by providing them with fundamental values on which to build their whole conception of life and human relations. Anne Braden writes, "I was a deeply religious child. I loved the services of the Episcopal church, and these services are rich with the words of brotherhood." Sue Thrasher traces the roots of her activism back to the church of her childhood: "It taught me some of the basic values I brought to the Freedom Movement—like the fatherhood of God and the brotherhood of man."[91] Ironically, the initial teachings of established Protestant religion, which were set in a segregationist framework, were a key factor in the rejection of the religious institutions that had provided them. As they grew older, the women found it increasingly hard to reconcile the message of universal brotherhood they had embraced with the reality of segregationist practices. At one point in their lives, they were necessarily brought to the same conclusion as Anne Braden: "White Southern society had injected much that was poison into my lifeblood.... But it had also had its ideals, and I had inherited those too. One of these was the principle that no man can live for himself alone, that each man has a responsibility to his fellow man ... and I knew that I must follow that ideal now or succumb to schizophrenia, as so many did." The reference to schizophrenia is used by other authors to describe the effect of segregation on white southerners. It is a central metaphor in Smith's work. Together with numerous images of fragmentation, it conveys the fundamental contradiction lying at the core of segregationist culture: "Minds broken. Hearts broken. Conscience torn from acts. A culture split in a thousand pieces. That is segregation."[92] When the contradiction between beliefs and acts became unbearable, white women broke with the establishment and joined religious organizations that offered an alternative view of human relations in keeping with the values they had first learned to cherish. Until World War II, the leading organizations of this kind were the YWCA and the Woman's Division of the Methodist Church. Following World War II, these groups were joined by United Church Women, the Fellowship of the Concerned, Councils on Human Relations, and the Student Christian Movement. Once the black liberation movement was a fully blown movement, a number of white women participated in it. The younger generation was especially attracted to SNCC, whose members were deeply religious in its initial years.

Finally, the last factor that played a significant part in white women's transformation was their experience of higher education.[93] Women's access to higher education remained restricted to a tiny minority in the South before World War II, as the region resisted the social and cultural changes that thrust the United States into the modern era. The region's leaders ostensibly rejected the liberalization of society that took place in the nation from 1920 on, a conservatism that translated into the maintenance of traditional gender norms, beginning with the assumption that higher education was not suitable for women. So, it should not come as a surprise that the few who did go to college should be enough influenced by the experience to choose a different path from their less well educated peers afterward. Whether they left the South to study or not, the young women first found themselves free from the direct influence of their family and of their community, which is obviously a common characteristic of all young people who go to college. In the case of these women, however, this new state of freedom was probably more crucial in their personal development owing to the rigidity of the etiquette they had had to respect thus far. Moreover, those who went to states where segregation was not the law were suddenly put into contact with white students who did not object to interacting with blacks, or were even led to interact directly with black students, as Durr's account shows. Living outside the South for a time also placed the students in a position where they could observe their native region from a new perspective, with distance, which made them more critical, as Lumpkin felt soon after entering Columbia University in 1918. "Until now, it came over me, I had never studied the South. I had never 'gone to the sources,' 'checked facts against hearsay,' sorted out 'unbiased from biased history.' . . . I began to doubt my own characterizations, and my fellows' as well. I soon became surfeited with the invariable echoes of the same old themes, and not a little impatient with our clearly-evident complacency."[94]

Those who remained in the South were obviously not forced to question the legitimacy of their native culture, but higher education nevertheless taught them to "use their minds," as Durr puts it.[95] College was a place of intellectual awakening, as many recognize, insofar as it encouraged questioning and discussion. In the context of the segregationist South, this was no insignificant fact. "For the first time in my life," writes Braden about her entering Stratford College in Virginia in 1942, "segregation became a topic for conversation. Then it was that the developing fluid began to work." Even if most women's colleges steered a cautious, conservative course in focusing on academic subjects, the students were encouraged to think about their culture, their society, and their history. Constance Curry, who attended Agnes Scott College in Decatur, Georgia, in the early 1950s, was expected to read and comment on a varied selection of books tackling the controversial issues of southern identity and race relations, from Wilbur Cash's highly critical *The Mind of the South* to U. B. Phillips's much more conservative *Life and Labor in the Old South*.[96]

One definitely liberal streak in the small world of women's colleges was cultivated by Methodist institutions, the leading one being Scarritt College in Nashville. Founded in 1892 in Kansas City, Missouri, as the Scarritt Bible and Training College and placed under the supervision of the Woman's Foreign Mission Society, it was originally designed to train Methodist women to become social workers in the broad context of the Social Gospel movement. It was moved to Nashville in 1924 to become Scarritt College, and asserted itself as a prominent institution in the regional higher education network. The college kept its social orientation, so that by the 1930s the sociologist Charles S. Johnson observed that "Scarritt had become one of the two most significant white educational institutions in the South in fostering a 'positive and dynamic response' to social issues."[97] The women who attended Scarritt found the means to apply to society the Christian principles they had been taught during childhood, instead of struggling with the contradictions of the segregationist etiquette. Thelma Stevens, who became in 1940 executive secretary for the Department of Christian Social Relations and Local Church Activities of the Woman's Division of the Board of Missions of the Methodist Church, found at Scarritt what she had not found in her church. She explained that "the church was isolated from life. It was a place where you go on Sunday morning and listen to the sermon that didn't mean a thing to you.... But the church didn't give a darn about those kids out there in that black school, that they got three dollars a year for their education, and the white children got from nine to twelve dollars, in that generation." By contrast, "the purpose of Scarritt was to stimulate you to understand the world in which you lived." So, Alice Knotts explains, "At Scarritt, Stevens entered an academic climate influenced by the Social Gospel and by forward-thinking southerners. She met professors who shared her theological understanding that people should be treated with justice regardless of race."[98] Some professors were a determining influence in the lives of their students. Of Louise Young, her sociology professor at Scarritt, Stevens says, "She helped hundreds of young women get new concepts of the meaning of working with people." A number of key professors became role models for the young women with whom they interacted.[99] Such relationships between teachers and students were definitely favored by the nature of women's education in the first half of the twentieth century. Indeed, as long as women and men attended separate institutions, the younger women could easily identify with their elders as spiritual daughters or sisters, which contributed to the emergence of female networks that were to play an important part later in the development of a specific activism.

The women who attended college in the 1950s and 1960s could go to women's or to coeducational institutions. If some found role models in teachers as the previous generation had done, the majority were influenced by student religious leaders who worked on southern campuses. In the decades following World War II, the Student Christian Movement, mainly represented by Young Men's Christian Association (YMCA) and YWCA infrastructures on campuses, provided inspiration to the white students who had received a segregationist education and were seeking ways of reconciling their Christian faith with their lives. The historian Sara Evans, who was herself a student at Duke University beginning in 1962, provides valuable insight into the determining role of religious leaders in the students' commitment to racial equality, drawing both from her personal experience and from her research on the subject. According to Evans, "This loosely defined 'movement' became more coherent in the early years of the cold war (1950s and 1960s) before dissipating in the 1970s, but its legacy remains a powerful part of the story of many movements for social justice that emerged in those same years."[100] The point is that, for both generations, it was not so much the nature of higher education as the environment and the climate it offered that played a crucial part in the process of unlearning the lessons of white supremacy.

Thus the autobiographical narratives and direct testimonies available today highlight a great number of commonalities between the two generations of white women who came to reject the racist assumptions of their native culture. All of them recall similar experiences that shook them into awareness at some point of their lives. Interracial contact, religion, and higher education stand out as determining factors in this process of emancipation. Moreover, the same women's trajectories reveal another common feature between them, their stories reflecting a dialectical link between their racial activism and their emancipation from southern gender norms.

Unlearning Ladyhood

Even if the social and cultural evolution of the twentieth century gradually undermined traditional norms and if the civil rights movement inflicted a severe blow to the traditional definition of southern womanhood, all the white women who became involved in interracial reform from the 1920s to the 1960s had to negotiate with the lady ideal in one way or another. As early conditions greatly differed from those of the 1960s, however, the two generations differed accordingly in their attitudes toward southern gender norms. Moreover, these attitudes were closely related to the approaches they favored in the struggle for racial equality. In any case, whatever their approaches and attitudes, most of the women who worked for racial justice in the South up to the 1970s went through a process of personal emancipation from gender norms as their fight against segregation inevitably led them to undermine the ideal of white southern womanhood.

Given the distinctive connection between race and gender characteristic of southern culture, any questioning of the racial order was bound to entail a questioning of the patriarchal order to which it was inextricably linked. In many cases, such questioning came as a by-product of racial activism since it clearly emanated from the women's commitment to racial equality. In others, it had always existed, but the women repressed it until their involvement in the civil rights movement brought it to the surface. Ultimately, most white women activists came to repudiate the ideal of the southern lady altogether, thus liberating themselves as women while fighting for the liberation of blacks.

Although southern women did not articulate any powerful critique of gender oppression before the 1960s—Lillian Smith standing out as the only exception—several members of the old generation identified the link between white supremacy and white patriarchy during the long civil rights movement but kept their views private. Interestingly, although they did not acknowledge this link publicly at the time, the few who later published autobiographies or memoirs did include and discuss the issue in their narratives. Virginia Durr's case speaks for others. The title of her autobiography, *Outside the Magic Circle*, testifies to the evolution of her outlook as it refers to her personal emancipation. The foreword explains that she once said:

There were three ways for a well-brought-up young Southern white woman to go.

She could be the actress, playing out the stereotype of the Southern belle. Gracious to the "colored help," flirtatious to her powerful father-in-law, and offering a sweet, winning smile to the world. In short, going with the wind.

If she had a spark of independence or worse, creativity, she could go crazy—on the dark, shadowy street traveled by more than one stunning Southern belle.

Or she could be the rebel. She could step outside the magic circle, abandon privilege, and challenge this way of life. Ostracism, bruises of all sorts, and defamation would be her lot. Her reward would be a truly examined life. And a world she would otherwise never have known.[101]

Durr's centering her autobiography on her identity as a white southern woman not only reveals the interconnection of race and gender in her own experience but also reflects a concern to tell the shared experience of a specific group, that of "well-brought-up young Southern white" women.

Sara Parsons draws the same parallel between individual and collective emancipation in her own autobiography in which she narrates her transformation from "southern lady" to political activist. Parsons establishes a close tie between her gradual involvement in the civil rights movement and her personal emancipation, but, rather than arguing that her growing racial activism caused her to reject gender norms by raising her female consciousness, she explains how the two processes coincided in her life and fueled each other. The turning point in her life occurred in 1953 when she realized that most of the women in her church's Women's Society were not registered to vote, and she successfully contacted the League of Women Voters to get them to register. "From this point in 1953 onward," she comments, "the steps in my long journey from complacent, middle-class southern housewife to liberal, integrationist politician came much more quickly." As she became more aware of the world surrounding her, she also realized she could play an active part in it: "When I look back on this period of huge transition in my life, I realize that the sense of being heard, of being accepted as having a brain, and of being capable of leadership fueled my budding political activity."[102]

The members of the younger generation went through similar experiences except that their repudiation of traditional standards occurred much earlier in their lives. It was also definitely more sudden than the slow process their elders went through, because the student movement in which they participated advocated immediate, radical change not only in race relations but in all forms of human relations. SNCC—in which many of this generation were involved—actually aspired to the creation of a new society rather than the reformation of the old. Thus the historian Sara Evans argues: "Building on their new strengths, looking consciously to new models both black and white, southern white women in SNCC as early as 1960 sensed that the achievement of racial equality required fundamental changes in sex roles. To them the term 'southern lady' was an obscene epithet." If SNCC constituted a specific ferment for the women's liberation movement, as Evans has shown, the broader black liberation movement definitely altered young white women's perception of themselves, whatever groups they joined. Margaret Rose Gladney, for instance, who was secretary of the Memphis Southern Christian Leadership Conference (SCLC) in 1968–69 (at the age of twenty-four), explains: "My feminist consciousness raising came right along with my search for an answer to racism, and ultimately and [sic] awareness of the interlocking directorate of race, class, gender, sexuality isms in our culture."[103] Dorothy Burlage describes at length her transformation from lady to woman in her personal account of her movement years. She explains that her questioning of southern norms of womanhood developed as her commitment to racial equality deepened: "As I got older and felt morally compelled to speak out about civil rights, my outspokenness conflicted with my training to be a southern lady, creating an internal struggle that began in college and continued during my years in the movement." Burlage stresses the fact that the movement constituted the catalyst of her rebellion against her native culture as she was all but a natural-born activist. She comments: "Although I was considered an anomaly by most of the southern white world, I continued to see myself as a personally conservative young woman who happened to believe strongly in civil rights."[104]

The liberating character of the civil rights movement for white southern women takes on still another dimension through the experience of Casey Hayden and Mary King, who reached a point in 1964 when they articulated a reflection on gender discrimination in the movement. The two young women were key members of SNCC at the time. The year 1964 was a turning point for them as well as for the organization, which was struggling to overcome the growing disillusionment, bitterness, and discontent that threatened its future.[105] It was in this context that Hayden and King put together a short paper entitled "SNCC Position Paper: Women in the Movement," which King had drafted. The core of the paper consisted in creating an analogy between race and gender discrimination based on the authors' experience in SNCC.[106] The point here is not to analyze at length this controversial episode of SNCC's history—this will be done in a later chapter—but to show that the members of the younger generation developed an acute gender awareness during the 1960s civil rights movement, the movement providing the conditions for the emergence and articulation of such an awareness. Mary King devotes a whole chapter of her memoir to the issue. After explaining, "my proximity to the suffering of blacks in the South and the creative ferment within the civil rights movement prompted a deep personal awareness of the condition of women," she goes on to emphasize the catalyzing function of the movement for her:

> Having deeply internalized Ella Baker's lesson that the oppressed themselves must define their own freedom, I felt I could not allow the civil rights movement to overlook fundamental questions that remain unanswered by our and other movement protests, conflicts, and revolutions: Who defines what it is to be a woman? Why must women form a second class? Who decides whether men and women are superior or inferior? Who determines the validity of another's existence?[107]

Hayden and King's paper thus emphasized the liberating character of the civil rights movement for women, by bringing to the surface a process the movement had triggered early on.

All in all, the evolution of these women demonstrates the causal link between their fight for racial equality and their personal emancipation from the gender norms imposed on them by their culture. The civil rights movement truly liberated and empowered them by providing the conceptual tools they needed to identify prejudices and denounce them as obstacles to the achievement of the aims the movement was aspiring to. The collective identity of white southern women thus underwent a gradual evolution from the early decades of the segregation era to the late 1960s. In the 1920s, before the expansion of antiracist activism across the region, white women were less defined as actual members of society than as an abstract construction buttressing the white supremacist order. As they committed themselves ever more strongly to racial equality, racial activists found their efforts increasingly hindered by the constraints of traditional white southern womanhood. The struggle for blacks' civil rights thus entailed a struggle against southern gender norms. By the 1960s, these women had turned from southern ladies to southern women.

* * *

The various life narratives and testimonies examined for this book unambiguously show that the establishment of segregation at the turn of the twentieth century and the defense of the system until the 1960s created a specific set of values and norms of behavior that intimately combined race, gender, sex, and class. White women found themselves at the intersection of these forces, which not only conditioned their position with regard to white men but also deeply affected their relationships with black women and black men. Race and gender roles became strictly codified, so much so that dissenting from white supremacist dogma became an extraordinary act of will. The women profiled in this book did dissent while remaining deeply attached to their region. All of them struggled against segregation in many different ways, but they experienced a very similar process of unlearning their white supremacist lessons when they became involved in the cause for racial justice. As the long civil rights movement developed, they also had to reconsider the ideal of southern womanhood that conditioned their behavior, ultimately bringing forth their own emancipation from white southern patriarchy. Whether they ended up undermining part of the ideal or repudiating it altogether, all of them ultimately became freer women as a result of their fight for African Americans' freedom.

2

Before *Brown*

Southern Lady Activism

The first generation of white women to become involved in racial reform emerged after World War I. The South of the 1920s differed strikingly from the rest of the United States in many ways. Since the Civil War, the southern economy had distinguished itself by its pervasive poverty due to a variety of factors. The abolition of slavery had entailed the establishment of the sharecropping system in agriculture and the development of a few labor-intensive industries in the sectors of tobacco, textile, mining, and lumber. The regional economy remained predominantly based on cotton production, with an industry heavily dependent on northern investments and without developed manufacturing infrastructures. Segregation and the dominant social conservatism maintained the majority of rural and industrial workers in poverty. As for politics, the system had been reshaped in the late nineteenth century by the restoration of white supremacy. The Democratic Party had effectively ousted the Republican Party from the region. Blacks had been deprived through a variety of devices of the voting rights gained after the Civil War. Unlike white primaries, which specifically excluded blacks from internal Democratic Party elections, literacy tests and the poll tax imposed by the states as a prerequisite for voting also theoretically affected a majority of whites, but local authorities mainly used them to bar blacks from registering. In sum, southern society was blatantly undemocratic in the first decades of the twentieth century.[1] To make matters worse, any change in these general conditions seemed all the more unlikely since southern culture was permeated by the doctrine of white supremacy and by the memory of the Civil War isolating southerners from national trends and maintaining the South in an antagonistic posture vis-à-vis the rest of the nation.

The following pages show how some white women responded to this situation and to the events of the three decades that led to the *Brown v. Board of Education* decision in 1954. Although women won a historic victory through the ratification of the Nineteenth Amendment in 1920, southern women basically remained confined to the traditional roles that their culture had assigned them, generally devoting their public activities to mission work. Their status and activities evolved, however, as a result of two key episodes of American history: the Great Depression and World War II. Starting in the 1930s, the Depression and the New Deal entailed a redefinition of the relationship between the federal government and the states, which directly affected southern society and politics. As for the war, it marked the beginning of a coordinated assault on segregation. As a new generation of black activists asked for the immediate end of Jim Crow, with the support of a tiny minority of whites, the federal government showed new signs of concern for civil rights, signaling the beginning of a new era. White women reformers responded positively to these developments, by shifting from a very paternalistic attitude to a genuine commitment to full equality, but they did so gradually and without publicity. All were first motivated by a deep religious faith, but they were inevitably drawn into politics through their commitment to racial justice.

Although the examples dealt with in this chapter are characterized by a great variety of outlooks, they share enough similarities to enable identification of a few distinctive features typical of the white southern woman reformer in the pre-*Brown* era. Whether they emphasized the religious, moral, economic, or political aspects of race relations and the means to improve them, all the women examined in this chapter shared characteristics that made them a unique brand of activists. Their activism was based on a multiplicity of paradoxes, insofar as they did not openly condemn segregation, nor did they reject their native culture, but they behaved in a definitely subversive way. They seemingly confined their action to the accepted fields of mission and reform work while committing themselves to highly political issues. They favored moral suasion and grassroots activities but supported national intervention in reform. They cultivated ladylike manners but behaved like true radicals. All these contradictory tendencies can be attributed to the context in which these women lived. As southerners, they seemed to have no alternative, but as lady activists, they paved the way for the next generation.

The Methodist women and other churchwomen who made up the majority of white female race reformers between the 1920s and the *Brown* decision devoted themselves primarily to reform work. This perfectly fit the traditional definition of women's roles as it did not encroach on politics, which remained men's reserved sphere. These women reformers, be they directly associated with religion or not, also benefited from the moral authority conferred on middle-class women since the Victorian era. Women being defined as naturally more virtuous and less prone to "vices" such as alcoholism or sex—an assumption they had confirmed by leading the temperance/Prohibition movements since the early nineteenth century—male-controlled public authorities viewed their reform-oriented activities as complementary to the action of politicians. It was precisely because they seemed to conform to racial and gender norms that these women could start to attack the system from within. In doing so, they gradually built extensive networks, asserted themselves as key actors in their communities, and began to redefine white southern womanhood in their own terms.

In the Name of God: The YWCA, Churchwomen, and the Commission on Interracial Cooperation

As white southern women spread the movement for social and racial reform over the South in the first half of the twentieth century, two organizations, the YWCA and the Woman's Division of the Board of Missions of the Methodist Episcopal Church, South, led the way. They represented thousands of women and resembled each other in many respects. In the South, the YWCA came to confront the issue of racism and segregation much earlier than all other regional reform groups. The association, which turned into a national organization in 1906 through the creation of the National Board, became an influential reforming force in the South. Starting in the very first decades of the twentieth century with the affiliation of separate "colored" branches—as they were called at the time—to the national body, it moved steadily toward desegregation. The national convention of 1946 officially adopted an "Interracial Charter" clearly condemning segregation. The charter had been drafted by the authors of a study conducted between 1940 and 1943 to assess the state of interracial relations across the nation's community YWCAs. The report published in 1944 recommended complete integration at all levels of the association, and its recommendations were adopted as official policy in 1946.[2] In spite of highly unfavorable circumstances, the YWCA laid the groundwork for the modern civil rights movement insomuch as it undermined segregation much earlier than all other southern groups. The main forces behind this process were, on the one hand, the constant pressure of black members, and, on the other, the student YWCAs that worked on southern college campuses from the 1920s on. A striking majority of the white women who participated in the struggle for racial justice in the region, from the beginning to the end of the segregation era, were either active YWCA members or close collaborators of the organization.[3] All in all, it can be said that the YWCA was among the most racially progressive organizations in the region during the pre-*Brown* era.[4]

The example of the YWCA testifies to the role of Christianity as a driving force of reform in the South. Another proof of this was the activity of churchwomen's groups in favor of racial equality throughout the segregation era. These groups gathered in thousands of Protestant white women, a majority from the middle class, who gradually expanded their traditional missionary work to favor desegregation before it became fashionable to do so. According to the historian Alice Knotts, between the 1920s and the 1940s Methodist women made up approximately half of all southern women involved in race reform and remained a force to be reckoned with until the 1960s. Knotts estimates their number at over 1,250,000 in the early 1950s.[5] Many of these women had close connections with the YWCA, and the evolution of their organizations followed the same course as the latter. In the name of God and Christian brotherhood, churchwomen occupied the forefront in social reform activities, inevitably leading them to condemn segregation as the major obstacle to human relations.

The late nineteenth century had witnessed the emergence of reform movements in which Protestant women had played an essential role. If the Progressive movement of the early twentieth century involved men and women alike in an attempt to cope with the excesses of urbanization and industrialization, major reform organizations such as the Woman's Christian Temperance Union (WCTU) were composed exclusively of women. Protestant women actually formed their own organizations out of frustration after being denied positions of responsibility by their churches. This was more particularly the case of Methodist women who became a major force of racial progress in the South in the early twentieth century. The opening, in 1892, of Scarritt Bible and Training College, which was to become a prominent institution in the region, secured the perpetuation of women's leadership for generations afterward.[6]

Methodist women's progressivism was certainly favored by the nature of their organization, which resembled that of the YWCA. The national network of women was headed by the Woman's Division of the Board of Missions of the Methodist Church (or Woman's Division), which was divided into the Department of Foreign Missions, the Department of Home Missions, and the Department of Christian Social Relations and Local Church Activities (CSR/LCA)—the last group being the main instrument of racial reform for southern churchwomen. The YWCA also functioned as a decentralized structure, leaving a high degree of autonomy to local branches. The Methodist national Woman's Division, like the YWCA's National Board, was not a coercive but a coordinating body, in which all levels of grassroots workers were democratically represented. Staff members did not dictate policy to the membership, and even had to adjust to local conditions in many cases.[7] Thus guided and supported by a solid organization, churchwomen could engage in a myriad of activities meant to improve human relations in their communities.

This democratic pattern constituted a factor of progress at times but could also turn into a liability. The YWCA operated on the Christian principle of universal brotherhood and favored all forms of discussion that might lead to better human relations, including race relations. In that sense the organization prodded women into challenging racism when and where they encountered it. On the other hand, owing to the decentralized pattern of the organization, the National Board could not coerce local branches into enforcing national decisions, which accounts for the fact that southern branches were much slower than others in desegregating their activities after the adoption of the 1946 Interracial Charter.[8]

The student YWCAs distinguished themselves for their early interracialism, which was precisely due to the great autonomy their leaders enjoyed. However few they may have been, these leaders were a key influence in the evolution of race relations in the interwar years. The obstacles and difficulties they had to face were real. They actually failed to convert the majority to their views until the post–World War II era, as shown by Frances Taylor, but they determined the course of progress. For about two decades, student YWCA leaders struggled with the following dilemma set forth in 1923 by Katharine Lumpkin (who served as national student secretary for the South from 1920 to 1925): "Is the way of progress to try to increase the number who are willing to act on their own convictions?" she asked, or "is it for those few who come to have some convictions because they have had a chance to form them to carry the many along with them, even tho the many does not yet share those convictions?" Lumpkin was deeply upset by this question and never found a clear answer to it. "As the secretary for 150 southern associations, she was their representative, not their dictator," writes Taylor. This tactical hesitation was due to the democratic functioning of the YWCA, according to which the members could not be forced to follow the leaders' policy. Yet the most advanced leaders finally managed to impose their position in 1944 when the Southern Regional Council withdrew its support from any student YWCA conference that maintained segregated practices.[9] Unlike student YWCAs, southern community YWCAs accepted de facto segregation in their structure and activities until the adoption of the Interracial Charter in 1946. This can be accounted for by the fact that local YWCAs depended on their communities for funds whereas the student associations were funded by the National Board.[10]

The vision of student YWCA leaders, like that of other YWCA staff for that matter, was directly influenced by the Social Gospel, which was at odds with the otherworldly views of southern Protestantism.[11] After World War I, the young women who joined the YWCA in the South could no longer ignore the discrepancy they observed every day between the teachings of Jesus and segregation practices. Katharine Lumpkin expressed the "need to be 'consistent' with what we believed." Like her fellow YWCA workers, she had inherited a deep religious faith from her southern Protestant education together with a white supremacist view of society, and the student YWCA, which she discovered in college, opened her eyes to the inconsistency of her general outlook. Taylor shows that for Katharine Lumpkin, as for Betty Webb and Augusta Roberts—student national secretaries from 1925 to 1926 and from 1939 to 1943, respectively—the student YWCA brought about "a sudden recognition of an incongruity between Christian doctrine and social practices." Thus the YWCA constituted the catalyst that led these young women to reject the white supremacist doctrine that they had been taught by a "triumvirate of southern institutions—family, church, and school."[12] The student YWCAs' approach to the issue of segregation was definitely radical. As early as the 1920s, the student national secretaries for the southern region played a key role in the dedication of their associations to racial equality while operating in a hostile context. Frances Taylor notes that seven of the twelve secretaries who occupied this position between 1920 and 1944 were southern-born whites.[13] These women's radicalism lay in the fact that, in the late 1920s, they adopted social equality—that is, full integration of all activities—as a goal and worked to convert their fellow southerners to their new vision.

The second step in the elimination of racism, after acquiring a new vision, was to act in conformity with it. The southern student YWCAs started interracial educational programs in 1922 with the double purpose of helping the students free themselves from the conservative religion and the racial prejudices they had been taught, and experiencing the interracial contact that southern society prohibited.[14] Thus the student secretaries organized visits by black speakers to white campuses, interracial study groups, and interracial conferences. Interracial contact seems to have been the most crucial factor of progress in the struggle against segregation and racism, not only within the ranks of the YWCA but for all the people and organizations that aimed at reforming southern society during the segregation era. Reporting on interracial conferences that had occurred in 1925 in Virginia, North Carolina, Georgia, and Tennessee, Betty Webb noted that "person after person said that the experience had been a real revelation." About the Nashville interracial study group she had organized in 1923 with her black counterpart Frances Williams, Katharine Lumpkin wrote, "it made me believe far more deeply than ever that to move forward in interracial understanding and education, there must be a multiplying of direct contacts, and opportunities for study and thought together." She added that this "is the truly fundamental approach to our situation." Lumpkin's conviction was confirmed by the experiences of hundreds of white women who had been raised to believe in white supremacy. Mary (Polly) Moss Cuthbertson, another student YWCA leader in the late 1920s and early 1930s, recalled being shocked into awareness by the first interracial meetings she had to attend as a member of the YWCA Southern Regional Council, whereas she had been "programmed into white supremacy" in her youth. She later enraged Governor Eugene Talmadge when she organized an interracial tea and discussion at Georgia State University in the academic year 1934–35.[15]

These individual stories show that the student YWCAs constituted an environment in which young women could develop dissenting views without paying the cost of unorthodoxy because the organization became an alternative community within which they could forge a unique collective identity. The strength of the association was to provide conditions in which they could not only share views but also support one another during emotionally straining experiences. This enabled them to overcome the isolation—even sometimes alienation—that their dissenting position could cause. Such was the case, for instance, of Katharine Lumpkin. She explained that her close friendships with other staff members sustained her in her work. She corresponded with Leslie Blanchard, the national student executive, "expressing both her joys and frustrations over the work in the South." Other southern secretaries, such as Elizabeth Webb (1925–26), Carrie Meares (1928–33), Elizabeth Smith (1929–33), and Augusta Roberts (1939–43), also relied on a supportive network of fellow staff members and "sister secretaries," as Frances Taylor calls them.[16] Thus the women of the YWCA created bonds as they became dissenters, a process that intensified with the development of antisegregation forces.

Another illustration of the YWCA's Social Gospel approach to society was the work of the organization's Industrial Division, which focused its efforts on labor reform. Some industrial secretaries proved as radical as student secretaries in their positions and activities, especially in the South. The scope of their action being limited by the constraints of legal segregation, reform-minded white southern women devoted much of their energy to the general improvement of blacks' condition and to women's labor issues—through which they could reach out to both white and black workers. Lois McDonald, Louise Leonard McLaren, and Lucy Randolph Mason served as YWCA industrial secretaries in their states.[17] The major part of their work consisted in promoting education and professional training for women workers. McLaren was the founder and director of the Southern Summer School for Women Workers in Industry (formed in 1927), in North Carolina. In the 1930s, McDonald was on the school's committee with another YWCA leader from Atlanta, Mary Barker. During the Great Depression, these women combined social and economic interventionism with the religious philosophy of the YWCA by applying the Christian ethic to the industrial world. They were closely connected with YWCA industrial clubs and established links with interracial organizations that shared their concerns, such as Highlander Folk School. Lucy Mason and another YWCA white woman who became a civil rights activist, Alice Norwood Spearman (later Alice Norwood Spearman Wright), became members of the school's advisory committee. Mason had started her own activist career by becoming industrial secretary for the Richmond YWCA in 1914. She took on the position of general secretary in 1923 and as such participated in the social and economic life of the community. She thought that "the YWCA cooperated effectively with many other organizations and spread its influence over a wide circle." She used this influence to promote measures in favor of the black community as part of the general improvement of social relations in her area.[18] Thus white women reformers' increased interest in the black community and racial issues was directly connected to their conception of Christianity as a dynamic instrument of reform. What distinguished them from the mainstream white society of their time was their increasingly assertive will to act consistently with their Christian ideals, leading them to break with the segregationist dogma.

As for Methodist white women, they first focused their efforts on spreading the Social Gospel across the South by creating settlement houses for white poor and working women, and then turned to the black population. The remarkable character of their action was that some of these settlement houses, such as the Bethlehem House of Nashville, founded in 1912, were managed by biracial staffs and boards, which was unique in the South at that time. Will Alexander, a Methodist minister who was to form the Commission on Interracial Cooperation (CIC) in 1919, did not miss this point when he declared that the Woman's Home Missionary Society "was the most progressive and constructive religious group in the South."[19]

In the 1920s, the CIC actually became one of the best channels of Social Gospel activism for women reformers. Born out of the efforts of a small group of white men led by Will Alexander, the organization was based in Atlanta. For twenty-five years, its members strove to promote racial harmony and cooperation, first by creating state and local interracial committees across the region, and then by conducting research and informing the public about the black community and opportunities for progress. Originally led exclusively by white men, the organization opened its central committee to black men in 1920, and admitted women after protracted negotiations in 1921. For all their open-mindedness and goodwill, the first leaders were steeped in segregationist culture and paternalism, so they were reluctant to admit blacks as full participants in policymaking, just as they hesitated to put white women in contact with black men for fear of violating the taboo of miscegenation. Hence, women were admitted only on a separate and unequal basis after a Committee on Woman's Work was created and placed under the authority of the central commission. The CIC's women's state committees were dominated from the beginning by white Methodist women, black clubwomen, and YWCA leaders. Baptist women were also fairly well represented.[20]

In a CIC pamphlet published in 1940, Jessie Daniel Ames, who had become director of the Committee on Woman's Work in 1929, and Bertha Newell, her close friend and work associate, summed up the achievements of women in the field of interracial cooperation. The authors insisted on the pioneering work of churchwomen, notably Presbyterian, Methodist, and Baptist associations, since the late 1910s. They had organized Christianity conferences, staffed summer schools and institutes interracially to train black women in community leadership, and helped them develop community centers for blacks. They had also sponsored study groups and community surveys that were used to lobby local authorities and to improve living conditions for African Americans. By offering their assistance to black women, white women ventured into an unknown black world, which in turn prodded them into further action. As the pamphlet stressed, "Further efforts to the welfare of Negroes grow out of the discoveries of conditions in home and community." Consequently, "They come to realize that so long as Negroes are disfranchised white people hold the keys to civic improvement and civic justice. Out of this realization of their responsibilities as citizens, white women go before local governmental agencies to present the needs of Negroes, not only in education but in community life."[21]

Thus the churchwomen of the CIC, although they were definitely more cautious and paternalistic than the student YWCA leaders, followed a similar path toward bolder interracial cooperation. Ames and Newell's 1940 pamphlet emphasizes the importance of interracial contact in white women's gradual evolution from a biracial outlook—based on the idea of cooperation within a segregated framework—to an interracial perspective—based on physical interaction between blacks and whites. The multiple testimonies compiled from the various states led the authors to conclude: "All along the way discoveries have been made and continue to be made as Negro and white folk work together; barriers of prejudice disappear; narrow paths become highways to understanding and mutual respect; wild animals of race hatred are driven back into their dens; people begin to catch a vision of a new earth where fear is banished."[22] It should be noted, however, that Ames and Newell wrote these words in 1940, nineteen years after the creation of the CIC's Committee on Woman's Work, revealing the progress white women had made since World War I.

Indeed, throughout the 1920s, the main outlook among white churchwomen was deeply paternalistic, as was the outlook of the CIC's white male leaders. As McDonough recalls, "The lessons of the 1890s—that segregation and disfranchisement were appropriate antidotes to the excesses of radical racists, that blacks did not desire social equality, and that whites would set the terms of gradual black uplift within a segregated society—were the bedrock of southern liberalism at the beginning of the twentieth century." This sense of racial superiority, combined with class consciousness in the minds of the white men who founded the CIC, shaped their conviction that they represented the best people of their communities, a conviction they definitely shared with churchwomen. Hence the founders' wish to bring together "the sanest, most Christian spirited white men" with "the most reliable colored men" matched the ambitions of the first director of the CIC's Committee on Woman's Work, Carrie Parks Johnson. For Johnson, as for the male leaders of the CIC, the key to progress lay in changing whites' racial attitudes toward blacks, rather than reaching out to blacks and whites alike.[23]

This was revealed by the circumstances in which the Committee on Woman's Work was launched. Black women approached white women in 1920 soon after failing to convince the YWCA to abandon distinctions in its treatment of black and white members. In July 1920, Lugenia Hope—the wife of Morehouse College president John Hope, who had become a prominent black community organizer in Atlanta—invited Carrie Parks Johnson and Sara Estelle Haskin—another Methodist YWCA leader—to the conference of the National Association of Colored Women (NACW) held at Tuskegee Institute. Impressed by this first meeting, which revealed to them qualities they had never expected black women to have, the two white women invited four of the latter to speak before a regional women's conference in Memphis in October, under the auspices of the CIC. The interracial encounter was a great success after the black speakers, especially Charlotte Hawkins Brown, told the white women of their plight under segregation and asked them to join black women in the fight against discrimination. The result was the creation of the Committee on Woman's Work by the CIC in 1921. From then on, the CIC organized regular "interracial" meetings, which usually consisted of inviting a few selected black members to speak to white women's groups. According to Jacquelyn Dowd Hall, "a number of incidents illustrate the subtle and not-so-subtle racist stereotypes under which black participants labored." For instance, Hall cites the white chair of the Interracial Woman's Committee introducing a black speaker to the CIC meeting of 1921. To Charlotte Hawkins Brown, Mrs. T. W. Bickett (Fanny Yarborough) warmly declared, "you are as fine as was my Negro mammy." On another occasion, a black woman was asked by a group of Baptist women to speak "about the work of the 'niggers,'" and they "instructed her to enter the meeting by the back door." These examples reveal that even the best-intentioned white women of the early twentieth century considered black women as inferior in one way or another. They also somewhat perpetuated the stereotype of the sexually depraved black woman, and "the belief that all black women were immoral and therefore not entitled to protection from sexual exploitation."[24] Carrie Parks Johnson clearly remained prisoner of her paternalistic views. Whereas black women asked for genuine collaboration, based on a specific list of grievances they had adopted at the Tuskegee conference, Johnson set her own agenda by being, for instance, more compromising than black women in her condemnation of lynching and by ignoring their demand for equal voting rights. She clearly did not intend to work *with* black women but *for* them and on her own terms.[25]

A few women, however, were perfectly aware of the problem and called for change in attitudes. This was the case of Lily H. Hammond, who, in a pamphlet published as early as 1917, identified white women as the main culprits in the perpetuation of racial discrimination and called on them to overcome their prejudices for the sake of humanity. She wrote: "The status of the Negro woman and the Negro home in the minds of the privileged white women will determine the status of the race." She stressed white women's primary responsibility for racial injustice by reporting the words of a southern Methodist leader who had not hesitated to indict them unambiguously:

"You white women," he had said, "are the main obstacle to Negro morality. You teach us men, and your children—your sons—that morality in a Negro woman is beneath a white person's notice." To a horrified audience that asked for explanations, he had added:

> For instance: You refuse to give a Negro wife her legal title of "Mrs." It's not a social matter, as so many think; it's a legal right, defining a legal status fundamentally necessary to civilization. But you Christian women refuse it to Christian women sufficiently handicapped, heaven knows, without this added difficulty. You make no distinction between the Christian wife and the mother of half-a-dozen haphazard mulattoes; they're all "Sally" to you. You say, in effect, that morality in a Negro doesn't count. You teach your sons that from babyhood. The Negro women pay for it; but by God's law your sons pay, too—pay a debt more yours than theirs. And the daughters they marry pay, too.

Hammond, by also condemning the "touching and universal cult of the Old Black Mammy," did not spare white women's consciences. In a strikingly straightforward style, she called for the burial of the stereotype: "She deserves a funeral, bless her; and she certainly needs one—a competent, permanent funeral that will not have to be done over again every few days." Unless white women took up this responsibility of theirs, black women would continue to hate them "for their scornful indifference toward a matter so tragically vital to the welfare and honor of both races."[26]

Hammond's call shows that churchwomen's endorsement of the Social Gospel involved the cultivation of a high sense of mission. Considering themselves as the moral guardians of society, first as elite white women, then as Christians, most of them were imbued with a righteousness that conditioned all their actions. Thus, from the early days of segregation on, they took on the fight for social and racial justice as their primary responsibility. Hammond's introduction to her pamphlet speaks for itself:

> The manners and morals of every community reflect the standards sanctioned or permitted by its privileged women. Individuals stand above this common level, blazing ethical trails into the unmoral wilderness of our wider human associations, and draw after them, here and there, adventurous groups; but there can be no mass advance until the

individual impulse toward righteousness, which is justice in its finest sense, is reinforced by a common standard embodying a force greater than the individual.

These common standards are furnished, actively or passively, by the privileged women, from whose homes they spread into the community. Racial adjustment, like many other moral issues, waits on the leadership of these women.

Hammond explicitly defined the racial question as a moral issue, which was highly unusual at the time. She was also highly class-prejudiced and paternalistic in her outlook, which could be said of many churchwomen of the pre-*Brown* era, although notable exceptions stand out.[27]

All in all, in spite of the limitations of deeply ingrained prejudice, from the early 1920s to the early 1940s reform-minded women used the CIC to encourage racial cooperation in their communities.[28] In that respect, many women who joined the commission in the 1920s and 1930s were ahead of their male counterparts—who did not focus their efforts on grassroots work—on the issue of racial cooperation. This may well have been a reason for men's reluctance to welcome them into their ranks in 1921. Alice Norwood Spearman, for instance, was very active in her work for the commission in South Carolina. So were Dorothy Tilly in Georgia and Jessie Daniel Ames in Texas.[29] The CIC actually provided female reformers with guidance and support. As the years went by, its main function became publicizing the work of interracial reformers by sponsoring community projects and by publishing pamphlets and reports to foster cooperation.

Churchwomen turned their Christian principles into action by joining most of the organizations that struggled for racial justice from the 1920s on. When they did not work for other organized groups, their main role consisted of developing church-related missionary activities and community work, with special emphasis on education and health care. As decades went by, however, the struggle against segregation became their priority, and they focused their efforts on interracial cooperation by setting up local interracial committees and holding interracial religious meetings and conferences.[30]

Dorothy Tilly's life illustrates how churchwomen's determination to apply Christian principles to race relations turned them into radicals in the movement for racial justice. She became the best-known Methodist leader in the region. Starting in the 1930s, she rallied thousands of women by organizing interracial conferences across the South in the name of Christianity. Her correspondence with hundreds of women testifies as much to her personal dedication as to the impact she had on other women. For instance, in a letter she wrote to one of them after an interracial conference she had organized in North Carolina in 1944, Tilly commented: "I never saw a group of finer and more intelligent women than those assembled at the Boat House that afternoon. I glowed with pride and thanksgiving as I saw them." Three years later, writing about the report of the President's Committee on Civil Rights (PCCR), to which Tilly had contributed as a member and which recommended federal measures against segregation, another woman declared, "Now it remains for us—the church women of this country—to put these noble phrases into action."[31] Tilly became a model and a source of pride for an outstanding number of southern women, as testified by Mrs. Gene Berkey, president of the Women's Chamber of Commerce of Atlanta. Making arrangements for a Southeastern Women's Exposition held in May 1948, she wrote to Tilly: "You are one of the most distinguished women in eight Southeastern States!! On nominating ballots returned from those sent to 500,000 members of Southeastern women's organizations, your name was among those most frequently mentioned as deserving special recognition for your achievements in your field of activity." Such popularity is all the more remarkable since Tilly was perceived as radical in the South because of her antisegregation views, as shown by the hate mail she occasionally received, as well as other correspondence.[32] In 1949, after President Truman's federal civil rights program was killed in Congress by southern segregationist leaders, Tilly formed the Fellowship of the Concerned (FOC), an organization of churchwomen that openly promoted interracial contact.

The impact of the most dedicated women on their organizations and ultimately on their communities became visible from World War II on. The adoption of the Interracial Charter by the national convention of the YWCA in 1946 and its consequences testify to this development. The process of integration was slow in the South, but it was carried out in spite of difficulties. Although the pattern of segregation prevailed in most southern YWCAs, the YWCA was far more likely to pursue racial integration than were other community agencies in the South; in Greensboro, North Carolina, for example, the YWCA opened its pool to blacks in 1952–53, when the practice was virtually unheard of in the South.[33]

The YWCA definitely owed its racial progressivism to the influence of its student branches. In 1949, the authors of an internal study found that community YWCAs followed the trends set by the student YWCAs in the previous decades. In describing how integration was achieved in YWCAs across the United States—with special attention given to the South, where segregation was still imposed by law—the report pointed out the detrimental effects of segregation, namely ignorance and misunderstanding between the two races, bitterness, and fear.[34] As for the best way to achieve integration in such conditions, the report's conclusions were strikingly similar to what had been observed through student YWCA work. The authors expanded at length on the crucial importance of leadership in providing guidance and a plan for action. Most of all, the stress was laid on the necessity to establish direct, physical contact between blacks and whites. This was the first basic principle to follow: "Face-to-face contacts are essential to progress." As Katharine Lumpkin and her fellow workers had learned in the 1920s, not only was it necessary for blacks and whites to sit, eat, and talk together at interracial meetings, but they also needed to work together if racial prejudices were to be eliminated. The 1949 report confirmed that "understanding between Negro and white volunteers, staff and girl leaders had come about to an appreciable degree whenever, and only whenever, they had worked together over a period of time on common projects. . . . In many cases where Negro and white persons had worked intensively on a special project they were first shy, then enthusiastic about their experience."[35] All things considered, this report testified that by the late 1940s, the YWCA was definitely ahead of mainstream society in the South as far as race relations were concerned. All southern individuals and organizations that openly took a stand against segregation before the *Brown* decision were labeled radical, and were so indeed, even if they shunned the label.

As for churchwomen, they consolidated their role in public life by creating the United Council of Church Women (UCCW), a national interdenominational body, in 1941. The UCCW, which became United Church Women (UCW) in 1950, was racially integrated from the start, and the women had to struggle with segregation laws and practices whenever they met for official meetings. In 1945, the organization officially decided that state councils that did not accept both races would not be affiliated with the UCCW, and a survey conducted in thirty-five communities revealed the damage caused by segregation. "These millions of wounds," the report concluded, "are forming a hideous cancer in the society of our day which, if not cured by the power of God working through us, will either split asunder or destroy it altogether." The same spirit of universal brotherhood led the Woman's Division of the Board of Missions of the Methodist Church to take an official stand against segregation by adopting a "Charter of Racial Policies" in 1952. Based on the premise that "God is the Father of all people of all races," Methodist women leaders pledged themselves to build "a fellowship and social order without racial barriers."[36] Thus having unambiguously positioned themselves by the early 1950s against the maintenance of segregation, a significant number of southern churchwomen signaled they were ready for the desegregation battle.

Churchwomen and YWCA leaders belonged to the same networks, and their constituencies overlapped. Many leaders, like Louise Young, Thelma Stevens, Dorothy Tilly, and Alice Spearman, actually worked for both networks. Given the strength of white supremacist ideology, the spirit and action of white churchwomen's groups, as of those of the YWCA, between World War I and the *Brown* decision definitely placed them on the radical side of social and political life. Their rejection of segregation as a violation of God's will, at a time when state segregation laws prohibited interracial contacts and were not challenged by outside pressure, clearly turned them into dissenters. Yet the religious dimension of their philosophy and activities wrapped them in a protective veil of respectability. Rather than seeing themselves as traitors or revolutionaries, they were convinced they were the representatives of the true spirit of the South, and they struggled to demonstrate that southerners were Christians before being segregationists. They did so by acting on their own through their independent organizations, but they also participated in all activities organized by other reform groups to promote racial justice in the region.

Moreover, owing to the interconnection of white supremacy and patriarchy in segregationist culture, white women's involvement in racial reform had inevitable consequences on their gender identity. The growth of religious female networks fostered a sense of solidarity as the women asserted themselves against white men's authority. From the 1910s on, Methodist white women distinguished themselves from Methodist male leaders by focusing their efforts on mission work in favor of the black community, and they claimed to represent a distinctive brand of Christian reformers at odds with the male-dominated Methodist church.[37] Race was not the primary concern of these reformist white women at the turn of the twentieth century, but their choice to direct their efforts toward the improvement of race relations at a time when interracial work was taboo strengthened their self-assertiveness. In that sense, early women reformers' racial activities contributed to their emancipation from gender norms by setting them apart from the male Methodist leadership.[38]

A similar sense of solidarity in the face of conservatism united the women of the YWCA, and more particularly of the student YWCAs. The YWCA sustained dissenting young women, notably through its campus activities, throughout the segregation era. It fostered an empowering sense of sisterhood that encouraged women—especially white racial dissenters—to act in accordance with their beliefs, knowing that they were not alone to hold views that differed from the segregationist dogma. As Mary Sims wrote in 1936 in the first history of the organization, "Women have found in the [YWCA] an opportunity to attack problems, to pursue new ideas, to work out new solutions in specific instances, and to dare the misunderstanding of the more static elements in community life."[39] Even after the expansion of the civil rights movement in the late 1950s and the 1960s, the YWCA remained a privileged place where young women nurtured relationships that challenged both racial and gender norms. Thus white women racial reformers started to emancipate themselves from southern patriarchy as early as the first decades of the twentieth century. Whether they belonged to churchwomen's groups, the YWCA, or both, they quietly created a new form of activism, questioning racial and gender norms in their own highly respectable way.

In the Name of Civilization: The Association of Southern Women for the Prevention of Lynching

That white southern female reformers were indeed a very peculiar brand of activists is demonstrated by the history of the Association of Southern Women for the Prevention of Lynching (ASWPL). The association was a direct outgrowth of the CIC since it was created in Atlanta at the initiative of Jessie Daniels Ames after she was appointed director of the Committee on Woman's Work. In 1930, the CIC changed directions by turning away from unproductive interracial fieldwork and by putting a new emphasis on research and publicity campaigns. In the fall of that year, Will Alexander established the Southern Commission on the Study on Lynching, headed by the sociologist Arthur Raper, together with the Commission of Law School Deans, charged with examining the issue from a legal perspective. Women were not invited to participate in the new venture. Throughout the 1920s, deeply ingrained prejudices had prevented white women reformers from responding favorably to black women's demands for support in causes that specifically concerned the black community, such as the fight against lynching. When, for instance, a group of black women had founded the Anti-Lynching Crusaders in 1922 and asked white women to become their allies in a campaign for a federal antilynching law, hundreds had officially expressed their support as individuals, but no white women's organization had joined the black women in the campaign. Although Mary Talbert, then president of the NACW, appealed to gender solidarity by declaring, "We have never failed you in any cause that has come to US, we do not believe that YOU will fail us now," white women did not prove sensitive to Talbert's call for actual cooperation.[40] Black women had to wait until 1930 for a new opportunity to rally white female reformers against lynching. They reacted to Alexander's initiative by protesting that white women, not men, were the key agents of change in the fight against lynching but had never responded to their repeated calls for action. When Mary McLeod Bethune, former president of the NACW, informed Alexander that she intended to issue a statement to the press urging white southern women to take up the fight against lynching, Ames stepped forward.[41] In November 1930, she and Alexander gathered twenty-six white women from several southeastern states in Atlanta, and the group founded the ASWPL, an organization exclusively composed of white women. The original group adopted a resolution in which they unambiguously condemned lynching as an act of barbarism for which no justification could be found, pledged themselves to act against it, and called community leaders to do the same in the name of civilization.[42]

In an unprecedented challenge to two pervasive myths of the New South, the rape myth and the presentation of lynching as the chivalric defense of white womanhood, the resolution adopted at the founding meeting read:

> Distressed by the recent upsurge of lynchings, and noting that people still condone such crimes on the ground that they are necessary to the protection of womanhood, we a group of white women representing eight Southern states, desire publicly to repudiate and condemn such defense of lynching and to put ourselves definitely on record as opposed to this crime in every form and under all circumstances. We are profoundly convinced that lynching is not a defense of womanhood or of anything else, but rather a menace to private and public safety, and a deadly blow at our most sacred institutions.[43]

In the following decade, the members of the ASWPL, led by Ames, Bertha Newell, and Dorothy Tilly, exerted direct pressure on local officials wherever and whenever they heard of an impending lynching. They called on sheriffs and other local public officials to do their duty by protecting the potential victims and deterring the formation of lynch mobs. They sometimes tried to prevent lynchings in person by standing in jailhouse doors. They also published pamphlets and fact-finding surveys about the ugly reality of this crime. The ASWPL grew rapidly. While 7,910 women had signed the pledge in 1932, the number had risen to 35,468 in 1936. Many law enforcement officers responded to the women by signing the pledge in turn. By 1936, 887 of them had done so. It is impossible to assess the exact impact of the association on the evolution of the lynching rate, but the fact is that the crime had virtually disappeared by 1942. Statistics tend to show that more lynchings were prevented in counties where the ASWPL was active.[44]

Methodist women formed the backbone of the organization, which was also supported by the YWCA. Ames and her closest collaborators—Bertha Newell, Louise Young, and Dorothy Tilly—were Methodist leaders. They rallied hundreds of state and local missionary societies to their cause. From her in-depth study of the organization, Jacquelyn Dowd Hall has concluded:

> In a generalized profile, an association leader would be seen, above all, as a woman active in a broad range of voluntary organizations. She would owe her primary allegiance to the women's work of the Methodist Church and she would be likely to occupy an elected position on the conference level of the Woman's Missionary Council. At the same time, she would belong to a local women's club or YWCA. She would be in

her late forties and would be married to a man who occupied a middle-level professional or managerial position. She would have attended at least one year of college, usually at a small southern women's school. She would not pursue a full-time career, but she would be more likely than southern women in general to have worked at least part of her life in a white-collar, sex-segregated occupation.[45]

After a decade of reluctance to antagonize white supremacist leaders by condemning lynching unambiguously and without reservation—an overwhelming majority of women remaining sensitive to the rape myth and the fear of miscegenation—elite white women finally responded to black women's demands and took up the fight against barbarism.

The ASWPL was both subversive and conservative in its policy and action. It was radical in the fact that it openly challenged a pillar of white supremacy, but it was conservative in that it did not go as far as calling for the elimination of segregation. Jessie Daniel Ames could be considered radical in her social views, but she was a pragmatist who sought to appeal to a majority of white southerners. She was convinced that lynching would not be eliminated as long as white southerners approved of it as a legitimate form of justice. This is probably the reason why she used the tactics of respectability by putting forward the ideas that lynching violated the fundamental principles of humanity and that neither the South nor the rest of the United States could afford to tolerate it without losing credibility. A typical argument of the ASWPL was that lynching "brings contempt upon America as the only country where such crimes occur, discredits our civilization and discounts the Christian civilization around the globe." The organization thus denounced the act of lynching for what it was, an act of savagery, and rejected the rhetoric of chivalry in an uncompromising style: "Public opinion," it argued, "has accepted too easily the claim of lynchers and mobsters that they were acting solely in the defense of womanhood.... Women dare no longer to permit the claim to pass unchallenged nor allow themselves to be the cloak behind which those bent upon personal revenge and savagery commit acts of violence and lawlessness." Such an indictment could not be considered a challenge to the southern way of life since it did not target segregation. Nevertheless, it had a definitely subversive dimension since it constituted a severe blow to the doctrine that buttressed the southern racial order, segregation included. Lillian Smith recognized the blend of respectability and subversiveness that characterized the ASWPL, to which she paid tribute in *Killers of the Dream*. She commented:

> They primly called themselves church women but churches were forgotten by everybody when they spoke their revolutionary words. They said calmly that they were not afraid of being raped; as for their sacredness, they could take care of it themselves.... Of course the demagogues would have loved to call them "Communists" or "bolsheviks," but how could they? The women were too prim and neat and sweet and lady-like and churchly in their activities, and too many of them were the wives of the most powerful men in town.

Smith actually pointed out the women's perception of themselves as everything but radical, for they did not seek to overturn the southern order: "Indeed, the ladies themselves hated the word 'radical' and were quick to turn against anyone who dared go further than they in this housecleaning of Dixie."[46]

The women's subversiveness lay in the unquestionable moral authority their status conferred them. When they called on law enforcement officers to use all their powers to prevent lynchings, the members of the ASWPL identified lynching as an act of barbarism that reduced lynchers to wild beasts. They did not approach the issue as a racial issue but as a moral one. As churchwomen, they exerted their authority over men by condemning all forms of excesses in which men were likely to indulge. From that perspective, the fight against lynching partook of the same moralistic rationale as the fight against alcoholism or the denunciation of violence against women. In addition, their repudiation of the rape myth as a pretext used by white men to murder black men while victimizing white women led them, according to Jacquelyn Hall, "to demand a single standard of morality: only when white men ceased to believe that 'white women are their property and so are Negro women,' would the racial war in the South over access to women come to an end. Only then could lynching cease and social reconstruction begin."[47]

However, the ASWPL's handling of the gender issue was ambivalent, for it conveyed both a form of respect for social standards and a break with cultural assumptions. On the one hand, its members officially endorsed the role women were supposed to play in society at that time. On the other, they undermined patriarchal norms by questioning the fundamental assumption that women's place was to remain under the protection of men. Thus Ames and other ASWPL leaders reasserted the primacy of traditional gender roles by claiming to be the moral guardians of society. Their resorting to moral suasion as a major instrument of reform could hardly be condemned as "agitation" since they behaved exactly as any perfect southern lady was expected to. Hall has shown that "neither Jessie Daniel Ames nor her followers rejected the norms of ladyhood outright; indeed the anti-lynching campaign relied for its impact precisely on its members' exemplification of this ideal." Yet the women who worked for the association subverted gender norms while claiming to respect them. In rejecting the so-called chivalry of white men, they stepped out of their position as vulnerable victims depending on white men for protection.[48]

Moreover, in insisting on the moral dimension of their action, the women made it clear that they did not challenge the regional political order. Ames's opposition to federal antilynching legislation confirmed that she aspired to reform the South from within while preserving its identity. Like a majority of white southerners in the early twentieth century, Ames was attached to states' rights and did not believe in the power of federal coercion to change minds and mores. In the 1920s, while a massive campaign was organized by black women to support the passage of the Dyer Bill, Ames fought for legislation at the state level. Then, in 1934, Ames convinced the ASWPL to keep a neutral position on the NAACP-sponsored Costigan-Wagner Bill, which was being debated in Congress. Her position isolated her from her fellow reformers, such as the national YWCA, the Woman's Missionary Council (Methodist Episcopal Church, South), and the CIC, all of which supported the federal measure. The ASWPL was divided and weakened by Ames's conservative position.[49]

On the whole, the ASWPL's discourse was ambivalent in the social and political context of its time. Even though the women wrapped their action in a veil of respectability, they undermined the norms they were supposed to respect. The very moment they directed their efforts toward influencing politicians and public opinion, they stepped "outside the magic circle" of domesticity, as Virginia Durr put it, to enter the realm of politics.[50] In doing so, they reached the limits of their accepted role as women and, willingly or not, became subversives in their communities. When they denounced the rape myth as a pretext to commit crimes in the name of white womanhood and when they rejected the so-called protection of white men, churchwomen publicly attacked southern politicians whom they held responsible for the crimes they were fighting. Indeed, in the 1920s and 1930s, while the NAACP and its allies strived to obtain the passage of federal antilynching legislation, southern politicians defended lynching as a legitimate means to protect white women from the assaults of black men. For instance, in 1930 South Carolina senator Cole L. Blease declared in a speech: "Whenever the Constitution comes between me and the virtue of the white women of the South . . . I say to hell with the Constitution!" To which Kate T. Davis, ASWPL state chair, responded: "Hundreds of thousands of white women in the South feel that the law . . . is their honorable and reliable protection and avenger. The women of the South are not afraid to stand by the Constitution." By contradicting southern politicians and repudiating their discourse, white women not only stepped out of the domestic sphere but directly challenged the power and legitimacy of those male leaders. In other words, they entered politics without claiming to do so.[51] Thus the members of the ASWPL were a definitely special brand of activists, a species that seemed to be endemic to the South, characterized by the same fundamental contradictions that lay at the core of southern culture. Lillian Smith did not miss the point when she described them as "lady insurrectionists."[52]

In the Name of Democracy: The New Deal and Social Reform

The Great Depression marked a turning point in the lives of many women born in the late nineteenth and early twentieth centuries. Owing to the pervasive poverty that had plagued its economy for decades, the South was more severely affected by the economic crisis than other regions. As the region sank into depression, the middle-class white women who were already involved in mission and reform work intensified their efforts and welcomed the New Deal as an opportunity to accelerate the democratization of the region. For others who had not been active in reform before 1930, the Depression acted as an eye-opener. They came to discover poverty, and were not long in realizing that the group most affected by economic injustice was the black population.[53] The Depression and the New Deal politicized southern women's activism, as their activities shifted from missionary work to participation in militant causes that reconnected the South to national social and political forces.

In this evolution, the women obviously followed regional, national, and international trends. The 1930s was a decade when Communism and Nazism rose to prominence in the world. In the United States, the Depression favored the radicalization of politics, with the emergence of an influential left-wing movement supported by Roosevelt's New Deal. In the South, it seemed at first that the New Deal would mostly benefit the rural economic elite that controlled its implementation. As the historian Patricia Sullivan has pointed out, "New Deal programs were a transfusion for the South. The Agricultural Adjustment Act, which created the Agricultural Adjustment Administration (AAA), boosted the sagging fortunes of landowners and introduced rationality and planning to halt the spiraling plunge of prices." Yet the new legislation also provided reformers with powerful weapons, such as workers' right to organize. So Sullivan adds, "At the same time, New Deal programs and legislation stirred the stagnant economic and political relationships that had persisted in the South, unchanged and largely unchallenged, since the dawn of the century. Federal work relief and credit, along with the legalization of labor unions, implicitly threatened the culture of dependency that had secured an abundant, cheap labor supply."[54] Many southern reformers endorsed the New Deal either by working for its agencies or by using its new legislation and programs to transform southern economic and political practices.

As for southern women, white and black, the election of Franklin Roosevelt brought them an unexpected ally in the person of his wife, Eleanor. The First Lady was indeed the real agent of racial progress in the White House during the Roosevelt era, and she formed privileged relationships with the women who called on her for support. A white woman of southern ancestry through her father, Eleanor Roosevelt gradually overcame her own prejudices in her adult life and became an increasingly vocal advocate of racial equality after FDR's first election.[55] In addition to being friends with black activists such as Mary McLeod Bethune and Pauli Murray, she developed close ties with white women like Dorothy Tilly, Lucy Mason, Virginia Durr, and Lillian Smith, and was unanimously admired by all other female reformers who drew inspiration from her. Understandably, she was hated by conservative southerners as, in Lynne Olson's words, "she was everything the compliant, sweet-talking Southern belle was not. And everything the belle might become."[56]

The advent of World War II confirmed the turning point of the 1930s. Americans' intervention in the war, which was presented by national authorities as a defense of democracy against totalitarianism, favored the emergence of a new generation of black activists who pointed out the contradictions between the United States' international discourse and the policy of segregation at home. This forced white southern racial reformers to face the issue more straightforwardly. The NAACP, founded in 1910, took on a new national dimension and significantly increased its influence after three decades of gradual, but limited, development.[57]

Finally, the New Deal and the war also represented a turning point in the history of white southern liberalism insofar as these events favored the rise of a more militant interracial movement that became more and more critical of segregation even though it did not openly call for its demise. The Southern Conference for Human Welfare (SCHW) reflected this evolution. Formed in direct response to the National Emergency Council's *Report on the Economic Conditions of the South*, which in 1938 had declared the South to be "the nation's number one economic problem," it brought together a wide array of southern liberals and radicals who saw in the New Deal an unprecedented opportunity to reform their region in all its economic, social, and political aspects.[58] The founding conference, held in November 1938 in Birmingham, was attended by between 1,200 and 1,500 delegates representing labor organizations, civic clubs, educators, churches, and politicians, from moderates to radicals—including a handful of Communists. Eleanor Roosevelt was present. Birmingham's city commissioner Eugene "Bull" Connor imposed segregation in the auditorium where the conference took place, and the SCHW resolved to hold nonsegregated meetings thereafter.[59] Between 1938 and 1948, the organization fought discrimination on the fronts of labor, education, farm tenancy, civil liberties, and, most of all, political rights. Its major action took the form of a long campaign calling for a federal measure to abolish the poll tax. Although many members left the SCHW in the 1940s because they found it too radical, especially in its tolerance of Communists, virtually all reform-oriented groups and individuals converged toward it in the late 1930s. Several of the women featuring in this study—Lucy Mason,

Josephine Wilkins, Lillian Smith, and Virginia Durr, to name but the most visible—were involved in it at one point or another of their lives.[60]

Among the various factors that influenced white southern female reformers during the Great Depression was the New Deal's focus on labor rights and labor legislation. Since labor reform had been a major issue for missionary associations since the early twentieth century, several women welcomed the New Deal as an instrument of change to be used in the South. As they became increasingly aware that economic inequality was closely connected to racial inequality in the region due to segregation, they came to associate the fight for racial equality with the fight for labor rights. Lucy Mason, for instance, testified in 1933 at the National Recovery Act code hearings in Washington, D.C., on behalf of the National Consumers' League and met prominent union leaders there. In 1937, she returned to Washington to speak before the Senate Committee on Labor in favor of the Fair Labor Practices Bill—which set up an eight-hour day, a forty-hour week, and a minimum wage for workers. On that occasion, she met John Lewis, president of the Congress of Industrial Organizations (CIO), who recruited her as the CIO's public relations representative for the South, where a major organizing drive was going on under the direction of Sidney Hillman. She worked for the CIO until 1951. Her work consisted in visiting unions as a "roving ambassador," as she described herself, to support and help them with whatever difficulties they might have, "in organizing, in living with the law, in finding their leaders, in linking their movement to the churches, or at least getting the tolerance of the churches, in adjusting the problems of race, and creating an interest in politics." So, as she explains, "I was not an organizer, but there were many ways in which I could help organizers and local union men."[61]

Mason's description of her work reveals that her position on race was part of a broader outlook that placed economic equality at the core of the democratic process. "As a southern woman," she wrote, "aware of the burden of history, and sensitive to changing patterns in our life, I have watched for and thought about the meaning of this vigorous union movement in the South, and especially of its role as a training ground for citizenship." Randall Patton has explained that Lucy Mason, like other CIO leaders, viewed "the southern race problem as primarily a *class* issue." In 1942, she argued that "unless blacks are organized and have economic equality . . . the employers will use them to undercut wages and lower standards for all workers." Mason's interracialism was the natural extension of her democratic ideals, and in 1949 she claimed, "The CIO has brought more hope for progress to Negroes than any other social institution in the South—and that, sadly, includes the church.... Our unions have stood four-square for equal pay for equal work. Negroes are included in all social security benefits, or in pension plans provided through union contract. Of first significance to Negroes is the acknowledgement of themselves as persons entitled to democratic respect." She did not emphasize race as a priority, but her action, like the CIO's policy in the South, challenged de facto segregation.[62]

Aware of the opportunities that the New Deal offered in the field of unionism, Mason and other female reformers began to envision the possibility of a movement for equality that could transcend race barriers in the South. Through her contacts with national politics, Mason came to see the federal government as an agent of change, as an ally, although she did not believe in coercion and insisted that southerners were to lead the drive for progress in their region. She especially appreciated the fact that "though the CIO was treated, when it appeared on the scene, as a dangerous alien, most of its leadership was southern, and its members came from all the southern states." A direct descendant of George Mason (author of the Virginia Declaration of Rights in 1776 and delegate at the federal Constitutional Convention) and a distant relative of General Robert E. Lee, she did not hesitate to put forward her southern credentials to defuse conflict with local community leaders. She recalls, for instance, convincing a prominent minister of the Southern Baptist Church to support labor's right to organize by first expressing appreciation for a picture of General Lee hanging in the pastor's home. "Dr. Barton was interested in this statement," she writes in her memoir, "and expressed the highest admiration of General Lee. I told him that Lee and father's mother, Lucy Randolph, were first cousins, and there were various other ties of kinship between him and both my mother and father. After that he beamed upon me and I was securely wrapped in the Confederate flag."[63] Her insistence on "southernness" was all the more natural since she was a typical southern lady. As such, she could play the card of respectability with potentially hostile men. She recalls how the director of the CIO's southern organizing campaign, Steve Nance, reacted on first seeing her: "I felt that he was mystified when Sidney [Hillman] presented to him, as one of his lieutenants, a small, white-haired, fifty-five-year-old woman who had never been in the labor movement." As Mason shared Nance's misgivings, she came back two months later to propose giving up her place to a man, to which Nance replied: "Lady, you are doing a real job and don't forget about it. Don't ever let me hear any more about your leaving this staff. You go places and do things the men can't do." Virginia Durr, who knew Lucy Mason well, confirms this point in her autobiography, when she explains that John Lewis, the president of the CIO, did not hesitate to hire Mason because "he immediately saw that Miss Lucy could be a great advantage in the South. As his public relations person Miss Lucy would be very disarming. All the fierce police chiefs and sheriffs and newspaper editors would be looking for some big gorilla to come in, and Miss Lucy would appear. She was the kind of perfect Southern lady for whom men would instinctively rise to offer a seat." Another anecdote confirms the idea that Mason's femininity was a distinctive quality that made her more effective than men in her work for the labor movement. During her first organizing trip to Charlotte, North Carolina, in the summer of 1937, she called on J. E. Dowd, managing editor of the *Charlotte News*. Mason first benefited from the fact that Dowd knew of her, as his wife had previously attended Mason's Sunday school class in Richmond. Then, as she was leaving, the editor told her, "You are a good advocate for the CIO." When she asked him why he thought so he replied, "You look mild." Thus Mason's ladylike manners definitely played in her favor when she engaged in her most militant activities. These reported conversations could be dismissed as simple anecdotes had they not been a common feature of white southern women activists' experience at that time.[64]

Other white women of Mason's generation followed the same course. Alice Spearman, for instance, found her first inspiration in the YWCA, organized and directed a dynamic state CIC in South Carolina, and in 1935 became state supervisor of workers' education for the federal Works Progress Administration (WPA). As such, she not only worked as a mediator between national and local policy but supported workers in strikes and encouraged interracial unions. She was also at one point South Carolina director of National Youth Administration camps for black and white girls. Another member of the CIC and friend of Lucy Mason's, Josephine Wilkins endorsed the New Deal as the best opportunity of democratizing the South. In 1937, she set up in her native state of Georgia a fact-finding program whose purpose was to "obtain factual information on 12 major aspects of Georgia from well-known

State authorities." The program, "based on confidence in the democratic process that knowledge will ultimately express itself in action," was sponsored by the Georgia League of Women Voters (LWV), of which she had been president since 1934, and was carried out by fourteen civic organizations from the Rotary Club to Federated Churchwomen through the Georgia Library Association. Wilkins's undertaking was so successful that it lasted more than the twelve months that had originally been planned. It was credited with initiating the passage of more than forty pieces of legislation during the administration of liberal governor Ellis Arnall. Wilkins had been urged into action by the National Emergency Council's *Report on the Economic Conditions of the South*.[65]

The Depression and Roosevelt's interventionist policy awakened in some women an interest in the political, rather than economic, dimension of inequality and discrimination. The examples of Frances Pauley and Virginia Durr are representative of this trend. Frances Pauley's gradual involvement in Georgia politics originated in the 1930s. She remembered the early years of her marriage as those of a typical housewife. She did not feel politically concerned until the Depression, "because actually looking after the family and looking after the things that were sort of at hand occupied my time." But in the mid-1930s, witnessing the poverty in the neighborhoods of Decatur, Georgia, where she lived, suddenly convinced her to act. It was not long before she and a group of local churchwomen had set up an interracial clinic with the combined help of local authorities and private contributors. "Our intent," she explained, "was to reach poor people and people that needed it. We didn't differentiate between black and white." These were Pauley's first steps in public work, and she became increasingly involved in politics afterward.[66]

As far as Virginia Durr is concerned, her first encounter with poverty occurred in the first years of the Depression when she volunteered for the Red Cross in an investigation of steel mill workers in the Birmingham area. Then came the election of Franklin Roosevelt. In May 1933, her husband, Cliff Durr, was offered a job in the new administration's Reconstruction Finance Corporation. They moved to Alexandria, near Washington, D.C. It was there that Virginia Durr was politically educated. She soon became a popular hostess for the new circle of southern New Dealers hired by FDR, which included Clark Foreman; Will Alexander, who had left his position as executive director of the CIC to head the Farm Security Administration; Aubrey Williams, of the WPA; and Joseph Gelders. She became friends with Foreman and Gelders, who contributed to the foundation of the SCHW. As she discovered the realities of labor conditions and industrial relations in the South, Durr became an ardent supporter of the New Deal. Her first political act consisted in becoming a volunteer for the Women's Division of the Democratic National Committee. There she started lobbying against the poll tax, not out of concern for blacks but because it was an obstacle to the vote of white women in the South. It took Eleanor Roosevelt and Mary McLeod Bethune to draw her attention to the fact that black voters also suffered from the device and that women should join with African Americans in the fight for political equality, which she did when she joined the SCHW.[67]

Several white southern women actually became interested in political equality as a result of the passage of the Nineteenth Amendment and came to realize that they shared interests with blacks since the regional suffrage restrictions—notably the poll tax—affected both population groups. This accounts for the fact that some women reformers used their local LWV and other civic organizations such as women's clubs to fight against political discrimination in the South, which had a strong racial dimension.

The fact that Josephine Wilkins was president of the Georgia LWV was no coincidence. As president of her state league, she organized meetings with legal and political experts to discuss New Deal policies and sensitize women about the issues of their day. Jessie Daniel Ames had been president of the Texas LWV in the 1920s and was treasurer of the Georgia LWV under Wilkins's presidency. Lucy Mason had been president of the Richmond LWV between 1921 and 1923. Alice Spearman was executive director of the South Carolina Federation of Women's Clubs in the early 1950s. These associations were reserved for whites and did not challenge segregation before the late 1940s, and even then only a tiny minority of local chapters did so. However, they contributed to the fight for political equality in the South at a time when southern politics were controlled by white supremacists.[68]

Inspired by the dynamism of public life in Atlanta—Decatur's adjacent city—Frances Pauley contributed to creating an LWV in DeKalb County, of which she became president in the 1940s. She then served as president of the Georgia LWV (1952–55).[69] As she put it: "I was interested in politics, and the league was one of the few ways that women could work." Pauley and her league soon became involved in local and state political fights. In particular, they organized in the early 1950s a successful campaign against the so-called unit rule, an electoral apportionment rule that favored rural counties at the expense of cities, thus preventing the more liberal and racially diverse urban population from exerting their influence in the state. This battle did not address the issue of race directly, but the exclusion of blacks from politics was the real stimulus behind it. Pauley was already ahead of many of her fellow workers at the time, as she managed to desegregate her league in 1947 soon after becoming its president. These first militant steps would prove decisive in her commitment to desegregation in the wake of the *Brown* decision. Pauley's example is typical of the way women's groups such as the LWV gradually turned into channels of racial activism in the South. Lucy Mason, who also worked with the LWV, thought that she shared with her fellow members "women's responsibility as citizens" to bring about progress.[70]

In shifting from socioeconomic issues such as lynching or labor reform toward the defense of political rights, white women joined the wave of political activism spawned by the Depression and the New Deal. During the war years, many of them focused their efforts on the fight against the poll tax, which had been plaguing southern politics since the late nineteenth century. In 1941, Virginia Durr became vice-chair of the National Committee to Abolish the Poll Tax (NCAPT). The NCAPT, created by California congressman Lee Geyers, was sponsored by a great variety of groups, the most notable being the NAACP, the American Federation of Labor (AFL), the CIO, and the National Negro Congress. Not surprisingly, the YWCA and the LWV also participated in the venture. The SCHW was not successful in its fight against the poll tax—as several bills that passed the House were killed by filibustering in the Senate—but the campaign contributed to building an ever-stronger coalition of black and white activists in the South and secured solid support for the struggle against discrimination at the national level. As Patricia Sullivan has observed, "The campaign for anti-poll-tax legislation initiated the nearly three-decade struggle to extend federal protection of voting rights to the South. It also linked southern-based efforts to expand voting rights with the political vitality of New Deal Washington." Indeed, when Josephine Wilkins wrote to Virginia Durr in 1943 of her growing conviction "that relief will come only through federal action or the threat of federal action," she was expressing the feeling of an increasing number of southern men and women who were getting tired of struggling alone against their native culture.⁷¹

The SCHW reflected the increasing involvement of white southern female reformers in politics, drawing together many of those examined in this chapter as well as others who shared their outlook. Many played key roles in the organization. The list of officers elected at the founding conference includes the names of Louise Charlton (U.S. commissioner in Birmingham), Mollie Dowd (National Board member of the Women's Trade Union League), Adolphine Terry (who was to play a prominent role in the battle for school desegregation in Little Rock twenty years later), Josephine Wilkins, Lucy Mason, and Virginia Durr. Others, such as Mary Barker of the Southern Summer School for Women Workers in Industry, did not serve as officers but became members of the conference. At the end of World War II, the organization joined other progressive groups in a massive voter education and registration campaign to defeat conservative forces in the South. The SCHW's state committees set up on that occasion exemplify the significant involvement of women and women's organizations in the conference. The Committee for Georgia was led by North Carolina native Margaret Fisher. Its board included Lucy Mason (vice-chair) and Josephine Wilkins, and it worked in collaboration with the Georgia LWV among others. Mary Barker was a member too. Virginia Durr was cochair of the Committee for Virginia. Another native of North Carolina, Mary Price, organized the North Carolina committee. In the words of Patricia Sullivan, that committee "was probably the largest and most active state committee." The dynamism of the North Carolina committee is confirmed by Christina Greene's research on the black freedom movement in Durham, North Carolina. Greene notes, among other things, that Mary Price benefited from the active support of the YWCA.⁷²

Finally, even Methodist women leaders turned to political issues around World War II. Dorothy Tilly, for instance, had endorsed the New Deal and had worked for several of its programs since 1934. She became friends with Eleanor Roosevelt and campaigned for federal anti–poll tax legislation along with other civil rights causes. Methodist women indeed reoriented their activism by working directly with the federal government in the 1940s. Alice Knotts found out that "in the years from 1943 through 1948 the Woman's Division had closer contacts with, and influence in, the executive branch of American government than at any other point in its history." Tilly played a key role in this influence. As Knotts adds, "Particularly through Eleanor Roosevelt, Dorothy Tilly, and Thelma Stevens, the Woman's Division increased its role as a liaison between local and federal agencies."[73]

This role reached its culmination when President Truman appointed Tilly to the PCCR in 1946. Tilly was one of the two southern members, and one of the two women, on the fifteen-member committee. The PCCR was to investigate the extent of racial discrimination in the country and make recommendations as to federal action against it. In its report, presented to Truman in October 1947, the committee condemned segregation as a violation of American democratic principles, called for its immediate end, recommended several measures such as federal legislation against lynching and the poll tax and a permanent Fair Employment Practices Committee, and reasserted the power of the federal government to protect civil rights.[74]

Dorothy Tilly and her fellow southerner, Frank Graham, were to provide inside knowledge of southern culture and society. Their presence also gave legitimacy to the PCCR at a time when segregationists used the notion of "outside interference" to oppose any federal intervention in the "southern way of life." Moreover, Tilly was considered an expert on lynching owing to her leadership in the ASWPL. She actually used her position to push for measures Methodist women had been seeking for years, such as the training of law enforcement officers against prejudice to prevent police abuses.[75] Tilly's experience demonstrates that by the late 1940s, even southern churchwomen who had always favored education, suasion, and local community work as a means to bring about progress had come to endorse federal intervention as a necessary tool in the democratization of southern society.

The evolution of most of the women considered in this chapter paralleled the evolution of the segregation issue, which took on an increasingly political dimension from World War II on. Indeed, in the postwar years, the Cold War and the intensification of anti-Communism complicated the racial situation in the South. The Cold War took on a distinctive dimension in the region because it directly influenced racial politics. On the one hand, it was used by many anti-Communist liberals like Lillian Smith to call for immediate integration so that the United States could stand internationally as the model of democracy it claimed to be in the face of Communist totalitarianism. On the other hand, anti-Communism became the main weapon of segregationists against all racial dissenters, as they systematically accused the latter of being

Communists, which led to many forms of harassment and repression against them.[76] The SCHW was the target of the House Un-American Activities Committee (HUAC) in 1947, contributing to its demise although it had already been weakened by other issues.[77]

Four years before the official dismantling of the SCHW, a new southern organization had been founded by middle-of-the-road liberals to take over from the CIC—whose spirit did not fit regional conditions anymore. The Southern Regional Council (SRC) was not a militant organization, did not tolerate Communists in its ranks, and did not take a strong stand against segregation at the time of its foundation.[78] Its purpose was to promote economic and social progress through education, which would prepare blacks and whites to accept each other when segregation ended—this was predicted to happen in the near future owing to the events of the war years. Indeed, the organization became involved in desegregation in the 1950s. The case of the SRC reveals how women contributed to the work of mixed organizations while reinforcing their own networks. Although the SRC's leadership was exclusively male, a small number of influential women played an essential part in it. Two of them, Grace T. Hamilton and Charlotte Hawkins Brown, were prominent black community leaders. Among the whites, Dorothy Tilly, Alice Spearman, and Josephine Wilkins provided essential contributions to the organization. Tilly, who headed the woman's work division of the SRC until her death in 1970, provided hundreds of contacts across the South on whom the organization could rely to build new community patterns as the movement against segregation spread. Soon after the creation of the SRC, Tilly reportedly asked to be hired on its staff because her husband—who had financed her activities so far—was running out of funds, and she wanted to continue community work. Guion Johnson, the wife of SRC's executive director, Guy Johnson, recalled that Tilly asked her to convince her husband to recruit her, putting forward as her main argument, "He needs a woman [on the staff]." Beyond its anecdotal character, Tilly's remark probably reflected a very practical reality insofar as women leaders like her were much likelier than men to influence the hearts and minds of local communities across the South, precisely because they had always worked at the grassroots level outside of the academic, business, and political channels traditionally reserved for men. Guion Johnson was impressed by the extent of Tilly's network: "I have seen her sit down with a stack of postal cards and her list of names when she would hear of something that needed to be done, and send out hundreds of cards to key women in the South."[79]

Josephine Wilkins provided the same community-oriented approach to the SRC's work, based on personal connections. She was among the founders of the SRC, served as its vice president for a time, and remained a member of its executive committee until her death in 1977—she had also been a member of the CIC.[80] As a former president of the Georgia LWV, among other positions of responsibility, she could reach out to a wide spectrum of the southern population through her women's networks. Her example illuminates the way women functioned within a great variety of civic and militant groups, liberal and radical, putting their specific skills to the service of those groups while nurturing special relationships between one another and quietly asserting their own collective identity as women.

The eulogies given in Wilkins's memory on June 3, 1977, stress the discrepancy that existed between her effectiveness and her discretion, qualities that turned her into a central figure of the SRC, although few people were actually aware of it. To John Griffin, she "was very skillful in working with people, and many of the contributions she made to the good causes she worked for are not on the record." Although she remained in the background, Griffin says, she was "at the very center of the creative and imaginative circle of individuals and groups who possessed real and social vision.... She was there among the most remarkable women leaders, like Mrs. Tilley and Mrs. Ames. She was there among the religious leadership and the business leadership, the editors and the writers, the scholars and the intellectuals—the best of the black community and the best of the white." Such quiet, unobtrusive, hardly visible influence seems to have been crucial in the ultimate success of the cause for racial justice in the South, and it was a characteristic of female action in the first half of the twentieth century. In his eulogy, Griffin quotes an Atlanta newspaperman saying, "Josephine Wilkins was a dangerous person, because under the charm and warmth of personality that could get things done so effectively there was a revolutionary philosophy."[81] Such an approach was typical of women's behind-the-scenes activism. Wilkins's correspondence confirms this as it includes letters to and from a large number of friends and fellow activists, such as Lucy Mason, Jessie Daniel Ames, Margaret Fisher, Eliza Paschall, and Virginia Durr. Wilkins's friend Grace T. Hamilton—who was executive director of the Atlanta Urban League from 1943 to 1961—confirms that Wilkins managed to transcend all barriers through friendship.[82]

Ultimately, one cannot close this chapter without examining one last example that does not fit in any predefined category and yet—again paradoxically—encompasses all the experiences of her fellow women activists. In 1943, Lillian Smith wrote in *Common Ground*: "I am a southern woman born in that region of all the earth where race prejudice is sharpest, where it has its bitterest flavor, its deepest roots, where the relationship of the two races has become so intertwined with hate and love and fear and guilt and poverty and greed, with churches and with lynchings, with attraction and repulsion that it has taken on the ambivalent qualities, the subtle conflicts, of a terrible and terrifying illness." Lillian Smith was an exception in that she expressed her dissent in a vocal, uncompromising way from the late 1930s to her death in 1966. She was different from other white women reformers in that she was an artist and an intellectual, and because she placed the individual at the center of her philosophical and political outlook. As "the quintessential atomized individual," in the words of Randall Patton, "Smith had no patience with ideologies or pragmatic political programs." In the 1940s, she was a board member of the SCHW for three years, but could not stand the internal ideological strife inherent in any such group and resigned in 1945. Having received a typical segregationist education, she rejected white supremacy in the 1930s and stopped practicing segregation in her personal life, but her significant contribution to the cause of integration lay in her writings. From the late 1930s on, she stood as the bad conscience of the white South.[83] Defining herself as a true liberal, she became the nemesis of segregationists, the rival of middle-of-the-road liberals, and a major inspiration for nonviolent freedom activists.

Smith stood out among southern women because she articulated a sophisticated reflection on gender as early as the 1940s and grounded her reflection on her critique of segregation. Like most women reformers of her time, she believed in the distinctively nurturing instinct of women, a feature that, according to her, had become prevalent in women's identity as a result of their age-long confinement to the domestic sphere. However, unlike leaders such as Dorothy Tilly who put forward women's nurturing qualities to extol southern women for their quiet achievements, Smith indicted women for not using these qualities in a more militant way. In 1941, she and her partner, Paula Snelling, wrote an article entirely devoted to women. The two authors declared: "While through the generations woman has borne, nurtured, and conditioned for better and for worse the raw material of humanity, she has contributed little else toward civilization." The best proof of this, they thought, was the proliferation of war and violence around the world—of which segregation was an avatar—which would not have occurred had women played their nurturing role. "For ten thousand years," they argued, "civilized woman's major job has been that of mother. As a brooder she has done her work honorably—measuring up well to the efficient gestation standards of female animals. But as a mother of human children she has learned little during the centuries." Writing in the context of World War II, Smith and Snelling blamed men's belligerent spirit on women: "It is an indictment of woman in her role of mother that millions upon millions of her sons today return to war and violence as the 'way out' of their deep trouble." As for white southern women, Smith held the majority of them responsible for the perpetuation of white supremacy since they conditioned their children into practicing segregation whereas they should have taught them love.[84]

She actually saw the specific status of southern middle-class white women as a powerful instrument to eradicate racism from their society and regretted the fact that so few used it as such. This was what she explained to Eleanor Roosevelt in a letter written in 1943: "I have been trying for six or seven years to prove to white southern women of my social class that we can speak out plainly about racial democracy; that we can take a public stand against discrimination and even against segregation without losing too much prestige and without suffering martyrdom." Smith did benefit from her status as long as she remained coeditor of her literary magazine and director of her summer camp for girls. After the camp closed and the magazine folded, however, she lost her respectable status as well as her financial independence, and as a result she became much more vulnerable to attacks.[85]

In the pre-*Brown* period, besides coediting the *North Georgia Review* with Paula Snelling between 1936 and 1946, Smith published articles in and outside the South, together with fiction. After the best-selling novel *Strange Fruit* (1944), which related the story of a lynching in a small southern town, she published her autobiography, *Killers of the Dream* (1949), a scathing critique of white supremacy that became the reference on southern culture for civil rights activists. Unlike other integrationist women, she clearly positioned herself as a dissenter, as she proudly wrote in 1961: "I realize that I have questioned deeply most of the moral foundations of the white race; during this time of change I am not their heroine. I have dissented more profoundly than any writer in this country." She developed an in-depth critique of southern society and culture while urging her fellow southerners to take personal action against segregation and prejudice. From the early 1940s on, she kept encouraging ordinary white southerners to break the racial etiquette in everyday life and exhorted civic leaders to take public stands against segregation. Appealing essentially to individual conscience, she indicted so-called liberals who condemned the worst manifestations of racial injustice but did not support immediate integration, and even less federal intervention to bring it about. In 1948, for instance, she despaired of the liberals' unwillingness to support President Truman's civil rights program in the face of segregationists' attacks. In an article entitled "Southern Liberalism" (a movement she included herself in), she deplored: "It is our caution, our lack of energy, our moral impotence, and our awful if unconscious snobbery, that make demagoguery unafraid of liberalism." Unlike white southern liberal journalists, such as Hodding Carter of the *Delta Democrat-Times* and Ralph McGill of the *Atlanta Constitution*, who disapproved of federal intervention in the states, Smith welcomed it insofar as the states violated the basic principles of democracy. Thus, in October 1948 she wrote about Truman in the prominent black newspaper the *Chicago Defender*, "I'm voting for him because I am a white Southerner and I am proud of the magnificent thing he has done in taking so brave a stand for the civil rights of all Americans. I think that he, as our President, has done my region great good by dramatizing democracy's belief in civil rights."[86] Indeed, although she defined herself as a liberal, Smith's explicit integrationist stance, together with her support of federal intervention, identified her as a radical in the context of the 1940s South. She served as a spokesperson for hundreds of white women who shared her views but were reluctant to express them as vocally as she did. She also powerfully articulated complex social and psychological mechanisms that many felt but were unable to grasp in all their implications. Lillian Smith was ahead of her time. She gave white racial dissenters a vision, and her influence extended to the post-*Brown* generation.

* * *

In conclusion, the pre-*Brown* era witnessed the emergence of a peculiar brand of racial activists, mainly represented by churchwomen's groups, the YWCA, the ASWPL, and the LWV. The women examined here, comprising the older generation of the present study, gradually turned from traditional social reform work to racial activism between the 1920s and the 1950s. These typical southern ladies abided by segregationist rules and stood as respectable members of their communities in their native region, but appearances were misleading. Indeed, while many of them were seen as the incarnation of southern tradition, they contributed to undermine the so-called southern way of life without losing their position of respectability. Their subversive character lay in the discrepancy between their manners and the nature of their actions. All of these women accepted, even claimed, their status as southern ladies, but used it against the white supremacists who had placed the protection of white southern womanhood at the center of their rationale. Without seeming to do so, they undermined both the racial and gender norms associated with the ideal of the southern lady. They did not attack segregation head-on but broke racial taboos within their organizations, while using their authority and influence to change white southerners' minds. They also conformed to gender norms by behaving as ladies, but they turned the passive figure of the endangered white woman into an active member of society eager to step down from her pedestal to become involved in all sectors of public life. In doing so, they opened cracks in the segregationist system and quietly started to upset the southern patriarchal order.

3

After *Brown*, Part One

The Tactics of Respectability

"Now is the time." These were the words with which Lillian Smith welcomed the *Brown v. Board of Education* decision handed down by the U.S. Supreme Court on May 17, 1954.[1] *Brown* marked the end of an era for the nation and for the South. If the Supreme Court had already undermined southern racial discrimination by declaring white primaries unconstitutional in 1944 and by ordering the equalization of educational systems in compliance with the "separate but equal" doctrine, it had never yet condemned segregation per se.[2] This was done in 1954. For all southerners, the *Brown* decision meant that the federal government was back after several decades of nonintervention. This event marked the culmination of a long litigation process started by the NAACP in the 1930s.

After the handing down of *Brown* II, mandating the desegregation of all public schools in May 1955, segregationists counterattacked and launched a movement of massive resistance to its implementation, reviving the interposition doctrine to support official disobedience to the Supreme Court. Segregationist leaders argued that the decision was unconstitutional, that the Court had fallen under the influence of Communists, and, most of all, that desegregation would entail "miscegenation," or "mongrelization," since black male students would seize the opportunity to have sexual intercourse with white females. Newly formed White Citizens' Councils exerted economic pressure on all supporters of desegregation—teachers and school boards receiving special attention. This so-called respectable resistance was reinforced by the revival of the Ku Klux Klan. As for state authorities, they openly challenged the Supreme Court by enacting measures with the specific purpose of circumventing implementation of the *Brown* decision and of repressing its supporters (such as the NAACP, which had initiated the *Brown* case).[3] Finally, southern politicians used, to an unprecedented degree, the black- and Red-baiting techniques that had been used in previous times against racial dissenters. As McCarthyism was waning in the rest of the nation, anti-Communism became the major weapon of segregationists against all supporters of the *Brown* decision.[4]

The *Brown* decision polarized positions on segregation in such a way that it became impossible to keep a middle ground. It provoked a crisis that ultimately drained the word "moderation" of its meaning, as liberal journalist Ralph McGill later regretted.[5] One had to take a stand for or against segregation. As the black-led civil rights movement unfolded, a majority of white southerners chose to remain silent.[6] Segregationist forces were so strong and the risk of repression or violence so high that fear prevented many from expressing themselves and was responsible for much apparent apathy. Most of the prominent white liberals who had warned against the dangers of immediate desegregation and federal intervention found themselves paralyzed and pushed to the sidelines, caught as they were between the advocates of resistance and the integrationists. By contrast, the stories of the minority who did speak and/or act for desegregation are tales of fear and courage.

White women racial reformers were definitely part of this minority. Having seen the writing on the wall since World War II, they had prepared themselves for the *Brown* decision, which they welcomed as a victory for human rights. Following the decision, they focused their efforts on securing its implementation. The decade between *Brown* and the Civil Rights Act of 1964 is a key decade in the history of white southern women's activism, because it brought together two generations that nourished each other in order to achieve the ultimate goal of full equality. In the late 1950s, the older generation born at the turn of the twentieth century was reaching an advanced stage of maturity while the new generation born around World War II was coming of age. This confluence of generations enriched white women's perspectives as their different approaches overlapped. As an element of continuity, the tradition of "southern lady" activism developed in the previous decades was perpetuated by the ongoing activities of existing and new organizations, while a new approach, based on confrontation, emerged from the radicalized post-*Brown* context. The two generations and the two approaches were not strictly separated, as some individuals of one generation took positions and resorted to tactics favored by the other, or embraced the two approaches alternatively depending on moments and situations. Some older women served as bridges between the two periods framing the *Brown* decision.

The present chapter examines the evolution of the older form of activism throughout the school desegregation crisis. It shows how existing organizations embraced the *Brown* decision by sticking to their indirect approach of suasion and lobbying, while new groups born out of the crisis proceeded from the same tradition of "respectable" dissent to support desegregation. All of these groups stressed their loyalty to the South and took pains not to antagonize white southerners and to avoid getting entangled in the black- and Red-baiting campaigns organized by the white supremacists. Moreover, the developments of the post-*Brown* decade reinforced the sense of recognition that had emerged among white female racial dissenters in the earlier period. Indeed, although women's organizations such as churchwomen's groups and the YWCA had not been created for the purpose of promoting racial justice, they had embraced the cause of racial equality earlier than other groups in southern society. In this countering of mainstream society, white southern women reformers united against the prevailing culture and developed a sense of solidarity and a common identity distinguishing them not only from southern white men but also from nonsouthern white women.[7]

Not Race but Human Relations

All the women's organizations that had worked for decades to improve race relations in the South anticipated the *Brown* decision in the early 1950s. In 1952, for instance, members of the executive committee of the General Department of United Church Women (UCW) adopted a resolution reaffirming the "inclusiveness of our Christian fellowship across denominational and racial lines." And they added, "we determine to take next steps toward the fulfillment of our Christian purpose." The members of UCW distinguished themselves by the boldness of their attitude in a context of growing regional defensiveness against change. UCW fully endorsed the *Brown* decision, and, in the ensuing years, leaders set up community workshops to facilitate its implementation. The basic premise underlying this grassroots work was that "essential to the success of any law is the willingness of the citizens to let it happen."[8]

It was in the same spirit that the Woman's Division of the Board of Missions of the Methodist Church adopted its "Charter of Racial Policies" in 1952, committing itself to "build in every area it may touch, a fellowship and social order without racial barriers." All schools and facilities administered by Methodist women were to be integrated, and local associations affiliated with the Woman's Division were asked to take a public stand for integration by ratifying the charter. They were also expected to prepare their communities for desegregation, laying special emphasis on public schools, and to press state and federal authorities into facilitating the process. On May 17, 1954, Methodist women were holding their annual conference and were about to discuss ratification of the Charter of Racial Policies when the Supreme Court handed down the *Brown* decision. Thelma Stevens and Susie Jones reacted immediately by drafting a resolution, which was adopted by the assembly. It was one of the most straightforward and unequivocal statements of support of desegregation by an organization, as its opening sentence read: "We affirm anew our determination to work with greater urgency to eliminate segregation from every part of our community and national life and from the organization and practice of our own church and its agencies and programs." The women present pledged themselves to work for immediate desegregation. In the following years, in collaboration with UCW, they organized local workshops, supported school board desegregation plans, pressed the Methodist Church to desegregate, lobbied federal politicians in Congress, and even organized an "open housing" campaign from 1957 on, having rightly identified the connection between school and housing segregation. Such a commitment was all the more significant since Methodist women had constituted since the 1920s a major segment of women's reform activism in the South, and their support of the *Brown* decision in the 1950s proved as pioneering as their efforts at biracial cooperation in earlier decades.[9]

Another illustration of churchwomen's anticipation and subsequent support of *Brown* was Dorothy Tilly's Fellowship of the Concerned (FOC), created in 1949. Tilly was then director of woman's work for the Southern Regional Council (SRC). After her work for the President's Committee on Civil Rights, Tilly set out to prepare the South for desegregation, while southern segregationist politicians, led by the States' Rights (or Dixiecrat) Party, rallied conservative forces to protect the "southern way of life."[10] Under the sponsorship of the SRC and the YWCA, and with the help of UCW, she created "a fellowship of Church women leaders of both races and the three faiths, concerned about their South." The participants of the founding conference signed the following pledge: "I AM concerned that our constitutional freedoms are not shared by all our people; my religion convinces me that they must be and gives me the courage to study, work, and lead others to the fulfillment of equal justice under the law."[11] The FOC had neither officers nor membership dues. Members were to meet each year at a regional conference to discuss ways of improving race relations, and were to spend the rest of the year putting their ideas into practice. One year after its creation, the fellowship had more than 4,000 members. In its first years, the FOC did not directly work for desegregation. Drawing from the action and spirit of the Association of Southern Women for the Prevention of Lynching (ASWPL), Tilly led hundreds of white women to exert pressure on courts and sheriffs so that black people would be fairly treated by the southern justice system. By 1953, however, Tilly knew that the *Brown* decision was pending. Thus, reporting on the 1953 conference, she wrote that "here the women planned what they would do in preparation for the decision." In the following years, every annual FOC conference was dedicated to the implementation of desegregation, and local chapters were founded throughout the region.[12]

As a leader of exceptional ability, Dorothy Tilly drove thousands of miles each year across the southern states to rally thousands of women of all faiths to the cause of integration. In a typical report covering the first quarter of 1956, she described her visits to Orlando and Daytona, Florida; Atlanta, Georgia; Richmond, Virginia; San Antonio, Texas; Columbia, South Carolina; Montgomery, Alabama; and Memphis, Tennessee. She went as an inspirer and supporter rather than as a leader, her whole conception of activism being based on grassroots work and adjustment to local conditions. She arranged discussion panels and provided inexperienced, uninformed women with civil rights literature, such as copies of Lillian Smith's pamphlet *Now Is the Time*. The correspondence she kept up during the school desegregation crisis shows that she was in permanent contact with local and state churchwomen. As staff member of the SRC and of the Woman's Division of the Board of Missions of the Methodist Church, she provided financial and organizational aid. UCW and Methodist women actually constituted the shock troops of the FOC. Tilly's correspondence holds hundreds of letters from all southern states in which local leaders reported on their activities, but also asked for support and comfort in hard times. Isabel Goldthwait, from Louisiana, Gertrude McCall, from Tennessee, Edith Dabbs, from South Carolina, Noreen Tatum, from Alabama, Anne Cunningham and Martha Burt, from Mississippi, and Fay Smith, from Virginia, were regular correspondents. When she spoke at workshops on "human relations"—a safe substitute for the phrase "race relations" during the school crisis—Tilly invariably resorted to the same set of arguments. The *Brown* decision was a blessing for the South because: it was moral; it was Christian; it was democratic; it was the best weapon against the spread of Communism around the world. Another outstanding leader who devoted all of her time and energy to prodding women into supporting desegregation was Thelma Stevens, executive secretary of Christian and Social Relations and Local Church Activities for the Methodist Woman's Division between 1940 and 1968. She did the same work as Tilly, with whom she corresponded regularly, and she is mentioned in many documents pertaining to the FOC.[13]

Thus, in the late 1950s and early 1960s progressive women's religious organizations joined forces to support the *Brown* decision and facilitate its implementation in the South. Moreover, southern Protestant women cultivated links with women of other faiths at the regional and national levels, notably with the National Council of Jewish Women (NCJW). They also worked with the Urban League and with the NAACP, which was at the origin of the *Brown* case and was severely hit by massive resistance measures.[14] NAACP representatives attended workshops on desegregation, where they exposed the legal and constitutional grounds for the Supreme Court decision. The YWCA carried on the campaign for integration it had initiated in the mid-1940s, and the American Friends Service Committee (AFSC), which had not been very militant in race relations up to that time, joined integrationist forces after *Brown*. Under the leadership of Jean Fairfax, an African American who was appointed national representative of southern programs in 1957, the AFSC set up school integration programs to support black parents who attempted to register their children in integrated schools and exerted pressure on white authorities. "Before the decade was out," writes Susan Lynn, "the AFSC was involved in school integration projects in nine states and over 200 school districts."[15]

Finally, leading white southern women reformers cultivated links with black women's organizations. Although segregation laws prevented interracial contact in public places and deterred interaction between blacks and whites in private life, the black and white women's associations that had developed separately in the South since the 1920s shifted toward increased cooperation under the influence of their boldest leaders. At the local and state levels, white women cooperated with black women's clubs and other civic groups. At the national level, some like Dorothy Tilly and Alice Spearman participated in events sponsored by the National Council of Negro Women.[16] A letter written by Mary McLeod Bethune to Dorothy Tilly in 1955 is illuminating in this respect, starting with these words: "My dear, dear Mrs. Tilly: It always gives me a great thrill to just hear your name or to have a line from you or a handshake. You came into my heart and into my life many years ago. You have been a great strength to me in so many ways. You have strengthened so sufficiently my confidence in the genuine interest of many Southern white women."[17] Interestingly, Bethune does not make southern white womanhood the central focus of her statement, but her shift from Tilly to southern white women implicitly enhances the specific identity of these women as a group. Personal friendship thus became an essential form of racial intercourse. The close ties white racial reformers and activists developed with their black counterparts fueled their antiracist activism just as it helped them draw the contours of universal sisterhood.

The same women who formed the ranks of UCW or Methodist women's associations also constituted the backbone of local and state Councils on Human Relations (CHRs) affiliated with the SRC. Some of these councils, which multiplied in the aftermath of the *Brown* decision, had existed since the 1940s as State Committees on Interracial Cooperation. Because the SRC was not officially a political organization but an educational one, and because it was vulnerable to legal attacks by segregationist authorities if it engaged in militant activities, state CHRs remained independent, autonomous organizations. However, as Eliza Paschall, executive director of the Greater Atlanta CHR from 1961 to 1967, remarked, "one of [the SRC's] major functions was to sponsor and encourage such councils." She further explained, "The relationship was not legitimized by bylaws and formal documents, but it was a strong common law relationship. As one Executive Director explained it, SRC received grants for field work which took the form of encouraging state and local Councils on Human Relations (Southern for 'race relations')." In the post-*Brown* decade, CHRs, whose actions were limited to nonpolitical activities owing to their tax-exempt status, struggled with local resistance to desegregation by combining the Christian arguments of churchwomen with a more pragmatic approach to community development. As a document issued by the Georgia CHR in the early 1960s stated, "The Southern Regional Council and its affiliates seek to be practical organizations, aiming at working solutions rather than spectacular pronouncements. They hold the belief that every community must ultimately find its own answers within the framework of law and conscience."[18] In keeping with this philosophy, state and local CHRs organized interracial groups whenever possible and supported all grassroots initiatives in favor of desegregation. After the school crisis, they supported the nonviolent movement throughout the 1960s.

Many women involved in other organizations were also members, if not leaders, of CHRs. Thus Frances Pauley and Eliza Paschall were, respectively, executive directors of the Georgia CHR and of the Greater Atlanta CHR in the 1960s after having served as presidents of the Georgia League of Women Voters (LWV). Alice Spearman Wright, who worked for the YWCA, the South Carolina Federation of Women's Clubs, and UCW, among many other groups, was also executive director of the South Carolina CHR from 1954 to 1967. Virginia Durr and Adolphine Terry were active in the Alabama and Arkansas councils, respectively. Rosa Keller, who struggled for the integration of the League of Women Voters of New Orleans (LWVNO) in the late 1950s, was also a member of the Louisiana CHR. Shannon Frystak notes that in the mid-1950s women actually represented a majority of council members in New Orleans. For all their reasonableness, CHRs were perceived as radical in most places, especially in areas of open massive resistance to desegregation. In Virginia, for instance, Armistead Boothe, the only politician whose name appeared on the original roll of the Virginia CHR—formed in 1955—asked to be dissociated from the organization for fear of bad publicity. Similarly, during the crisis in Little Rock, Arkansas, Velma Powell, an original founder of the Women's Emergency Committee to Open Our Schools (WEC), left the newly created group because, as secretary of the interracial Arkansas CHR, she might be a liability.[19]

If women's major contribution to racial progress was through religious organizations, however, nonreligious women's groups such as the LWV also played a part in the general movement for desegregation, but they were more divided than churchwomen on the issue. Indeed, some local leaders who had come to repudiate segregation by the early 1950s pushed their leagues toward outspoken support for desegregation, but they were not always successful. The Georgia LWV, led by Frances Pauley between 1952 and 1955, did take a stand in favor of the *Brown* decision when it was handed down. Its action in the months preceding the decision actually foreshadowed this stand, as the LWV campaigned against a proposed state constitutional amendment that would have allowed the replacement of public schools by private schools funded by the state—the main purpose being to avoid desegregating the schools in the event of a repudiation of segregation by the Supreme Court. The February 1954 issue of the *Georgia Voter*, the league's publication, offered a detailed analysis of the amendment and demonstrated the danger it represented for Georgia's public school system. The LWV deliberately dissociated the issue of public education from that of segregation. It declared, "THIS AMENDMENT IS A SCHOOL QUESTION, NOT A SEGREGATION QUESTION." The league tried to reassure the population about the impending Supreme Court decision in order to prevent a massive rejection of it: "Segregation in public schools has been questioned. Georgia is not involved at this time and need not act until she is. . . . Theoretically a suit could be instituted against each school in Georgia—a process that would require years. A time-lag is built-in. No impending crisis looms." Yet the women also took care to prepare the white community for change: "We must realize that the decision of the Court will have an impact on Georgia, *one that will spread over many years*." Indeed, less than a month after the *Brown* decision was issued, the Georgia LWV joined the United Churchwomen of Atlanta and of Georgia in their support for the decision. They signed an official statement, which they sent to Governor Herman Talmadge on June 8 and read before the Georgia Education Commission on June 25, 1954. After declaring, "As law-abiding organizations, we will gladly take part in planning how Georgia may best meet its responsibilities consistent with the highest law of the land," they suggested the appointment of an interracial committee to "work out methods that will best fit local conditions," and added, "It is the obligation of state leadership to make that possible." Frances Pauley explained later that although they emphasized the importance of preserving public education, everybody understood that the real issue was desegregation. "In April 1954," she recalled, "the league had its convention, and after a very heated debate, we took a stand for public schools, which really meant integrated schools."[20]

For all their progressive gestures on school desegregation, in 1954, southern LWVs still remained all-white organizations—Pauley's De Kalb County LWV standing out as an exception—whereas the national league's by-laws stipulated that membership should "not only be representative of the community," but should be "community-wide in its interest in setting up programs."[21] In the decade from the mid-1950s to the mid-1960s, local leagues struggled to adjust their practices to their proclaimed democratic principles but were sometimes defeated by internal and external resistance. One of the largest, the Atlanta–Fulton County LWV, unexpectedly voted to open its membership to blacks during its annual meeting in 1956, provoking the resignation of its president, its vice president, and six board members. The motion to integrate the league was actually proposed by a northern woman who had recently moved to Atlanta. The debate between supporters and opponents of the motion was lively, but the motion finally passed after a few hours. Sara Mitchell Parsons, a middle-aged housewife and mother of three who had recently joined the league, "did not hesitate one second." She recalls, "With a strange surge of joy I said 'aye.' To be proud of yourself in a crisis is a wonderful feeling." Parsons owed the LWV for her subsequent involvement in civil rights activism. "The League changed my life," she said. "From being bored with playing bridge and attending garden club meetings, I became involved in issues vital to the quality of life in my community." In 1958, she became president of the Atlanta LWV for a two-year term. She recalled that "virtually every issue that we studied in order to educate the public had racial overtones. The LWV helped persuade the Atlanta school board to adopt a desegregation policy, and we were adamant that funds should be more equitably distributed among white and black schools." Empowered by this first experience, she was elected to Atlanta's Board of Education in 1961 as an integrationist candidate, and for seven years she confronted her conservative fellow board members by herself, until she resigned to follow her second husband to California.[22]

The LWVNO was less successful in integrating its own ranks but supported the *Brown* decision against the forces of interposition. The LWVNO was created in 1942 on an all-white basis because, as one of its integrationist members, Rosa Keller, admitted, "obviously the forties were no time to be breaking the racial barrier." After a failed attempt at integration in 1947 by Emily Blanchard, a former president of the Louisiana LWV and member of the Southern Conference for Human Welfare, Keller held an integrated meeting at her home to consider opening membership to black women. This was in 1953. Like Frances Pauley in Georgia, Keller was well ahead of a majority of her fellow league members and prodded them into bolder action. "As past president of the integrated New Orleans YWCA and president of the New Orleans Urban League," Shannon Frystak writes, "she believed that integration was the only path for a political group such as the LWV." Keller shared this view with the then president of the LWVNO, Mathilde Dreyfous. Many league members were concerned that integrating the membership might kill the organization owing to the hostility of the local population to integration. In keeping with its noncoercive policy, the national league advised the New Orleans leaders to promote meetings open to all races at nonsegregated places before encouraging blacks to join. This course was adopted until 1955, when five black women became members. By this time, however, Louisiana's legislature had enacted new segregation laws to prevent implementation of the *Brown* decision, making interracial activities virtually untenable. With a significant drop in membership during 1956, the leaders reluctantly abandoned their policy of integration, and did not resume it until 1963.[23]

Thus the situation in New Orleans contrasted with that of the Atlanta LWV. In Atlanta, even if integration provoked a temporary crisis, it did not endanger the organization since the local context was generally more favorable. As Pauley recalled about her league, they certainly lost some members as a result of their racial policy, but they gained ten times as many in return. In any case, even if the LWVNO had to yield over the issue of membership, it confronted local and state authorities by supporting school desegregation. Together with other organizations like the NCJW, the Louisiana Education Association (LEA), and the YWCA, the LWVNO adopted a resolution supporting the *Brown* decision. "In fact," notes Frystak, "a number of progressive-minded groups such as the LWV, the NCJW, and the YWCA made the Supreme Court decision a priority on their organizational agendas."[24]

The experience of the LWV in Louisiana sheds light on the determining influence of local factors on the activities of progressive groups in the immediate post-*Brown* context. In that respect, policies or attitudes acceptable in some places might prove to be dangerously radical in others. In Durham, North Carolina, for instance, black women's organizations pressured white women's groups into accepting integration. As a result, several African Americans joined the local league in the 1950s without triggering significant opposition.²⁵ In the Deep South, where resistance was the most active and where state authorities officially adopted interposition measures, organizations such as UCW, the NAACP, or CHRs, to name but a few, were the direct targets of repression and intimidation, inevitably curtailing their efforts. Mississippi was one of the most repressive states, as Florence Mars, a white integrationist, testified: "In the weeks following the [*Brown*] decision I discovered that approval, or even acceptance, of the Supreme Court decision would not be tolerated. After commenting that the Jim Crow laws had made a mockery of the Constitution and being met by surprisingly unfriendly responses, I ceased to express my opinion."²⁶ Such hostility was due in great part to the national influence of Senator James Eastland, a close associate of Joseph McCarthy. A member of the Senate Internal Security Subcommittee (SISS) since 1951, Eastland became its chairman in 1956. He used the committee to harass integrationists throughout the South during that period. After the Supreme Court issued the *Brown* decision, he kept attacking the Court as being "indoctrinated and brainwashed by left-wing pressure groups," and openly called on the South to disobey. In 1955, he asked before the U.S. Senate: "Who is obligated legally or morally to obey a decision whose authorities rest not upon the law but upon the writings and teachings of pro-communist agitators and people who have a long record of affiliations with anti-American causes and with agitators who are part and parcel of the communist conspiracy to destroy our country?" Mississippi was also the state where, in 1954, the first White Citizens' Council was formed. Eastland actively supported the White Citizens' Council movement. Eastland's anti-integration crusade was no lonely battle, as other prominent southern politicians, such as Senators Herman Talmadge of Georgia and Strom Thurmond of South Carolina, resorted to the same techniques to discourage compliance with *Brown*.²⁷

White Citizens' Councils were a source of much concern for Mississippi churchwomen, as Dorothy Tilly's correspondence reveals. In her report for the first quarter of 1956, however, Tilly found that the most critical situation was that of South Carolina, because of the combined assaults of the White Citizens' Councils and "undercover propaganda" against churchwomen "and the Church in general." In that state, as in other areas where massive resistance was strong, conditions that had seemed fairly favorable in 1954 worsened with the rise of resistance and reached a desperate low in 1960. The state council of UCW, for instance, which had been "a flourishing organization" up to 1955 under the leadership of Edith Dabbs, had taken by 1960 "a very defensive position" in reaction to the attacks of the *Charleston Courier*. In some places like the city of Rock Hill, CHRs were forced into inactivity by intimidation. Numerous letters sent to Dorothy Tilly from other states described the same acts of intimidation. The Louisiana women were frightened by the "horrible and extreme things that are being done in this state by the [White] Citizens' Councils now springing up like mushrooms." In Montgomery, Alabama, Virginia Durr recalled that "about a hundred women, black and white, from all over the state," held interracial prayer meetings for a while. One day, a segregationist newspaper editor took all the license numbers on their cars during the meeting and published their names and addresses in his newspaper. The subsequent harassment, she commented, "broke the group up. We never met after that."[28]

Fear did not completely paralyze the women, however, even if it definitely limited the scope of their activities. In fact, massive resistance directly affected the tactics that progressive southerners used to achieve desegregation. Moral suasion, which had been white women's major instrument of reform since the 1920s, was all the more resorted to after intimidation inhibited many individuals who would not have opposed integration in safer circumstances. Churchwomen appealed to Christian love to overcome the barriers that prevented acceptance of desegregation. They assumed that they could persuade southerners to overcome their prejudices just as they had done for themselves earlier in their lives. Thelma Stevens, for instance, had invited Dorothy Tilly in 1930 to break the taboo of eating with a black person. As Alice Knotts explains, "Appealing to a higher calling of Christian faith, Stevens encouraged Tilly to overcome her fear of breaking a racial taboo, and accompanied her in the experience. . . . This became the model of social transformation used by both Tilly and Stevens as they helped lead Americans on one of the largest projects ever attempted to change American attitudes about race." Even the leaders who tended to be bolder than others recognized the necessity of winning hearts and minds as a priority. For instance, Frances Pauley, who became executive director of the Georgia CHR in 1961, traveled across the state as the nonviolent civil rights movement developed. Although she supported the direct action campaigns set up by newly formed groups, she did not join them but rather continued the grassroots work of persuasion that had been started by churchwomen in the previous decades. As she explained later, "I felt my major job was to try to form this bridge, to try to get blacks and whites together, and no matter what I went into that was the first thing we did."[29]

Moreover, the systematic accusations of Communism used by segregationists to repress integrationists led the latter to play the tactic of political moderation to avoid harassment. Although their goal was desegregation, the various organizations considered in this chapter did not present it as such. Words such as "integration," "desegregation," "race," and, of course, "Communism" even became taboo. As Eliza Paschall noted, the phrase "human relations," used extensively after World War II, meant in reality "race relations." In order to achieve their aims, integrationists deliberately refrained from using direct references to race in their public statements. Sara Parsons describes this tactic at length in her memoir. When she ran for a seat on the Atlanta Board of Education in 1961, she was coached in her campaign by her friend Helen Bullard, another liberal white woman who worked in public relations. The first handout card they created for the campaign read: "We need a Qualified, Dedicated, Experienced, Capable Woman on the Atlanta Board of Education." She commented, "Not one of these words in any way alluded to my liberal, integrationist beliefs." Reflecting on articles published later during the campaign, she noted: "None of these write-ups mentioned 'integration' directly, but as I've said, there were code words such as 'all,' 'equal,' 'change,' and 'improve,' and everyone could read between the lines." This was obviously necessary to be elected. In Little Rock, Adolphine Terry had long repudiated white supremacy when the school crisis burst out in 1957. She led the white women's campaign for the integration of schools, as will be shown in the next pages, but she was opposed to adopting an official integrationist stance in the fight. And yet when a reporter visited her in her house and, seeing the portrait of her Confederate father, asked her why she was involved in the crisis, she answered: "My dear, I am an integrationist!"[30]

Finally, in response to organized white resistance, supporters of integration invariably insisted in their private exchanges on the necessity for discretion. For instance, when the leaders of the LWVNO attempted to integrate their group in late 1954, an internally circulated document warned: "Please do not discuss this problem with any non league members as publicity and inevitable misunderstanding at this time could do much damage." In a similar vein, the national LWV's executive secretary wrote to Frances Pauley in 1956, "It is . . . important, we think, that at this time no special publicity be given to those Leagues with Negroes in their membership." As for the Mississippi churchwomen who wrote Dorothy Tilly about the climate of fear spawned by the White Citizens' Councils, they did not give up all action but stressed the need for nonpublicized meetings. Admitting that "any publicity or public statement at this time would be no good there," Elizabeth Noble, the state president of the Mississippi Council of Churchwomen, told Tilly that "such meetings as this one you are calling are helpful in this connection." Isabel Goldthwait expressed the same view concerning the situation in Louisiana.[31]

Speaking and acting in favor of the *Brown* decision in the South between 1954 and 1964 thus was an act of courage. Edith Dabbs, who helped found a council of UCW in South Carolina in the early 1950s, actually remarked that it did take courage "merely to belong to the organization against the pressure of general public opinion."[32] Hundreds of women demonstrated such courage by participating in activities sponsored by the FOC, UCW, Methodist women, the LWV, the various CHRs, and other local groups. They were not all deeply committed to integration, but they were led throughout by a few leaders who were true integrationists and did not hide it. These leaders made a difference by struggling quietly but determinedly for total equality. They were not crusaders, but they were not compromisers either. They stood as living examples and sources of inspiration for the masses of other women who only needed guidance and the certainty that they were not alone in disapproving of white supremacy.[33] Samples of letters of appreciation are far too numerous to be listed here, but the following extracts speak for themselves: to Edith Dabbs: "I was so stimulated by your state meeting I could not sleep that night.... Some of it was too strong for me and in retrospect I question, but I *liked* the challenge of new approaches and I *want* to grow. That was a growing experience"; to Dorothy Tilly: "Thank you so much for the inspiration and information of the meeting last Thursday and Friday. It was what I needed to take the next steps in action toward desegregation"; to Frances Pauley: "Without you—and what you are doing—I and the others like me would not know where to turn for guidance and leadership. You are a real and definite sustaining force, giving each of us, as Councils or as individuals, that added support we all need to let us know we are not alone." Of Adolphine Terry, Sara Murphy has written, "Terry's outspokenness made it easier for some of the rest of us to stand for what we believed as well." Of Thelma Stevens, Alice Knotts says, "An exceptionally articulate champion of human rights, Thelma

Stevens was known by thousands of Methodists and other churchwomen and was in popular demand to address conferences and workshops."[34] Apart from a few exceptions like Tilly, these women did not make the headlines. They were not public figures, but they definitely contributed to the movement for desegregation by effectively combating apathy in their communities.

Saving the Schools

After the Supreme Court decreed in May 1955 that the states were to desegregate their public schools "with all deliberate speed," the battle for implementation began. Supporting the *Brown* decision was one thing, putting it into practice was another. Between late 1957 and the mid-1960s, the desegregation of southern public schools triggered riots, open confrontation of state and federal authorities, and the closing of schools in several places across the region. These events gave white women a new reason to challenge white supremacist authorities in their distinctive, southern, ladylike way. Drawing from the tradition of respectable militancy they had built up in the previous decades, a handful of them launched a movement to "save the schools" in direct opposition to massive resistance. The movement started in the fall of 1958 as a reaction to the closing of schools in Little Rock and in Virginia. While women created organizations to reopen the schools in places where they had been closed, others took preventive steps to avoid school closings in Atlanta and New Orleans. These parallel save-the-schools groups ultimately rallied thousands of white women to the cause of school desegregation, even if only a minority of them were really committed to integration.

Whereas the Virginia Committee for Public Schools (VCPS) was led by men, the organizations that grew up in Arkansas, Georgia, and Louisiana were controlled by women and strikingly resembled each other.[35] They relied on the same women's networks of churchwomen, YWCAs, LWVs, and CHRs, and they adopted the same tactic of respectability. Although these movements could be deemed conservative as compared to the black-led nonviolent movement that gained momentum in the same years, they were nevertheless part of the progressive forces at work against white resistance.

The *Brown* decision was the result of a long legal battle initiated by the NAACP in the mid-1930s. Whether they liked it or not, southerners knew that the segregation era was coming to an end. While opponents of segregation were impatient to hear the Supreme Court condemn it as unconstitutional, segregationist leaders devised means to circumvent the expected decision. Many states actually worked to equalize their black and white school systems in the hope that blacks would prefer to attend new, well-equipped segregated schools rather than registering at older integrated ones.[36] Some state authorities also adopted provisions allowing them to replace their public school systems by private ones should the Supreme Court order the integration of public schools. Thus, between 1954 and 1956, the states of Georgia, Virginia, Alabama, Louisiana, Mississippi, South Carolina, and Arkansas adopted interposition measures and devised legal means to allow their state authorities to order the closing of public schools in case of a court order requiring desegregation.[37]

In spite of these acts of defiance, desegregation plans were devised in many places, including those where resistance was being organized. In Virginia, the Commission on Public Education, appointed by Governor Thomas B. Stanley in 1954 and chaired by state senator Garland Gray, first recommended a moderate plan of token desegregation, which charged local school boards with assigning pupils to schools on a "nonracial" basis and recommended the provision of tuition grants for parents who did not want their children to attend integrated public schools. By the summer of 1956, however, the Virginia legislature had entered upon its interposition program, and the Gray commission had retracted its recommendations. The General Assembly decreed that schools where integration occurred would be placed under the control of the state and would be closed "until the governor could reestablish segregation under the police powers of the state." The situation initially seemed more favorable in Arkansas, where the state authorities were not as massively opposed to desegregation as those of Virginia or of the Deep South—although the adoption of an interposition amendment to the state constitution clearly stated where their loyalties lay. Governor Orville Faubus, who had earned a reputation as a business-oriented moderate, declared in March 1956 that segregation was "a local problem" and added that it could "best be solved on the local level." For its part, the Arkansas legislature adopted a pupil-assignment law giving local boards full authority to act.[38]

Little Rock's school board reacted to the first *Brown* decision by announcing its will to comply, and, a year later, proposed a plan of gradual desegregation, from the integration of one high school in September 1957 to that of elementary schools in the fall of 1963. Local resistance undermined the plan, however, entailing the well-known troubles of Central High School and the federalization of the National Guard by President Eisenhower. White resistance intensified as the months passed by, and in August 1958 the Arkansas legislature voted to authorize the governor to close any school threatened by violence or integration. On September 12, in response to a federal district court order to integrate, Faubus ordered the closing of Little Rock high schools. On the same day, Governor J. Lindsay Almond Jr. closed the first Virginia school in Warren County. He went on to close eight more in Norfolk and Charlottesville in the following days. The two governors' measures were approved by referendums.[39]

Although resistance to segregation clearly was the majority position in Little Rock and Virginia in the fall of 1958, a number of white citizens were not ready to sacrifice their children's education to segregation. This was illustrated by the creation of "save-our-schools" groups. In Virginia, the VCPS was organized in December 1958 to coordinate a number of groups that had emerged in the localities concerned by school closings. In Little Rock, the battle for public schools was waged by the WEC. These organizations campaigned to convince the white power structure that closing the schools would prove more damaging than accepting controlled integration. They organized publicity campaigns, supported moderate candidates against segregationist leaders in elections, and lobbied local and state authorities. After months of intense struggle, they won the support of the business elite and parent-teacher organizations. Schools started to reopen in Virginia in February 1959, and in April the state legislature adopted a new plan of token integration. In Little Rock, a coalition composed of the WEC, the Parent-Teacher Association (PTA), the Chamber of Commerce, and other prominent civic and religious groups won the replacement of segregationists by moderates on the city's school board in May 1959. As a result of this victory, Central High School and Hall High School reopened in August on a token integrated basis.[40]

The reopening of Little Rock's schools would probably not have occurred without the dedication of a few white women who had decided to take action a year earlier. On September 12, 1958, the day Governor Faubus closed the schools, Velma Powell, Vivion Brewer, and Adolphine Terry met at Terry's house to discuss ways of mobilizing women "concerned about the matter of race relations." Terry wrote in her diary: "It is high time for the moderates to be heard from." Fifty-eight white women answered the call on September 18 when the WEC was officially founded. Sara Murphy, who served on the board of the new organization, remembers that the original name was the Women's Emergency Committee to Save Our Schools, but that it was changed after the founders learned of a "Save Our Schools" committee being formed in Louisiana. In fact, the New Orleans Save Our Schools (SOS) committee did not officially come into being until February 1960, with the help of the SRC. The founders of SOS, Gladys Cahn and Rosa Keller, had been working for the implementation of the *Brown* decision since 1954, and wanted to avoid the same pitfalls as Virginia and Little Rock by furthering, "by all proper and legitimate means, the continuation of a state-wide system of free public education." The creation of Help Our Public Education (HOPE) in December 1958 in Atlanta was motivated by exactly the same concerns. Maxine Friedman and Muriel Lokey had been the first initiators of the effort to rally moderate citizens to the cause of public education when Atlanta's schools were threatened with closing.[41]

The creators of HOPE feared that a pending court decision might entail the closing of all schools as a result of interposition measures enacted earlier by the state legislature. Atlanta's power structure was not vocally opposed to integration, and Mayor William Hartsfield had proclaimed the city "too busy to hate," but interposition measures passed by state and county politicians could have easily affected Atlanta. Immediately after the creation of HOPE, women started lobbying the legislature in favor of preserving the public school system. They also set up publicity campaigns to rally the white population to their cause, and extended their influence statewide by creating chapters throughout the state. The former president of the Georgia LWV—from 1952 to 1955—Frances Pauley, contributed greatly to HOPE's expansion by mobilizing the network of women with whom she worked. The women's campaign to win over Georgia's population and state authorities to the preservation of public schools bore fruit after more than two years when, in early 1961, the state legislature repealed the interposition measures it had passed in 1956. Atlanta's public schools were integrated in September 1961. At that time, HOPE gave way to Organizations Assisting Schools in September (OASIS), an umbrella agency coordinating approximately "fifty civic, religious, and youth-serving Atlanta agencies" that aimed at the "peaceful and orderly acceptance of desegregation."[42]

In New Orleans, SOS was founded in February 1960 after federal district judge J. Skelly Wright had ordered the city's school board to prepare for desegregation. The school board reluctantly started to work on a plan to desegregate two schools in a working-class neighborhood but counted on the state government to resort to interposition measures to prevent compliance with the court order. The deadline for integration was November 14, 1960. In the summer of that year, the Louisiana state legislature and Governor Jimmy Davis engaged in a showdown with Judge Wright. The members of SOS started lobbying the legislature as early as February 1960. Then, during the battle between the courts and Louisiana authorities, they campaigned with the help of the LWV for respect of the desegregation plan. In spite of their efforts, writes Shannon Frystak, "the majority of white citizens of the state seemed intent on defending segregation and defying the directives of the Supreme Court and the state courts." On November 14, the admission of four black girls to the two selected integrated schools triggered riots. In the following days, most white parents withdrew their children from the two schools, while the black pupils were harassed every day on their way to school. The women of SOS escorted the black families for days before federal marshals took over, and they later concentrated on convincing the community of the harmful effects of boycotts while supporting the integrated schools whose funds had been frozen by the state. Finally, after months of campaigning, new schools were successfully integrated in September 1961. After further efforts to educate white Louisianans about the detrimental effects of the crisis, and since the process of school integration continued after the crisis, SOS disbanded in 1962.[43]

The examples of Little Rock, Atlanta, and New Orleans testify to the vitality of white women's activism during the desegregation crisis. Starting as small groups of dedicated individuals, the WEC, HOPE, and SOS evolved into powerful organizations that definitely influenced the local course of events in their communities and in their region. At their height, the three organizations claimed memberships of more than 2,000, close to 1,200, and 30,000, respectively.[44] The WEC, HOPE, and SOS shared many characteristics, the first one being the predominance of women within their ranks. HOPE and SOS included a number of men but were definitely managed by women who represented a large majority of their memberships. The WEC, as its name indicates, was exclusively female. All groups were socially homogeneous as they attracted mainly members of the middle and upper-middle classes. Most of the members were Protestant but a significant number of Jews were also involved. Many were housewives married to businessmen, educators, or professionals. Obviously, since the organizations were set up by women, their membership and constituencies overlapped with those of the LWV, the YWCA, churchwomen associations, the NCJW, the American Association of University Women (AAUW), PTAs, and interracial reform organizations such as the Urban League and the NAACP.[45]

Another striking characteristic common to the three groups—which also applied to the VCPS—was their all-white policy. The rationale behind this deliberate choice relied on several arguments. The first one was that segregation was a system that had been imposed and was being defended by whites, who controlled the whole power structure. Thus it seemed logical that whites should be the ones to dismantle the system they had built. Behind this argument lay the idea that the whites in power would only respond to other whites' pressure since the black population had no significant political influence at the time. In a letter to Rosa Keller about SOS, for instance, Paul Rilling, field director for the SRC, wrote, "It is assumed that the attitude of Negro leadership is on record, that white persons will have more success with white legislators, and that it needs to be demonstrated that *white* people are interested in keeping the schools open regardless of the segregation-desegregation issue." The issue was discussed with black people, as Frances Pauley remembered. Pauley had promised to herself in 1954, "I was not going to belong to, give my efforts to, give my money to, or support in any way anything that was segregated." When the leaders of HOPE asked her to join, she objected to excluding blacks from the group, but she recognized that "this was a political issue, and at that point it looked like maybe this would be the best way to go, tactically." Moreover, black people she knew "agreed that what we wanted to do was keep the schools open and that tactic seemed to be the best." In Little Rock, Adolphine Terry implored her friend Daisy Bates not to come to the organizational meeting of the WEC. Bates, an NAACP leader, had earned a national reputation at that time for having taken the first nine black students of Central High School under her protection. Terry argued that an integrated organization would fail to attract a large number of white women who might be won over to the cause of public schools, and "she needed a core of white women with enough influence, clout, and drive to pull others in." Sara Murphy writes, "Bates said that because she trusted Terry, she supported what Terry was doing." Besides the purely tactical dimension of such a segregated policy, another argument put forward by Terry was that white women were more fit to do the job than other population groups owing to their specific status in southern society. She explicitly referred to Jessie Daniel Ames and the ASWPL as "a model for action in this present crisis."[46]

"Respectability" was a major concern for the women who engaged in the battle for open schools. As schools concerned the community as a whole, victory in the battle between the proponents of massive resistance and those of controlled integration depended on public acceptance. Moreover, the black- and Red-baiting techniques of the segregationists made any dissenter all the more vulnerable to accusations of radicalism. Thus "save-the-schools" groups adopted the same tactic of respectability as many moderate integrationist groups, by adopting a southern, white, middle-class, Protestant, and conservative profile. As an illustration, when it came to choose an official chairperson for HOPE, Rebecca Dartt notes, "Fran Breeden seemed the logical choice. She had perfect credentials for the job: she was southern, having been born and raised on Florida's Gulf Coast; Protestant; charming; articulate; and unknown in Atlanta." Nan Pendergrast, one of the founders of HOPE, was, in her own opinion, "the natural choice to head the Speakers' Bureau." The daughter of an old, prominent Atlanta family, she often introduced her talks with the story of her grandmother's birth on the day of the battle of Atlanta. The grandmother, she explained, had been born in the basement of the house "because the Yankees were occupying the rest of the house." Such an introduction made it difficult then to label the speaker an "outside agitator."[47]

In the same vein, save-the-schools groups cultivated the notion of domesticity, for instance, in organizing meetings in their members' homes, which often took the form of tea parties. This was how HOPE managed to grow from a handful of concerned mothers into a mass organization. Frances Pauley and Betty Harris, HOPE's executive director, organized teas across Atlanta in the early months of 1959. Harris, a Georgia native born to a family of Methodist preachers and educators, was still another of those women who used their status to challenge white supremacy in an acceptable way. A friend of Lillian Smith, she was a Girl Scout professional who had started to work for racial equality well before the *Brown* decision. As Rebecca Dartt—Harris's daughter—points out in her study of HOPE, "She had the advantage over many recent newcomers to Atlanta in facing this deep-seated emotional issue with her fellow Georgians." The "tea strategy," as Dartt calls it, relied on favorable press coverage to attract new followers, a strategy that could not fail when "the *Atlanta Journal* society section ran a photo of Pauley and two other well-dressed women, wearing white gloves, pouring and receiving tea from a silver tea service." In a similar tribute to legendary southern ways and manners, Little Rock's WEC held its most important gatherings at Adolphine Terry's house, an old white-columned mansion built in 1840, with the cook and the gardener performing their domestic tasks in the background.[48]

The "tea strategy" clearly shows that HOPE leaders deliberately adjusted means to circumstances in order to achieve their aims. Pauley, for instance, unambiguously aimed at full integration, but in a letter to another organizer in which she discussed the selection of speakers for a future meeting, she advised: "I believe Jim Dorsey would be better than Morris. In the first place Jim is a conservative who wants open schools. He will appeal to the middle of the road people and to the segregationist more than Morris." The leaders of the WEC had the same preoccupations as those of HOPE. Jewish members, especially, although they were key figures in the organization, insisted on remaining in the background because they were not considered "true" southerners by the mainstream society and wanted to avoid "giving extremists a further excuse to attack either the Jewish community or the WEC." As for SOS, one of its members, Peggy Murison, explained that "people didn't want to give the impression that this was an extreme liberal assault on the community," however puzzling the notion of extreme liberalism might be. Indeed, the Orleans Parish School Board asked the organization to limit its Jewish and its liberal membership, to no avail.[49]

Obviously, respectability in 1958 was incompatible with interracialism. Thus just as integrationist groups had replaced the phrase "race relations" with "human relations" in their public discourse, save-the-schools groups removed the issue of race from their campaign literature. This policy was deliberately adopted as a means to avoid harassment as well as to attract the largest number of supporters. In Little Rock, Sara Murphy recalls that the founders of the WEC "had first envisioned starting a committee for racial harmony, but because of the crisis they had decided that this in itself would create opposition, so the focus for the new group was to be 'strictly aimed at saving the public schools.'" In her first statement to the press, Vivion Brewer, the

WEC's chair, could not be more explicit: "We stand neither for integration nor against integration. We are not now concerned with this. Our sole aim— I repeat—our sole aim is to get our four high schools open and our students back in their classes." In all subsequent campaigns, flyers invariably featured the same message: "NOT For Integration, NOT for segregation, FOR Public Education." HOPE's rhetoric was the same, as a typical published statement read: "HOPE, Inc. does not propose to argue the pros and cons of segregation vs. desegregation, or states rights vs. federal rights. It has one aim—to champion children's rights to an education within the state of Georgia." As for SOS, Murison said, "They wanted it to look like we were just keeping the schools open, although in the back of our hearts a lot of us were assaulting the bastions of segregation." In Virginia too, the initiators of VCPS's organizational meeting on December 6, 1958, wrote: "We are not meeting either as segregationists or integrationists."[50] The refusal to deal with integration at all was clearly meant to defuse negative reactions both inside and outside the organizations, which had been specifically formed to solve the school crisis. Whereas the leaders aimed at more than the preservation of schools, many members did not.

However, although the women of save-the-schools movements were divided over the issue of integration, they all shared the same preoccupations as mothers. Motherhood was indeed a key factor in the involvement of many nonpoliticized women who took their first steps in political life to save public schools. It was also a key factor for longtime activists who had always put forward their womanhood to claim responsibility in educational matters. For those who had struggled in the 1930s for children's rights, or for the improvement of black and industrial education, the battle for integration was a matter of continuity. Women had always been recognized as the guardians of education, so it was natural that when the educational system was threatened, they should lead the fight to rescue it.

With hindsight, it seems that the achievements of save-the-schools movements surpass their weaknesses. On the weak side, although the WEC and VCPS played a crucial part in the reopening of schools in Little Rock and Virginia, and although HOPE and SOS convinced the communities of Atlanta and New Orleans to accept desegregated schools rather than no schools at all, school desegregation remained limited to tokenism until the early 1970s. Moreover, by the time these groups disbanded between 1961 and 1963, segregation was still the law in the southern states, and nonviolent protesters were being brutally repressed—sometimes murdered—by local authorities. According to Sara Murphy, many of the white women who had campaigned for the preservation of public education "were 'single issue' conservative women from the community who had originally lined up for one cause—to open the schools." They returned to their homes after obtaining just that. The tactics adopted by these organizations clearly limited their achievements, as Frances Pauley recognized in January 1961. "Hope," she wrote, "has been handicapped in being for one purpose only—that of keeping the schools open." But she added, "I think if we had not had a single purpose we could not have been as useful as we have." The all-white policy also had its obvious limitations. Many women remained prejudiced since they did not have the opportunity to interact with black people. For instance, a WEC member who attended her first interracial conference in 1960 could not find the courage to invite a black person for a coffee at a Woolworth's lunch counter. She was not hopelessly racist, as her attending the conference showed, but her work with the WEC had not encouraged her so far to break racial taboos.[51]

That said, for many other women the achievements of the fight for public schools were immense. At the community level, the organizations managed to lead voters to repudiate their segregationist leaders in favor of moderate ones. Indeed, writing to Vivion Brewer in December 1959 to congratulate her after WEC-supported candidates defeated segregationists in the election of a new school board, Henry Woods remarked: "I have never seen a more apathetic electorate; that your organization was able to turn out almost 9,000 votes in the face of such apathy is a little short of miraculous." In her assessment of SOS, Shannon Frystak stresses the extraordinary dimension of this movement given the unfavorable context in which it grew. She writes that "drawing on the long tradition of female activism in Louisiana since the 1930s, women in the 1960s were on the frontlines of the fight for change during the school desegregation crisis. They not only escorted the children to and from school in an extremely dangerous and hostile environment, but also subjected themselves, and their families, to death threats, harassment, and physical and verbal abuse." Frystak finds that the tactics adopted by SOS were adapted to the context, because "they worked within the system, not without it."[52] Her statement applies to most of the first generation studied in this book.

Achievements were also outstanding on the personal level. Not surprisingly, many of the women who played key roles in save-the-schools organizations joined or supported the civil rights movement in the 1960s. Some, like Frances Pauley, Nan Pendergrast, and Eliza Paschall, had already broken free from segregationist culture when the school crisis occurred, so that they naturally shifted from the integration of schools to the fight against overall segregation. Pauley was connected with the Student Nonviolent Coordinating Committee (SNCC) and with Martin Luther King Jr., among others; Pendergrast was a member of the Georgia CHR, the NAACP, the National Urban League, and the Southern Christian Leadership Conference (SCLC); Paschall, who was executive director of the Greater Atlanta CHR in the 1960s, corresponded with Martin Luther King Jr. and with SNCC leader James Forman. Alice Spearman also used her position as executive director of the South Carolina CHR to support the student movement in her state.[53]

Other women, like Sara Murphy, had not been actively involved in militant activities before, and underwent a deep transformation as a result of the fight for open schools. Reflecting on it years later, she explained that by late 1962, when she ran for a position on Little Rock's school board, she had partly overcome her prejudices, but she did not identify herself as an integrationist. "The word 'integration,'" she wrote, "evoked images of intermarriage and Communism in the still-emotional climate in Little Rock." Murphy's full transformation occurred in 1963, in the aftermath of her action with the WEC, when she learned about a Kansas City women's group named Panel of Americans, which organized interracial, interfaith panels where individuals of each racial or religious group represented on the panel exposed their personal experience of prejudice. Murphy promptly set up a similar group in Little Rock, which took the name of Panel of American Women (PAW). The panel was meant to awaken as many white people as possible to the common humanity of all individuals, as "Little Rock was split into two communities that did not communicate or know enough about each other to solve problems together." Murphy and her fellow panelists drove across the state in the mid-1960s to educate people about the virtues of an integrated society. Little Rock's PAW was successful in converting a number of Arkansas whites to integration, and it directly inspired other women who created similar panels in Memphis and New Orleans.[54]

Finally, as Murphy also pointed out, the white women who first committed themselves to the integration of schools extended their commitment to the nonviolent civil rights movement by serving as channels of communication between direct action activists and local white communities. Commenting on her new relationship with black activist Gwen Riley, of PAW, Murphy observed: "I met civil rights leaders from across the South in Gwen's kitchen who were working with Negail [Gwen's husband] to plan sit-in strategies for college students at the lunch counters in Kress and McClellan's downtown. From them I learned more about the civil rights movement and how important it was to have a bridge like the panel to interpret it back to the community at large." This was the case for many other women who participated in the organizations studied here, from churchwomen to the LWV through the NAACP and others. The personal papers of these women testify to the close relationship they established with the civil rights organizations that led the black liberation movement throughout the 1960s. They not only provided advice but also comfort and help in hard times.[55] Last but not least, in helping their communities cope with the desegregation crisis, lady activists became political actors and acquired an undeniable degree of expertise and influence in society. Besides empowering them politically, their work for racial justice forced them to confront the stereotypes of their culture and to repudiate them publicly. Commenting on the work of Little Rock's WEC, for instance, Sara Murphy writes: "I think the organizing became a personal crusade for women. They had been kept silent, held down, put into stereotypes, and not listened to for so long that by the 1960s they were heady with their own power."[56] Murphy's comment ultimately stresses the fact that the women who struggled to "save" southern schools started to liberate themselves from the gender restraints of their culture.

The Southern Lady: A Double-Edged Sword

The battle for schools pulled together great numbers of women who were not political activists but entered politics when they realized that white resistance jeopardized a pillar of their society, public education. During the crisis, they asserted themselves as women without ever repudiating the ideal of the southern lady. On the contrary, they used the ideal as a weapon to counter segregationists, thus undermining southern patriarchy without rejecting it altogether. Armed with their moral authority, their status, and their manners, they confronted white supremacist leaders and emancipated themselves by deliberately redefining ladyhood to their advantage.

One of the most conspicuous assets of lady activists up to the 1960s was their emphasis on children and the preeminence of motherhood and education in their public discourse. For instance, after 1954 Dorothy Tilly redirected the efforts of her FOC toward convincing southern parents to accept school desegregation as a chance for children to grow up in a better environment. She argued that "these twelve million children—Negro and white—will be the victors or victims of change, in proportion to how well the parents and teachers prepare them for this new venture in brotherhood and neighborliness." Tilly and the FOC focused primarily on children and consequently on women, whom Tilly considered to be the key agents of change through their educational role. Thus she especially advised women to teach their children the values of an integrated society and to steer their husbands into accepting change, because "husbands could learn indirectly from their children." Tilly was not alone in considering women as essential in the fight for integration. Lillian Smith, who before the *Brown* decision had already stressed the necessity for southern women to speak out against white supremacy, welcomed churchwomen's support of desegregation as evidence of women's moral superiority over men. In 1956, she wrote to a member of a northern Quaker group who had proposed to help in the desegregation process: "I wish I could tell the country about the fine courage of our young preachers and of some of our older ones. And the women, bless them, how steadily they work down here. This confusion is caused largely by white men, not by white women." The convergence of Tilly's views and Smith's comments confirms the idea of a distinctive female approach to segregation.[57]

Such emphasis on women's moral responsibility—which could be traced back to the early days of women's activism—was characteristic of "lady activism," as is well illustrated by the words of Roberta Church—then minority consultant for the Department of Labor—who spoke at a meeting of the Urban League of Greater New Orleans in 1959. She said that women had the power to "exert great influence both as individuals and through their organizations by taking the initiative in the community to stand for high moral principles in all areas, and by moulding public opinion to support this stand."

She deemed it important "that women accept this responsibility for it is they who should see to it and insist the proper moral tone prevails in the home, the community, and the nation." Such an argument was all the more powerful in the segregationist South, where motherhood was extolled as the primary quality of a respectable woman.[58]

Motherhood was also a major strength for the women of save-the-schools groups who fought for the implementation of the *Brown* decision in the late 1950s and early 1960s. Most of these women first became involved in the movement for school desegregation out of concern for children and education. Such concern was a driving force behind Little Rock's WEC, Atlanta's HOPE, and New Orleans's SOS.[59] As one of HOPE's statements to the press underlined, the organization's single aim was "to champion children's right to an education within the state of Georgia." The members of all save-the-schools groups emphasized the nurturing role of women in society, which they often associated with a concern for education, peace, and harmony. The best incarnation of this trend was Nan Pendergrast, who gave birth to seven children while working actively for many causes and organizations. She was a founder and board member of HOPE. A respected member of the Atlanta white elite, she was featured regularly in the pages of the *Atlanta Constitution* as a model mother and wife who devoted her life to human causes in a constructive way without threatening prevailing social norms. In the 1960s, she was involved in Atlanta's Partners for Progress. This group of women sent black and white members to eat together in restaurants in support of desegregation. The third of seven principles they put forward in one of their statements reads: "We are aware that all women are deeply concerned that every child in Atlanta be allowed and encouraged to grow up in a climate of good will, and an atmosphere of calm acceptance of the responsibility of being a good citizen."[60] Thus it is clear that motherhood constituted a means for lady activists to assert their controversial views during the desegregation era. This dimension of women's activism was all the more respected since it reinforced the traditional definition of women, deflecting any accusation of radicalism or subversion.

In addition to showing a natural concern for children, being a middle-class married woman in the segregated South made it easier to dissent from prevailing views insofar as it provided relative protection from retaliation. Several testimonies suggest that women were freer than their husbands or their fellow male activists to break the racial etiquette or to take a public stand in favor of integration or racial equality because they did not depend on public acceptance for their livelihood. Dorothy Tilly, for instance, "linked her public identity with that of her husband." In the words of Edith Riehm, "She put this image to good use in her reform efforts by quietly challenging southern society from within the safe and gendered boundaries that circumscribed the life of a proper southern lady." Tilly actually explained that her husband, Milton, a businessman, was responsible for her involvement in mission work by deliberately driving her through Atlanta's poor neighborhoods to shock her into action. He reportedly told her: "I thought if you saw the people hurting long enough, that you would hurt, too—and if you hurt bad enough, you'd do something about it! *I can't do it myself,* but I'll make it possible if money is needed for you to get involved. I'll back you!" Milton remained faithful to his word and supported his wife's work until his death in 1961. As another illustration, Nan Pendergrast retrospectively remarked that her "social standing and wealth seemed to protect [her] from ugly opposition." She could devote herself to the struggle for racial justice in the 1950s thanks to her "blessedly supportive husband," who was a prominent businessman.[61]

The idea that, until the 1960s, women could afford to do what men could not is confirmed by the testimonies of other women. Louise Young, for instance, another Methodist woman who taught at Scarritt College in the 1920s, explained in an interview: "When I asked an older woman one time why it was that southern men let their wives do these things that were so outrageous you know, like various race relations things . . . she said, they're so glad that they can do things, the women can do things their husbands couldn't get away with." Echoing Lillian Smith's views, Young added that owing to their domestic status, women had a more personal approach to human relationships: "A southern woman, middle-class . . . was very much protected and her contacts were personal relationships. . . . And she saw life personally and was sensitive to personal needs. Now the man on the other hand had to bring in money and so forth, so he was exposed to much rougher tougher world."[62] Similarly, during the school desegregation crisis, the women who led the save-the-schools movement thought they could afford to do so whereas their husbands either approved and stayed behind the lines for fear of retaliation or else opposed their wives' action and drifted away from them.

As women's activism expanded, the idea that women had a different approach to social issues gained ground. Interestingly, while this development tended to encourage men to consider women's work as marginal at best and, as a result, to keep women away from their own sphere of action, women used the same idea to claim higher effectiveness in the fields they considered important and to assert themselves in the political sphere. Edith Dabbs, who served as state president of UCW in South Carolina in the 1950s, attributes the success of UCW in her time to its outstanding efficiency, due, according to her, to "the close and free communication between . . . state and national levels." In the 1950s, UCW was an autonomous organization, but it was placed under the authority of the National Council of Churches, led by men. As Dabbs recalls, there was a classic saying at the National Council of Churches: "When an apparently insoluble problem came up and the men had wrestled with it to the point of frustrated exhaustion, they sometimes gave up on a curious note. 'It's hopeless,' one of them would say. 'I see no possible answer. Let's turn it over to the women. They don't understand that these things can't be done and they just go straight on and do it anyhow.'" To Dabbs as to other women activists, this eccentricity of sorts was the strength that made the difference between men's conservatism and women's true adherence to democratic and Christian principles, and ultimately created the conditions for change.[63]

Adolphine Terry, of Little Rock, had the same distinction in mind when, in the late summer of 1958, as it became clear that Little Rock's schools would not reopen as usual, she put on her hat and white gloves and called on journalist Harry Ashmore at the *Arkansas Gazette*. "Mr. Ashmore," she told him, "the school situation is absolutely intolerable. It is perfectly evident that the men are not going to do anything about this. I've sent for the young ladies"[64]—by which she meant that the WEC was being launched.

Churchwomen from all denominations had asserted themselves as a specific reform group through the years since the early decades of the twentieth century. Initially maintained in a subordinate position by male leadership, they broke free from church authorities by devoting themselves to increasingly militant reform work that ended up in challenging the foundations of segregationist society. Edith Dabbs introduces her short unpublished memoir of UCW—written in 1972—with a brief history of churchwomen sounding more like a women's manifesto than a historical review. She pits women against men to describe the growth of churchwomen's groups as a process of emancipation from men. Men, she argues, "decreed the hierarchy among themselves and allowed the hand-maidens to do much of the work while trying very hard to keep a tight lid on their women-folk." In an explicit indictment of male religious leaders, she claims that "they underestimated the power and dedication leashed in those Christian women growing increasingly restless to be about their Father's business without the restriction of having to play church by masculine rules." She then explains that the creation of the interdenominational United Council of Church Women in 1941 represented the logical outcome of the women's increased vitality: they finally "decided to come together for greater efficiency and strength."[65] It is important to note that Dabbs does not blame men for discriminating against women per se but for thwarting their reform impulses. Given that Dabbs and South Carolina's UCW devoted most of their time to the fight against segregation in the 1950s, her account highlights the dialectical link between the women's commitment to racial equality and their emancipation from the male leadership.

Women's increasing militancy on race at mid-twentieth century actually consolidated the female networks created in the previous decades, on which the post–World War II civil rights movement could rely for its own expansion. As white women's groups concentrated their work on desegregation, the specificity of their activism came to the fore. Although it was not publicized owing to its apolitical, community-oriented character, such activism was very effective in the sense that it provided the opportunity to mobilize large numbers of people across the region in a short lapse of time. As for women's achievements within mixed organizations, they were not immediately recognizable because they were based on private, unofficial work and relationships dependent on the networks they built throughout their lives, but they were undeniable.[66]

For all their discretion, the women who engaged in controversial activities or behavior were perfectly aware of their distinctive position as female reformers and used it as part of their tactics, one of their favorite weapons being the image of the southern lady. Some, like Tilly, were undoubtedly deeply attached to their status and held it as a matter of principle to dress and behave in accordance with it. As an illustration, Guion Johnson, a historian born in 1900 in Texas who studied at the University of North Carolina at Chapel Hill and married the sociologist Guy B. Johnson, remembered Tilly as "a sweet little southern woman with a soft voice, small features." "And," Johnson added, "she dressed like a belle." Johnson came to live in Atlanta in 1944 when her husband became the first executive director of the SRC. There, Tilly recruited her to work for the Georgia Conference on Social Welfare. In the following years, Johnson and Tilly closely collaborated, touring the state to favor the development of community welfare programs. Johnson remembered: "In fact, she said to me that she disapproved of my severe clothes, my tailored clothes, She said, 'When you go out to do battle, you must dress for the occasion.' So, she wore frilly hats with flowers and lace on them and frilly dresses and always with white gloves, and she was accepted by the sheriffs and the commissioners and the city councillors."[67]

White gloves were a standard prop for many women activists of the older generation, as the protagonists often mention them in memoirs or interviews. Nan Pendergrast, for instance, described her action with Partners for Progress in these words: "We would be very well-dressed.... That almost dealt me out. I remember that we had to wear white gloves." White women particularly cultivated the stereotypical image of the southern lady to deter violent reactions or mere hostility. Frances Pauley emphasizes this dimension in her account of women's lobbying actions with Georgia politicians. For instance, in June 1954 Margaret MacDougall, leader of UCW, read a public statement supporting the *Brown* decision before the Georgia Education Commission on behalf of several groups, including the Georgia LWV of which Pauley was president. Pauley explains: "We chose her because she's so sweet and such a lady." The commission then questioned the presidents of the various organizations that had endorsed the statement. Pauley remembers that the experience was especially painful because it was a very hot day and she was "dressed in navy blue trimmed with white, and white gloves, white shoes, and white hat." On another occasion, during the school desegregation crisis in Atlanta, HOPE sent members to the state legislature to stage a protest in defense of public schools. While the two senators of the state were visiting the legislature to speak about schools, the women quietly sat in the gallery and waited until the senators started to speak. "We told everybody to dress very nicely and wear white gloves and told them not to say anything—not to boo, not to clap, not to do a thing." Then they took everybody by surprise when they "took out their signs—'We want Public Schools'—" in a dramatic gesture of defiance. It was in the same spirit that the leaders of Little Rock's WEC orchestrated a lobbying campaign during the 1959 session of the Arkansas legislature. One of them argued: "I can testify from personal experience that legislators turn pale when they see a group of polite but determined women descending on them. Perhaps it brings sudden memories of their mothers, urging them to do the right thing!" So Irene Samuel, who was in charge of the operation, "selected a group of attractive young WEC workers who spruced themselves up in heels, white gloves, and their best dresses to run interference for the others." These examples show that women activist groups deliberately played with the image of the lady for tactical purposes. Pauley recognized it when she commented later, "HOPE was very genteel. We operated in a very nice manner; it was a little bit hard for people to get at us."[68]

There is no doubt, then, that the lobbying activities of all women's groups, however moderate they may have claimed to be, directly challenged the traditional definition of women's role in society. Pauley's example, although far from being the only one, is one of the most telling. She developed outstanding political skills, first as president of the Georgia LWV, then as HOPE's major lobbying agent. The reactions of male politicians at the time testify to the subversive character of the LWV's activities in the 1950s, Pauley recalling, "the men didn't like us, called us the 'Leg of Women Voters.' They were making fun of us, as I imagine they did even more with the early suffragists." Interestingly enough, while Pauley often stresses the impeccable manners she and her fellow activists cultivated in all their actions, she remembers that league members virtually lost their ladyhood in the eyes of their opponents as a result of their involvement in politics. Commenting on the politicians who sat in the Georgia legislature, she noted: "They didn't admire us like some other women who visited the legislature." The other women did not come to lobby the legislature but to bring cookies to the men during sessions. When Pauley finally expressed her opinion by saying to one of the cookie bearers, "You make me ashamed to be a woman," the woman replied, "I'm not a woman, I'm a lady." Pauley had clearly been unconscious of the inevitable shift from lady to woman that her political activities had entailed. A few years later, Pauley returned to the legislature on HOPE's behalf. "The men Frances could corner," writes Rebecca Dartt, "were offered the facts and expert opinions on the issue before them. Sometimes she tried to persuade them to vote yea or nay on a particular bill, and spoke of what the consequences would be if the bill passed or not.... She did all this politicking without a care to fashion, except for wearing white gloves, a must for southern ladies at the time." Yet wearing white gloves, as the previous example shows, was not enough to hide the fact that Pauley was threatening the existing order through her action.[69] The same ambivalence characterizes Dorothy Tilly, who continued to cultivate her ladyhood while increasingly encroaching on the men's sphere. Although she centered her action on mission work as a prominent Methodist leader, this position allowed her to be appointed by President Truman in December 1946 to his Committee on Civil Rights. Tilly thus came to incarnate the paradox of white southern female activism since, on the one hand, she represented the "quintessential southern lady," as Edith Riehm puts it, and, on the other, she participated in the work of a federal committee that helped the president elaborate his highly controversial platform for the 1948 election.[70]

Eventually, in some instances, ladyhood clearly became a hindrance to the women's growing commitment to desegregation, which led them to throw away the mask of respectability they had worn up to the 1950s. Sara Mitchell Parsons is a case in point. Her emancipation from traditional gender norms would probably have occurred even without the advent of the civil rights movement, but it would have been much slower and arguably less far-reaching than it actually was in the context of desegregation. Parsons's commitment to racial equality constituted a crucial factor in the deterioration and ultimate demise of her first marriage, as her husband vainly tried to prevent her from challenging the segregationist power structure while she became ever more assertive in return. On January 5, 1964, she wrote in her diary: "Ray has become even more resentful of my political life, especially my liberal-radical leanings. I have become increasingly aware of a serious undertow of disaffection." Her election to the board of education also contributed to her personal liberation, as she earned a salary for the first time in her life. She comments, "To me, the salary meant that I was more than Mrs. Ray Mitchell, more than the good, quiet corporate wife, more than a mother of three and the manager of a household (albeit one now virtually empty, both physically and emotionally), more than a volunteer with opinions people could take or leave." Stepping out of the domestic sphere by taking a job, although it constituted in itself a challenge to prevailing gender norms, might have been tolerated as an act of eccentricity. Using this job to promote school desegregation was unforgivable. Indeed, when she publicly committed herself to desegregation, Parsons repudiated the ideal of white southern womanhood to which her husband and her parents expected her to submit. The February 12, 1964, entry of her diary reads: "My mother and mother-in-law are both like my husband in one way: they don't approve of my social or political life." Commenting later on her mother's pressure to make her wear a hat to a social event they had attended together, she added: "I knew then that the way she wanted me to be—a properly dressed, socially prominent matron—wasn't me at all."[71]

The rejection of her family's outlook went along with a rejection of her local church, whose members, unlike their minister, supported segregation during the desegregation crisis. In this case, too, she explicitly attributes this change to her growing involvement in the civil rights movement. She recalls, "the civil rights era raised fresh questions for me about the church." After a few years, her new racial views and militant activities led her to stop attending church. "I was clearly out of step with local beliefs," she writes. "My convictions and my theological readings were pulling me away from my family's beliefs and especially from the particularly strict religious beliefs of my husband. But I had long known better than to discuss my lessons with Ray."[72] Thus Parsons's retrospective comments make it clear that her involvement in the civil rights movement made it impossible for her to continue to respect the traditional standards of white southern womanhood as defined by segregationist culture. She became estranged from her family when she joined women's organizations such as the LWV or churchwomen's groups, which challenged the racial status quo at a time when white community leaders supported it.

* * *

In the final analysis, the *Brown* decision marked a turning point in the history of white southern female reformers because it led them to express their dissent from the segregationist dogma openly, even if they did so in a nonconfrontational way. Although the nature of their activism did not change fundamentally, the desegregation crisis placed them at odds with their communities and forced them to reconsider their relationships with their fellow southerners. Before 1954, interracial work had been part and parcel of their reform activities, seeming to be the natural extension of their traditional missionary role as southern ladies, and everybody had accepted it as such. This had allowed them to undermine segregation from within without openly condemning it. After 1954, racial equality officially became their primary focus. Their support of the *Brown* decision automatically turned them into open dissenters, forcing them to devise a whole strategy to keep their influence and achieve their aims without losing their status. Thus the figure of the southern lady became a weapon in their gloved hands, which they deliberately used to counter white resistance. In some instances, however, the weapon turned into a liability. In any case, the lady strategy had its strengths and its limitations, but it definitely consolidated white female networks, and favored the assertion of a new white southern female identity.

Nevertheless, if these lady activists clearly represented a majority of white female reformers in the South at mid-twentieth century, whose outlook was rooted in the reform movement of the interwar decades, they were not the only female representatives of white southern antiracism in the post-*Brown* era. For all its homogeneity, the older generation of white women activists also included a few individuals who, in the face of white resistance and intimidation, opted for direct confrontation with segregationist forces. As the modern civil rights movement gained momentum in the wake of the *Brown* decision, these outspoken dissenters enthusiastically embraced the black cause and, as a result, often lost their position of respectability.

4

After *Brown*, Part Two

Open Confrontation

In the wake of the *Brown* decision, the Montgomery Bus Boycott that started on December 5, 1955, brought together the legal forces of the NAACP and a new form of protest based on massive, nonviolent resistance to injustice. The boycott constituted a turning point in black southerners' history, for it was the first massive black protest involving the near totality of a local black population, whose unity and determination did not falter from the very first day to the final victory.[1] The women's organizations that first concentrated their efforts on the implementation of the *Brown* decision contributed to desegregation by playing the card of moderation and, as such, did not openly support the new wave of protest initiated by the Montgomery boycott. Another brand of white women activists responded to the *Brown* decision and the rise of the black movement by playing a different card. These women had close connections with moderate women's groups, but they also spoke and acted as individuals in a straightforward, militant way. They openly stood on the black side in the battle for human rights and advocated integration, going against the grain of their society.

An important dimension of the new protest movement against segregation was the centrality of religion in it, which made it especially appealing to white women reformers. Unlike mainstream white southern Protestantism, which ignored the social implications of Christianity, southern black religion was a driving force in the improvement of blacks' social status, and ultimately in the fight against discrimination.[2] After the Montgomery Bus Boycott, church mass meetings became a distinctive feature of the civil rights movement and maintained a strong sense of unity. Martin Luther King Jr.'s Southern Christian Leadership Conference (SCLC), like the Congress of

Racial Equality (CORE), combined the concepts of Christian love and nonviolence to confront segregation in the South. This form of protest broke with former attitudes—notably with the NAACP's legalistic strategy—and was immediately recognized as radical by white supporters and opponents alike. The Student Nonviolent Coordinating Committee (SNCC), founded in April 1960 under the guidance of Ella Baker—a pivotal figure in the NAACP and the SCLC—also grounded its action in Christian ideals and resorted to nonviolence as a tactic to confront segregationist laws.[3] Unlike King's SCLC and the NAACP, however, SNCC immediately distinguished itself in the nonviolent movement by its political radicalism due in great part to its being formed by students. Another fundamental difference with previous challenges to segregation in the South was that the new movement was a black movement—although open to whites—and that it was entirely controlled by blacks. In that respect, the Montgomery Bus Boycott confirmed that blacks had taken the lead in protest against segregation and that whites had lost the initiative for change. This was a crucial development because it reversed the roles in the fight for racial equality. The few whites who joined the civil rights movement after Montgomery became minority members in a majority-black structure, which deeply altered their perception of themselves and their relationship with blacks.

The black liberation movement pulled together a multiplicity of individuals and groups in a large number of places. In addition to the SCLC and SNCC, CORE and the NAACP organized local campaigns or participated in actions set up by the recently formed southern organizations. The Southern Regional Council (SRC), Councils on Human Relations (CHRs), the National Student Movement, student YWCAs, the American Friends Service Committee, Highlander Folk School, and the Southern Conference Educational Fund (SCEF)—which will be dealt with in later pages—closely supported the movement.[4] After the sit-ins and the Freedom Rides, SNCC and CORE complemented their direct action operations with voting registration and political education campaigns in Mississippi, Louisiana, and southwest Georgia, where white resistance was the strongest. The civil rights movement continued, with the Albany Movement, the March on Washington, the Mississippi Freedom Summer Project, the Mississippi Freedom Democratic Party (MFDP), and the Selma, Alabama, demonstrations.[5] This joint assault of black southerners on segregation—with the aid of black and white southern and nonsouthern volunteers—obtained the passage of the 1964 Civil Rights Act, banning segregation in all public places across the nation, and of the 1965 Voting Rights Act, prohibiting all voting restrictions. The Twenty-Fourth Amendment to the Constitution, ratified in 1964, abolished the poll tax.

Southern whites' responses to these events were diverse. While the majority remained passive and silent, a small minority supported and/or joined blacks in the nonviolent struggle, and another fraction, small in numbers but very effective since it included local politicians and law enforcement officers, resorted to violence and terrorism to try to defeat the movement.[6] Violence was an omnipresent, day-to-day feature of the 1960s movement, especially in the rural areas of the Deep South where SNCC, CORE, and the NAACP organized voter education campaigns between 1961 and 1964. Throughout these years freedom workers responded to segregationists' attacks by nonviolent determination. As for those whites who disapproved of segregation, they adjusted in a variety of ways to the evolution of events from the Montgomery Bus Boycott to the advent of Black Power in 1966.[7] In 1955 and 1956, when the Montgomery Bus Boycott took place, many prominent white liberals, seized by fear in the aftermath of the *Brown* decision, had considered King and the NAACP as extremists because they called for immediate desegregation.[8] The liberals welcomed the sit-ins more favorably as the students did not disrupt the usual order of things on a large scale and took personal risks to denounce a blatant injustice in a highly dignified way. As the black movement radicalized under the influence of the students, however, white liberals came to consider King as a moderate on the racial issue, condemned the radicalism of SNCC and CORE, and turned away from the movement after the passage of federal legislation.[9]

As far as white women reformers are concerned, the transition from "southern lady" activism to open radicalism was a natural by-product of the political radicalization caused by the modern civil rights movement. Indeed, in the 1950s—and even earlier in exceptional cases—several members of the older generation of white southern women who disapproved of segregation confronted white supremacy head-on, becoming alienated from other whites. Unlike other women reformers who worked behind the scenes and held publicity as a liability in the post-*Brown* context, they stood up against their communities by articulating a severe critique of segregationist culture and by urging white southerners to repudiate segregation not only for the sake of blacks but for their own collective redemption.

These women saw themselves as ordinary citizens motivated by human equity, but they were perceived as radicals owing to their public support of integration. Some, like Lillian Smith, Sarah Patton Boyle, and Juliette Hampton Morgan, can be defined as moral radicals for their focus on the psychological dimension of segregation, for their stress on the notion of white guilt, and for the priority they gave to individual conscience in the fight against racism. Others, like Anne Braden and Virginia Durr, shared some aspects of Smith's, Boyle's, and Morgan's moral outlook, but would better be described as political radicals because they set their denunciation of segregation within a broader critique of southern society and politics, and because they were active in militant organizations. Most of all, Braden and Durr, as well as a few others, did not object to collaborating with Communists or "fellow travelers" in the fight against racial injustice, although they did not believe Communism was the answer. Instead of distancing themselves from Communism in response to Red-baiting, they publicly stood up against the segregationists when the latter harassed them, which definitely placed them on the side of radicals.

Given the pervasive character of white supremacy in southern society up to the 1960s and the very small number of racial dissenters in the region, close ties developed between the few whites who worked against segregation during that era, since mutual support was essential to resist white supremacist repression. This was all the truer for women who not only shared with male integrationists the ostracism reserved to all dissenters but also had to cope with the constraints of gender, which further limited their status in their communities. Thus the most radical women who became involved in the struggle against segregation, and who antagonized their communities as a result, developed personal friendships that nourished their activism while increasing their awareness of gender constraints. Such personal relationships played an important part in these women's emancipation because they reinforced the already strong ties that women's networks had created since the 1920s. Hence, the civil rights movement and the resistance it met created conditions in which these women supported and encouraged one another, and were led, ultimately, to confront southern gender norms openly.

Moral Radicals

From the 1950s until her death in 1966, Lillian Smith denounced the "conspiracy of silence" that played in favor of segregationists in the South.[10] Through this phrase, Smith meant not only that moderates and liberals harmed their region by remaining silent instead of supporting integration, but that the same people contributed to silencing the few white integrationists like her by dubbing them extremists. As a writer, she was the most articulate of the individuals I have called "moral radicals," and she directly inspired them as their personal histories during the post-*Brown* crisis show. Unlike the women examined in the previous chapter, Smith and other moral radicals spoke and acted primarily as individuals rather than through organizations.

A major characteristic of Smith was her isolated position not only in the white community but in liberal and militant circles as well. This isolation—which turned into alienation as the years went by—can be accounted for by several factors. In the first place, Smith distinguished herself from the racial reformers of the 1940s by defining segregation as a moral issue, whereas others saw it as a social, economic, or political one. In her numerous articles as well as in *Killers of the Dream*, the autobiography she published in 1949, she described at length the devastating psychological effects of segregation on black and white children. In language clearly influenced by psychoanalysis and wrought with disturbing images, she equated segregation with a disease, or a "spiritual lynching." As early as 1945 she described it as "an insidious, slow, creeping disease that destroys a child's emotional tissue, sapping his strength, making him a weak thing for life in a world that requires, above all else, psychic strength and maturity."[11] Such an approach was virtually unheard of in the South at the mid-twentieth century, as the reception of *Killers of the Dream* shows. For middle-of-the-road liberals like Ralph McGill of the *Atlanta Constitution*, Smith was dangerously irrational, as his reaction to her book revealed: "A woefully unsound book," he wrote. "Miss Smith is a prisoner in the monastery of her own mind." He reproached Smith for hardly ever getting outside and then "seeing only wicked things to send her back to her hair shirt and the pouring of ashes on her head and salt in her own psychiatric wounds." For many other southerners, however, she was a prophet, and her book was an eye-opener. For instance, in contrast to McGill's review, Juliette Morgan, the daughter of an old privileged southern family living in

Montgomery, Alabama, wrote in a local newspaper that Smith's work was "packed with powerful arguments about the racial question."[12]

Another disturbing element of Smith's work for many of her contemporaries was her insistence on white guilt and her very negative depiction of the South at a time when southern segregationists extolled the southern way of life and liberals danced on the tightrope of condemning racial injustice while disapproving of federal coercion in the name of states' rights. Smith definitely stood in the 1950s as the bad conscience of white liberals, and they responded by shunning her at best when they did not reject her altogether. Her voice was all the more unsettling as she continued to denounce liberals' silence, thus holding them responsible for massive resistance to desegregation after the *Brown* decision. The fundamental difference that distinguished her from mainstream liberals and from the majority of women reformers was her conviction that the only way to achieve integration was to speak up in favor of it in order to strike consciences. Hence her publication of *Now Is the Time*, a pamphlet urging the implementation of the *Brown* decision, in 1955. The pamphlet was used by Dorothy Tilly in her "Fellowship of the Concerned" workshops, but it was removed from southern bookstores without justification a few months after its publication.[13]

Moreover, Smith not only lashed out at white supremacy but also dissented from liberal orthodoxy by indicting moderation in the polarized context of the late 1950s. In December 1957, in the thick of the school crisis, she bitterly denounced the moderates' attitude: "They are cautious, they move inch by inch, and only when pushed from behind; and that is their privilege. But they refuse to let others move faster, or to speak more clearly and perhaps even more persuasively than they." Indeed, when the leaders of the Montgomery Bus Boycott were criticized for their allegedly extremist attitude, Smith enthusiastically endorsed the fledgling nonviolent protest movement as the embodiment of the moral radicalism she advocated. In response to the critics who equated the extremism of the segregationists with that of the integrationists, she articulated a definition of positive extremism that left no doubts as to which side she was on. In December 1956, she addressed the participants of the Montgomery Bus Boycott in the following terms: "You have been extremists: good, creating, loving extremists and I want to tell you I admire and respect you for it.... You have dramatized, for all America to see, that in times of ordeal, in times of crisis, only the extremist can meet the challenge.

The question in crisis or ordeals is not: Are you going to be an extremist? The question is: What kind of extremists are you going to be?" Juliette Morgan, who lived in Montgomery, was deeply impressed by this address. After the Montgomery Bus Boycott, Smith—who had joined CORE's advisory committee in 1946—actively supported Martin Luther King Jr. but also the workers of SNCC and CORE until the civil rights movement shifted toward Black Power. She publicized the movement whenever she could, notably by publishing a short book, *Our Faces, Our Words*, in 1964.[14]

Finally, Smith's radicalism was all but political, as she believed the primary condition for progress was individual moral growth. This passionate individualism turned her into a fierce anti-Communist—although she unambiguously combated McCarthyism. The epitome of the "Cold War liberal," she saw Communism, like segregation, as destructive of the human spirit, and after the *Brown* decision she hammered out the idea that desegregation was the best weapon of the United States against the international spread of Communism.[15]

After the publication of her novel *Strange Fruit* (1944) and of *Killers of the Dream* (1949), Smith earned the reputation of being a lonely voice in the wilderness of southern racism. Although she was confronted with the attacks of segregationists who tried to silence her, she was heard and admired by many integrationists who did not dare to speak up but read her works. She could also rely on a national audience for support and recognition. This was not the case of two other white dissenters who provoked the wrath of their contemporaries when they expressed their views in local newspapers. Sarah Patton Boyle and Juliette Hampton Morgan shared with Smith the conviction that segregation was a moral evil, and they appealed to whites' consciences to eradicate it, but they paid a high price for their outspokenness.

Juliette Morgan's life exemplifies the process of personal transformation from southern belle to racial activist that many white women went through between the 1930s and the 1960s. When the desegregation crisis started in the mid-1950s, she was working as a librarian in Montgomery. Born in that city in 1914 to a southern aristocratic family, she received a typical segregationist education and earned a master's degree from the University of Alabama in 1935. She began to question white supremacy in the aftermath of the Scottsboro Case. In the mid-1930s, she became involved in the social and political issues of her time through the local Democratic Club and its circle of New Dealers. She joined the Women's International League for Peace and Freedom—which distinguished itself by being racially integrated—and signed the pledge of the Association of Southern Women for the Prevention of Lynching (ASWPL) in 1937. In 1939, she started to write regular letters to the *Montgomery Advertiser* to denounce the injustice of segregation. In 1941, she joined the newly formed local segregated chapter of United Church Women, where she became familiar with, and soon fascinated by, the work of Lillian Smith. She also met Virginia and Cliff Durr at that time. In 1942, she was not yet a full-fledged integrationist, but she supported antidiscrimination measures such as a federal antilynching law and the abolition of the poll tax. She supported President Truman's civil rights program in 1948. In late 1946, she completed her psychological reeducation by participating in the creation of an interracial prayer group that soon boasted of nearly 100 members, including Virginia Durr, Coretta Scott King, and Juanita Abernathy. She was also a founder of Montgomery's Fellowship of the Concerned chapter.

When the *Brown* decision was handed down, Morgan not only worked actively with the state chapter of the Alabama CHR in favor of its implementation, but she publicly called for, in the *Montgomery Advertiser*, the adoption of a gradual desegregation plan, which caused her library superintendent to ask her to refrain from making controversial public statements again. It was finally the Montgomery Bus Boycott that precipitated the last stage of Morgan's rejection of white supremacy, and alienated her so deeply from her native community that she could no longer endure it. On December 13, 1955, the following lines could be read in the *Montgomery Advertiser*:

> Not since the First Battle of the Marne has the taxi been put to as good use as it has this last week in Montgomery. . . . The Negroes of Montgomery seem to have taken a lesson from Gandhi—and our own Thoreau, who influenced Gandhi. Their own task is greater than Gandhi's, however, for they have greater prejudice to overcome. . . . It is hard to imagine a soul so dead, a heart so hard, a vision so blinded and provincial as not to be moved with admiration at the quiet dignity, discipline, and dedication with which the Negroes have conducted their boycott. . . . Instead of acting like sullen adolescents whose attitude is

"make me," we ought to be working out plans to span the gap between segregation and integration to extend public services—schools, libraries, parks—and transportation to Negro citizens.

Her long letter triggered a nasty campaign of harassment by the segregationists. Her superintendent did not fire her but made her promise not to publish any more letters. As white resistance intensified in 1956, Morgan agonized over her promise while she witnessed the riots that prevented Autherine Lucy from attending the University of Alabama in February and the effective suppression of all white liberal forces in Montgomery. She supported the boycott by driving black maids to and from work. She felt desperately guilty on hearing Lillian Smith's address advocating positive extremism. Finally, in January 1957 Buford Boone, publisher of the *Tuscaloosa News*, asked Morgan for permission to publish a letter she had privately sent him in appreciation of his stand against the White Citizens' Council. She accepted. The ensuing harassment, together with the pressure exerted on the library to have her fired, led her to resign on July 15. On July 17, she committed suicide.[16]

Sarah Patton Boyle did not kill herself, but after waging a sixteen-year battle against the total incomprehension of her fellow white southerners, she sank into disillusionment and withdrew from the social world. Like Morgan, she was the descendant of an old southern upper-class family, but she did not experience the same gradual awakening to the evils of white supremacy. From her birth in Virginia in 1906 until the registration of African American Gregory Swanson at the University of Virginia in 1950, Boyle remained a standard product of segregationist culture. Her life was suddenly transformed in 1950. The immorality of segregation abruptly dawned on her as she learned of Swanson's admission to the University of Virginia. After she had approached Swanson in such a paternalistic way that he dismissed her in anger, she gradually became aware of the extent of her racist indoctrination and undertook to unlearn her prejudices by taking actual lessons from Thomas Jerome Sellers, a sympathetic local black editor. From then on she wrote articles and letters to editors in which she candidly expressed her views in favor of integration. She welcomed the *Brown* decision with much enthusiasm. When the Gray commission, appointed by Governor Thomas B. Stanley, held hearings in November 1954 on the issue of school segregation, Boyle overcame her fears and was among the handful of whites—with Mrs. A. J. E. Davis, of the Arlington

Council of Church Women—who spoke in favor of desegregation.[17] Events took on a dramatic turn in February 1955 when the *Saturday Evening Post* published one of her articles under the title "Southerners Will *Like* Integration." Reactions were not long in proving she had been far too optimistic, and she became the target of violence, ostracism, and harassment. In addition to burning a cross in her yard, segregationists bombarded her with hate mail and phone calls. Although she was severely hurt by such hostility, Boyle did not yield to pressure. She went on speaking out to convince Virginians of the immorality of segregation. She toured the state as a representative of the Virginia CHR but left the organization in 1960, finding it too moderate in its stance. She then participated in several episodes of the civil rights movement, from the March on Washington to the march of protest after the shooting of James Meredith in 1966, including a demonstration against segregation, ending up in jail in 1964.[18] In the early 1960s, she joined the NAACP and was a member of the Virginia advisory committee of the U.S. Commission on Civil Rights.[19]

Unlike Morgan, Boyle acquired a national reputation as an integrationist by publishing a best-selling autobiography, *The Desegregated Heart: A Virginian's Stand in Time of Transition*, in 1962. She also wrote *For Human Beings Only*, a manual on integrated racial relations published in 1964. As its title suggests, *The Desegregated Heart* served a double purpose. In the first place, it was a means for Boyle to expiate her racial sins through confession. She does so in the book by describing her original segregationist identity and her transformation after her 1950 epiphany. This "conversion narrative," as Fred Hobson has called it, leads to redemption in the last part of the book. The autobiography, however, also has the collective function of redeeming the white South as a whole by addressing white southerners' conscience in a time of crisis. Boyle clearly establishes herself as a typical product of segregationist culture but also as the living proof that prejudices can be overcome, notably through religious faith. Although Boyle's original optimism did not survive the nonviolent movement and white resistance, her moral and religious stance placed her within the same philosophical current as Lillian Smith and Martin Luther King Jr., who recognized a kindred spirit in her.[20]

As can be seen in their personal histories, Morgan and Boyle were very different in many respects, and yet they both ended up as outcasts as a result of their stand on segregation. One major common point they shared with

Lillian Smith was their highly critical depiction of the South and the stress they put on southern white guilt. For instance, writing in the June 3, 1952, issue of the *Montgomery Advertiser,* Morgan denounced the state Democratic Party's white supremacist motto as "an insult to the colored races and a disgrace to whites." Comparing the South to Nazi Germany, South Africa, and Stalin's Russia, she expressed her disgust for the "savage old mores of the South, otherwise referred to as 'our Southern traditions,'" adding that such traditions "would be far more honored in the breach than in the observance." As for Boyle, she wrote in her autobiography: "The segregation robot, once set in motion, controls the segregator as well as the segregated with an iron, mechanical hand which will not be stayed for mere broken bodies, broken hearts, or sympathy.... In my very viscera I became sick at these injustices—of which I had known nothing at all before."[21] In the climate of regional defensiveness that prevailed in the 1950s and early 1960s, such words sounded like a declaration of war and were answered as such.

Another major characteristic justifying the identification of Morgan and Boyle as moral radicals was their insistence on the necessity of breaking the silence in order to defeat segregation. They agreed with churchwomen that winning hearts and minds was the primary condition of racial progress, but they disagreed on the means to use to achieve integration. In a context of fear and intimidation, they argued, it was essential to counter the loud voices of the segregationists by speaking up even louder to win over the so-called silent South to the cause of human justice. In an open letter to Governor Folsom published on July 28, 1955, Morgan observed: "I just don't see letting the most backward and retarded politicians speak without any answer from the other people of Alabama." The notion of courage—and its opposite, cowardice—was as central in Morgan's letters as in Smith's articles. Like Smith, Morgan kept complaining about liberals' failure to lead the fight against white supremacy. On April 10, 1956, she wrote to her cousin Paula Morgan: "I am so ashamed of Alabama I don't know what to say. And I'm more ashamed of the people who know what's right and are just playing safe by silence." Boyle was equally enraged by Virginian conservative and liberal politicians who either advocated resistance to integration or remained passive and silent. She indicted them in her autobiography for their sorry testimonies at the November 1954 hearing on school desegregation: "Not only our Southern tradition of kindness and courtesy, not only the ideals of our nation and our professed religion, but also even minimum standards of civilized citizenship were desecrated by Virginia's elected representatives that day, and those whose duty was to oppose them blandly implied by tone and words that it was all quite allowable and that the desecraters merely held 'different opinions' from their own." Setting the liberals' position against the standards of Christianity and morals, she added: "Across my mind marched the words from Revelation, '... thou art neither cold nor hot... I will spew thee out of my mouth.' There was something morally nauseous about this timid half-lifting of a tiny, limp flag of decency when the need was for a trumpet call and a dramatic unfurling of the banner of professed faiths." Liberals were worse than cowards, she concluded, as they simply placed their safety above moral values. Patty Boyle, like Juliette Morgan and Lillian Smith, placed moral principles above everything else in life. This is the reason why she retreated from civil rights activism in 1967. "I have always believed in total commitment... and I was sure I was right about the brotherhood of man, and about the moral underpinnings of the Movement. When the original idealism of the revolution began to dissipate, I ceased to be creative."[22] Deeply disillusioned, she found refuge in religion.

Smith, Morgan, and Boyle can be singled out as moral radicals because of the way in which they expressed their dissent, and especially because they antagonized their communities and stood alone against them rather than sacrificing their principles. They were certainly not unique in their primarily moral approach to segregation, as the study of the next generation will show. Even within their own generation, however, other women actually shared some aspects of their outlook, but differed from them insofar as they combined moral arguments with political action in the fight against segregation, and were much less isolated than they were in spite of the ostracism they had to face due to their positions.

Political Radicals

The best incarnation of the blend between moral and political activism was Anne Braden. Born in 1924 in Louisville, Kentucky, and raised in Anniston, Alabama, she really was at the crossroads of the older and younger generations of white southern women activists, as she was already a mature woman when the students entered the black liberation movement in the early 1960s but was much closer to them in outlook than she was to the older generation. In 1958, she published a memoir under the title *The Wall Between*, in which she related the persecution she, her husband, Carl, and her black friends Andrew and Charlotte Wade had suffered in 1954 when they breached the pattern of housing segregation in Louisville. Like Lillian Smith's *Killers of the Dream* and like Boyle's autobiography, *The Wall Between*, published in time of crisis, was an act of personal catharsis through which a white woman expiated her original sin of racism, but it was also a critical examination of southern society and culture, as well as an appeal to whites' consciences urging the repudiation of segregation in the name of universal brotherhood. Moreover, the book described and denounced at length the black- and Red-baiting techniques of the segregationists.

Typically, Braden came to reject her segregationist education on reaching adulthood. As with all the other women of this volume, the spark of her racial activism was the Protestant religion in which she had been raised. Her description of segregation and its effects echoes Smith's writings. The words she uses, such as "poison," "guilt," "schizophrenia," convey an image of the South as a sick society in need of shock treatment. Braden's book ends with the same insistence as that of her fellow crusaders on the necessity to speak out against the segregationists' resistance. The basic rationale for such a stance is based on psychological arguments, since the author presents speaking out as the only way to draw the masses out of apathy: "If liberals all over the South sit silent," she argues, "they leave a vacuum. Human society, like nature, abhors a vacuum, and today the forces preaching white supremacy in the South are presenting their campaign as a great crusade, breathing a new life into the old myth, giving it a new and immediate fire it has not had for generations." She goes on to observe, "The movement for equality, for a world where all people can live together in harmony, could be presented in that way too. But today in the South it is only among the Negro people that this is happening; among the white people the only real crusade in sight is that of the white supremacists." It is interesting to note that Braden encouraged a crusading spirit whereas churchwomen like Dorothy Tilly and Thelma Stevens played it down in exactly the same period. Clearly, while the two latter women pursued the same goals as Braden and other radicals, their tactical choices led them to avoid being identified as crusaders.[23]

In addition to her outspokenness, Braden articulated the same critique of gradualism as Smith. Her main objection to gradualism was practical. Referring to segregated race relations, she declared: "I know of no gradual method to change the pattern." According to her, the problem did not lie in the ideal of gradual change but in its practical impossibility. "How could Autherine Lucy have gradually entered the University of Alabama?" she aptly asked, "although, when one stops to think of it, what could actually be more gradual than one Negro student entering a university? But the entrance itself could not be slow and gradual—no more than any Negro anywhere could gradually move into a previously all-white neighborhood." In other words, change, by definition, could not be gradual, as the switch from a segregated to a desegregated pattern would "always seem startling." Thus, she concluded, there was no reason to ask for more time since delay would never solve the problem.[24]

Although Virginia Durr was no crusader, she was as outspoken and as radical as Braden in her political views. Durr was twenty-one years older than Braden and already had a career of political activism behind her when the desegregation crisis began. Through her work for the Southern Conference for Human Welfare (SCHW), she had led the national campaign against the poll tax in the 1940s, and she had asserted her Popular Front views by associating with Henry Wallace and his Progressive Party in 1948. She was also strongly supportive of her husband, Cliff, when he left the Federal Communications Commission (FCC) in disapproval of President Truman's loyalty program at the onset of the Cold War.[25] Actually, in an effort to avoid worsening Cliff's already weakened economic situation by appearing too radical in her views and actions, Virginia had retired from political activism, and in 1951 they had come to live with Cliff's family in Montgomery, Alabama, after nearly twenty years spent in Washington, D.C.

While Durr had embraced integration and left-wing causes in the 1940s, Braden turned her moral radicalism into political activism by directly confronting segregationist forces as an individual in 1954 and, from 1957 on, as field secretary for SCEF, an integrationist organization. When the Supreme Court delivered its first decision in the *Brown* case, Braden lived in Louisville, Kentucky, with her husband, Carl, and their two young children. A journalist by training, she had worked as a reporter for several southern newspapers before marrying and engaging in public relations work for trade unions in Louisville, which were racially integrated. As she explained, "the great attraction was that here were white people who were willing to take a stand against segregation." As her husband introduced her to left-wing circles, she was indeed less attracted by their politics than by their integrationist policy. The couple worked for the NAACP and welcomed the *Brown* decision with enthusiasm. By that time Anne was already identified as a radical by the white community owing to her straightforward support of immediate integration. "I could not see the argument of waiting and taking the more prudent way," she recalls. "If segregation in the parks was wrong, it should be ended now. And if segregation in the hospitals was wrong, it should be ended now. If segregated schools were wrong, they should be integrated now—before any more children grew up absorbing the poison I had absorbed." What probably singled her out from many other white supporters of *Brown* was her propensity to turn her opinions into concrete action: "Whenever the opportunity arose to tug at the roots of segregation, I had to act and act now. Everything in my life, past and present, demanded it."[26]

In 1957, Anne and Carl Braden joined the staff of SCEF, then administered by James Dombrowski. Anne was appointed editor of the organization's paper, the *Southern Patriot*. In 1965, they became SCEF's executive associate directors and remained so until they resigned in 1973. SCEF died of internal strife a few years later. SCEF had originated as an outgrowth of the SCHW, in which Lucy Randolph Mason, Josephine Wilkins, and, most of all, Virginia Durr had actively participated. Durr had been on SCEF's board in its early years but had resigned in 1950 because she did not want to jeopardize her husband's business by being identified with radicalism.[27] Created in 1946 on the recommendations of Josephine Wilkins as the heir to the dying SCHW, SCEF was intended to carry on the work initiated by the parent organization, but Dombrowski, its director from 1947 on, refocused the new organization on the single issue of desegregation.[28] SCEF worked for the implementation of the *Brown* decision, and it became, in the words of the sociologist Aldon Morris, a "halfway house" for the civil rights movement. Among all groups that played significant parts in the movement, SCEF was the only interracial civil rights organization in which white people—Anne Braden among them—occupied key leadership positions. From 1960 on it worked in close collaboration with SNCC. Its major function was to publicize the movement through the *Southern Patriot*, edited by Braden, which became "a conduit of news on race for a variety of other small publications, especially for African

American newspapers that were short-staffed and dependent on news services for stories." More specifically, Braden considered that SCEF's main job consisted in reaching out to whites so they would embrace integration as the new southern way of life. With Highlander Folk School—which was also led by whites but was a tax-exempt educational institution—SCEF built bridges between the black-led student movement and whites dedicated to integration. Braden explained in 1963:

> Highlander and SCEF, as the older of the organizations, are able to provide contacts and know-how that are invaluable to a movement of this kind.... SNCC supplies the enthusiasm and the man and woman power which makes it possible to move large groups of people to register to vote, picket, sit in, march, and generally protest their lack of freedom. Not that SCEF and Highlander people don't have the enthusiasm; the appeal of the young people in SNCC simply moves people into action more quickly.

Most of all, SCEF, like Highlander and SNCC, distinguished itself from other groups by "not excluding people from taking part in activities because of their alleged politics or lack of them."[29] This statement refers to the issue of anti-Communism and the problems it posed to the civil rights movement at large in the 1950s and 1960s.

Braden's and Durr's association with SCEF, which combined political and racial radicalism, turned them into privileged targets of the leaders of massive resistance. On several occasions in the 1950s and 1960s, they found themselves in the midst of "antisubversive" campaigns orchestrated by Senator Eastland. Durr was drawn out of her temporary retreat when, in the spring of 1954, Eastland subpoenaed her and four SCEF board members—including president Aubrey Williams and executive director Jim Dombrowski—to a hearing of the Senate Internal Security Subcommittee (SISS) in New Orleans. The hearing's official purpose was to expose SCEF as a Communist-front organization. In reality, although it is impossible to prove, it is highly probable that Eastland, one of the most influential southern segregationist politicians, intended to discredit and intimidate supporters of desegregation in anticipation of the pending *Brown* decision. Durr had resigned from the SCEF board in 1950, but she was sister-in-law to Supreme Court Justice Hugo

Black. Eastland may have calculated that by accusing Durr of Communism, he could "cast doubt on the Court" by association and weaken its position in the predicted battle over school desegregation.[30]

In any case, the hearing was a fiasco for the senator. Eastland relied on Paul Crouch, a former Communist Party member and a favorite government witness in many earlier congressional hearings, to charge the SCEF members with having been members of the Communist Party in the New Deal years. Some, like Dombrowski, denied this allegation while declaring their socialist leanings. As for Virginia Durr, moved by "anger and rage," she prepared a statement that she handed to the press after Eastland denied her permission to read it. The statement was a scathing denunciation of the SISS and a clear rejection of its legitimacy. The following extract illustrates the political principles underlying her position:

> This Hearing is no valid exercise of the investigatory powers of the United States Congress, but a kangaroo court where people, called as witnesses, are being tried as criminals, as traitors to their country, without any of the safeguards set up around such trials by the Constitution of the United States. . . . I wish to state for the record that I do not recognize the power of this Committee to try me as a traitor. I refuse to accept its jurisdiction. If there are any valid charges against my patriotism, I demand a trial in open court with proper legal safeguards. . . . I do not plead the provisions of the Fifth Amendment against self-incrimination. I am not a Communist nor have I ever been one. I only ask that I be accorded a fair trial in open court and not be subjected to the indignities and the disgrace of this public lynching of my life and reputation. I am invoking all other provisions of the Bill of Rights and of the Constitution which I believe are designed to protect citizens against outrages of this kind.

The last sentence of the statement reveals the confrontational dimension of her stance: "I refuse to submit to the authority of this Committee and I stand in utter and total contempt of it." As Eastland did not let her read her statement, she stood up to him question after question by systematically stating her refusal to answer. She actually answered "no" to the two key questions, "Are you a member of the Communist Party?" and "Are you under Communist Party discipline?" because she could not afford to harm her brother-in-law's position on the Supreme Court by leaving doubts as to her belonging to the black-listed Communist Party, but to all other questions she defiantly replied: "I stand mute." And to make her contempt clear, her husband remembered, "Every now and then she'd take out a compact and powder her nose. It drove them into a rage." Cliff Durr, who was a lawyer, participated in the hearing as Aubrey Williams's counsel. He was allowed to cross-examine Crouch after his testimony. When Crouch stated at one point that Durr himself had been a member of the Communist Party, Durr seized the opportunity to take the stand and declare under oath that he had never belonged to it. Then he told Eastland that one of the two witnesses had obviously lied and should be indicted for perjury. At the end of the day, Eastland admitted that he had lost the battle. He was discredited for once.[31] Nevertheless, the New Orleans hearing was a severe blow to SCEF, to the Durrs, and to integrationists at large. The report reasserted SCEF's connection with the SCHW, which had been officially labeled by the House Un-American Activities Committee (HUAC) as a Communist-front organization, so that the Red taint created by the hearing never dissipated. The mere fact of holding a hearing at all was enough to ruin the reputation of the accused and to cause them to lose their standing in their communities. Although Durr was not personally harassed by official authorities anymore, persecution of SCEF continued into the 1960s.[32]

In still another assault on SCEF, on October 4, 1963, local and state police raided the organization's headquarters based in New Orleans. Louisiana representative James Pfister, who chaired the Louisiana Joint Legislative Committee on Un-American Activities (LUAC) and acted in concert with Senator Eastland, charged executive director Jim Dombrowski and two white civil rights lawyers with violating Louisiana's antisubversive law.[33] Having secured the help of SNCC and the SCLC, the Bradens and their lawyers took the case to federal courts, which in 1965 put an end to the prosecution on the grounds that it infringed on First Amendment rights. Between the 1963 raid and 1965, however, Pfister had had time to state in a published report that SCEF was "in fact a Communist Front and a Subversive Organization." He added: "The Southern Conference Educational Fund is managed and operated by Communist [sic] and has obvious multiple connections with other Communist Front organizations." Pfister went on to smear the SCLC and SNCC by pointing out their close connection with SCEF.[34]

The direct link between anti-Communist harassment and the integrationist views of its targets was revealed by the ordeal the Bradens went through in 1954, which Anne related four years later in her memoir. When Andrew Wade, a black electrician she and her husband had met in their work for a local union, asked them to buy a house on his behalf in an all-white neighborhood, she did not hesitate. The Bradens bought the house and transferred its title to the Wades in May 1954. In June, the house was dynamited. In the ensuing trial, they were all confronted with the hostility of local officials. Instead of investigating and prosecuting the authors of the crime, the court's grand jury charged the Bradens and other witnesses with sedition in relation to alleged Communist activities. In December, Carl was convicted and sentenced to fifteen years of imprisonment. In 1956, following a Supreme Court ruling invalidating state antisedition laws, the sentence and charges were dropped. Throughout this period the two couples suffered harassment and intimidation at home from local segregationists enraged by their action. Wade finally sold the house and left. This typical campaign of black- and Red-baiting was only the first in a series of assaults orchestrated by the leaders of massive resistance in the late 1950s and throughout the 1960s.[35]

The Bradens, SCEF, and Virginia Durr were among the handful of southerners who refused to exclude Communists from their ranks or to reject them in any way. SCEF, which was directly accused of being a Communist-front organization, answered by coupling the fight for civil rights with an aggressive defense of civil liberties. Thus, when Jim Dombrowski—whom the Bradens did not know personally but who, out of principle, had helped them in the Louisville sedition trial—proposed that they work for SCEF in 1957, Anne found in this new job a good opportunity to put her ideals into practice. As her biographer explains, "SCEF had the perfect blend of militancy and idealism to suit her."[36] SCEF was also a connecting link between Braden and a few other white women who believed anti-Communism was as harmful to democracy as racial discrimination. Josephine Wilkins and Virginia Durr had been founding members of the organization, and, although evidence is missing as to whether Juliette Morgan was a member, it is known for a fact that she was involved in it through her friendship with Durr and Aubrey Williams.[37]

If being an integrationist was radical in the context of the post-*Brown* South, being tolerant of Communism constituted the ultimate test of political radicalism in the 1950s. In that respect, Braden and Durr were definitely radicals as compared to other white female integrationists, all the more so as they stood up publicly against accusations of Communism, not only by refusing to condemn Communism as a crime but also by counterattacking anti-Communist forces on the grounds that they violated the U.S. Constitution.

Eight days after the publication of Anne Braden's *The Wall Between* in 1958, she and her husband, Carl, were subpoenaed to a HUAC hearing held in Atlanta on July 30. Anne's appearance was postponed, and Carl refused to answer the committee on First Amendment grounds. In 1959, he was convicted of contempt of Congress and sentenced to a year in prison. In 1961, the U.S. Supreme Court upheld the conviction. Carl entered prison on May 1 while Anne launched a campaign for clemency to which Martin Luther King Jr. agreed to associate his name in spite of the charges of Communism he was already facing. Anne also participated in a national campaign organized by the newly created National Committee to Abolish HUAC (NCAHUAC). Although the clemency petition failed to convince the Kennedy administration to intervene, it succeeded in attracting more than 1,000 signatures from more than forty states.[38]

It is clear that the anti-Communist hunt launched in 1954 in the South specifically targeted outspoken integrationists. What is also clear is that this harassment only boosted the determination of individuals like Anne Braden and Virginia Durr to defeat their attackers by fighting back. The two women became friends in 1956 when Anne and her husband toured the South to publicize their first experience with official harassment. They supported each other in the post-*Brown* decade as they struggled not only against harassment but also against ostracism and sometimes alienation from their communities. Their confrontational stance put them at odds with liberal and moderate integrationists who avoided unfavorable publicity and, most of all, did not combat—even sometimes collaborated with—anti-Communist forces. In 1959, for instance, Durr wrote to her friend Clark Foreman, former president of the SCHW: "I have tried joining things, Church groups, League of Women Voters, Human Relations Council, AAUW [American Association of University Women], Legislative Council, even the Society for the Prevention of Cruelty to Animals, but with the same result in all of the groups, no one is unpleasant but nothing ever comes of any of it, no one calls, no one comes, no one asks me to call, it is simply non-recognition."[39] This testimony proves that Durr's stance was of a different kind than that of her "respectable" counterparts, although she had been raised as a lady and was identified as such in society.

Durr as well as Braden witnessed the conservative turn taken by the national NAACP and liberal groups after several southern states directed their antisubversive assault against the NAACP from 1956 on. In Louisville, where the Bradens had been active members of the association, the leadership asked them to leave or at least move into the background in 1957 because they had become a liability. As the civil rights movement developed in the 1960s, the NAACP and SCEF displayed open hostility to each other, although some of their members maintained friendly personal relations. Durr also deplored the fact that the NAACP indulged in Red-baiting in the 1950s instead of uniting with people sympathetic to the black cause, but the intensity with which some prominent white liberals such as editor Ralph McGill attacked Communism and all fellow travelers embittered her even more, as it did Braden. The liberal SRC, itself accused of Communism by "antisubversive" committees, distanced itself from SCEF and individuals who did not condemn Communists. Durr and Braden profoundly differed from other integrationist women such as Lillian Smith on the issue of Communism.[40]

In the face of massive white resistance and lack of support from mainstream liberals, Braden and Durr resorted to various forms of action. Braden launched a civil libertarian crusade as black- and Red-baiting led her to couple the fight for civil rights with the defense of civil liberties. From the late 1950s on, she wrote petitions and pamphlets, delivered speeches, organized conferences, and publicized her cause in the *Southern Patriot*. She articulated a powerful critique of McCarthyism, southern style, and exposed the techniques used by segregationist inquisitors to ruin integrationists' efforts by identifying them with Communists. The main thrust of her argumentation was that HUAC and its southern counterparts not only resorted to lies but also systematically violated the First Amendment when they subpoenaed citizens to ask them questions about their opinions. As she wrote in her "Petition for Clemency" to President Kennedy, "the very asking of such questions by a governmental committee denies a citizen the freedom of speech and association guaranteed by the First Amendment to the U.S. Constitution." A pamphlet published by SCEF after Carl Braden's conviction for contempt was entitled "My Beliefs and My Associations Are None of the Business of This

Committee," in reference to a statement the latter had made before HUAC in 1958. Braden had then added: "And I stated my grounds on the First Amendment, on the grounds that the question has no possible pertinency to any legislation." The pamphlet also emphasized how southern committees infringed on First Amendment rights when they asked for NAACP membership lists and when witnesses who refused to comply were convicted of contempt—which had become a common tactic in the late 1950s.[41]

Braden obviously positioned her fight in a national perspective, as her main arguments relied on the respect of the U.S. Constitution. She also worked with national organizations such as the NCAHUAC and the Emergency Civil Liberties Committee—with which Durr was also associated—but her appeal was essentially focused on the South and more particularly on the white South.[42] Durr, for her part, was more pessimistic than Braden about the possibility of eradicating southern racism from within, which convinced her that only federal intervention would overcome resistance. Her assessment of the southern situation led Durr to act for integration in two ways after 1954. On the one hand, she helped the black movement by interacting personally with many of its members—she was especially close to Rosa Parks, Johnnie Carr, Coretta Scott King, E. D. Nixon, and Ralph and Juanita Abernathy—and by publicizing it among the northern circles she had kept in contact with since returning to live in Montgomery.[43] On the other hand, she used her connections to lobby northern politicians in favor of federal intervention against southern resistance.

When Rosa Parks was arrested on December 1, 1955, Parks and Virginia Durr were already friends. Cliff Durr assisted Fred Gray, the lawyer who represented Parks in the legal procedure that accompanied the Montgomery Bus Boycott. Virginia worked as her husband's secretary and helped the boycotters in any way she could. She also wrote dozens of letters to northern friends in which she interpreted the new protest movement as a formidable historic development that was already giving whites a lesson in human dignity. "They all laugh at me when I praise them," she wrote, "and say they're fighting for my freedom as much as for their own."[44] After the boycott, she continued to support the civil rights movement.

Aware that whites did not have a place on the frontline of the southern movement, she used her lobbying skills and her political connections to stir federal authorities into action. She more particularly relied on her friendship with Lyndon and Lady Bird Johnson to press Lyndon into using his political leverage to promote civil rights.[45] Starting in 1959 in the thick of massive resistance, she kept urging him to use his influence as majority leader of the U.S. Senate. In one of her letters she summed up her arguments in simple, straightforward terms: "I go on the premise that you and I agree that the Southern system of segregation has to end. I do not think it can all be left to the U.S. Supreme Court with the accompanying demonstrations and resistance and defiance of the law and that Congress *must* act." She later turned to Burke Marshall, assistant attorney general in the Kennedy administration, to convince him of the necessity of providing freedom workers with federal protection.[46]

In the final analysis, Braden's and Durr's radicalism lay mainly in the fact that they advocated total and immediate integration and did so in an outspoken way, that they socialized with black people who welcomed them within their ranks when they were ostracized by whites, and that they considered segregationists more dangerous for democracy than Communists. Although they were not attracted to Communism, they nevertheless embraced the views of the Old Left associated with the New Deal. During her campaign against HUAC, Braden declared: "It matters not that some of us disagree profoundly with the philosophy of the Communist Party—and I happen to be one who does. But if we had a free and civil libertarian atmosphere in America... then these disagreements could be discussed." She added: "When a civil libertarian atmosphere is restored in America, when the cobwebs of McCarthyism are swept away, when a man can be a Communist if he wants to and continue to be considered a human being, then at that time we'll gladly state our differences with Communism in any public forum and happily debate real issues with anyone who is interested." Durr never hesitated to discuss Communism like any other political ideology. In 1953, she explained in a letter to a scholar who was writing a book on Henry Wallace's Progressive Party: "At one time I even thought to be [a Communist] was the only way to salvation, and the reason I did not become one was not that I did not believe in Socialism, I do. But I think their political approach for this Country was all wrong." Indeed, it is probably their placing the issue of racism within the broader perspective of social and economic inequality that endeared the Communists to some students in the civil rights movement. Writing about the Braden couple, Catherine Fosl observes: "The upsurges of the Depression and postwar era were not animated by the very same impetus as that which ignited the 1960s civil rights movement, but Anne, Carl, and a few others like them were important bridges linking the two [Old Left and New Left] movements and eras." Virginia Durr, who accommodated SNCC youths in her house, was among the few others mentioned by Fosl.[47] Braden's and Durr's tolerance of Communism definitely singled them out in the context of their time and distinguished them from a majority of white women reformers. However, they also shared many features with lady activists. For all their radicalism, Braden and Durr, just like Smith, Boyle, and Morgan, remained true representatives of white southern womanhood, but their militant stance on race implied a constant struggle against southern gender norms.

From Race to Gender

Through their open confrontation with white supremacy, the women examined in this chapter, be they moral or political radicals, were bound to reconsider, and ultimately redefine, their status as white women in the segregated South. Although Durr was the only one to broach the issue directly in her autobiography, the others experienced a similar process of personal emancipation during the fight for racial equality, as their correspondence shows.

In the context of southern segregationist society, racial dissenters found themselves at odds with their communities. When they were not involved in organizational activities, they were likely to experience a strong sense of isolation—if not complete alienation—as a result of their unorthodox views. White women responded to these conditions by sharing their experiences and supporting each other within their minority circle. Private correspondence constituted a privileged channel to exchange views, many women finding comfort and encouragement in the sustained correspondence they cultivated with female friends.

In October 1956, Sarah Boyle wrote Virginia Durr to thank her for expressing her support. Boyle and her family had been harassed by extreme segregationists and ostracized by the rest of the community since the *Saturday Evening Post* had published her integrationist appeal under the title "Southerners Will *Like* Integration." Boyle and Durr did not know each other personally, but as a former victim of white supremacist repression—notably the Eastland hearings of 1954—Durr sympathized with Boyle and all other victims of segregationist resistance after the *Brown* decision. In her response, Boyle could express ideas and feelings that she could not share with anybody in her immediate surroundings. She identified her community's silence as the main cause of her predicament. "My chief disillusionment," she wrote, "has been along the line of those who I know are with us but who will not risk a finger nail [sic] to defend the principles which they believe in as stoutly as I do—the people who believe I'm right, yet will not be seen with me on the street." She had not expected the crisis that the *Brown* decision triggered, and she suddenly lost her position as a respectable southern lady to become an outcast, confessing, "I have been deeply shocked to learn how utterly without moral courage most modern Americans are, and above all I was not prepared for the silence of the good willed." In such circumstances, Durr's support took on a crucial dimension, and Boyle ended her reply writing, "I'm deeply grateful for your letter. It was gracious of you to write to me."[48]

Actually, as the desegregation crisis drew together the members of the integrationist white minority, women were more likely to turn to other women for support. They all belonged to the various women's networks that had grown in the previous decades, creating a sense of recognition between them even when they did not identify it explicitly as such. Durr's letters to Josephine Wilkins confirm this point. The two women became acquainted through their common participation in civil rights reform activities and developed a special relationship as a result of it. One particular example highlights the nature of their connection. Durr wrote to Wilkins in 1961. She was then active in the Alabama CHR, an affiliate of the SRC, but she and her friends from SCEF were deemed too radical by many SRC members—including the fiercely anti-Communist Tilly—owing to their tolerance of Communism. In her letter, Durr asked Wilkins whether she could use her influence to convince her SRC associates to stop Red-baiting her friends and to unite forces with them against the "real bad guys instead of weakening the southern liberal movement." "I have done what I could," she said, "but I am not 'in' with the SRC as you are and while I am tolerated, still I do not feel I am really trusted as being 'one of us.'" The two women were not close friends but knew each other well enough to support each other mutually and possibly connect distrustful groups through their relationship. Durr ended her letter by stating, "I hope our friendship will one day have a chance to grow and flourish as I never am with you but that I feel it would if we had a chance." More significant, in a letter written in 1960, Durr wrote, "We have lived through so much together and I hope our mutual friends and experiences will draw us closer together. At least we can say that we have not led a dull life like so many of our bridge playing friends."[49] This sentence reveals that Durr identified their activism as a distinctive feature that differentiated them from other women. She thus implied that the white women who committed themselves to the fight against white supremacy escaped the traditional sphere of southern womanhood as a result.

As a political radical, Durr was certainly more subjected to ostracism than less controversial integrationist figures, heightening her sense of isolation in the 1950s and 1960s. The correspondence she kept during these years reveals how her commitment to the desegregation movement turned her into an outcast and led her to reflect on her status as a white southern female dissenter. Especially interesting is the fact that although she did not elaborate a full-fledged critique of the condition of white southern women in the segregated South, her position during the desegregation era made her aware of the painfully paradoxical situation in which white women found themselves. In some letters, she emphasized the suffering they had to endure, as, for instance, when she wrote to Jim Dombrowski in May 1968, "I think so many Southerners especially women are in love with death and suffering and their highest ambition is to be known as 'brave sufferers.' I hate it."[50] After her husband, Cliff, left his position on the FCC in protest against President Truman's loyalty program, they had moved back to the South to live at Cliff's parents' house in Montgomery, Alabama. Although Cliff's family were not extremists in their defense of segregation, they nevertheless disapproved of federal intervention and, most of all, of Cliff and Virginia's activism. Virginia thus witnessed the growth of the black movement from the Montgomery Bus Boycott to the late 1960s surrounded by disapproving, if not openly hostile, people. At the same time, she made her own individual contribution as a white sympathizer by building bridges between the black movement and its potential white southern and national allies. This was how she became friends with Anne Braden, who was going through a similar experience in Louisville, Kentucky.

The letters the two women exchanged during that period reveal how the desegregation crisis heightened their awareness of the link between racial and gender oppression in segregationist society and ultimately led them to emancipate themselves from the constraints of white southern womanhood. If the bulk of Durr's correspondence focused on the issues of civil rights and racial equality in the South, she nevertheless indulged occasionally in digressions revealing her frustration, even anger at times, at the treatment of white women by segregationist society. In most cases her reflections about women derived from her reporting of race-related incidents. Durr found in Braden the confidant she needed in a time of crisis, explaining in 1960, "I think a woman needs another woman as a close confidant and friend. But there are so few women I can confide in or who would even know what I was talking about and have any sympathy or understanding of it." Thus being a woman was not the only reason why Braden had become her closest friend. Durr also recognized in Braden a kindred spirit in a hostile world. In the same letter, she even went so far as to write that "the Southern White Woman ... suffers more or certainly as much under segregation as the Negro. . . . I think Lillian Smith did something of this in *Killers of the Dream* but she did not go beyond the Freudian approach, and that is only part of it, but a big part." Such a statement not only suggests that Durr underestimated the effects of segregation on African Americans' experience but also that her own suffering as a woman ran deep in her consciousness.[51]

In the thick of the desegregation crisis, the two activists deepened their reflection on womanhood. Durr wrote to Braden in 1960: "We do come from very similar backgrounds, we do have very similar outlooks. You are younger ... but I think we both have a feeling, a deep and passionate compulsion, to help the people of the South and most particularly the white women of the South, whose lives have been so starved and twisted by the kind of life they have had to lead." Durr described her personal experience as typical of that of all white women born and raised in the segregated South, as she went on: "I know how painful it is to have your own mother so full of fears and ... terror ... and frustration, as it was to me to have my mother and my sister in the same situation. Of course this sense of fear and terror and frustration and futility is what I call the despair I have to fight against." This aspect of white women's lives was a logical part of segregationist culture that associated race and sex in so many ways. Durr had come to recognize this by 1960. After Juliette Morgan committed suicide in 1957 because she could not stand the pressure exerted by the white community on integrationists like herself, Durr wrote to Braden about white southern women: "The death wish is so strong in many of them and rightly so because they have been so shut off from life. I don't just mean sex frustration, although that is part of it, but I mean just as Negroes have been barred from life or they have tried to bar them, so have the women been barred from life so often, or the life they have been offered has been nothing but cotton candy."[52] The analogy between white women and African Americans is symptomatic of the interconnection white supremacy created between them.

One year earlier, Braden had confided in Durr about being deeply upset after Morgan's suicide. "I think the reason I feel so strongly about it," she wrote, "is that I feel so strongly that I could so easily have been Juliette Morgan, and that my life could have gone just like hers.... There was so much in her early life that was so exactly like mine: the same social environment, the same intellectual bent in a society that puts little premium on these things for women, and yet approves of and helps her as long as she stays within certain bounds." She went on to explain that the difference between Morgan and her was that, unlike Morgan, she had never intended to go back to her native town of Anniston, Alabama, after college. "I knew I had to get away. I can see now, looking back on it, that what I was trying to get away from was the prison our society shuts a woman up in." She then referred to the destructive mother-daughter relationship that segregation tended to create in view of the fact that dissenting daughters like Morgan, Braden, and Durr—who also alluded to this in her own letter—often became estranged from their parents as a result of their choices. "I don't think there is any doubt that Juliette Morgan's mother killed her," she wrote. "She [the mother] was a victim too—in ways I'm not completely clear on, because I don't know enough of the background yet. But I guess I feel strongly about this aspect of it too because again there's an apparent parallel with my only [sic] life—or rather, an opposite. Instead of my parents killing me, I am killing them." Finally Braden explicitly attributed these troubles to segregation, noting that "the real villain in this whole situation is a social system—a system based on exploitation, which destroys human relationships." She concluded, "Segregation of course is the precipitating factor because it is here that the exploitation hits its worst extreme and so all our conflicts crystalize around it."[53] The connection between gender and race in segregated society could not be more explicit. Such a correspondence reveals not only how segregation adversely affected the condition of white southern women but also how racial dissenters developed an acute awareness of this phenomenon. The letters they exchanged during the civil rights movement reveal that discussing the events of the period led them to reflect on their personal experiences and inevitably exposed to them the direct link between their struggle against segregation and their own emancipation as white women.

Lillian Smith also kept a rich correspondence through which she tried to break what she considered a conspiracy of silence against southern dissenters. As in Durr's case, most of Smith's nonprofessional letters were centered on the issue of segregation, but she nevertheless dedicated a significant part of them to a reflection on women, with a special emphasis on white southern women. In a 1943 letter, presumably addressed to a black northern newspaperman, she complained: "So few Negroes in the North believe in the integrity or good faith of a southern white woman. . . . You see—for a southern white woman to take a stand and speak out requires of her the willingness to run grave risks to her prestige, reputation, and so on." After explaining that she understood the skepticism of black people in that respect, she added: "Sometimes, though, I get awfully tired of taking the verbal blows meant not for me, personally, but for Southern womanhood in general."[54] As Smith, Durr, and Braden further explored the meanders of white womanhood, they extended their perspective from their personal experiences to the collective experience of white women born and raised in the segregationist South. Thus out of their exchange emerged a will to act against what they identified ever more clearly as a form of oppression. Indeed, after Juliette Morgan's suicide, Durr and Braden contemplated writing a book on southern womanhood that would denounce the damages segregationist culture inflicted on white women, an idea that finally remained unfulfilled.[55]

The study of these women's correspondence demonstrates that, while concentrating their efforts on the fight against white supremacy, they increasingly questioned the specific implications of segregationist culture for white women. However, apart from Lillian Smith, the individuals dealt with in this chapter did not confront white patriarchy openly and straightforwardly. Despite their obvious radicalism, they did not go so far as to reject the image of the southern lady. Thus, when it came to gender, the most radical white female reformers shared common features with the more moderate members of their generation, with whom they cultivated close ties. Along with a reluctance to reject the lady ideal publicly, they privately expressed a sense of female recognition, based on the growing conviction that their gender and race turned them into a distinct kind of activist. Braden mentioned the issue in a letter to a male colleague in 1959. "All my experience in the integration movement," she wrote, "has led me to the firm conviction that the most convinced and dedicated people are women; this applies to both Negro and white women." Most of the time, however, women reserved such meditations for their female friends. Correspondence thus contributed to reinforcing the spirit of sisterhood first fostered by the growth of female organizations. Durr's above-mentioned exchanges with Josephine Wilkins illustrate this point, as does Smith's friendship with Margaret Long, to whom she wrote in October 1961, "You and I are about the only two people on earth I know who can talk on paper."[56] Actually, in spite of their open rejection of racial and political conformity, these radicals did not reject the definition of womanhood that prevailed in their time.

In addition to interacting with other white women reformers, they shared with them some key characteristics directly associated with traditional womanhood. For instance, Lillian Smith's scathing denunciation of white southern patriarchy did not prevent her from extolling women's nurturing instincts. She did not have children, but placed children at the core of her conception of the ideal society, granting as much importance to education as "lady activists." She put her philosophy into practice in the 1940s as director of the Laurel Falls Camp for girls. A fervent follower of modern psychology and psychoanalysis, Smith experimented with new educational approaches to foster children's creativity and to break down the psychological barriers erected by segregation. According to her, no society could grow into a great civilization unless it allowed its children to grow into whole human beings. In 1948, she wrote in the *Chicago Defender*, "It is not easy to face up to the bitter fact that democracy cannot work unless its citizens are mature; that citizens cannot mature unless they are free to grow; that they cannot grow unless they are whole; and they cannot be whole as long as they are segregated on any level of their life. There should be signs all over the world: TAKE CARE, CHILDREN GROWING." This emphasis on children partook of her moral radicalism as she summed up her philosophical outlook: "To me, the growth of a child is the essence of morality: what makes a child grow is good; what kills a child's growth is bad."[57] As for Boyle, Braden, and Durr, they were married, had children, and fulfilled their roles as wives and mothers. Owing to their involvement in many organizations, Durr and Braden constantly struggled to combine their militant activities with their family lives. Durr educated her own daughters according to traditional southern standards while always insisting on the importance of respecting "good manners" and social expectations in all circumstances. One of her daughters remembers that she "was a strong supporter of the women's movement and yet she always told her daughters 'first you must get a man before you can be liberated from one.'" Durr may have presented her advice as a joke, but her life and private writings indicate that she believed what she said and held ambivalent views on the issue of gender conformity. Braden also complied with the norms of ladyhood. As her biographer, Catherine Fosl, observes, "she struck some [SNCC] students who met her as a kind of renegade southern lady: soft-spoken, well-mannered, 'ladylike' even—yet driven by some inner flame to bring down segregation. . . . Although Anne rejected the lion's share of southern white ideology, her personal style was one that expanded rather than defied popular notions about southern 'ladies.'" Fosl rightly argues that "Anne's class privilege, enmeshed with her race, gender, regional background, and perhaps even marital status, created for her a kind of shield many other activists simply did not enjoy." She goes on to explain, "Up to a point, she was freer to criticize regional conventions, and she maximized that discursive space, still benefiting in a small way from the kind of male 'protectionism' toward elite southern white women that she herself decried and that the historian LeeAnn Whites has identified as shaping gender relations in the South since the Civil War."[58]

Ultimately, the members of the older generation liberated themselves from southern gender norms in a gradual way. Their involvement in the civil rights movement caused them to grasp the interconnection of race and gender in southern society and thus to identify the constraints of white southern womanhood, until they reached a point, late in their lives, when they repudiated the ideal of southern womanhood altogether. Virginia Durr traces the process in her autobiography, published in 1985. Like many members of her generation, she came to reject the image of the southern lady in stages as the resistance of white supremacists to desegregation hardened. The 1954 New Orleans hearing—during which Senator Eastland tried to prove that Durr and other integrationists had close ties to the Communist Party—constituted an important step in her evolution. Indeed, her refusal to answer Eastland's questions and her public defiance of such a prominent politician contrasted with her ladylike manners to the point of undermining her image. After the hearing, the Durrs lost in part the respectability they had enjoyed as members of the old white elite. Yet Virginia commented: "In a way, I was grateful that my cover as a nice, proper Southern lady was blown by the hearing, because then I could begin to say what I really thought." Still she did not give up her white gloves or her manners.[59]

In 1962, massive resistance to desegregation led Durr to express her dissenting views as a white southern woman. During the school desegregation crisis, white supremacists had been waving the old specter of miscegenation. They had presented resistance as the only way to protect white girls from contact with black boys and to prevent interracial sex. Durr responded by writing an article entitled "In the Name of Southern Womanhood," in which she took over the fight of the ASWPL. In an explicit parallel with the 1930s, she wrote: "As we women once were used as the rationale for lynching, now we are used as the rationale for segregation. I think it is about time we stopped permitting our name to be thus shamefully and senselessly bandied about." The article is strikingly hostile to white men, especially to white politicians, whom Durr subjects to ridicule. In the face of what she considers mere hysteria, she calls for women's unity: "It seems to me it is time for southern white women to band together once again and in a very lady-like way tell our loud and valiant defenders that our virtue is in no danger, that we can protect it very well by ourselves and that we do not need all these indignant champions to do it for us." She thus rejects the legitimacy of southern white men's position of authority by adopting an openly antagonistic stance: "Let us proclaim to these white men that we will no longer stand for them to take our name in vain to keep segregation."[60] Durr actually goes an important step farther than the ASWPL in condemning segregation. She also pits men against women in an uncompromising and militant way, but she still abides by the ideal of the lady. Durr's article thus testifies to her discontent with white women's position in segregationist culture, but it also reveals her acceptance of gender norms, at least on the surface, as late as 1962. It took her more than twenty years to complete her emancipation. In 1971, she broached the issue directly in a new article aptly entitled "The Emancipation of Pure, White, Southern Womanhood," signed under her maiden name, Virginia Foster. In this later piece, the sixty-eight-year-old activist finally put together her private thoughts on the interaction of race and gender in her native culture, and she explicitly linked her personal emancipation to her breaking of racial taboos, thus confirming that one could not exist without the other. The publication of *Outside the Magic Circle*, her autobiography, in 1985, represented the last stage of her evolution. Ultimately, although Durr never became a militant feminist, she came to recognize that her lifelong commitment to racial equality altered her identity as a woman as it led her to reject the submissive role she should have assumed had she respected the prescriptions of her culture.

* * *

In sum, the moral and political radicals dealt with in this chapter not only bridged two movements and two eras, they also bridged two generations of white southern women reformers. The activists shared characteristics with the two generations. Like the typical members of the older group, they belonged to the social elite, had been raised as perfect southern ladies, and used their status to undermine segregation while enjoying relative protection from repressive segregationist forces. On the other hand, they shared with the younger generation a compulsion to speak out and act in conformity with their ideals even if this implied open confrontation with both their communities and segregationist authorities. This radical stance had direct consequences on their personal evolution because the hostility and repression they met led them to ponder their identity, and more particularly the deep causes of the personal and collective crisis they were going through. From this reflection emerged the idea that they could not win the fight against segregation without emancipating themselves from the prescriptions of white southern ladyhood. They would have to wait until the late 1960s, however, before taking such a step. Focusing on the struggle against racism, they embraced the direct action movement of the 1960s as the best incarnation of their moral stance and identified the white female students who joined the movement as their spiritual daughters. It is to this new generation that the following chapter is devoted.

FIGURE 1. Dorothy Rogers Tilly. Photograph, Dorothy Rogers Tilly Papers, by permission of Manuscript, Archives and Rare Book Library, Emory University.

FIGURE 2. Juliette Hampton Morgan, circa 1935. Photograph, Lila Bess Olin Morgan Family Papers, by permission of Alabama Department of Archives and History, Montgomery.

FIGURE 3. Lillian Eugenia Smith, 1944. *World Telegram* photo by C. M. Stieglitz. Library of Congress Prints and Photographs Division.

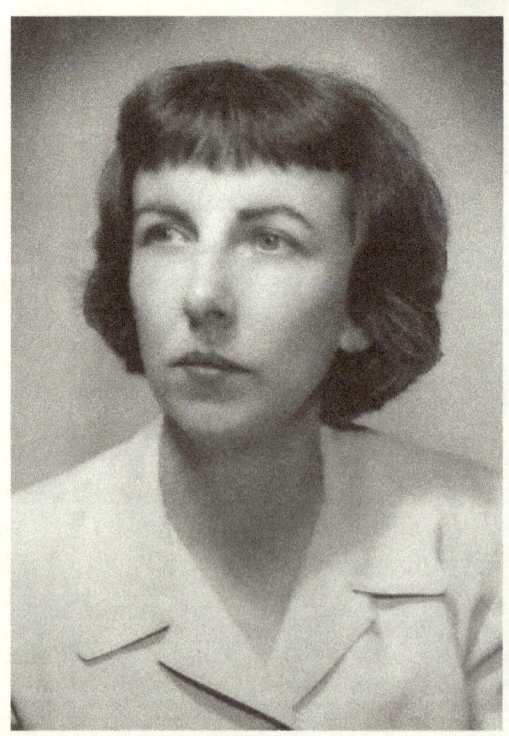

FIGURE 4. Margaret Long, 1950. Photo courtesy of Valdosta State University, by permission of Margaret Burr Leonard.

Above: FIGURE 5. Nan Pendergrast, 1956. "Thrower for Congress" tea, Atlanta. Randolph Thrower ran for the U.S. Congress on the Republican ticket against the incumbent segregationist, James C. Davis. Nan Pendergrast is standing fourth from left. Estate of Randolph W. Thrower.

Left: FIGURE 6. Women's Emergency Committee to Open Our Schools members, Vivion L. Brewer, Adolphine Fletcher Terry, and Pat House (*left to right*), November 2, 1963. Photograph from *The Embattled Ladies of Little Rock*, by Vivion L. Brewer, QED Press/Cypress House/Lost Coast Press, California U.S.A. By permission of Margaret A. Rostker, Executor, POA, Trustee.

Right: FIGURE 7. Anne Braden and Ella Baker leaving the library, Highlander Folk School, Monteagle, Tennessee. By permission of Highlander Research and Education Center.

Below: FIGURE 8. Anne Braden in the Southern Conference Educational Fund (SCEF) office, where she edited the organization's newsletter, the *Southern Patriot*, n.d. By permission of Wisconsin Historical Society, WHS-55103.

FIGURE 9. Frances Freeborn Pauley (*far left*), Fisk University Race Relations Seminar, 1961. From the Race Relations Department of the United Church Board of Homeland Ministries records. By permission of Amistad Research Center.

FIGURE 10. Joan C. Browning (*far right*), Fisk University Race Relations Seminar, 1962. From the Race Relations Department of the United Church Board of Homeland Ministries records. By permission of Amistad Research Center.

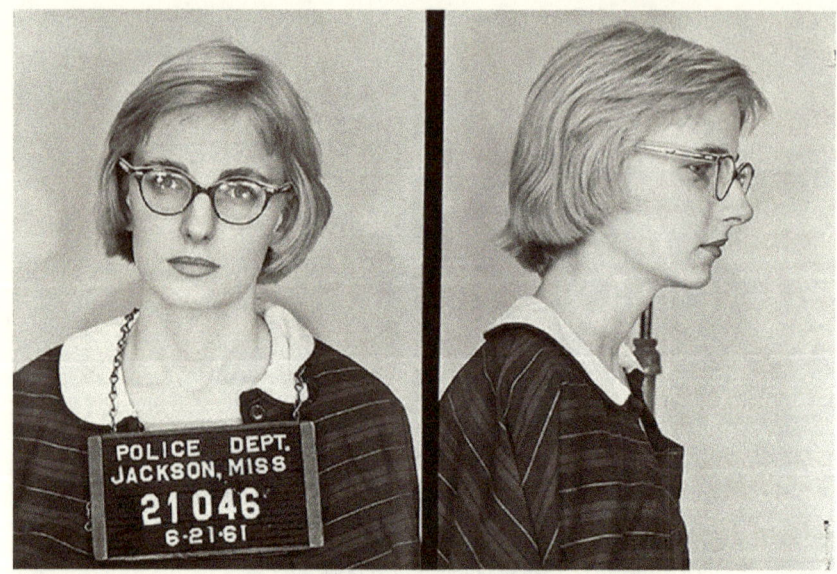

FIGURE 11. Margaret Burr Leonard, Freedom Rider, Jackson, Mississippi, June 21, 1961.

FIGURE 12. Joan Trumpauer Mulholland, Freedom Rider, Jackson, Mississippi, June 8, 1961.

FIGURE 13. Joan C. Browning, 1962. Photo courtesy of Joan C. Browning from personal collection.

FIGURE 14. Dorothy Dawson Burlage. Photo courtesy of Dorothy Dawson Burlage.

FIGURE 15. Constance "Connie" Curry, Atlanta, 1973. Photo by Penny Weaver, courtesy of Constance Curry.

FIGURE 16. Sara Mitchell Parsons and Angela Davis, 1977. Photo courtesy of Perry Mitchell, Executor, Estate of Sara Mitchell Parsons.

FIGURE 17. Casey Hayden, Students for a Democratic Society reunion, 1988. Photo by Michael Gaylord James from his forthcoming *Pictures from the Long Haul*.

FIGURE 18. Mary Elizabeth King, Mexico, 2013. Photo credit: Noah Friedman-Rodovsky. Courtesy of Mary E. King.

FIGURE 19. Margaret Burr Leonard during a voter registration drive conducted in Greensboro, Georgia, by the Democrats during the Obama campaign in 2008. The book Margaret is holding in the photo is *Breach of Peace: Portraits of the 1961 Mississippi Freedom Riders*, by Eric Etheridge. Photo by Carl McGrath, courtesy of Margaret Leonard.

FIGURE 20. Joan C. Browning and Joan Trumpauer Mulholland, 2011, at National Endowment for the Humanities showing of film, *Freedom Riders*, sponsored by Congressional Black Caucus. Photo by Autumn G. Shelton, courtesy of Joan C. Browning and Joan Mulholland.

Above: FIGURE 21. Four friends commemorating the 1960s struggle, Chicago, filming of the Oprah Winfrey television show, April 2012. *Left to right*: Rev. Dr. Patricia A. Jarvis, Joan C. Browning, Faye Powell, and Cinda Kinsey. Courtesy of Patricia A. Jarvis, Joan C. Browning, Faye Powell, and Cinda Kinsey.

Right: FIGURE 22. Nan Pendergrast continued her fight for civil rights, peace, justice, and the environment for decades after her work with H.O.P.E. She is shown here early in her nineties. Photo by Mark Pendergrast. Courtesy of Mark and Nan Pendergrast.

FIGURE 23. Virginia Foster Durr and her four daughters on her ninetieth birthday. Birthday party held at Lucy and Sheldon Hackney's House, August 1993. From collection of photos of Virginia "Tilla" Durr (*bottom right*).

5

The 1960s Movement

Modern Abolitionists

In October 1960, Lillian Smith participated in the first conference held by the fledgling Student Nonviolent Coordinating Committee (SNCC) in Atlanta. She had been invited to speak as a longtime advocate of integration. Among the 140 or so delegates and observers present at the conference was also Anne Braden, representing the Southern Conference Educational Fund (SCEF). Smith spoke the following words to the black and white students: "We of the older generation cannot go on that great journey with you... but there is something we can do: We can make of our lives, our knowledge, our experiences, our wisdom... a bridge, a strong, sure bridge over which you can cross into the new, unmade world." She addressed the younger generation as a whole, but her statement is perfectly relevant to the history of white southern women activists of both the segregation and desegregation eras. Smith and Braden definitely stand out as bridges between the older and younger generations. Having confronted segregation for years against the grain of their own generation, they embraced the new movement and became mentors for the following generation.[1]

In a statement of purpose adopted in April of the same year, the founding members of SNCC had defined the new organization as nonviolent, independent, and action-oriented: "We affirm the philosophical or religious ideal of nonviolence as the foundation of our purpose, the presupposition of our faith, and the manner of our action. Nonviolence as it grows from Judaic-Christian traditions seeks a social order of justice permeated by love. Integration of human endeavor represents the crucial first step towards such a society." The students had described their goal and action as the actualization of moral ideals, declaring: "By appealing to conscience and standing on the moral nature of human existence, nonviolence nurtures the atmosphere in which reconciliation and justice become actual possibilities."[2] In the subsequent four years, the black and white members and followers of SNCC acted in strict accordance with their ideals and managed to create conditions for what they called the "Beloved Community." Among them were a significant number of young white women who were drawn to the new movement during their college years.

Women in the new generation of female white racial activists found themselves in college in the late 1950s and early 1960s, when the national Student Christian Movement became more visibly committed to desegregation and when black students started direct-action demonstrations in southern cities.[3] These young women, supported by the most militant members of the older generation, embodied a new form of racial activism not based on suasion but on direct confrontation with segregationist forces. This generation distinguished itself from the former in various ways. For one thing, it was much less socially homogeneous. Whereas the older women were almost all of similar socioeconomic backgrounds—that is, belonging to the middle and upper classes—the freedom activists of the 1960s came from all social backgrounds, from the lower to the upper class. Like the members of the older generation, those of the new had been conditioned by segregationist norms since childhood. Yet apart from this common culture, they did not share the social interests and commonalities that elite white women had shared in the first half of the century and which had brought them to work together in women's organizations. What united the members of the new generation was a deeply felt philosophical and religious idealism that reached full maturity during their college years and soon proved incompatible with segregationist culture. The new generation was also very young. Unlike their predecessors, whose involvement in the racial struggle had often been gradual and in many cases had occurred at an already mature age, the new activists discovered the 1960s protest movement—which served as a catalyst for their commitment—on college campuses. They threw themselves into the movement out of moral compulsion. In doing so, they broke with their native communities and started up a new life in accordance with their ideals. As students, young white women were naturally drawn to student organizations. Many of them became familiar with the interracial movement through student YWCA chapters. The typical course of action was then to volunteer for SNCC or the

Congress of Racial Equality (CORE). SNCC was undoubtedly the organization where most young white activists could be found in the first half of the 1960s, but they usually did not limit their activities to a single group. They also worked with the National Student Association (NSA), groups affiliated with the Southern Christian Leadership Conference (SCLC), the NAACP, Councils on Human Relations (CHRs), and a myriad of lesser-known civil rights associations. All in all, whites only made up a very small proportion of the 1960s movement, which became even tinier when limited to white women.[4] Yet this handful of individuals had a specific role to play and was distinctive enough to be recognized as a significant portion of the movement as a whole.

The evolution of the younger generation confirmed the existence of a distinctive form of white female activism within the long civil rights movement. Through their participation in the events of the 1960s, these women fully asserted and emancipated themselves individually and collectively, becoming a community of sorts within the broader civil rights movement. Thus the 1960s movement constituted the last stage in the construction of white southern sisterhood, which, for many women, ended up in full liberation from southern gender norms.

The Movement as Catalyst

All the members of the new generation saw their lives transformed by the events that occurred in the early 1960s, instantly drawing them into a world they had not been aware of earlier. They then participated in the various actions set up by the main organizations making up the movement, either as staff members of the organizations or as volunteers. Constance "Connie" Curry definitely belonged to the new generation, but, being born in 1933, she was not a student anymore when the sit-ins started. Given this distinction and the nurturing role she played from the birth of SNCC until 1964, Curry stood apart from the rest of the white female participants in the civil rights movement. Like older women, she can be defined as a bridge, but she was a bridge between different people and spheres rather than between different generations. She graduated from Agnes Scott College in Georgia in 1955, spent a year in France as a Fulbright exchange student, and, after a year at Columbia University, she became national field representative for the

Collegiate Council of the United Nations. While in college, she was drawn to the NSA, and in 1953 she was elected chair of the Great Southern Region for the organization. The NSA had been founded in 1947 as an association of student governments pledged to guarantee "to all people, because of their inherent dignity as individuals, equal rights and possibilities for primary, secondary, and higher education, regardless of sex, race, religion, political belief, or economic circumstances." Every year the NSA held its National Student Congress in August on a midwestern campus. At the 1957 Congress, as massive resistance to school desegregation was gaining momentum, the delegates adopted a statement that explicitly condemned segregation in education and called for its elimination.[5] Between 1960 and 1964, Curry worked for the NSA as director of the Southern Student Human Relations Project (SSHRP), or Southern Project, based in Atlanta. Her main work consisted in organizing summer seminars where she and a few other adults taught black and white southern students how to overcome their racial prejudices and how to interact as human beings in a nonsegregated setting. At the end of the seminar, the students went on to attend the NSA Congress and then returned to their campuses to put their new philosophy into practice.

The development of the Southern Project coincided with the spread of the sit-in movement and the creation of SNCC in April 1960. Instantly attracted to the new protest movement, Curry was present at SNCC's founding meeting. She and Ella Baker were elected adult advisers shortly after the first meeting, which made Curry the first white member of SNCC's executive committee. As she became involved in SNCC, Curry played the role of an observer rather than that of a direct-action activist. She reported on the southern student movement for the NSA and other organizations outside the South. In 1964, she was hired as southern field representative for the American Friends Service Committee (AFSC) and concentrated on helping black families implement school desegregation in Mississippi, where white resistance still prevailed. She first worked with a group of white women, Mississippians For Education, led by Winifred Green, who directly drew their inspiration from Little Rock's Women's Emergency Committee to Open Our Schools and Atlanta's Help Our Public Education.[6] Constance "Connie" Curry became a friend and mentor to the white female students who participated in the black liberation movement. This can be illustrated by the fact that three of the women who constitute the sample analyzed in this chapter—Casey Hayden,

Faye Powell, and Joan Browning—attended her NSA-sponsored Southern Project seminar in 1960, 1961, and 1962, while another one, Dorothy Dawson Burlage, worked for Curry's Southern Project in 1962.

The Southern Project and the NSA were part of the organizations that provided several of the young women discussed here with the opportunity to step into the civil rights movement. One of Curry's earliest recruits, who became one of her best friends, was Sandra "Casey" Cason—who took the name of Casey Hayden after marrying Tom Hayden in 1961. By the time she was recruited by Curry for her seminar of 1960, Casey Hayden had already been active in the interracial movement for a couple of years. She had enrolled at the University of Texas (UT) at Austin in 1957 and became a regional leader of the student YWCA as well as a national leader in the Student Christian Movement. Hayden's roommate at UT was Dorothy Dawson—Dorothy Burlage after her marriage to Robb Burlage in 1963. During her first college year in a small private women's school (1955–56), Dawson had attended an integrated regional NSA meeting. She transferred to UT in 1956. Together, the two students became involved in the activities of the integrated Christian Faith and Life Community (CFLC), and they soon moved to the CFLC's building, which was the only integrated housing facility on campus. Hayden and Burlage participated in sit-ins and other direct-action demonstrations in Austin in 1960. Hayden then met Curry, who was searching for participants for her annual summer seminar, and they immediately connected.

The Southern Project was a turning point in the lives of many of its participants. It was certainly so for Hayden. Curry's seminar not only drew Hayden directly to SNCC, of which she became a key member, but it also propelled her into the national student movement when she delivered a passionate speech at the NSA Congress urging support for the sit-ins. As she mesmerized the founders of Students for a Democratic Society (SDS)—starting with her future husband Tom Hayden—she drew the attention of northern students to the fledgling nonviolent movement, establishing a precious connection between the southern movement and other student organizations.[7] As for Dawson Burlage, after graduating in 1959 and spending a couple of years at the University of Illinois as a YWCA program director and at Harvard Divinity School as a graduate student, she left Boston in the fall of 1961 for Atlanta, where Curry hired her for her NSA Southern Project. Her decision to move back south was directly related to the events that had occurred since her graduation. She had participated in CORE direct-action activities at the University of Illinois. Outraged by the attacks on Freedom Riders in Alabama in 1961, she had organized a civil rights group in Boston to mobilize northern support of southern freedom activists. She had also attended the 1960 NSA Congress and joined SDS. The NSA offered her the opportunity to join the southern movement. One of her major contributions consisted in supervising an NSA interracial voter registration project in North Carolina in the summer of 1962.[8]

If the NSA played a decisive role in the involvement of several young white women in the antiracist movement, SNCC attracted virtually all of the members of the younger generation studied here. Between 1961 and 1965, Hayden first worked for Ella Baker on human relations projects. Her main function consisted in organizing workshops on southern campuses, where she favored the emergence of a new philosophy of human relations based on nonviolence and universal brotherhood. In addition, she worked for a great variety of SNCC projects, both as an observer and as an organizer—she participated in Freedom Rides, in Mississippi Freedom Summer literacy projects, as well as in the challenge by the Mississippi Freedom Democratic Party (MFDP) to the Mississippi delegation at the Atlantic City Democratic National Convention. Finally, she played a key role as SNCC's northern coordinator from 1963 on. As for Dawson Burlage, her decision to go south in 1961 was directly related to her growing involvement with SNCC.[9]

Unlike Hayden and Burlage, Sue Thrasher, born to a working-class family of West Tennessee, did not suddenly immerse herself into the civil rights movement but gradually became involved in it through contact with the major black-led organizations. She entered Scarritt College in Nashville, Tennessee, in the fall of 1961. Far from being militant at heart, she was sensitive to discrimination but was reluctant to challenge segregationist authorities and prevailing norms of behavior. However, after attending an SCLC-sponsored mass meeting that "changed [her] for ever," she became, little by little, involved in SNCC and in the local Nashville Christian Leadership Council, an affiliate of the SCLC. The bombing of Birmingham's Sixteenth Street Baptist Church in September 1963 shocked Thrasher into stepping up her commitment to the black cause. Outraged by southern white racists' assaults on the nonviolent movement, she "made a silent vow to make [her] own voice heard."[10]

Mary King worked for SNCC from June 1963 on. She describes her experience in the civil rights movement in a powerful memoir, *Freedom Song*, published in 1987. King was a southerner through her father, but she was born and raised in New York, her father being an expatriate southern Methodist minister. She entered the civil rights movement in the spring of 1962. A student at Ohio Wesleyan University, she went on a study tour to Nashville, Atlanta, and Tuskegee, Alabama. It was on that trip that she met Atlanta's civil rights leaders, notably SNCC's James Forman and Julian Bond, as well as Casey Hayden and Connie Curry. In June of the same year, she accepted Ella Baker's offer to replace Hayden on her YWCA Human Relations project. She joined the staff of SNCC's Atlanta office a year later. She worked with Julian Bond for SNCC's communications department. Her role consisted in collecting and spreading information about the movement by distributing news releases and writing special reports about the various ongoing programs. Communications were a key factor for the success of the movement since national media coverage was initially very limited.[11] Lastly, Jane Stembridge was also the daughter of a southern Protestant minister. A native of Virginia, she was a student at Union Theological Seminary when Ella Baker recruited her in 1960 to occupy the position of office secretary during the first months of SNCC's life. She played a key role in the building of SNCC's organization after its foundation meeting in April 1960.[12] All the women mentioned above shared the experience of joining SNCC in its early years out of a will to repudiate their segregationist education.

In some instances, the rejection of one's native culture was only possible through direct action rather than coordinating or office work. Joan Trumpauer and Joan Browning, both natives of rural Georgia, are cases in point. Trumpauer was still a teenager when the school desegregation crisis broke out. Living then in northern Virginia, she witnessed white resistance. "I knew something was terribly wrong in the South," she writes. "Both as a Christian and as a southerner, I felt that when I had a chance to do something to change things, I should do it." She goes on to explain that the chance came with the sit-in movement at Duke University in Durham, North Carolina. When local black students started the sit-ins in 1960, she and a few other whites joined them. She soon left Duke for Washington, D.C., where she was hired by the SNCC-affiliated Nonviolent Action Group (NAG), an organization based at Howard University. Her application to Tougaloo College in the spring of

1961 was motivated by her conviction that black students should not be the only ones to bear the burden of desegregation by applying to all-white colleges and that "whites had to make the journey, too." In early June, she seized the opportunity to translate her ideas into action by participating in a Freedom Ride with other NAG members—including future SNCC chairman Stokely Carmichael. They took the train from New Orleans to Jackson, Mississippi. They were arrested and sentenced to two months in prison. Trumpauer spent the summer in jail, first in Jackson, then at Parchman Penitentiary. She was released just in time to start classes at Tougaloo. She spent the next three years on the front lines of the Jackson direct-action movement working for SNCC and CORE before returning to Washington, D.C.[13]

Joan Browning's case presents striking similarities with Trumpauer's. Like Trumpauer, she was born to a lower-income family of rural Georgia. Like Trumpauer, she left college in 1961 after violating the racial etiquette. During her second college year at Milledgeville's Georgia State College for Women, she and her white college friend, Faye Powell, first went to a black church, and then attended the Paine College Student Christian Conference in Augusta, Georgia, which was not acceptable for their school authorities. Browning was not expelled but was informed she would not be welcome back after the summer. Like Trumpauer, Browning was moved early on by a compulsion to act in accordance with her ideals, whatever the consequences might be. On December 10, 1961, she and seven other SNCC Freedom Riders left Atlanta on a train bound for Albany, Georgia. They were accompanied by Casey Hayden, who served as designated observer.[14] The Freedom Riders were arrested on arrival and spent a week and a half in Albany's jail. The catalyst for Browning's involvement in the nonviolent movement was the Paine College conference that had taken place earlier that year. There she learned about Christian nonviolence both in spirit and in body while participating in the direct-action demonstrations organized in Augusta. It was there that she attended her first church mass meeting, and met Connie Curry and other whites involved in Curry's Southern Project—Curry was the designated observer at the Augusta sit-ins. As a direct consequence of these events, in the fall of 1961 Browning volunteered for work at SNCC's Atlanta office and was elected vice-chair of the new Greater Atlanta Student Council on Human Relations, of which she became chair the following year. In this position she set up interracial college projects and participated in the Atlanta movement. She continued working for a variety of antiracist organizations until the late 1960s. In 1968, she contributed to sending an alternate Georgia delegation to the Democratic National Convention in Chicago but stopped believing in electoral politics for a time after the assassination of Robert Kennedy. She never gave up social justice activism, however, and even ran for election to the West Virginia House of Delegates in 2006 and 2008.[15]

The above examples show that SNCC was a major factor in the commitment of the younger generation of female racial dissenters. SNCC, however, could not be present everywhere in the South, and even in places where it was present, other groups worked against racial discrimination related to segregation. Thus, in some specific areas, other civil rights organizations attracted the few white southern women who wanted to make their contribution to the movement. In Jackson, Mississippi, for instance, the youth branch of the NAACP was especially active. Mississippi was perhaps the most dangerous place for civil rights activists in the early 1960s as it was the state where the traditional rural, white supremacist elite was the most entrenched and where outside influence was the weakest. Given these conditions, it took an exceptional amount of courage to dissent from the racial orthodoxy and to challenge segregation in any way, be it by forming interracial church groups, by creating CHRs, or by organizing voting registration campaigns or direct-action demonstrations. Ed and Jeannette King, both native white Mississippians, had such courage. They had entered the civil rights movement during their student years at all-white Millsaps College in Mississippi. Ed had participated in the Freedom Rides of May 1961 and had been denied ordination by the Methodist Church as a result of his advocacy of integration. In January 1962, the couple moved to the campus of majority-black Tougaloo Southern Christian College, near Jackson. From 1962 on, they participated in the Jackson movement. They joined the Jackson NAACP youth group, which was more militant than the adult group, and took part in the various direct actions organized between 1961 and 1963 to desegregate public facilities in Jackson. From late 1963 on, they were key participants in the organization of the MFDP. While Ed ran as MFDP candidate for lieutenant governor in a freedom ballot campaign, Jeannette developed Freedom Schools for the Mississippi Summer Project. At the end of the summer, she was elected MFDP delegate to the Democratic National Convention. After the disillusionment of defeat in the challenge, Jeannette worked for a federal Head Start program, the Child Development Group of Mississippi. The couple left Jackson for New Orleans in 1967.[16]

The organization that led the nonviolent movement in New Orleans was not SNCC but CORE. While a dynamic group of black women energized the New Orleans CORE chapter, three white students distinguished themselves for their dedication to the local sit-in movement. Margaret Burr Leonard was born into a liberal Georgia family, whereas Connie Bradford came from a traditional, conservative background. As for Jill Finsten, she was of Jewish Canadian origins but moved to Florida with her family at the age of fourteen. The three of them were students at Newcomb College, located on the campus of Tulane University, when they joined CORE to participate in direct-action campaigns in 1960 and 1961. Leonard later went on a Freedom Ride from Atlanta to Mississippi. She explains that she had to overcome her fear of being killed, but that her interest and support for the civil rights movement was stronger than fear.[17]

The many personal testimonies and other archival sources available point to a few sets of common features that shaped the identities of the freedom activists. In the first place, they were all moral radicals in the sense that they gave priority to ideals over social norms of behavior. Another major characteristic of these activists was that they were a handful of white women in a black movement led by black men, which placed them in an unprecedented minority position and reversed their status—they lost the dominant status they had always enjoyed as whites in a segregationist society to become equal, even in some cases subordinated, to blacks in the movement. Finally, as their moral idealism urged them to repudiate the "southern way of life" without compromise, all of them were considered traitors by other southern whites and many developed an acute sense of alienation, all the more so since the original movement that had welcomed them ended up rejecting whites, turning them into total outcasts.

Christian Existentialists

Christian ideals directly inspired all forms of antiracist activism that developed in the South during the segregation era. This characteristic applies tenfold to the generation of the 1960s. While many of the young women had their first interracial awakenings through student YWCAs—notably

Casey Hayden and Dorothy Burlage—they all nurtured the Christian ideal of universal brotherhood, which they had learned in Sunday school in their youth. Thus, when they found themselves on their own in college towns and when black students based their protest action on the same ideal, they were instantly drawn to them. Religion pervaded the civil rights movement, from mass meetings to office work. For instance, Howard Zinn quotes Bob Moses—who first went South in 1960 to work at SNCC's Atlanta office—describing his work with Jane Stembridge in these terms: "SNCC and Jane Stembridge were squeezed in one corner of the SCLC office.... I was licking envelopes, one at a time, and talking—Niebuhr, Tillich and Theos—with Jane, who was fresh from a year at Union [Theological Seminary.]" Of Stembridge, Curry writes: "Jane, pixie and poet, was wide-eyed and full of Christian existentialism and faith in the movement."[18]

The Christianity that moved the students to act, however, was not so much a religion as a moral, even a philosophical imperative. Rather than centering their faith on God, they focused on human relations and on the notion of brotherhood. The young women's views coincided perfectly with those of SNCC's founders, who strove to create the "Beloved Community." Dorothy Burlage described it in the following terms: "The Protestant Church's influence faded as the Freedom Movement became more relevant to addressing the ethical issues that concerned me. I was at home with the ideals of the Southern Freedom Movement, with its religious tradition and its commitment to nonviolence and creating a Beloved Community. The movement became my spiritual home." The Freedom Movement actually offered a new ethic of which Christianity was an essential dimension but not the only one. Joan Browning embraced the "radical Christian ideals" that Martin Luther King Jr. and other black leaders "were circulating throughout the South." "Increasingly," she writes, "I found my spiritual exploration turning from organized Christianity to activism and into existentialism and eastern mysticism." In her application form for the NSA's Southern Student Human Relations Seminar in 1962, she stated: "While the New Negro is coming of age in the South, I would like to try to create a New White citizenry which will accept the Negro not only as an equal but as a brother." Browning's college friend Faye Powell, who attended the seminar in 1961, put forward Christian motives as her primary reason for applying.[19]

The second fundamental dimension of the movement's ethic, which could not be dissociated from Christianity, was nonviolence and its ultimate implication, the possibility of dying for one's ideals. The radicalism of the modern civil rights movement lay in great part in the physical risk that the demonstrators were ready to take. Casey Hayden writes that "nonviolent civil disobedience created a new community of folks willing to risk everything for their beliefs." Browning explains, "I was attracted to the Freedom Movement and to the people in it whose commitment to a just society led them to willingly face death." Sue Thrasher experienced a similar feeling: "There was something very powerful in the act of confronting segregation, in standing up and saying, 'No more,' with the body. It was very different than the endless talk about interracial gatherings and working behind the scenes." As Thrasher points out, nonviolent direct action fused mind and body in such a way that it made all socially constructed norms irrelevant. Hence, it forged the fundamental difference between the new and the old generations of white female activists. To the new generation, social norms and practices were not a factor to be taken into account in the fight against racism. As an illustration, here are Browning's reflections during her stay at Paine College in the spring of 1961:

> I want to fail. Unusual, isn't it, when all the world wants success.... I want to fail to retain and develop a typically Southern prejudice based on qualities that are not important.... I want to fail in my attempts to assure myself of the validity of leaving it up to someone else to correct social evils. I hope I will be unsuccessful in my attempts to rationalize until my Christian convictions are obscured in my escape from Christian responsibility. And having distorted my beliefs to read "Let Someone else do it" I would fail to stand safely in the shelter of public opinion and criticize or join in the cry to "crucify" those who are conscientiously living their convictions.

Browning and her fellow activists believed that they could not commit themselves to the movement without taking risks. But they did, and they became, in Hayden's words, "new people, free of the old stereotypes of gender, class, and race."[20]

The driving force behind the young women's activism was a blend of religious faith, moral principles, and philosophical aspirations. Casey Hayden recalled that those in the 1960s civil rights movement absorbed the works of liberal theologians such as Paul Tillich and Reinhold Niebuhr and of existentialist philosophers such as Jean-Paul Sartre and Albert Camus, and then "debated how to use their tenets in the fight for social justice." In one of her essays, she describes nonviolence as "a presentation or demonstration of oneself." She explains: "By acting in this clear, pure way, in which the act itself was of equal value to its outcome, and by risking all for it, we were broken open, released from old and lesser definitions of ourselves in terms of race, sex, class, into the larger self of the Beloved Community. This was freedom as an inside job, not as external to myself, but as created, on the spot and in the moment, by our actions." When she spoke at the NSA Congress in 1960 to urge the organization to support the sit-ins, she made a moral appeal. She justified the violation of segregation laws by stating: "If the pattern is unjust or a person doesn't agree with the relations, a person must at times choose to do the right rather than the legal. I do not consider this anarchy, but responsibility." She also emphasized the ethical value of action: "An ideal can be transmuted into action . . . a just decision can become a reality in students walking and sitting and acting together." Finally, she recalled that Henry Thoreau had refused to pay his taxes because he disapproved of his government supporting slavery and had been jailed for his act. She then asked her student audience the same question that Thoreau had asked Ralph Waldo Emerson when the latter had come to visit him in jail: "What are you doing out there?" Her appeal proved successful since not only did the NSA vote to empower its officers to publicize and financially support the southern student movement, but also the fledgling SDS established close links with SNCC after hearing her speak.[21]

Up to the mid-1960s, the SCLC, CORE, and SNCC embraced nonviolence as a philosophy and used it as a protest tactic against the segregationist system. They drew their inspiration from Thoreau and Gandhi as well as from the Bible. This accounts for the power of attraction that these organizations, especially SNCC, exerted on the southern white students who were searching for a way to cope with the contradictory forces at work in their native culture. White women were probably more sensitive than white men to this religious-oriented philosophy insofar as southern society and culture had favored the development of close ties between women and religion. Not surprisingly, the white female students who had painfully realized that their churches did not practice the brotherhood they preached and who had turned to the YWCA for better answers to their questions found in nonviolence the means to act according to their religious ideals. Thus when the nonviolent movement spread, they turned to blacks for redemption.

Minority Status

As Lynne Olson points out, "The early white women in SNCC made clear they had not come to the movement to play Lady Bountiful in the cause of racial justice, as some of their nineteenth-century sisters had done. They were not there to dominate or dictate or lead. They were there to serve. And in serving, perhaps they would find their own freedom." This reversal of roles and status represented another break with traditional white southern female activism. Whereas previous racial reform movements had been controlled by whites, the modern civil rights movement was a black movement that attracted a small number of whites. When they joined the movement, those whites broke ties with the world in which they had been identified with the dominant group to enter a different world in which they constituted a visible minority.[22]

One major reason why white students became involved in the civil rights movement—and this is true of men and women alike—was their realization that the black people who constituted this movement were not the stereotypical, irresponsible, second-class citizens they were supposed to be according to segregationist standards. Sue Thrasher remembers her moment of revelation occurred while she was a student at Scarritt College. She reluctantly accepted to follow an older Scarritt woman to a mass meeting organized by the Nashville Christian Leadership Council, which proved to be a pivotal moment in her life: "It was the first time I had ever heard black people speak for themselves," she writes. "The first time I understood in even a small way the meaning of freedom and equality. The first time I got any real inkling about the costs and the pain of segregation. It was my dazzling moment of clarity." Nan Grogan's epiphany occurred during the March on Washington, in 1963. A native of Virginia and a student at Mary Washington College, in Fredericksburg, she had never "known blacks as equals," until she spent the summer of 1963 in Washington, D.C., working for a government agency. She told the historian Gregg Michel that the March on Washington revealed "to her for the first time that black Americans throughout the nation—including in her native Virginia—were engaged in a broad-based struggle for equal rights. Energized by this discovery, she returned to school and immediately joined the YWCA race relations committee on campus." She went on to work for SNCC and the movement.[23]

As they became better acquainted with nonviolent black activists, the young women came to see them as morally superior to the whites who accepted segregation as a way of life. They realized that, as white women, they had everything to learn from black people in matters of human relations.[24] Thrasher took her lessons in nonviolence from John Lewis. Up to 1963, the year she graduated from Scarritt, she did volunteer work for the SCLC and SNCC but, still fearing the consequences, did not dare to participate in their direct-action campaigns. It was during those years that she learned about the nonviolent philosophy from local black leaders, and in particular from Lewis, who was then a major figure in the Nashville movement. Browning experienced similar revelations at the Paine College Conference in 1961. Later assessing the impact of that conference, she said, "I understood that racial segregation kept me imprisoned. That it violated my rights as a citizen. That it rejected the values I had learned from my family, my schools, and the Methodist Church." In contrast to most of the whites she knew, she added, "the people on the other side of the color line were warm, genuine, welcoming." She herself felt inferior to the Paine students, as the following notes reveal: "These dynamic young people who are really basing their lives on something ultimate which to them is very real rather than the stumbling general belief and the open-for-faith-ness I have. By evaluating these people and seeing their sacrifice and personal suffering and by comparing myself, I feel that I fall *far* short of the ideal." These words reveal how far the younger generation was from the paternalistic attitudes of the pre-*Brown* era. Browning also learned much from black people during her jail experience as a Freedom Rider, as did Joan Trumpauer. In a letter she sent to her friend Faye Powell from Albany's jail, Browning wrote: "These kids on the ride and others closely connected with our group are wonderful. I've probably said this before but put it in the record again. I think that if these people label whatever the intangible is as Christianity, then there is hope for the faith." Trumpauer kept a diary during the first two weeks she spent in jail in Jackson in 1961. She was never to forget the spirit the Freedom Riders maintained there. Commenting on her experience, she writes: "The singing, worship, and the continual flow of new Freedom Riders made it one of the most inspirational times of my life."

Jeannette King expresses a similar feeling in a personal account of her experience published in 2010. She recalls as the catalyst of her commitment the interracial meetings black and white students held at Tougaloo. "In a short space of time," she writes, "these meetings accomplished what all the religious (do unto others) and social (be kind to everyone) ideas had just talked about."[25]

Because their skin color identified them with the oppressor group, white women felt humbled by the movement that welcomed them. They saw themselves as adopted children in a loving foster family. Casey Hayden thus describes her position: "As a white southerner, I considered the southern Freedom Movement against segregation mine as much as anyone else's.... However, when I worked full time in the black community, I was considered a guest of that community, which required decency and good manners, as every southerner knows." Dorothy Burlage relates that her mother disinherited her after she settled in Atlanta to work for the movement. Yet in spite of the sadness the gesture caused in her, Burlage felt enriched by her new life: "It gave me overwhelming joy to live in a time when my life seemed to make a difference and I could share my idealism and commitment with some of the best and brightest young people in the country. This network of friends and coworkers became my family."[26]

In addition to forcing them to humility, the women's white skin constituted a real danger for their fellow black activists insofar as segregationist culture proscribed any personal contact between white women and black men. The dedication of the white women who joined SNCC in its early days was deeply appreciated by the black activists, but everybody was aware that they represented a liability for civil rights workers who organized grassroots activities in rural areas of the Deep South. As Belinda Robnett found out, "By their presence, openly visible White women intensified the hatred aimed at all field workers." In the Deep South, where SNCC organized major direct-action and voter registration campaigns, the mere fact of a black man and a white woman riding in the same car could provoke a lynching. The white southern women who became involved in the movement were perfectly conscious of this. Curry recalls that when she would drive to South Carolina with Hayden and Reggie Robinson, who was black, the two women sat in the back and the man put on a cap to pass as a chauffeur. Burlage confirms that "the presence of a white woman with black men was inflammatory for most southern white people." In a recent interview, she narrated an incident involving Septima Clark, Andrew Young, Dorothy Cotton, and herself. They were driving to Dorchester, Georgia, when they saw a shack burning on the side of the road, with two babies sitting on the porch. While Young and Cotton jumped out of the car to rescue them, Burlage could only lie down on the floor to avoid being seen with her black friends. She knew she had no choice because her presence in the car put them all at risk. As another example, writing about her Freedom Ride and subsequent imprisonment, Browning notes: "Ironically, being the white girl was fraught with special dangers, for me and everyone around me." In a letter where she related the events, she commented on the white policemen's reactions on seeing her: "I caused a hell of a disturbance. It seems that never in their experiences has a white girl—especially such a quiet, soft-spoken, all-American type—been involved." As a result of this specific characteristic, white women were hardly ever assigned field work, or when they were, they were not sent to areas where white supremacy was deemed too solidly entrenched to guarantee their safety as well as that of their co-workers. This is the reason why the NSA's Southern Project board chose to send Burlage to North Carolina rather than to Mississippi for the registration project she was to supervise in the summer of 1962.[27]

Thus, owing to their white skin, everybody agreed that white women were not to play the same role as black men and women in the civil rights movement. For one thing, it was deemed safer for all that they should do office rather than field work, or that when they participated in direct action they should serve as observers rather than as actors. Casey Hayden expressed a definite uneasiness at working with rural black people because she was conscious of perpetuating "visions of white superiority." She added, "I was also conscious, and had been since I first arrived in Atlanta in 1960, of the danger I spread around me as a highly visible blonde white woman. It was fine with me if other white women wanted to work in SNCC projects in these killer little towns, but in good conscience I couldn't endanger my black companions, especially the guys, in this way." Such comments prove that the specter of lynching still haunted white women and black men as late as the 1960s. Thus it was usually as observers that Curry and Hayden traveled extensively across the Deep South in addition to doing office work. Jane Stembridge became SNCC's first office secretary in June 1960. Mary King was hired in June 1963 to assist SNCC's press secretary, Julian Bond.[28] In addition, Hayden made it clear that safety was not the only reason for such a choice. The definition of white women's status in the movement was also a matter of principle: "My appropriate role," she writes, "was to work behind the lines, not to be a leader in any public way. In fact, one of the major goals of SNCC was to create a new kind of black leadership."[29] Although other women do not express this idea as clearly as Hayden, they all implicitly share her view. As the liberation of black southerners depended on their empowerment as an oppressed community, it was important that white southerners should stay in the background.

Some of the women dealt with in this chapter took this assumption one step further by becoming actively involved in the creation of a new all-white organization named the Southern Student Organizing Committee (SSOC) in 1964. The purpose of this group was to offer white southern integrationists the opportunity to contribute to the liberation of black people without infringing on blacks' leadership. The idea of reaching out to whites was exactly what had motivated Anne Braden to work for SCEF. It was also the goal that Sue Thrasher, one of Braden's protégés, intended to achieve when she contributed to the founding of SSOC in 1964 and became its executive secretary.[30] In 1964, Thrasher became friends with Anne and Carl Braden, who helped her and other students to found SSOC. Connie Curry also supported the move as a way to complement the work of the NSA's Southern Project. Thrasher was elected executive secretary for the new organization and held that position until 1966, when she moved to Washington, D.C., to work for the liberal think-tank Institute for Policy Studies. During the Mississippi Freedom Summer, she and SSOC set up "white folks'" projects aimed at getting the white population involved in the civil rights movement.[31] Other white female students joined SSOC. Nan Grogan, who had become an activist after witnessing the March on Washington in the summer of 1963, was among them. Another activist, Anne Cooke Romaine, was born in Atlanta and grew up in North Carolina. Her father was a liberal North Carolina state senator during the 1950s. Having originally thought of becoming a Presbyterian missionary, she became seriously interested in civil rights in 1963, and started her activist life upon entering the University of Virginia as a graduate student in history. She met her future husband there, and in 1964 they participated in the founding of SSOC.[32]

The initiative to create a southern organization appealing specifically to white students grew out of concern among the few young white activists like Thrasher who had participated in the early 1960s movement—notably through SNCC, the NSA, and SDS—that white participation was too weak. They believed that a potential existed for more white involvement in the southern movement in spite of the apparent indifference of predominantly white southern campuses. "It wasn't so much about creating an organization," Thrasher recalled. "It was about how you involve more whites in the civil rights movement and pull them to the other side so that they're not against what's going on. And if they're a little bit hesitant, then the organization could provide a way for them to move into more activism and be a support group." Nan Grogan considered SSOC as "a thing to penetrate the white campuses in the South." It also provided an opportunity to break the isolation felt by many white students who wanted to act but did not dare to oppose their communities alone. As Mary King observes in her memoir, "The isolation felt by thoughtful southern whites who questioned racial segregation was paralyzing."[33]

SSOC's founding meeting on April 4–5, 1964, was organized by Thrasher's group of Nashville white students who were anxious to coordinate the various white student college groups that had appeared across the South to support the civil rights movement. Anne Braden and Connie Curry helped in publicizing the meeting. Also in the original Nashville group were Robb and Dorothy Burlage, active with SNCC and cofounders of SDS.[34] Two of SSOC's founders, Sam Shirah and Ed Hamlett, had worked as SNCC field organizers on a White Southern Student Project conceived by Anne Braden in 1961 and funded by SCEF. This original connection between SNCC and SSOC showed that most founders of SSOC believed in SNCC's ideals but thought their contribution to the black cause would be more effective if they worked independently to attract moderate white students who deemed SNCC too radical. Although some, like Anne Braden, feared that the integrationist spirit of the movement might be lost with the creation of an independent white organization and pleaded for SSOC to become an affiliate of SNCC, the former option was retained and approved by SNCC leaders, including Stokely Carmichael, Ella Baker, Bob Moses, Ruby Doris Robinson, and Connie Curry. Thus SSOC became SNCC's white sister organization in the southern student movement. Remembering the debates, Thrasher writes: "I was so focused on the need for white southerners to work with other white southerners that it took me years to understand why some people considered this a bad idea." Another reason why Thrasher was so keen on creating an independent organization was her concern to preserve the nature of SNCC as a black-led movement. Indeed, although she wanted whites to be active in the black cause, she did not want them to occupy leadership positions: "My sense was that it was our place to work with other white students and not to be messing around in the black movement and telling people what to do because that's exactly what happened in SNCC. I mean, white people really took leadership roles [in SNCC]. And I never saw that as being my job." Thus Thrasher's view of her role in the black liberation movement resembled that of most of her fellow white female activists, and she found in SSOC the best way to put them into practice. She worked for the organization until the spring of 1966.[35]

Thus whatever the channels they chose and the positions they held in the movement, white southern female activists saw themselves as participants of a different kind who refused to occupy the front stage. "I viewed myself as a support person," writes Hayden. Burlage also uses the phrase "support person" to define her role, to which she adds the image of the bridge, a metaphor that can indeed be applied to many white southern women activists.[36] Curry took on an all but official bridging role when she became an adviser for SNCC, a role confirmed by all the other positions she held during the same period. Her NSA Southern Student Human Relations Seminar achieved much more than interracial communication. In a 1960 report, she explained the meaning of the seminar: "Although the participants generally acknowledge the harmfulness of segregation, it was the common sharing of joy and anger and tears that brought true acknowledgement of each other as human beings and the commitment to somehow make this kind of sharing possible in the South." The seminar had very practical consequences, as she added: "Moreover, this kind of understanding has indeed proved fruitful, since it is safe to say that practically every participant has continued his interest in human relations, and at least twelve of them [out of sixteen] have made specific contributions in human relations work on their campuses or in their communities." Some, she said, had participated in direct actions. She concluded with those words: "In the past months this relationship has meant that I have solid contacts in nine Southern states—contacts who are willing to cooperate with the Project and on whose work the Project has been able to build."[37]

Curry's reflections prove that she and other white women constituted chain-links between the civil rights movement, the white southern community, and the rest of the nation. Julian Bond, a central figure of SNCC, thus described Curry's position in a letter to a friend: "Connie was a bridge between the overwhelming number of black sit-in students and white students who were predisposed to join with us. And she got us into the NSA network. It was an invaluable resource for recruiting money and political support [and] provided the basis later for Friends of SNCC groups on college campuses. She publicized the sit-in movement within the NSA network, interpreted it, and created an audience for us that might not have been there." Bond's assessment could also be applied to Hayden and Burlage. As members of SNCC and SDS, they could secure the support of northern students for the southern movement by publicizing it on northern campuses. This twofold involvement also led Burlage to focus on the role of white students in the southern movement—as SDS was a majority-white organization—which accounts for her involvement with SSOC. As for Jeannette King's view of her own role, though more prosaic, it partakes of the same dynamic, as she recalls: "My most vivid memories of spring 1963 to summer 1964 are those intense conversations held around my dining room table over food and drink. . . . Tougaloo's campus and our house were safe havens for many of the people coming into the state for part-time volunteer work." Even for the minority of white women who participated in direct-action field operations, like Joan Browning or Joan Trumpauer, their white skin played a specific role in the demonstrations. Indeed, some of the organizers assumed that the presence of white students on the side of blacks could arouse the sympathy of some whites who remained passive out of fear. This was what Bill Didley, a black leader from the Paine College group, told Browning. She reports: "He thinks that our being southern white students from southern colleges helped raise the consciousness of people in Augusta, added to the Freedom Movement's credibility, and led some white people to be sympathetic to the students' cause."[38]

Ultimately, the 1960s generation of white southern women activists experienced what their elders had not: they lived for a time in a southern community of brotherhood where race, class, and gender differences were almost erased. They would probably all recognize themselves in Casey Hayden's description of SNCC's essence: "We actually experienced freedom and equality—in race, in gender—not completely, but perhaps as close as it gets. We actually experienced integration. We may have been the only people in this country who ever really have."[39] Yet this extraordinary achievement had a price since, when they first broke with their native segregationist culture to join the movement, they became outcasts from the white world. Then, when the movement changed and gradually shifted to Black Power after 1964, they became aliens in the black world. Thus being white integrationists in the segregationist South cursed them with a fundamental contradiction that could hardly be resolved without loss.

The Price of Commitment

Many white racial activists first experienced a sense of loss when their families rejected them for their commitment to the civil rights cause. Such a rejection was not systematic, as Curry, Thrasher, and Jeannette King, for instance, maintained good relationships with their parents even if they disagreed with them. For others, such as Browning or Burlage, their activism entailed a long-lasting estrangement from their families. However, even when parents and relatives accepted their daughters' violation of segregationist culture, the white community at large condemned and often harassed them. The historian Gregg Michel stresses the fact that estrangement from the white community was a common feature of SSOC members as white southern dissenters. For instance, as Nan Grogan commented on the aftermath of the 1964 Freedom Summer, northern volunteers returned to their communities to be welcomed as heroes whereas southern volunteers went back home to "ostracism and pain." Dorothy Burlage explained: "As you got deeper and deeper into the movement you, in fact, did burn your bridges.... We lost our ties to the system."[40]

The feeling of alienation only grew as the activists realized that their white skin singled them out among their black counterparts and could never be totally forgotten, however tolerant and welcoming blacks were. For instance, in a 1963 letter to Lynne Strauss—the chair of Ohio Wesleyan University's Student Committee on Race Relations, which supported the sit-ins—Joan Browning described "the agonizing loneliness and isolation of the 'new' Southerner who is freed of racial or ethnic bigotry and is alone." She added: "We are denounced by friends and family as traitors, distrusted by Negroes, and misunderstood by non-Southerners who fail to understand how we can simultaneously reject the 'Southern Way of Life' and cling sentimentally to the South and love this corner of the globe." Browning's correspondence in those days reveals acute suffering. In June 1962, she wrote to Vincent Harding, who was then at the head of the Mennonite House in Atlanta: "There is no Southern white person today who does not suffer in one form or another from the discriminatory custom so deeply ingrained into our mores. In short, it is hell to be a white Southerner today." Browning had to leave the region for a while, as she recalls: "I felt suffocated in the South."[41]

Alienation from the white community was compensated for a time by the real sense of brotherhood that the movement managed to create between 1960 and 1964. Then, after the ordeal of Freedom Summer in Mississippi and the passage of the federal Civil Rights Act, which prohibited segregation in all public places, the movement lost its uniting purpose, and white activists became irrelevant in black organizations. Hayden remembers: "This was the period of SNCC's transition out of our nonviolent, interracial culture. I watched, conflicted and depressed, as that fabric unraveled, empathizing with the feelings expressed and sure that the public implications were tragic." Hayden's journey from segregationist to integrationist society, though vital to her development as a full human being, proved to be an alienating experience: "I had moved farther and farther out, onto the margins of the culture, into the center of the movement, leaving everything behind. I was standing on the ground of the Beloved Community, but that ground eroded. Spun out into the world at large by the accelerating force of a social revolution I had helped create, I crashed and burned. There was no going home again. I lost everything." As extreme as it may seem, the nature of Hayden's experience was not unique. Indeed, even if some white southern activists successfully negotiated the shift from nonviolent interracialism to Black Power in the late 1960s, they all went through estrangement to varying degrees. When Dorothy Burlage looked at herself by 1970, she noted that she was "not a typical southerner, not a northerner, not an academic, not a liberal, not a leftist, not a hippie, not a feminist. I wasn't black, but I didn't feel very white. I did not fit anywhere." Joan Browning expresses the same sense of "not belonging." She explains that in participating in the movement, "I lost my only real opportunity for a higher education, and I was alienated from my church. I experienced a lifelong separation from my large and loving family, and was set apart from the world in ways that affected all my relationships and employment options. For me, and for many other women like me, participation made us outcasts—women without a home." Jeannette King, for her part, started to feel estranged in 1965: "To me, the Movement in Mississippi was SNCC, but there was no place for a white southerner to fit into the organization as it began to change.... Once again, I was on the outside."[42]

However, this moment of loss should not be interpreted as an end but as the beginning of a new life. Indeed, for most white southern women activists, the black liberation movement meant liberation from segregationist culture, expiation from white guilt, and a sense that a fully integrated society was possible. After the demise of the movement, they went on to live up to their ideals in the larger society. Browning explains: "I have shelved that part of my life that was formative, transformative, that set the course of my future. I still witness to the values that brought me to the Freedom Movement." Thrasher expresses a similar feeling: "The Freedom Movement offered us the vision, a glimpse of what we could be, 'a Beloved Community' that transcended difference. Perhaps we didn't know how to make it happen, but I doubt that any of us has lost the power of that vision. It is still something I hold on to." Burlage declares that the movement made her grow: "It helped me learn to follow my own vision," she writes, "have a political voice, and develop leadership skills. And it helped me abandon some of my restrictive southern upbringing in personal relationships."[43]

Moreover, although the rejection of the integrationist ideal by Black Power advocates hurt them, they nevertheless understood this move as the logical outcome of white resistance and of the persistence of racism in spite of the victories of the civil rights movement. Besides, whereas the Black Power movement excluded whites from its ranks in late 1966 as a matter of official policy, most of the interracial friendships that had grown out of the early 1960s struggle survived. Curry does not seem to have gone through the same trauma as others, which can probably be accounted for by the fact that she had occupied the position of adviser rather than that of field activist. She was also less vulnerable because she worked for many different groups that did not embrace the Black Power ideology in the late 1960s. The AFSC, for which she started to work in 1964, stuck to the interracial faith. So she remembers: "When Stokely Carmichael, chairman of SNCC, issued his call for Black Power in 1966, I was neither surprised nor alarmed. I understood the new emphasis on Black Power within some ranks of the movement; dashed dreams, broken heads, and loss of faith can demand a new strategy." Without generalizing, it seems fair to say that Curry shared this view with several white southern radicals who embraced the civil rights movement in the 1960s. This is definitely true of Anne Braden, who continued to interpret Black Power from her SCEF position to convince the white activists that the new development should not deter them from carrying on the fight for justice.[44]

Eventually, the 1960s generation represented the ultimate level of dedication to racial equality in the sense that their involvement in the civil rights movement superseded their other activities, including family life. To a certain extent they stood as the heirs of the older generation of white southern women activists. They had grown up in the same segregationist culture, and, most of all, they held spiritual values as a fundamental frame of reference that influenced all their attitudes in life and society. On the other hand, the members of the new generation broke with the tradition of white southern female activism by opposing their culture in open defiance of its norms and by leaving their communities rather than compromising their ideals. This was made possible by the advent of the modern civil rights movement, to which some members of the older generation also contributed in various ways. The young women who came of age in the late 1950s and early 1960s found in these new conditions the opportunity to repudiate segregation in a radical, uncompromising way. The formation of SNCC in 1960 was crucial to the new generation as it provided them with a vision that coincided almost perfectly with their attitude to life. Casey Hayden summed it up well: "The SNCC I knew was radically humanistic, placing human values above those of law and order, insisting that values could and should be acted out to be realized. One's actions were in fact the source of the unity of ends and means."[45] The new generation's radicalism lay in this total identification of ends and means, which clearly departed from the tactical concerns of previous reform or protest groups. The young women also distinguished themselves by aspiring to much more than racial equality. Their ultimate goal was not mere desegregation but brotherhood in its literal sense. Such was the meaning of the "Beloved Community," which was not an empty catchword but a spiritual, physical, social, and political alternative to the society they knew. Unlike their elders, they did not call for racial reform but for a revolution in human relations. Jane Stembridge summed it up: "Love alone is radical. Political statements are not; programs are not; even going to jail is not."[46]

Nevertheless, even though the younger generation appeared as fundamentally different from the older in goals as well as in manners, the two were closely connected by deep common features. As the post-*Brown* decade drew old and young together in the fight against racism, the civil rights movement revealed a thread of continuity between the respectable activism of the former and the revolutionary activism of the latter. This thread, which ran deep under the surface of events and attitudes, was the specific identity all those women shared as white southern women struggling with the race and gender prescriptions of their society and culture. Their commitment to racial justice entailed a process of collective emancipation from those "southern scriptures."

The Blooming of Southern Sisterhood

Unlike the members of the older generation who did not meet on a daily basis and consolidated ties through participation in common activities outside their homes, or through correspondence, the young women who experienced the civil rights movement in the 1960s lived together within the movement's community and faced physical danger in their day-to-day confrontation with white supremacists, strengthening their bonds. Yet the post-*Brown* civil rights movement bridged generations, as the older activists mentored the younger, providing them with material and moral support. The older generation in particular provided role models for the students, who suddenly moved from the sheltered certainties of their family environment to the intense, challenging, and totally unknown world of the black movement. Thus the struggle against racism reinforced the bonds of white southern womanhood to the point that these women ended up openly challenging male supremacy along with white supremacy.[47]

At about the same time as their elders were drawing close to each other through writing, the members of the new generation were embracing the modern civil rights movement. With the foundation and expansion of SNCC, new concepts and new forms of action transformed the struggle against segregation into a movement for the creation of a new society. The 1960s movement, the ultimate goal of which was the advent of the "Beloved Community," started by putting this ideal into practice in its grassroots operations, so that its participants not only worked but also lived together wherever the action was. Besides, as SNCC concentrated its efforts in the rural Deep South, where white resistance was the strongest, its staff and volunteers lived under the permanent threat of death. For the young white women fresh from college who participated in the movement between 1960 and 1964, these conditions favored the emergence of a unique sense of sisterhood.

Being a minority as white women in a movement led by black men naturally drew these women close to one another. This was especially true in the initial stages of the movement for the few white southern female students who suddenly stepped out of their white world to join black students. Casey Hayden writes: "The southern white women were my base community inside the movement in these early days. I lost touch with them when I moved to the blackside in the Deep South later, all except Jane [Stembridge], who also made that move." Ties were reinforced by the fact that the handful of white female volunteers who joined SNCC between 1960 and 1963 started by working at the Atlanta office and shared apartments in the city for varying periods of time depending on the evolution of their work for the organization. Such were the cases of Casey Hayden and Mary King, Dorothy Burlage and Joan Browning, Connie Curry and Jane Stembridge.[48]

Thus, as they lived and worked together, some of them became friends and exchanged views and feelings on a great variety of subjects, including their condition as women. When they did not actually share apartments, they exchanged letters, which served not only as a way to support each other and to overcome the anxieties caused by the dangerous circumstances in which they found themselves but also as a means to share their experiences as women. As an illustration, when Dorothy Burlage married in December 1963 and became torn between her wish to conform to traditional married life and her militant aspirations, she turned to her friend and former college roommate Casey Hayden: "Occasionally," she writes, "I would stop [ironing] and write to Casey, saying something was wrong with all this. She and I corresponded frequently during this period, sharing our thoughts about the role of women in the movement." It was during that period that Burlage, Hayden, and King read Simone de Beauvoir, Doris Lessing, and other feminist writers, which led them to develop a new awareness of gender issues through discussing their readings. Hayden recalls being especially impressed by Lessing's *The Golden Notebook*. She was living in Atlanta with Mary King in 1963, and reports: "Mary read the book too. On the basis of our shared Y experiences and this book we engaged men and women in conversations about gender, much as I had engaged SDS women in Ann Arbor earlier."[49]

In her memoir of the movement, King devotes several pages to Jane Stembridge and their correspondence when King was working for SNCC's communications office and Hayden and Stembridge were in Mississippi. Stembridge, the second white member of the staff after Hayden to move to Mississippi, was given the charge, in late 1963, of preparing a training manual for volunteers arriving the following summer. "Jane was torn by her own search for identity," King writes, "as a woman, as a white southerner in conflict with the immorality of segregation, and as a poet-philosopher in a movement she feared in danger of becoming mechanistic." Stembridge's letters to King were a way to reflect on the nature, goals, and actions of the movement as well as on herself and her native region. "Paris must be preferable to Greenwood," she observed, "but when I was in Paris they burned a bus in Alabama and I came home—*home*?" In another letter from Greenwood, Mississippi, she shifted from factual report to introspection: "I wanted to write something for you about food and clothes, but it is hard for me to be a writer of leaflets. I am such a bad politician. Lillian Smith, call her Miss Lil for warmth (she likes it too), told me that when I begin to be political, I begin certainly to lie because poetry is in opposition to ideology."[50]

The same blend of personal and political concerns characterized the letters Joan Browning sent to Faye Powell from the jail she had been locked up in after participating in the Albany Freedom Ride of December 10, 1961. While she was in jail, Browning wrote letters to her friend in Macon, Georgia, not so much to find comfort—although this was an obvious function of the letters—as to testify to the courage of the freedom activists who were in prison with her. On December 12, 1961, she gave Powell instructions: "First—save all the things I write you—I may need them later to get exact information when writing my memoirs or something." Moreover, because Browning and Powell were two dissenting young white women who, on the one hand, had become estranged from their white communities, and, on the other, did not have the same background as black activists, they could only rely on each other to make sense of the experiences they were going through. After coming back to Atlanta, Browning wrote Powell: "I would so much like to see you. I'm going insane because there's no one who really understands that I can talk with—or to." Thus the two women became tied by a unique bond out of their common commitment to human rights. In addition to Powell, Browning became friends during the movement with Casey Hayden, Connie Curry, Mary King, Diana Ellison, Margaret Long, and many other white women.[51]

This example shows that an important function of correspondence for the women of the younger generation, as for their elders, was to enable them to convey their dissenting views to sympathizing fellow southerners, who were all the more likely to understand because they were also white women. The letters Connie Curry received as director of the Southern Student Human Relations Seminar demonstrate this point. After the seminar, many female students wrote Curry to thank her and, more significant, to voice feelings they could not express to anyone around them. Thus Valerie Brown, a student at Texas Christian University, wrote her on September 14, 1960: "Connie, will you come see me soon? I do hope you'll find it possible to travel this way sometime this year soon. It's so hard to find someone to talk to who isn't afraid of being real." Judy Carter, from the University of Alabama, thanked Curry for her "understanding and sympathetic ear." Faye Powell—Joan Browning's friend—wrote Curry in September 1961 to confide about being sick and hurt back home because of segregationists. Actually, Hayden and Browning both became friends with Curry after attending the seminar in 1960 and 1962, respectively, while Dorothy Burlage became Curry's assistant on the Southern Student Human Relations Project in the winter of 1961–62.[52]

Curry's central role as bridge leader within the 1960s movement points out the last important by-product of white women's commitment to racial justice: the creation of bonds between the two generations during the post-*Brown* era. Although Curry belonged to the younger generation, she was significantly older than the others who were in their college years when the movement started—Curry having left college in 1957. If most SNCC members, men and women, black and white, saw a nurturing figure, if not a mother figure, in her, white women considered her as a protective big sister whom they could both identify with and seek advice from. Several older women who already had a long career of activism behind them when the students stepped in became mentors to the new generation. They were role models and provided emotional comfort when needed, but they also spurred young women into asserting themselves within the movement. In addition, they helped the latter grasp the complexity of their status as white southern women and free themselves from it.

A large number of personal testimonies on the 1960s movement describe the determining influence of the YWCA and other religious leaders on campuses. Casey Hayden and Dorothy Burlage both identify Rosalie Oakes, from Virginia, as an inspiring figure. She was a "mentor" to Burlage, a "role model" to Hayden, who adds that Oakes was "the first of the many women of the Y who inspired" her.[53] In addition to the numerous religious advisers who helped female students find their way during their formative years, prominent older activists provided support and inspiration by accompanying the young through their progression once they found themselves in the thick of the movement. Given the small number of women of the earlier generation who participated in the modern civil rights movement, all of those who did take part in one way or another served as role models for younger white female activists but are not recognized as such, either because they were not public figures or because they were not directly involved in the movement. Frances Pauley, for instance—who was director of the Georgia CHR between 1961 and 1967—features on the list of Joan Browning's role models. Browning describes her as a "very important person" to her in those days and later. Although Pauley's name does not appear in historical accounts of the 1960s movement, she was present and active in Albany in 1961 and 1962 and, according to Browning, tried to do whatever she could—along with Ella Baker—to help the Freedom Riders who were jailed. Another little known but influential member of the older generation was journalist Margaret Long. She was director of information for the SRC between 1961 and 1967, a position that included serving as editor of the organization's publication, *New South*. Browning cites her as important. Long actually embodied the link between the two generations since her daughter, Margaret "Sissy" Leonard, participated in actions with CORE and SNCC, thus drawing Long close to the student activists of the 1960s. Long's correspondence during the decade reveals that she did not limit her role to reporting on the civil rights movement but also became friends with many of its members, notably young white women. She encouraged young authors to publish on the South and the movement in a creative and militant way. "What a grand cadre of older women we had behind us," Browning notes. She points out other women as role models, including Connie Curry and Virginia Durr. "Important to my breaking out of my cage of race," she reflects, "was meeting Connie Curry. She showed me, by example, how an admirable white woman could free herself from racial restrictions." On Virginia Durr's death, she wrote the following words: "Though I saw her only a few times, Virginia Durr was prominent among those white women who inspired me." For Browning, "By their life and witness," such women "proved that one could be white, southern, and female without being racist."[54]

Two names stand out in the mass of personal accounts available: Lillian Smith and Anne Braden. Even if few of the young women actually met Smith, who was seriously ill with cancer by the early 1960s—she died in 1966—several of them identified her writings, notably *Killers of the Dream*, as a catalyst in their realization of the racial and gender currents running through the depths of southern culture. Curry, Burlage, and Browning explicitly identify her as a guiding spirit, while Smith's correspondence includes letters testifying to her friendship with Jane Stembridge, whom she especially encouraged to develop her artistic soul. She also discussed the philosophy and tactics of the fledgling student movement, providing support at a time when Stembridge doubted her abilities in her key position as SNCC's first office secretary. "Everything seems to me, at this distance, to have been managed beautifully. And this is YOU, Jane," she wrote her in October 1960. "No one in the movement seems to me as important in the Atlanta situation as you. So don't worry about it. You are exactly where you are needed; what you do can determine whether the movement fails or succeeds."[55]

As for Anne Braden, Sara Evans describes her as "perhaps the most important adult white woman to young southern activists throughout the sixties." She was all the more so to women as she "provided a model of an adult woman, with three children, whose life was totally immersed in the struggle for racial equality." She was especially close to some young women with whom she kept up a regular correspondence. Stembridge was one of them. In her biography of Braden, Catherine Fosl writes: "From the beginning of their work together, the depth of Anne's dedication to social change impressed Stembridge, and she saw Anne as 'a person beside whom I have always measured my commitment.'" In 1960, Stembridge wrote Braden to discuss her recent decision to participate in the next sit-ins planned by SNCC. In her letter, she credited Braden's book, *The Wall Between*, with prodding her into action. She thanked her for writing it. Another of Braden's protégés, Sue Thrasher, recalls how the older woman encouraged her to write for SCEF's newsletter, the *Southern Patriot*. Braden also played a central role in the formation of SSOC, of which Thrasher was a founder. Thrasher explains how Braden bridged the gap between old and young generations of activists: "[She] told me one time in no uncertain terms that my generation was not the first actively to oppose segregation and that I owed it to myself to find out more about the radicals of the 1930s."[56]

Along with older white women, Ella Baker served as a mentor to all the young women, black and white, who worked with her in the civil rights movement. Baker's relationship with white women in the civil rights movement actually points to the fact that female antiracist activism not only bridged generations but also races, and in the process reshaped the definition of southern womanhood. As Baker's biographer, Barbara Ransby, notes, "To young women, black and white, Baker embodied the possibility of escaping the restrictions that defined conventional femininity."[57] Ransby does not limit her reflection to the South, but her statement is especially relevant to black and white southern civil rights activists. Through their involvement in the 1960s movement, young white women not only naturally forged special bonds with each other but also became aware of their common points with black women. This helped them bridge the gap segregation had created between them.

Interracial friendships were key in the building of southern sisterhood. Many white southern women unlearned racism through personal contact with black activists who became their friends. If such friendships had existed since the early days of the student YWCAs, they became more common and were greatly facilitated during the 1960s civil rights movement. These relationships show that even if white women did not identify with black women as fully as they did with other white women—for the obvious reason that the two groups had radically different experiences—blacks and whites nevertheless supported one another as women sharing interests and goals. For instance, Anne Braden and Septima Clark—a key black member of the SCLC who set up Citizenship Education Programs—relied on each other for comfort and encouragement. Clark especially had a hard time coping with what she perceived as a lack of recognition on the part of the SCLC's male leadership. In 1961, when Clark was considering leaving the movement and joining the Peace Corps, Braden responded: "Our part of the country needs you, Septima, more than any one person that I can think of right now.... Don't let things get you down. You can't always see the good that you're doing until you look back at it from a distance. But I don't know of anyone who has made the contribution that you have." Braden was also the one friend who managed to persuade Ella Baker to take some rest after eye surgery in the summer of 1960. The two women spent a few days together in a wood cabin. Barbara Ransby reports that "Anne and Ella sat on the long front porch of the house in the evenings talking about the direction of the movement and about their own lives and families. Ella enjoyed a glass of expensive Jack Daniels whiskey—one of the very few indulgences she allowed herself—as Anne sat next to her sipping a glass of wine." As the historian comments, "The two women warriors were refueling themselves physically and emotionally for the battles that lay ahead." Four years later, it was Baker's turn to comfort her friend through hardship when Braden's eleven-year-old daughter, Anita, died of primary pulmonary hypertension.[58] Baker was also friends with members of the young generation. Of particular interest here are the friendships she developed with Connie Curry, Casey Hayden, and Dorothy Burlage. In her autobiographical essay, Burlage declares: "My relationship with Ella Baker marked the reshaping of my relationships with black people, allowing the kind of open communication I had always wanted but not been able to have as a child." Her statement reveals the dynamic function of interracial friendships in the transcending of racial barriers during the segregation era. These were typical of southern female activism during the segregation and desegregation eras. In a recent interview, Burlage further commented on the importance of personal interracial contacts in the struggle against institutionalized racism, by explaining that "the personal trumped the political." She meant that, for decades in the segregated South, personal contact had been the only way to overcome the racial barriers fixed by law.[59]

As another example of interracial bonds, Septima Clark also developed a lasting friendship with Virginia Durr, at the urging of whom she joined the National Organization for Women (NOW) in 1968. Lynne Olson observes that "both then in their late sixties, the black daughter of a former slave and the white granddaughter of a former slave owner said they had become members of the organization for the same reason: the subordination of women by men." Clark later associated black and white women in her defense of women's rights: "This country was built up from women keeping their mouths shut. It took fifty years for women, black and white, to learn to speak up."[60] It is not stretching the facts to assume that Durr's and Clark's female assertiveness had grown out of their interaction within the civil rights movement. Beyond the personal value of individual friendships, the kinship that connected black and white female activists who had been drawn together by the cause for racial justice contributed to heighten their gender awareness, which ultimately surfaced in the late 1960s.[61]

Liberation: From Southern Ladies to Southern Women

The movement of the 1960s undoubtedly fostered a new sense of sisterhood among the women who participated in it, even if race continued to separate black and white women in many ways. For white southern activists at least, this growing awareness of their female identity ended up in a repudiation of the gender norms still prevailing at the time. Thus the process of female emancipation that had started in the earlier decades was completed in the 1960s.

Dorothy Burlage's experience is especially revealing. Her marriage to Robb Burlage in December 1963 precipitated her full emancipation from gender norms when she suddenly stopped the militant activities in which she had participated: "I lost my footing in political work," she recalls, "not because of Robb, but because I became confused. I had learned in my southern upbringing that marriage was not just a way to legalize a love relationship, but a job description—to be a helpmate to my husband." Yet it was not easy to *stay* in the background. She goes on to describe her new domestic life as a struggle between her will to conform to cultural norms and her own aspirations. She recalls dividing her time between ironing her husband's shirts and reading the seminal works of the new generation of feminist writers. With hindsight, she comments: "My marriage and struggle for an identity in that framework forced me to address the tangle of gender, racial, and class issues in the South, especially as they influenced my own life." She recalls that she reached a new stage of awareness at that point: "Somehow I had always intuitively understood that there was a connection between the segregation of blacks and the creation of suffocating roles for white women. . . . It was Lillian Smith's *Killers of the Dream* (1949, rev. 1963) that clarified for me the function of women's roles in maintaining segregation." Yet she still hesitated to repudiate her upbringing, as she observes: "I found it easier to see the problems of how women were socialized, particularly those of us brought up with the southern lady myth, than to change my attitudes and behavior." She finally did change them by going back to work for the movement after a few months, thus completing her personal emancipation.⁶² The position paper Casey Hayden and Mary King submitted for debate at SNCC's Waveland retreat in 1964 proves that Burlage was no isolated case. In their "SNCC Position Paper: Women in the Movement," the two young women mainly stressed the analogy between racism and sexism they had become aware of as a result of their involvement with SNCC.⁶³ They insisted more particularly on work discrimination as they believed their contribution to the movement was not recognized in its full dimension because they were women. They thus declared: "This paper is presented anyway because it needs to be made known that many women in the movement are not 'happy and contented' with their status.... It needs to be known that just as Negroes were the crucial factor in the economy of the cotton South, so too in SNCC, women are the crucial factor that keeps the movement running on a day-to-day basis. Yet they are not given equal say-so when it comes to day-to-day decisionmaking." The authors were aware that the struggle against gender discrimination was not the priority at that time because conditions were not ripe for such a fight. Yet they seized the opportunity offered by the Waveland conference to express their concern freely in order to attract attention to the issue. In the concluding paragraph, they wrote: "Maybe the only thing that can come out of this paper is discussion—amidst the laughter—but still discussion." They hoped women who still did not recognize the issue would become aware of discrimination, declaring in their last sentence: "And maybe sometime in the future the whole of the women in this movement will become so alert as to force the rest of the movement to stop the discrimination and to start the slow process of changing values and ideas so that all of us gradually come to understand that this is no more a man's world than it is a white world."⁶⁴ Rather than expressing a complaint, such words constitute a call for positive action, a wish to build on the black liberation movement in order to complete the transformation of human relationships that had started with the fight against racism.

The paper, which is considered today as a founding text of the women's movement, went almost unnoticed at the time Hayden and King wrote it. Although some SNCC staff truly appreciated it, the prevailing reaction—as they had anticipated—was laughter. One year later, the two friends drafted a second paper in which they appealed to women as a group. In "Sex and

Caste: A kind of memo from Casey Hayden and Mary King to a number of other women in the peace and freedom movements," sent to the women of SDS, the NSA, the Northern Student Movement, the Student Peace Union, and SNCC, they expanded on the analogy between racism and sexism—although they did not use the latter term for the simple reason that it did not exist at the time. In addition, they called for more discussion about the issue in American society at large and for cooperation between women, especially black and white women, in the struggle for equality. They wrote: "Perhaps we can start to talk with each other more openly than in the past and create a community of support for each other so we can deal with ourselves and others with integrity and can therefore keep working."[65]

The interpretation of these two documents has been marked by controversy. With the development of the women's rights movement in the aftermath of the civil rights movement, historians—especially women—associated concepts with Hayden and King's views that the authors did not deem relevant in the context they had known. Among those misconceptions was the idea that women in SNCC naturally aspired to positions of leadership but were deliberately maintained in subordinate roles by male leaders. King corrects this view, as far as she is concerned, by writing:

> Our status in the movement was never the issue. Furthermore, this distortion overlooks the truly significant roles women played, the responsiveness of SNCC to women leaders before such an issue had been articulated, and the fact that, by and large, the movement was peopled by women; worst of all, it belies the seriousness and earnestness with which women in SNCC were involved and denies the important debate within SNCC that gave rise to our two documents.

As for Hayden, she echoes King's remarks by writing about the 1964 paper: "As the paper has entered the literature of feminism over the years, some historians have wondered if it exposed a struggle for power or leadership. Nonsense. We were all white. None of us were after leadership. That was for blacks. I believe we were speaking not for our private self-interest, but for all women, to share what we saw: that gender is a social construct, as is race."[66]

Another misinterpretation that the two women have taken pains to correct is the idea that they considered SNCC at the time as a patriarchal organization whose male chauvinism had alienated them over the years. They reacted in particular to the widely circulated account of a scene in which Stokely Carmichael had cracked a joke during the Waveland retreat, declaring in a roar of laughter that "the position of women in SNCC was prone," which caused hilarity in the group he was relaxing with after a day of debate. Hayden and King, who were part of the group, heartily defend Carmichael against charges of male chauvinism. Hayden declares, "Stokely sounds like a sexist, pure and simple, to any outsider. But he was quite the opposite.... Stokely was a friend of mine. We crossed paths in many settings, and talked often about many subjects. After he went to Africa, he sent me long letters on Marxism and feminism," to which King adds, "Casey and I felt, and continue to feel, that Stokely was one of the most responsive men at the time that our anonymous paper appeared in 1964." The issue of sexism within SNCC remains controversial to this day because it tends to tarnish the image of the organization by implying that it was not as egalitarian as it claimed to be. While it would be absurd to maintain that SNCC was immune from sexism, it is probably fair to say that its democratic functioning, especially the egalitarian streak that ran through the organization, encouraged women to challenge all the forms of discrimination they could identify, including gender prejudices. In fact, Hayden and King's critique can be considered a tribute to SNCC's essential spirit, as King comments: "The early SNCC values of personhood had nourished Casey's and my changing sense of ourselves. As old-timers, relatively speaking, Casey and I also thought we would take some responsibility to influence the debate on SNCC's identity and future." King describes the movement as a period of ferment for other social movements, including feminism: "While the civil rights movement and the people in it mirrored the conventions and stereotypes of the larger society, that movement was at the same time giving rise to a challenge from within it that would contribute to produce a successor movement." As for Hayden, she sees their critique as "a fine example of how the tools developed in analyzing racism were translated, inside SNCC itself, into an analysis of gender." She comments: "We had pierced the racist bubble and were seeing clearly. All things were open to question. As Bernice Reagon has said, 'SNCC was where it could happen.'" Dorothy Burlage also emphasizes the positive dimension of her own experience by observing retrospectively that she did not feel inhibited in any way, but that the movement provided the opportunity to break free from southern ladyhood. Belinda Robnett has found that other women's testimonies corroborate the above. She concludes that "rather than feeling oppressed and sexually exploited, the Black and White women interviewed for this study felt empowered by their participation in the Student Non-Violent Coordinating Committee, seeing themselves as unhampered by sexist constraints."[67] Thus, beyond the denunciation of sexism, white women's initial demand for gender equality, together with their retrospective comments, reveals the catalyzing role of the 1960s movement in these women's personal growth.

* * *

In conclusion, the younger generation of white southern activists was composed of students who spontaneously joined the nonviolent movement because it started during their college years, corresponded to their ideals, and provided the instant opportunity to repudiate their white supremacist education. Like their elders, second-generation activists were primarily motivated by moral ideals. Unlike them, however, they were not leaders in the struggle, nor did they benefit from any moral authority as white women. Moreover, the members of the younger generation did not respect southern social and racial norms. They deliberately chose to break segregationist laws in public and to go to jail if necessary. In doing so, they became alienated from their native communities, but forged bonds that liberated them from white supremacist culture. Finally, the 1960s movement brought forth a strong sense of sisterhood among the members of the younger generation, just as it reinforced the female bonds created in the previous decades. As a result, by the end of the segregation era, white southern women activists could seize the opportunity to escape the narrow definition of womanhood in which they had been trapped for more than a century. For many of them, the fight for racial equality had turned into a fight for human equality.

6

A Peculiar Brand of Feminism

By the late 1960s, white southern women still constituted an identifiable group distinct from the rest of the American female population. Although they had followed national trends by asserting themselves in a male-controlled society, few of them actually joined the radical feminist movement represented by women's liberation groups in the 1970s. Yet virtually all the previously examined antiracist activists who experienced the post–civil rights era fought for gender equality and strongly identified feminism as a central issue in their lives. The reasons for such a stance are to be found in these women's southern identity.[1]

The first factor accounting for this distinctiveness was the complex relationship of white southern women activists with their native region. Indeed, just as their identity was divided by their double status as oppressors and victims, their attitude to the South was characterized by an ambivalent tension between an urge to rebel against their culture and a sense of belonging to it, a tension reflecting the weight of southern history since the Civil War and affecting their definition of themselves. These women's attitude regarding gender issues paralleled their attitude regarding race insofar as they challenged the southern patriarchal order while claiming to reform it—to redeem it as far as many of them were concerned—not to destroy it, out of a deep attachment to their culture. From that perspective, the national feminist movement seemed in some respects irrelevant to their fight.

The second factor of distinctiveness—directly linked to the first—was the primacy of race over gender among southern female activists during and after the struggle for racial equality. This characteristic is obviously due to the extreme form of racial oppression that existed in the South in contrast to other parts of the United States. In a society where racism justified the lynching of black men in the name of the protection of white womanhood, it was hardly conceivable on the part of white women to equate sexism with racism. So, if many white female racial activists struggled with the constraints of gender during the fight for racial justice, they did not put this issue to the fore for some time. Ultimately, when legal segregation was abolished and when the feminist movement arose, they publicly endorsed the concept of gender equality and became committed to the cause of women's rights but saw the fight against sexism only as a corollary of the ongoing fight against racism, which remained a sore issue in the South in spite of the gains of the civil rights movement.

The unique character of white southern feminism was finally demonstrated by southern women's attitudes to the women's liberation movement. Indeed, the national movement that emerged from the 1960s was led by middle-class white women who had not experienced southern racism firsthand, and clearly gave priority to the fight against gender oppression over the fight against racism. As a result, many southern women, white and black, did not sympathize with this movement. Thus it appears that the women's liberation movement strengthened the bonds of southern sisterhood by pitting black and white women from the South against the most vocal national white feminist leaders.

Southern Women and the South

Here are the words Eliza Paschall wrote around 1970 for the *Great Speckled Bird*, a counterculture newspaper established in 1968 in Atlanta: "The main problem of the southern white woman, quite seriously and with no malice, is the southern white man.... Just as we say that whites cannot be free until blacks are free, we can say that men cannot be free until women are free. So help us down the statue, will you? As Lillian Smith so well pointed out in 'Killers of the Dream,' it's cold and lonely and not much fun on a pedestal."[2] This statement shows that, by the late 1960s, after more than a decade of struggle against segregation, Paschall had become a feminist. Her denunciation of female oppression, however, remained anchored in her southern experience. Her words point to the fact that, through her involvement in the civil rights movement, she was emancipated not so much from patriarchy per se as from white southern patriarchy. This was also the case of most of her fellow white female activists.

A major distinctive feature of white southern female activism in race relations was its nonconfrontational approach, based on the assumption that racial dissenters were not apostates but prophets in their beloved South. This characteristic can actually be extended to southern white women's activism in all other spheres, including gender issues. On the one hand, the women who challenged southern orthodoxy during the segregation era distanced themselves sufficiently from their native culture to challenge its norms, even to turn to outside forces such as the federal government or national organizations to defeat southern racism. Yet, on the other, they remained fundamentally loyal to the South and clearly identified with their fellow southerners when it came to defining themselves either in the course of informal exchanges with fellow southerners or nonsoutherners, or through autobiographical writing. Their personal evolution through the years of their adult lives was thus marked by a permanent tension between an urge to assert themselves as individuals—and as women—and a deeply ingrained sense of community bonding them to "their" people—that is, southerners.

Owing to their dissenting views on race, many of the white women considered in this book could appear as disloyal to their native culture. This trait was especially salient among the most radical female activists of the older generation such as Smith, Durr, and Braden. The bleak portrait of the segregationist South these women drew stood in stark contrast to the idealized picture conveyed by the myths of the Old South or the Lost Cause that remained powerful well into the twentieth century. Beyond the critical look they cast on their society, their relative lack of loyalty showed in the perspective they adopted throughout their adult lives, a perspective that crossed regional barriers to consider the South as an integral part of the nation.

Racism constituting their primary target, they presented the South as the region of the United States the most affected by it and called attention to the southern segregationist system as a dangerous disease for the whole nation. For instance, in 1953 Durr wrote to her friends Clark and Mairi Foreman, describing the region as a "vermiform appendix... swollen and tight with green, nasty, filthy, smelly pus and germs." She added: "[It] can infect the whole nation if we don't operate on it."[3] Durr's correspondence during the post-*Brown* decade reveals her somber vision of the South. During the school desegregation crisis, she wrote to Clark Foreman: "I think we have raised up a breed of real Nazis down here. I think it is the fault of your people and mine, the slave owners and the 'good families' who looked down on the Negroes, and you know it is true." In 1959, she did not seem to see any way out of the crisis, writing again to the Foremans: "Until people in the rest of the country realize that this southern situation is part of the overall rottenness that infects the country and stop thinking of us as different and do something toward making the Federal government and northern industry stand up and take definite action, all the pious good wishes really don't make any sense."[4] Durr and other women activists struggled in particular to correct misinterpretations about the South that resulted from the extremely polarized dimension of the debates about desegregation. They combated on two fronts to prove to the rest of the nation that a significant proportion of whites were not segregationists and needed outside help. They also wanted to show that middle-of-the-road liberals who did not favor federal coercion during the school desegregation crisis tended to overemphasize southern whites' readiness to implement the *Brown* decision.

The article Eliza Paschall wrote for the May 1960 issue of the *Atlantic Monthly* echoes Durr's point of view as it reflects her attempt to differentiate herself from the so-called southern point of view in the thick of white resistance to desegregation. The article starts with these words: "It is common practice among Southern spokesmen to refer to the 'Southern point of view.' Our Capitol in Atlanta resounds with speeches which say that all Georgians agree. And it is always stated or implied that what they all agree on is that our present system of a legally racially segregated society is best." Paschall goes on to expose her dissenting view: "I am a Southerner. From *my* point of view, not only does the U.S. Supreme Court have jurisdiction over Georgia, but the school decision was a correct one." In response to the various arguments put forward by the opponents of desegregation, she declares: "I do not set my standards of morality by what others do, in the North or in Chicago or in South Africa. I set them by what I believe in my heart, and I do believe in my heart that segregation is a disease that affects all parts of a being, human or political." She then distances herself from the southern white majority and from the opinion leaders who take this majority as their standard: "I do not agree with the 'realistic liberals,' who daily play the game which has as its primary rule: To be influential you must stay in the group. What influence do we have if we constantly yield to the pressure of 'This is not the time. It would cause trouble'?" Finally, in the closing sentence of the article, she blends her southern identity with her American one by asserting: "There is another Southerner whose view I would accept as my own. That Southerner is George Washington. The words are 'Let us raise a standard to which the wise and honest can repair.' The standard is the Constitution of the United States."[5]

The white women activists who were in the habit of corresponding with national politicians and opinion leaders struggled to convince them to stop compromising with the segregationist South, insisting on the fact that the South owed allegiance to the United States and its Constitution. Just as Durr corresponded with national politicians asking them to resort to federal means to break massive resistance, or as Braden set up national campaigns to guarantee the constitutional liberties of dissenters inside and outside the South, Paschall wrote to officials of the Kennedy administration to prod them into exerting pressure on southern authorities in favor of desegregation.[6]

The women tended to write in an increasingly reproachful tone as the desegregation crisis deepened in the early 1960s. For instance, in her letters to Burke Marshall—assistant attorney general for civil rights for the Kennedy administration—Durr expressed disapproval at appointments in the South of federal judges known for their segregationist leanings: "I believe you to be an honest man, I hear you are," she wrote in 1961, "and I think Robert Kennedy wants to do a good job, but how can we believe in any speeches when the MEN who are appointed are the worst enemies of integration?" In the same vein, Paschall wrote to Dean Rusk, secretary of state, in 1962, asking for the State Department to send representatives to Atlanta to discuss the local situation with the city's leaders—something federal officials refused to do unless they were formally invited. Her argument went as follows:

> We may be "underdeveloped" but we are not a foreign country, and it seems unnecessarily formal for the American government to wait for an invitation to send someone here in its behalf. The South has made progress, as any person who has been sick and is "getting better" has made progress, but—and I say this as a lifelong resident of South Carolina and Georgia—to permit us the luxury of setting our own pace of progress so completely out of step with the rest of the world is to grant to the South special privilege beyond the point of kindness.[7]

Paschall and others also resented the national media's tendency to publicize the positive image of the South provided by prominent southern liberals.

As Durr witnessed events from her parents-in-law's home in Montgomery—from the bus boycott to the Selma-to-Montgomery march of 1965—she despaired of southern whites' capacity to change, and she found in particular that the national media were too complacent with white resistance. She remarked to Clark Foreman: "I read the Sunday [*New York Times*] and the Nation and the New Republic and Izzy [I. F. Stone] and the Guardian and whatever else comes to hand, and I am continually amazed at the wishful thinking on the part of the rest of the country. They hail with delight when one Negro child among hundreds gets into a school, and do not realize nor seem to care that the screaming women in New Orleans are not just a small minority but represent the majority sentiment." As for Paschall, she complained to national newspaper editors about the rest of the nation being too understanding with white southerners. "As a native southerner," she wrote to John Oakes, from the *New York Times*, in 1962, "I think that non-southerners do us and the rest of the nation a great disservice to praise us for—what?.... If the rest of the nation would begin to expect more of us, demand more of us and stop 'understanding,' we might demand more of ourselves." Paschall went a step further in her "disloyalty" to the segregationist South when she wrote to Robert Hutchins, of the Fund for the Republic: "I think we should celebrate the Civil War centennial by having the rest of the country remember and act on the fact that the south [*sic*] lost the war! We are part of the United States and you all should expect us to act like Americans! You should *demand* that we act like Americans."[8]

To a certain extent, it can be argued that white southern women's activism was more radical in meaning than that of their male counterparts in all other racially progressive groups, which can also be attributed to women's more exacting loyalty to their region inasmuch as they seemed to be readier to challenge majority opinion. Guy and Guion Johnson provide an interesting illustration of this point. The couple was quite representative of southern white liberalism at mid-twentieth century. Guy was a prominent sociologist from the University of North Carolina at Chapel Hill, which was seen as a beacon of liberalism in the segregated South. In 1944, he was elected first executive director of the Southern Regional Council (SRC). The SRC's declared purpose was the achievement of "democracy and equality of opportunity," but the council did not initially condemn segregation as such. Johnson, like his SRC associates, sincerely believed in racial equality but was convinced that segregation was too entrenched in southern culture to be abolished immediately. According to the writer John Egerton, "Johnson was highly regarded in the black academic world, not only as a good scholar but also as a decent fellow, fair-minded and sympathetic," but he and other gradualist liberals were criticized by more advanced racial activists for compromising with an unjustifiable system. After Lillian Smith and black professor J. Saunders Redding publicly criticized the SRC in the magazine *Common Ground* for its failure to condemn segregation, Johnson responded in the next issue of the magazine that it was "more realistic to base a movement on the support of thousands who are willing to do something than on a few lonely souls who denounce injustice but are powerless to do anything about it." This position actually became untenable by the early 1950s, when the SRC shifted to the integrationist side, losing many of its white members in the move.

In contrast, Guion Johnson, who worked with Dorothy Tilly and was involved in social welfare, did not believe in gradualism. She commented on her husband's views in these terms: "His philosophy at that time was one of gradualism. That you cannot force the change upon an unwilling people. That it must be by enlightenment and education, that you gradually get a change and any change that comes gradually rather than quickly or dramatically is the change that is lasting." She disagreed with his position, saying: "I think there comes a time when some dramatic change must be made. And my own experiences have illustrated that." She was referring to a time at Chapel Hill when she had managed to obtain the creation of a child care center open to black children by ignoring the threats of a prominent white woman who could have used her influence against her.[9]

As far as the SRC is concerned, key women like Josephine Wilkins and Margaret Long—but also Frances Pauley, Eliza Paschall, and Joan Browning who headed Councils on Human Relations (CHRs) affiliated with the SRC—were closer to the radical wing of the civil rights movement than the organization's leadership. Wilkins was involved in the Southern Conference Educational Fund (SCEF) and was friends with individuals whom the SRC kept at a safe distance, such as James Dombrowski and Clark Foreman. Durr's letter to her in relation to the organization's hostility to radicals confirms that she was not identified with the moderate line of the SRC, which was clearly defined as conservative by the members of SCEF and the Student Nonviolent Coordinating Committee (SNCC).[10] The same observation can be made concerning other periods and groups. For instance, in 1920 the first executive director of the Commission on Interracial Cooperation, Will Alexander, supported the admission of women to the organization against the will of a majority of men because he had earlier realized that Methodist women were more committed to racial justice than men were. Actually, his first contacts with African Americans occurred when he became a member of the board of the Nashville Bethlehem House, which was administered by Methodist women. In 1930, a report on women's status in the church commissioned by the Methodist Woman's Missionary Council confirmed Alexander's opinion by asserting, "Women are more fearless in their attempts at civil and political reform ... because they are freer from entangling political alliances or obligations, and because they are less hampered by business interests and economic interrelationships."[11] Southern Methodist women proved that their loyalty to the southern dogma was limited when they became involved in federal efforts to undermine segregation in the 1940s.

Nevertheless, if white women reformers tended to be bolder than their male associates during the segregation era, the majority who favored suasion over confrontation always took care to adjust their activism to southern conditions, which is well illustrated by Tilly's attitude as one of the two southern members of the President's Committee on Civil Rights. As a southern woman, she expressed her disagreement about the tactics favored by the majority of the committee. She made it clear she was opposed to the continuance of segregation, but she rejected the idea of coercion as counterproductive owing to the South's attachment to states' rights and to the depth of racial prejudices in all southerners' minds. She was convinced that a frontal attack on segregation would "undo the social progress the South has made in the last twenty-five years." Admitting that "we cannot avoid facing the segregation," she suggested that the report "make it with a different approach," based on persuasion, an approach she had used for decades as a churchwoman.[12] However, when the final report openly called for the immediate end of segregation, she did not dissociate herself from it. From then on, she was seen in the South as a radical. Segregationists started harassing her, whereas hundreds of Methodist women expressed their admiration and thanked her for participating in their name in such a glorious action. Interestingly, one of the letters suggests that Tilly may have underestimated the readiness of some southerners to eliminate segregation, as its author wrote: "I was so glad your Committee used the word 'immediately' in regards to abolishing segregation. We too often try to excuse our inactivities, absolving our selves from all blame by thinking and preaching that action must not take place until the next generation."[13]

Tilly's example shows that, as paradoxical as it may seem, even when female activists distanced themselves from their native culture by calling for reform and outside help, they never stopped asserting their southern identity as well as their attachment to their region, placing themselves in a somewhat schizophrenic position. This applies particularly to those who wrote autobiographies or memoirs in the thick of the struggle against segregation. In her reflection on gender identity, Lillian Smith described autobiography as a privileged form of writing for women because, according to her, women were abler than men to apprehend the deepest meaning of life and death, and, most important, they approached life and the world in a more individual, personal way than men. As a result of these distinctive qualities, Smith continued, women were more likely than men to dissent from the culture in which they had been raised. From that perspective, autobiography could be interpreted as the assertion of the author's individuality against the culture of her community. In 1962, she thus declared in a speech: "Southern women have never been as loyal to the ideology of race and segregation as have southern men. The southern woman has always put the welfare of one individual above the collective welfare or collective values."[14] That a significant number of white women—notably Katharine Du Pre Lumpkin, Lillian Smith, Sarah Patton Boyle, and Anne Braden—wrote their autobiographies between 1946 and 1962 testifies to the situation of crisis in which they found themselves as integrationist women in a segregationist society. Through these personal narratives, they could assert their identities as racial dissenters and as white women raised in a white supremacist society while setting their experience within the collective frame of southern history and culture. This allowed them to liberate themselves from the norms of segregationist culture without repudiating their southern heritage.

The historian Elizabeth Fox Genovese has pointed out the distinctiveness of southern authors in the field of female autobiography. According to her, rather than emphasizing their gender identity in their writings as female autobiographers usually do, southern women define themselves first as members of the southern region: "Even after the abolition of slavery and the defeat of the South, southern women remained uncommonly concerned with the history of their region as an aspect of their own identities. For many generations, no southern woman autobiographer wrote of her self [*sic*] without explicit reference to social and historical conditions." This statement perfectly fits the four books published by Lumpkin, Smith, Braden, and Boyle in 1946, 1949, 1958, and 1962, respectively.[15]

The first characteristic of these works is that they reflect in their very titles the collective perspective chosen by their authors. The four titles actually do not refer directly to the authors' lives but to the segregated South of which the authors are an integral part. As Jacquelyn Dowd Hall rightly notes, through the title *The Making of a Southerner*, Lumpkin does not ask "Who am I?" but "Who are we and how can we use both memory and history to reinvent our regional identities?"[16] As for the other titles, they do not point to the authors' lives but to segregation. Smith's *Killers of the Dream* and Braden's *The Wall Between* refer to the destructive dimensions of the system, while Boyle's *The Desegregated Heart* focuses on her rejection of it. If Boyle seems to present her story as an individual act of emancipation, however, she places it in the collective perspective of her state and her community through the subtitle, *A Virginian's Stand in Time of Transition*.

Autobiography serves several functions in the case of these women, the first one being to identify the causes of their moral ordeal as white southerners and to escape the influence of their culture through the expiatory act of writing. Hence their insistence on the determining role of southern education and its main institutions—the family, church, and school.[17] While describing the elements of segregationist culture common to all southerners, the authors subtly proceed to distance themselves from this culture by inserting comments stressing the contradictions inherent in it without indicting their fellow southerners explicitly. Lumpkin, for instance, plays on the pronouns "I" and "we" to convey the idea that, although she clearly establishes herself as a victim and considers all other southerners as such, she also points out a collective guilt shared by all whites, which each individual should face as she does. Smith also alternates the use of "I" and "we" throughout her narrative. She announces in the opening pages: "In this South I lived as a child and now live. And it is of it that my story is made. I shall not tell, here, of experiences that were different and special and belonged only to me, but those most white southerners born at the turn of the century share with each other." Boyle makes it clear in a preliminary note to her volume that she does not stand in opposition to her native region: "The book is not an indictment of the South, of my community, of any organization, or any individual."[18]

Beyond personal emancipation, the four authors clearly aimed at redeeming the South from its sins, which accounts for their insistence on their "southernness." The publication of their personal stories during the desegregation crisis represented a militant act. It constituted a means to prove to other southern whites that they could reject white supremacy without losing their southern identity. Thus the women set themselves up as "models of the possible" by depicting their conversion from racists to integrationists.[19] To make their point, they took pains to show that southern culture contained within itself the seeds of redemption, thus invalidating the idea that repudiating white supremacy was an act of betrayal. Accordingly, Lumpkin declares in the last pages of her book: "We may say of the very ideals of my personal childhood rearing that they were potentially explosive taken in their combination.... We may point to religion, and the way it was turned around on itself—for me, I mean—so that its high authority was fallen back on to justify the very acts which our Southern teaching had told us were unjustifiable." She concludes by pointing to the existence of a different South, peopled with black and white individuals believing in universal equality, a South that could prevail if given the chance: "It took a fresh reading of our past to find buried there not a little that told of the strivings of these various Southerners after a different South. As it came about, it was this different South that in the end drew me towards my refashioning, even as my Old South receded even farther into history."[20]

Smith resorts to a more indirect way of conveying the same fundamental belief in the existence of a nonracist South, as she relates how she helped white girls who attended her summer camp in the 1930s and 1940s to unlearn the lessons of white supremacy. Recalling her conversation with one of them, she writes: "'You have to remember,' I said, 'that the trouble we are in started long ago. Your parents didn't make it, nor I. We were born into it.'" She closes the story with these words: "We were tired. It was late. I told her we would talk again another time. I told her there were ways out of the trap, things were changing a little, and people could change anything, even segregation, if they really wanted to."[21] As for Braden, she reflects: "White Southern society had injected much that was poison into my lifeblood.... But it had also had its ideals, and I had inherited those too. One of these was the principle that no man can live for himself alone, that each man has a responsibility to his fellow man." In her concern to downplay the radical dimension of her fight so that her readers could identify with her, she goes on to write: "Many people have tried to explain me by saying I learned the things I believe in from the radical movements of our day. But the basic things I know and believe in I learned, paradoxically enough, from the institutions of the white South." She then shifts from her own experience to the collective potential for change: "I find that I cannot completely write off the undeveloped potential of a society that still at least teaches its children a sense of obligation to all other children of the world."[22]

Boyle's narrative is probably the most pessimistic one because she wrote it after going through the ordeal of massive resistance, harassment, and failure to rally her community to her cause. Yet, like the other authors, she credits southern culture with providing her with the fundamental moral values that ultimately led her to commit her life to racial equality. Referring to her aristocratic lineage, she describes the vision she had inherited of the ideal man: "He was one whose glory was an inner glory, one who placed culture above prosperity, fairness above profit, generosity above possessions, hospitality above comfort, courtesy above triumph, courage above safety, kindness above personal welfare, honor above success." In spite of her undeniable bitterness in the face of the bigotry she had directly suffered from, she admitted to having "a feeling of roots reaching far back—and far forward—into history." She explained: "I was taught to think of myself as a part of the very backbone of Virginia, which was the backbone of the South, which was the backbone of the nation, which was the backbone of the world. In the years ahead, when Southern editorial pages not infrequently demanded that I leave the South, I was grateful for the indoctrination that my roots were strong and deep."[23] Thus, even when they despaired of the white South's potential for redemption, the white women who wrote about their experiences never contemplated repudiating their southern roots as an act of personal liberation.

As for the others who did not undertake to write about themselves during the desegregation era, they nourished the same perspective as southern women intent on redeeming their beloved South. In her study of the student YWCA in the 1920s and 1930s, Frances Taylor emphasizes the student secretaries' concern to serve as role models for other white southern students:

Appreciative of the fact that their own beliefs and actions carried them far from the traditional path for white women set forth in southern lore, the southern secretaries went to great lengths to trace their radicalism back to some aspect of their southern upbringing. By parading their southern credentials, the secretaries wished to demonstrate to young white college women the strong possibility of their own conversion. Repeated instruction in white supremacist ideology, in the Confederate Cause, and in the tenets of fundamentalist Christianity justified their claims to being true southerners who had every right to stand in judgment of their native region.[24]

Indeed, Katharine Lumpkin, who served as secretary in the 1920s, adopted the same posture in her work for the YWCA as she did years later in her autobiography.

Identification with southern tradition gave these dissenting southern daughters legitimacy while enabling them to negotiate their own conversion, implying a permanent inner struggle. Even after World War II, whereas the civil rights movement gained momentum, the women who supported the implementation of the *Brown* decision by no means rejected their southern heritage. Some may have overacted their role as perfect southern ladies out of tactical concerns, but there was never any doubt as to their identification with the South. As an illustration, Sara Murphy, of the Women's Emergency Committee (WEC), remembers that WEC meetings were held in Adolphine Terry's living room under the portrait of Terry's father in Confederate uniform. "His portrait established that we were not outsiders plotting against the South," she writes, "but indigenous women who knew it was time to change. There was something reassuring and solid about having him there, but something even more solid and reassuring about his white-haired, gracious descendant, whose sparkling eyes and slight smile told us that she was already chuckling inwardly about what she knew we could do together." Among the younger generation, Joan Browning once observed about Anne Braden: "[Anne was] one of the small group of [older] women who showed me that one could be a loyal Southerner and a respectable woman while fighting for social justice. The fact that Anne was Southern to the bone and had that wonderful slow Southern speech helped me redefine myself."[25] There is no doubt, then, that the white women who stood up to segregationists did not so much repudiate the South as they did one particular South, the racist South, in which they did not recognize themselves, convinced as they were that the nonracist South was only less vocal.

This attachment to the South came out whenever white southern women found themselves in the presence of northerners or in a position to compare northerners and southerners. For all their opposition to segregationist culture, they did not hesitate to take their stand as southerners, all the more so when northerners expressed contempt of or hostility to the South. In 1936, for instance, Juliette Morgan wrote for the *Montgomery Advertiser* a half-serious response to a statement made by a northern woman, in which the latter had criticized "the whining, complaining and complacency" of southern women. Morgan described the woman (and northern women) in these words: "We Southerners know her type well, . . . energetic, immaculate, sturdy, honest, democratic, and keen, but often brusque, officious, pushy captains of industry with the voices of drill sergeants. We could learn from them, and we know it—most of us. They could learn from us, and they don't know it. And that's where we have it over them."[26]

Virginia Durr was much more serious-minded when she wrote to a *New Yorker* journalist who had talked with her husband and her in 1960 as part of an investigation of the racial situation in the South. Virginia was indignant at him for publishing the conversation, which the couple had wanted to stay off the record given the hostility they were suffering from at the time. She wrote: "We told you we stay here because we like the people here, in spite of our disagreements, they are our own people. I will say in all sincerity that we feel in the Southern people some sense of personal loyalty and integrity in personal relations." She then shifted from the individual case to a collective attack: "We much prefer to trust ourselves to them, rather than to northern 'liberals' like yourself who do not hesitate to sacrifice individuals to a 'cause' in their own interest. We also prefer to be hit from in front rather than from the rear." Durr confirmed her identification with the South on several occasions, as when she wrote to her friends Glenn and Vann Woodward in 1967:

> I really have come to the conclusions that reconstructed Southerners are the most attractive people there are, they are not self-righteous like so many of our Yankee friends, they know from experience the ease of evil ways, and the difficulty breaking away from them, all of us have had

to pay for our convictions so they are not held lightly, and I am of the opinion, which of course is very conceited that we emancipated Southerners are really prizes!

Durr obviously sensed at heart what Vann Woodward had conceptualized as "the burden of southern history." Her daughter recently summed up the paradoxical nature of her position in the following terms: "She was by nature contradictory and controversial as she tried to find balance between her intellectual and spiritual needs and her fury and sadness at not belonging to a society which she simultaneously condemned and yet for which she wanted approval."[27]

Finally, the members of the new generation, although they challenged southern tradition in a more open way than their elders, also felt a strong sense of identification with the South and tended to affirm their southernness when it came to defining themselves. As an illustration, when Joan Trumpauer was jailed with a group of Freedom Riders in June 1961, she wrote in her diary: "I think all the girls in here are gems but I feel more in common with the Negro girls & wish I was locked with them instead of these atheist Yankees—particularly when they sing."[28] Such a statement reveals that southern culture was a stronger influence than race in the shaping of some southern women's identity. Drawing a similar contrast between southerners and northerners, Joan Browning wrote to Vincent Harding and a group of northern volunteers based in Atlanta:

> If I could say one thing to you, as "damn Yankees" coming to work in the South, the land I dearly love, it would be this: As you witness every day the evils which the white Southerner has inflicted upon his darker brother, maintain some awareness that the white Southerner has suffered in this system. Too many Yankees have a missionary zeal for destroying the system which has some inherent evils admittedly, and their zeal blinds them to the awareness that Southern people are basically good, cordial, hospitable people. The tales of "Southern hospitality" are real and are reflective of a gentle people. In your efforts to reform the South, work with the thesis that the system, not the people, is evil.

Browning's insistence on white southerners' inherent "goodness" reveals her profound attachment to her regional identity. Her letter actually recalls the autobiographical narratives previously examined by revealing white southern women's unique position. Just like her elders, she rejected key elements of her native culture, but grounded her action in the culture itself, moved by feelings and ideas she had first experienced as part and parcel of her southern identity. To put it another way, she found at the core of southern culture the inspiration for destroying the unacceptable traits of this culture. This is what Browning means when she says retrospectively, "I was not rebelling against my culture, merely trying to help overcome its most glaring faults."[29] However, such a position could appear untenable, for white supremacy was so closely identified with the "southern way of life" in everybody's minds that destroying one might necessarily imply destroying the other. Hence there was a definite ambivalence in those women's position.

The gap between northern and southern freedom activists widened after the massive influx of northern white volunteers to Mississippi in 1964. As a result of this development, the small group of white southern women who had worked with SNCC since the early days of the organization felt estranged from their northern counterparts. Southern activists knew that the presence of white women among blacks in the Deep South was not to be taken lightly. In contrast to women of southern backgrounds such as Casey Hayden, Connie Curry, Jane Stembridge, Dorothy Burlage, Joan Browning, and Mary King, most of the northern white women who volunteered to participate in Freedom Summer in 1964 ignored the prescriptions of southern culture, which could have tragic consequences. Curry later explained: "That's what used to make us mad about some of the White women who would come from the North. This was all very new and very romantic and very titillating for them. And a lot of us resented the fact that they didn't know that they were putting these young Black men at high risk." As Belinda Robnett found out in the interviews she conducted for her study: "White women raised in the South approached the movement with a knowledge of the region's social taboos and norms. According to the interviewees, both Black and White northern newcomers were unfamiliar with southern ways of life and history.... Southern White women—more than those from the North or other regions of the United States—understood these southern strictures." Dorothy Burlage recently reinforced this idea by observing that black and white southern women distinguished themselves from nonsoutherners by having the same religious background, commitment to family, food habits, and manners.[30] Such differences testify to the preexistence of a southern sisterhood within the civil rights movement, based on a cultural background that set black and white southern women apart from their nonsouthern sisters. As a matter of fact, the black and white women who had grown up in the segregated South and struggled together for racial equality in their region shared a common outlook, a common attitude to life, a common definition of activism as community-oriented, and a common conception of leadership as based on grassroots work.

Finally, whether considering the older or the younger generation, one invariably finds out that southern white female dissenters constantly struggled with an inner tension between, on the one hand, a will to assert themselves as individuals by confronting their native segregationist culture and, on the other, a fundamental identification with their region mainly inherited from history. Their moral conscience placed them at odds with the collective ideology of the white South, an ordeal that long prevented them from challenging all social norms in an outspoken way. This was true of gender as well as of racial norms.

Race over Gender

White southern women's perception of themselves and of their gender could not be dissociated from their southern identity, meaning obviously that it could not be dissociated from race either. This characteristic makes it difficult to apply to them the now classical concepts of sexism or patriarchy commonly used to account for women's evolution in the late twentieth century. Most of the white women who fought for racial equality in the South up to the late 1960s can be defined as de facto feminists inasmuch as they undermined, and in many cases rebelled against, traditional gender norms. Yet at first sight they do not seem to qualify as full-fledged feminists. As far as the older generation is concerned, some of its members participated in the feminist movement of the early twentieth century, and many of them were concerned about their female status in a society led by men. The members of the younger generation experienced the second wave of feminism that originated in the 1960s and embraced the cause of women's rights in the process. Yet many gave priority to race over gender in their struggle for equal rights.

Although the conditions of southern politics and culture in the early twentieth century did not favor the development of a strong feminist movement in the region, several first-generation reformers embraced the fight for women's political rights. Jessie Daniel Ames, for instance, was a suffragette leader in Texas in the 1910s. Adolphine Fletcher Terry, whose sister was president of her local suffrage league in Little Rock, Arkansas, participated in equal rights campaigns with her. Virginia Durr's introduction to political activism took the form of volunteer work for the Women's Division of the Democratic National Committee in the late 1930s. She explains in her autobiography that there were no southern women at that time on any local Democratic committees in the South, which led the Women's Division to center its work on the problem of the poll tax. Durr observes that blacks' voting rights were not the issue then: "The goal of the Women's Division was to get rid of the poll tax so that Southern women could vote. There was no mention in the Democratic Committee at that time of black people. And there were no Negroes around the Women's Division. Of course, very few black people in the South voted, but the Southern white women didn't vote either."[31] After the passage of the Nineteenth Amendment, many white southern women who gradually became involved in racial reform also struggled for women's civil rights by joining the local and state Leagues of Women Voters, as did Jessie Daniel Ames, Lucy Randolph Mason, Josephine Wilkins, Adolphine Fletcher Terry, and Frances Pauley, among others. Given these facts, it would not be accurate to assert that southern women were not interested in women's issues. In fact, although they were not vocal in this field, they were nevertheless concerned enough to participate in civic groups early in the twentieth century, and, when their involvement in racial reform increased, they naturally blended the two causes of racial and gender equality in their activism. Durr recognized this point when she retraced her personal experience. Commenting on her New Deal years, she reflected: "I was also slowly becoming something of a feminist. I had had a great resentment, I now realize, of the role that Southern girls had to play. Nice Southern girls were supposed to try to get husbands, and so they were always fooling the men and being pleasant and putting up with almost anything to be popular." The women cited above would no doubt have agreed with this statement. As for Durr, she adds: "My resentment hadn't come to the surface yet. It was still gestating inside of me. But I must have felt it, because I plunged into the fight to get rid of the poll tax for the women of the South with the greatest gusto."[32]

Through these comments, Durr reveals a typical feature of white southern women's positions on gender before the 1960s—that is, a striking discrepancy between their public and their private discourse on the issue. Actually, if one considers those who expressed their views in public life or in published writings, one will hardly find any open reference to gender, whereas the same women's private correspondence tells an altogether different story. This does not apply to the literature of the Association of Southern Women for the Prevention of Lynching (ASWPL) since the organization based its action and discourse on the denunciation of false chivalry, but the irony is that in doing so the members of the ASWPL precisely rejected the gendered rhetoric of southern womanhood. Even Lillian Smith, who stood as an exception in many respects and denounced patriarchy early in her career, proportionally devoted a strikingly small part of her published writings to the issue of women. When she did broach the issue, as in *Killers of the Dream*, she systematically combined her reflection on gender with her reflection on race. Leaving aside one essay cowritten with Paula Snelling in 1941, it was only in the early 1960s that she devoted full speeches and essays exclusively to women.[33]

Two reasons seem to account for this gap between public and private discourse. On the one hand—as Durr's above-mentioned comment clearly reveals—the women were not fully aware before the 1960s of all the implications of their female identity in their lives. On the other, supposing that they were, they were not ready to challenge their society by voicing their frustration or discontent aloud. Significantly, when Durr's friend Jessica Mitford encouraged her in 1960 to write her autobiography, she responded: "I really don't think I have the time, energy or discipline to do it. Then I lack what you have in such abundance, and that is the courage to tell the truth about people and my life. I still live among them, I have not escaped them as you have and never will."[34] This statement reveals that as long as the civil rights crisis lasted, the pressure for social conformity was such that writing about oneself amounted to an uncommon act of courage. It was all the more so for female racial dissenters who took the twofold risk of breaking racial and gender taboos by expressing their deepest personal views.

As a matter of fact, several women of the two generations published autobiographies or memoirs, either during the crisis, as did Lumpkin, Smith, Braden, and Boyle, or years after the end of the civil rights movement and the development of the second feminist movement, as did, notably, Durr, Parsons, King, Hayden, Curry, Burlage, Browning, and Thrasher. A comparison of the two groups of works illuminates the evolution of white southern women's identity in relation to their treatment of race, gender, and southern culture. In the earlier works, the authors set their narrative within the framework of southern society and culture. Their main emphasis is on the culture of white supremacy. Thus their self-definition hinges primarily on their southernness and on their whiteness. If the notion of womanhood is not altogether absent from the books, it only appears marginally and in an impressionistic way. Lumpkin, for instance, devotes a little more than a page to describing the somewhat ambivalent nature of her family's position on the issue of women's place. "In some sense," she remarks, "it remained with us the woman's part to sit silent when men were speaking; not to pit our opinions against the more knowing male's; indeed, to look on woman as a figure on a pedestal—Southern woman, that is—to be treated accordingly; even to regard her as a creature of intuition, who was meant to lean her feeble strength on the firm, solid frame of a male protector and guide." But she adds: "Yet in our family circle the something different had crept in to counter this. It was a saying with us, carrying all the weight of my father's prestige and my mother's training: 'Those who have brains are meant to use them;' As a result, no real distinction in this regard was made between boys and girls." Note that even in this passage, which is just about the only one referring to womanhood, Lumpkin does not write in the first person but describes the family's view through the use of a collective "we."[35]

Smith's *Killers of the Dream* and Boyle's *The Desegregated Heart* devote more space to the constraints of southern womanhood, but they do not dissociate the concept from white supremacist culture. Braden's case is even more telling as it reveals a deliberate effort to tone down an acute feminist consciousness in order to give priority to the cause of racism. This seems to have been a common tendency among many women activists of the older generation. While Braden's memoir, *The Wall Between*, is virtually devoid of references to her gender, her behavior and her private correspondence throughout her adult life testify to her concern to assert herself as a woman. She could not be more explicit when she wrote to a friend in 1962: "Women, like Negroes, still aren't totally free.... In fact, I think that my next crusade—after we integrate—will be to see if we can't win real freedom for my sex. In a way, I'm working on the two battles simultaneously, I guess." Her biographer remarks that she "possessed a gender consciousness that in 1960 far exceeded that of most SNCC students, and few of the younger women probably realized at the time what an unconscious model of female opposition she functioned as for them." Braden did not publicize this gender consciousness, however, although she expressed it occasionally in private.[36]

In 1963, for instance, SNCC and SCEF were looking for a new white person to replace Robert Zellner as director of a project in Mississippi.[37] Braden thought of Dorothy Burlage and of Joan Browning, among others, but SNCC's chairman, Chuck McDew, was clear in his refusal to give the position to a woman. Braden reported the incident to Browning in a letter: "I recall last spring, when they thought Bob was going back to school *this* year, Chuck McDew asked me to be on the lookout for somebody for them, and I said, 'It doesn't have to be a man, does it?' Whereupon he looked at me in horror, as if to say 'What other kind of creature is there in the world?' So to explain myself further, I said, 'I mean, it could be a girl, couldn't it?' At that he looked even more horrified and answered in just one word: 'No.'" Braden goes on to comment: "My feminist blood was boiling—but at that moment we were in the courthouse in Magnolia, Miss., of all places, for the McComb trials, and surrounded by the enemy, so I did not feel that it was the time or place to have a full-dressed argument with him. So I just said, 'OK. But when you all get ready to fight for the whole human race, let me know.'" Braden's private account proves that her unconditional support for SNCC and her choice to give priority to the fight against racism did not prevent her from disapproving of what she perceived as a form of gender discrimination, which accounts for her warning to Browning: "If you should apply though, you should probably be prepared to have to overcome their male supremacy." In this particular incident, Braden might have misinterpreted McDew's refusal as sexism whereas it could well have arisen from SNCC leaders' sensitivity to the real risks civil rights workers were running in Mississippi at the time, and they were reluctant to send women to reputedly dangerous areas. In any case, the point is that Braden *was* concerned about gender even though she played her concern down.[38]

The women of the older generation actually evolved toward a gender-oriented discourse after the early 1960s. Especially interesting is the contrast between the autobiographies published since then and those published earlier.

Durr's and Parson's are two cases in point. Durr published *Outside the Magic Circle* in 1985. Parsons published *From Southern Wrongs to Civil Rights* in 2000. By that time, the two women had witnessed the federal abolition of legal segregation and the growth of the women's liberation movement, inevitably impacting their general outlook. As a result, although their narratives, like earlier works, remained deeply rooted in southern culture, the emphasis had shifted from race and the South to gender and the South. The title Durr had initially chosen, *The Emancipation of Pure White Southern Womanhood*, speaks for itself. As for Parsons, she writes in her introduction: "I want readers to see the movement and its key personalities from my perspective as a woman and a southerner." This change in perspective attests to the evolution of the authors' perception of their gender between the segregation era and the post–civil rights movement era.[39]

Although Durr and Parsons were clearly not ready at mid-twentieth century to tell their personal stories as southern women, their private writings show that they were concerned about their white female identity long before the issue became public, but that they reserved their militant energy for the racial issue. Parsons went public on race in the early 1960s when she was elected to Atlanta's Board of Education as an integrationist candidate. She obviously concentrated on race throughout the 1960s, but the diary she kept in 1964 reveals that she was privately fighting to emancipate herself as a woman throughout the battle for racial equality. It is significant that she included extracts from this diary in the memoir she published in 2000.

Her personal emancipation could only be completed after the actual publication of her story. She could then cast a different look on her experience through the civil rights movement by incorporating into the memoir the impact of the women's movement on her evolution. Thus she devotes a whole chapter to the issue of gender. In "Men Don't Like Women on Boards," she not only reflects with hindsight on gender discrimination at the time she became involved in the movement, but she also uses her example to emphasize the specific contribution of white women to the struggle against segregation. She notably writes: "Although Atlanta's white, liberal-on-race women have never received credit, I believe that we made a real contribution. While we may not have been heroes on the front line, we offered heavy backup support for those who were. We helped black civil rights workers bring about integration of schools and public accommodations, often at considerable personal cost."[40]

Up to the 1960s, Durr made herself known for her radical views on segregation and never broached the issue of gender in public. Yet her correspondence during the desegregation crisis demonstrates that even if she gave priority to the fight against racism, she struggled constantly with the issues raised by her being a white woman born and raised in the segregated South. In 1961, she wrote to Jessica Mitford, who had expressed a wish to write a book about the South: "In fact 'Southern Womanhood' would be a real field. Think of the contrast between fact and fiction there! . . . I think the South is so complex and varied that you will have to try to get it through some one angle and it may be that the women of the South will be the best angle to see it clearly." Thus Durr may have rebelled against her native culture in many ways, but she could not conceive of exploring southern identity without studying southern womanhood—by which she definitely meant "white womanhood."[41]

The evolution of Durr's attitude regarding the issue of gender shows up in the few already mentioned articles she published in the 1960s and 1970s. The resurgence of the rhetoric of chivalry and defense of white southern womanhood that accompanied resistance to school desegregation seems to have been the catalyst for her new stance on the issue. Indeed, the piece she wrote in 1962 for *New South*, "In the Name of Southern Womanhood," is significant of a shift in her general outlook. Interestingly, she still identified herself as a southern lady at that time, and the use of a pen name (Eliza Heard) suggests that she was reluctant to take a public stand on this issue. Yet it constituted a first step in her public involvement in women's issues. She took the next step in 1971 with the publication of "The Emancipation of Pure, White, Southern Womanhood" under her maiden name, Virginia Foster. The final publication of her full-length autobiography—based on oral interviews conducted between 1975 and 1977—in 1985 completed a process started decades earlier.[42]

The members of the younger generation did not have to repress their feminist impulses for as long as their elders because the women's liberation movement emerged in large part from the civil rights movement in which they participated. The white southern women who joined blacks in the civil rights movement of the 1960s actually found in the movement the means to liberate themselves from traditional gender norms along with other norms, as Hayden's and King's examples have shown, but the struggle against sexism never superseded the fight against racism in their experiences. As a matter of fact, when they analyzed the movement decades later, Hayden and King adopted a similar perspective to that of Parsons and Durr, for they included an examination of gender in their narratives, which otherwise emphasized the significance of their white southern background in their lives and activism. If gender clearly features as an important dimension of all late twentieth- and early twenty-first-century narratives, it is only one among others, namely race, class, and southern culture. This characteristic is what distinguishes many white southern women from the activists who launched the women's liberation movement in the late 1960s and led the fight for gender equality in the following decades.

Southern Women and the Women's Liberation Movement

"We women in SCEF agree with you that 'sisterhood is powerful' and we consider all of you in the New York women's liberation movement our sisters. Therefore, we feel that it would perhaps be helpful to our mutual understanding if you knew a bit of the history of the development of SCEF's women's liberation project and the thinking of the SCEF women on this question."[43] These were the words Anne Braden wrote circa 1970 to Kathie Amatniek, a former white volunteer in Mississippi who became a leader of the new feminist movement in New York. As it turned out, the cultural gap that seemed to prevent mutual understanding between northern and southern women activists continued to separate the two groups in the following decades. As the women's liberation movement developed and as its vocal radical wing singled out patriarchy as the most fundamental form of oppression in all societies, many southern white female activists could not see the point of turning away from the cause to which they had dedicated the major part of their early years and which they considered far from settled.

By the late 1960s, gender had no doubt become a central issue for white southern women activists. Hayden and King had written their memo in 1965 in an attempt to get women to unite against discriminatory social patterns, a document that is considered by many as a manifesto for the women's liberation movement.[44] Women's liberation groups were formed across the South. The women of the Southern Student Organizing Committee (SSOC) organized a conference on women's liberation in Atlanta. The letter of invitation they sent to hundreds of female students across the South explained: "In response to increasing discussion and concern about women's problems, in society and in the movement, many women, actively working for social change on southern campuses, have expressed interest in coming together to further the dialogue." According to the historian Christina Greene, "between 120 and 180 women from eleven southern states met in Atlanta from February 7 through 9, 1969, for the first southern meeting on women's liberation." Anne Braden, who was present, recalled that "the participants were all white and almost entirely middle class." Throughout the year, women organized liberation groups on southern campuses in Arkansas, Mississippi, North Carolina, Virginia, and South Carolina.[45] Several of the women who had participated in the civil rights movement became involved in women's organizations. Sue Thrasher recalls that she joined such a group in Atlanta as well as the Women's Caucus of the underground newspaper the *Great Speckled Bird*. Eliza Paschall was also involved in the *Great Speckled Bird*. In addition, she served as national secretary of the National Organization for Women (NOW) in the early 1970s. She also worked for the Equal Employment Opportunity Commission (EEOC) between 1966 and 1984—she notably served as regional representative of the Federal Women's Program in Atlanta. Paschall was also appointed to the Georgia Commission on the Status of Women, one of the many state commissions established in the 1960s after President Kennedy appointed the first one at the national level in 1961. As another example, Mary King was a founder of the National Association of Women Business Owners, and became its president in 1976. She received a Distinguished Achievement Award from the Women's Equity Action League in 1977; was a member of the U.S. delegation to the multilateral World Conference on Women, Copenhagen, in July 1980; and was inducted into the National Women's Hall of Fame in 1992.[46]

Yet the issue of racism remained the main concern for southern women. Cynthia Washington, a former black member of SNCC, explained in 1977: "To me, it was not a matter of whether male/female oppression existed but one of priorities. I thought it more important to deal with the folks and the system which oppressed both black women and black men." Several of the white women who had worked with SNCC shared Washington's view. In her later thoughts on the 1965 memo, Hayden stresses both the importance of gender in her eyes and her refusal to consider it in an exclusive way. She describes the text in these words: "It doesn't blame anyone, but suggests women organize themselves toward ownership of this issue and their lives. It reflects both a realization of the gendered self as a political reality and a struggle against the tendency to see everything through the lens of that realization." Braden's letter to Amatniek echoes Hayden's remark, broadening the perspective of women's liberation to an improvement of society and ultimately of humankind at large: "We [SCEF women] believe profoundly that women organized can change not only our own situation but the entire world—and certainly the South in which we work." Braden and other southern activists did not separate women's issues from other issues, as the new radical feminists did. The corollary of this view was that women's liberation did not necessarily require focusing on women's issues: "We believe that for many women the starting point of this new freedom and strength may not start with a so-called women's issue at all."[47]

Such divergence in views was first of all ideological, as SCEF was a radical leftist organization whose main target by the late 1960s had become capitalism, but it was also due to the southern context in which white women had come to face the issue of gender identity and emancipation. They actually sensed the differences separating them from the white women who lived in other parts of the country. Burlage recalls that, although she became involved in the women's movement, she did not identify with "northern" women. She was "repulsed," she says, by their "anger" and "stridency." In her 2000 essay, she explains: "As a southern woman, my issues seemed different from those of the northern SDS women I knew in Washington." The difference, she adds, was one of cultural background: "Coming from liberal or left-wing families where they were encouraged to be political, they resented the limitations they felt in SDS. I usually felt, in contrast, that I needed to struggle with myself against the limitations of my Old South upbringing, and even then, most of the southern white women in the movement with whom I was friends were from homes that were more liberal than mine and in which it was more acceptable for them to be politically outspoken." As for Joan Browning, her response to the question of what her position on feminism had been since the emergence of the women's liberation movement was: "It ain't my movement. My efforts center always on overthrowing white supremacy."[48]

Southern women's relative lack of identification with Betty Friedan's *The Feminine Mystique*, first published in 1963, partakes of the same distinctiveness. Friedan's book, which became a major reference for the new generation of feminists, described the condition of middle-class, suburban white American women in the post–World War II era. Not surprisingly, black women did not recognize themselves in this depiction of womanhood, and neither did many white southern antiracist activists—although there were exceptions.[49] Sue Thrasher remembers: "I read *The Feminine Mystique* when I was working for SSOC, desperately looking for something that would tell me I wasn't crazy for feeling angry at times. But Betty Friedan's words weren't for me; they did not speak to a farm girl who grew up working the land and whose mother labored in a factory." Mary King confirms this view when commenting on her own feminist awakening during her exchanges with Casey Hayden and Dorothy Burlage. "Betty Friedan's *The Feminine Mystique*, which sent shock waves across American suburbs that same year, seemed irrelevant and marginal to us," she writes. "Although I later realized its significance with some sectors of American women, it was amazing to us that black women in the United States were not cited once. . . . Friedan's suburban emphasis seemed out of touch with the social and economic issues that concerned us and utterly unrelated to the questions of political and personal self-determination that were beginning to preoccupy us." Thrasher's and King's reactions to Friedan's work, by emphasizing the author's ignorance of economic and racial factors in her reflection on oppression, reveal the impact of their southern background and of the civil rights movement on their general outlook. Because the movement had first focused on segregation, a system that crystallized racial, social, and gender oppression, southern activists were more aware than others of the interconnection of these factors in human relationships. King elaborates on the issue in her 1987 memoir, urging the women's movement to broaden its perspective, and, more particularly, to combat racism as strongly as sexism: "The best gauge of the success of our democracy and the true measure of justice in the United States is still the status of America's black community. Covert forms of racism need the attention of women, and no women's movement in the United States can be viable without a strong alliance to overthrow racial injustice and a clear presence of black women."[50] Thus, if there is no doubt that the white women activists of the South embraced feminism in the 1960s, it is also clear that they did not follow the main line of the women's liberation movement. Interestingly, just as white southern women had shared more commonalities with black southern women than with nonsouthern women during the civil rights movement, some proved closer to black feminists than to white radical feminists when the women's movement developed. bell hooks's own critique of *The Feminine Mystique*, published in 2000, illustrates this point. She notably rejects the universalist tendency of second-wave feminism. "A central tenet of modern feminist thought," she writes, "has been the assertion that 'all women are oppressed.' This assertion implies that women share a common lot, that factors like class, race, religion, sexual preference, etc., do not create a diversity of experience that determines the extent to which sexism will be an oppressive force in the lives of individual women." hooks's refusal to give systematic priority to sexism in the defense of women's interests partakes of the same rationale as that put forward by white southern female activists. She goes on to describe her realization of the gap between white women and herself in the early 1970s. "When I entered my first women's studies class at Stanford University in the early 1970s," she writes, "white women were revelling in the joy of being together—to them it was an important, momentous occasion." She comments: "I had not known a life where women had not been together, where women had not helped, protected, and loved one another deeply. I had not known white women who were ignorant of the impact of race and class on their social status and consciousness." But she adds the following qualifying note: "(Southern white women often have a more realistic perspective on racism and classism than white women in other areas of the United States.)"[51] hooks's critique of modern feminism hinges on the same arguments as that of the white southern women quoted above. Thus it seems that the cultural divide between North and South that had appeared during the Mississippi Freedom Summer of 1964 also applied to the feminist movement that developed later. In fact, white southern women's experience of segregation not only made them aware of the interconnection of race and gender but also led them to realize the link between racism and classism, as bell hooks notes, when they became involved in the struggle for blacks' rights. Consequently, after the 1960s civil rights movement, many devoted their energies to the struggle for economic and social justice closely connected to the struggle against racism, rather than concentrating on gender equality. This is especially true of Anne Braden, Virginia Durr, Sara Parsons, and Frances Pauley, of the older generation, but the same observation applies to several younger activists, notably Dorothy Burlage, Connie Curry, Joan Browning, Sue Thrasher, and Casey Hayden.[52]

Southern feminism finally set itself apart when the radical feminist movement focused its efforts on the denunciation of rape as the ultimate manifestation of patriarchal oppression. According to the prominent feminist Susan Brownmiller, "The brilliant, visionary strategy of radical feminism was to conceptualize sexual violence as the key link in the pattern of male domination and to attempt to put an end to it for all time." In 1975, Brownmiller published a groundbreaking work on the issue, *Against Our Will*, in which she placed rape in a political and historical perspective in order to demonstrate that rape was a political crime. In chapter 7, "A Question of Race," she more specifically discussed the legacy of slavery in the South, the use of rape and lynching as instruments of oppression against black people as well as the discriminatory use of the death penalty against black men convicted of rape. She dealt at length with the Scottsboro Case of 1931, in which six African Americans were sentenced to death on the charge of attempting to rape two white women. She also dealt with the case of Willie McGee, a black man executed in Mississippi in 1951 on a rape charge, as well as with the Emmett Till case of 1955, in which two white men were acquitted after murdering a black fourteen-year-old boy who had whistled at a white woman. While she acknowledged the specific character of the issue in the South, she accused the Communist Party and the leftist groups and individuals that had defended the Scottsboro boys in 1931 of tackling rape as an issue only because the accused were black men. Indeed, after the Scottsboro Case, civil rights and civil liberties groups associated with the Left had constantly denounced the use of the rape myth as a privileged weapon of the white supremacists in the South. As far as Emmett Till was concerned, Brownmiller observed that, given the legacy of southern history, the black boy who had been lynched for whistling at a white woman could only have been aware of the political character of his attitude, as he no doubt "understood that the whistle was no small tweet of hubba-hubba or melodious approval for a well-turned ankle." According to Brownmiller, Till shared with his murderers the idea that the white woman was the white man's property. Thus, the author argues, the whistling "was a deliberate insult just short of physical assault, a last reminder to Carolyn Bryant that this black boy, Till, had in mind to possess her."[53] Brownmiller's treatment of these two cases outraged many people, notably among the Left.

In 1977, Anne Braden published a virulent critique of Brownmiller's book, denouncing its "recurring tendency to ignore racism as a primary force in this country." Braden obviously wrote as a representative of the radical Left, and the reasons that she opposed Brownmiller were first ideological, but she also emphasized her concern to answer Brownmiller as a southern woman. She stated: "Racism is not some abstract concept invented by the left for its own gain. It *does* exist. The 'rape cases' inspired action and became famous not because they were unusual but because they exemplified the terrorism which upheld political and economic power relationships in the South." She refuted Brownmiller's accusations by declaring: "Instead of manipulating people, the left's defense efforts offered black and white women a way to fight back together." She then shifted to her southern identity: "For me, as a white Southern woman, this social analysis was sensible and liberating. It no longer left me individually guilty for the racism that was destroying us all. Individual guilt is a dead end; it offered no possibility for collective action. The social analysis, however, meant that if I repudiated my complicity in racism, I could be free."[54]

The notion of white guilt is central to understanding Braden's and other white southern women's attitudes on the issue of rape since the women who rejected racism struggled with an acute sense of participating in the oppression of black people in general and black men in particular. "Blacks were being killed," says Dorothy Burlage, "women were not." In a previous pamphlet addressed to white southern women, Braden had already expressed her sense of guilt, writing: "I am writing to you, my white sisters throughout the South, to ask you to join with me and others in a campaign to free Thomas Wansley.... Whether we like it or not, he is in prison because of us. He is a victim of the myth of white Southern womanhood." Wansley had been jailed in Virginia on a rape charge. Braden went on to describe rape as "traditionally a crime in the South if the accused was black and the alleged victim was white, but never a crime if the victim was black and the attacker was white, and scarcely noticed if both parties were white, or both black." She used the Wansley case to clarify her views about white women's identity:

> I believe that no white woman reared in the South—or perhaps anywhere in this racist country—can find freedom as a woman until she deals in her own consciousness with the question of race. We grow up little girls—absorbing a hundred stereotypes about ourselves and our role in life, our secondary position, our destiny to be a helpmate to a man or men. But we also grow up white—absorbing the stereotypes of race, the picture of ourselves as somehow privileged because of the color of our skin. The two mythologies become intertwined, and there is no way to free ourselves from one without dealing with the other.

Braden thus explicitly conditioned white women's liberation to their repudiation of racism. She was not the only one to interpret rape as she did. In 1958, for instance, upset about a series of dubious court cases in which black adolescents had been executed after being charged with rape, Virginia Durr had written to Jessica Mitford, "I sometimes feel we southern white women are some kind of obscene goddesses that they make these burnt offerings to, 'Burn the Nigger, burn the Nigger' is what you hear when one of them comes up and there is something so awful and horrible about it, especially when no white man ever gets the death penalty for rape in any case and of course when it occurs with a Negro woman they never even believe it is rape."[55] In this letter, Durr expressed the contradiction that lay at the core of her white southern female identity, as she alternately described white women as victims and oppressors.

Since they could not but feel directly guilty for the killing of black men in their names, it is no wonder that Durr, Braden, and their likes should have been reluctant to hold all men responsible for the oppression of all women in society. To Braden, on the contrary, the defense of black men accused of rape in the South was an act of personal liberation, not a form of passivity or complicity with patriarchal oppression. In the same article in which she argues with Brownmiller's thesis, she explains that her own "moment of freedom came in 1951." After the execution of Willie McGee in Mississippi, Braden and a delegation of white women tried to see the governor of the state to express protest. At some point, a local policeman threatened to kill her, shouting, "You are not fit to be a Southern woman," to which she replied, "No, I'm not your kind of Southern woman." This was the beginning of her road toward redemption. "Suddenly," she comments, "I knew I was on the 'other side.' The other side not just from that cop but from all the rulers of the South who treated black people like children and put white women on pedestals and turned on both in fury when they asserted their humanity. For me, it was a point of no return." Braden stresses the contrast between her experience in the McGee case and Brownmiller's interpretation of it: "To my amazement, she views the Willie McGee case, which provided my road to freedom, as just another example of the male-dominated left using a rape case as an organizing tool for its own benefit." The difference between the two women here is definitely more cultural than ideological.[56]

Braden certainly distinguished herself from a majority of white southern women by her radicalism, but a specific episode concerning the Georgia Commission on the Status of Women proves that the legacy of slavery, segregation, and lynching continued to influence women's issues in the South after the end of the civil rights movement. In April 1974, Eliza Paschall, who was a member of the commission, received a draft of a report on rape about to be published. The commission had conducted a study of rape in Georgia in an attempt to draw public attention to the issue and to destroy the myths surrounding the crime, notably the idea that the victims were often suspected of "asking for it." The first set of statistics cited in the report is based on race and indicates that "rape is predominantly an intra-racial crime—that is, committed by black men against black women and by white men against white women." The preeminent place of racial statistics in the text is certainly no coincidence as the draft goes on to comment: "With the majority—75%—of the reported rapes being intra-racial, rather than inter-racial, the belief that rape is predominantly a crime of black men against white women is, therefore, a myth." However, in the final version of the report published later, this sentence was edited out of the paragraph.[57] This leads to two conclusions. First, the explicit mention of the "black rapist" myth reveals that the authors of the draft were conscious enough of the persistence of the myth to feel the necessity to denounce it. Second, one can infer that the latest developments of the national women's liberation movement, notably the rise of rape theory and the antirape campaigns set up by feminist organizations, were gaining ground in the South, in spite of a lingering regional distinctiveness, and that the myth of the black rapist was indeed receding. Thus, the editors of the report did not find it worth mentioning any longer. So if there is no doubt that the southern women—black and white—who became involved in women's issues in the 1970s, like those who sat on the Georgia Commission on the Status of Women, followed national cultural trends, they still distinguished themselves in the post–civil rights era by a great sensitivity to race when it came to tackling women's issues.

Ultimately, an essential reason why a significant number of the white women who fought for racial equality in the South came to criticize some aspects of second-wave American feminism is that their view of human relations rested on the concept of racial integration, which most of them certainly applied, like Casey Hayden, Mary King, and Lillian Smith, to all forms of social categorization, be they race, class, or sex. When asked whether she would describe herself as a feminist, a radical feminist, or neither, King responded, "Feminist," but added: "Feminism is but a partial concern; it does not have the same instrumental potential as the field of gender for injustices lined to one's gender and the impact of gender socialization. More to the point, the coherent emergence of gender studies over the past four decades has become a more potent and cross-cutting analytical tool than feminism, which is but one slice." King's experience of the civil rights movement actually led her to devote her work to the field of building peace as a comprehensive development, the success of which in large part depends, according to her, on the empowerment of women. She describes her evolution in the following terms: "I have used my experiences in the U.S. civil rights as a platform, a launching pad, for working on social justice, gender equity, and advancing the study and practice of nonviolent action throughout the rest of my life." As for Hayden, she insists particularly on the significance of the civil rights movement for her personal development as a human being rather than a woman. "I could break taboos effortlessly," she recalls, "and I could escape the claustrophobia of my experience of the culture of the white South." Instead of pitting women's rights against other groups' rights, Hayden explains how she came to embrace the concept of integration as an abolition of all the barriers southern culture had erected in her former self: "Women's culture and black culture, merging for me in the southern freedom movement, especially in SNCC, free of the constraints and values of the white patriarchy, would lead the way." King and Hayden thus stand as the natural heirs of Smith, who once summed up her views in very simple words: "It all comes down to our mutual willingness to become human: to think of ourselves first as human beings and second as women and men, and third as being different in appearance and talents and abilities and insights."[58] Such a statement may sound commonplace, even clichéd, to our contemporary ears, but it was all but so in the South of the early 1960s, as all the women featured in this book knew.

* * *

In the final analysis, for all their differences, at the end of the segregation era and in the aftermath of the civil rights movement, white southern female activists embraced feminism but distinguished themselves from the national feminist movement. As southerners, many of them were closer to black southern women than to other American women in their general outlook, owing to the continuing hold of race over public southern matters. This distinctiveness was mostly cultural, as black and white women of the South had all become aware, by the late 1960s, of the specific interaction of race and gender in their native culture and of its impact on their respective identities. Even though they remained separated by different experiences, and if other factors, such as class, constituted an important dividing line between them, southern women tended to concur in their criticism of radical feminism, viewing it as a movement that ignored the interests of many American women. In fact, this peculiar form of feminism somehow anticipated the evolution of social and political thought at the end of the twentieth century. After all, the interconnectedness of race, class, and gender, which has come to occupy a central place in the current public and scholarly debates, is what southern women have experienced firsthand in their native region for generations.

Conclusion

The history of white southern women dissenters throughout the segregation era stands as a multifaceted and liberating journey. From the early reformers of the 1920s to the freedom activists of the 1960s, the women involved in the struggle against racism went far beyond contributing to the liberation of black people in their region. Their participation in the long civil rights movement ultimately liberated them from their own condition as white women raised in a white supremacist society.

In the first place, all the women under study found in their racial activism a means to come to terms with the guilt induced by their whiteness, which identified them with the oppressor group in the South. Devoting their adult lives to undoing the wrongs of the southern white community offered them the opportunity to cope with their original sense of participating in the oppression of black people by the mere fact of being white. They were thus able not only to expiate their individual sin but also to claim to redeem the entire white South and liberate their native region from its historic burden. These women went through a variety of personal journeys, but in their collective evolution, their history is clearly marked by a process of gradual emancipation from racism.

Liberation from a southern female identity in patriarchal society marks the second form of emancipation they underwent. In spite of many differences in outlooks and varying degrees of gender awareness, the white women who embraced the cause of racial equality in the segregationist South were fated to face and challenge the constraints of white southern womanhood on which the whole rationale of white supremacy was grounded. Thus, whether they consciously rebelled against patriarchal norms or not, all of them undermined southern gender orthodoxy when they turned the ideal of the southern lady upside down to use it against white supremacists or to repudiate it altogether. In the process, they asserted themselves as women and emancipated themselves from a culture that had maintained them in a subordinate position through a falsely chivalrous rhetoric aimed at preserving the domination of southern society by white men.

These two processes were interconnected in so many ways that it is impossible to establish a clear causal relationship between them. On the one hand, women's commitment to racial justice entailed their later commitment to women's rights, which is corroborated by the successive developments of the civil rights movement and of the feminist movement in its wake. That women's participation in the fight for African Americans' civil rights precipitated their emancipation as women is clear. On the other hand, it can be argued that in a significant number of cases, gender awareness—and more particularly the awareness of their unique, problematic status as both oppressors and victims—led some white women to become active in racial reform at a time when such a stance was highly subversive. In other words, the combined factors of gender and race played a part in those women's racial activism. The present study underscores how white women reformers became more radical than their male counterparts as the civil rights movement developed.

Obviously, the degrees of emancipation reached by the various individuals concerned vary significantly according to factors other than gender and race. Indeed, several personal testimonies attest to the high cost they had to pay for their racial conversion. Moreover, if most of them managed to unlearn their own racist prejudices, they remained constrained by the prejudices of others, black and white. Whiteness often remained a liability in the quest for universal brotherhood, as the collective experience of racism continued to weigh on race relations. On the one hand, for many blacks, white skin remained a strong reminder of past racial oppression even after the official abolition of Jim Crow. On the other, in the eyes of segregationists still numerous in the late 1960s, white identity required conformity to racial orthodoxy and was used to condemn and ostracize white integrationists as traitors to the South. These qualifying remarks should not be interpreted to suggest that these women's efforts were a failure, however.[1] The point is that the white women reformers studied in this volume undertook an empowering inner transformation that enabled them to solve on a personal level the fundamental paradox of being oppressors and victims at the same time.

In addition to achieving personal emancipation, this particular brand of white southerner played a key role in the southern struggle for racial justice throughout the segregation era. As racial dissenters belonging to the dominant group, they built bridges between the white power structure and regional integrationist forces, not only by paving the way, in the early period, for the post-*Brown* civil rights movement but also by working on the community level before and after the pivotal decade of the 1950s. Ironically, although they were in many respects more active than white men in racial reform and civil rights activities, these women remained "invisible revolutionaries." According to Joan Browning, "The earliest Civil Rights histories used the most accessible evidence, which concentrated on events covered by the national media and on leaders. Those national media writers were men, and they identified leaders who were men. The metaphors were those of athletic contests or wars. This is history as keeping score between winners and losers."[2] The invisibility of women in the historiography of the civil rights movement has already been discussed at length, the main factor accounting for it being the dominant position of men in society until the second wave of feminism, which started in the late 1960s, and the male perspective that prevailed in scholarship until the 1990s. As for the white southern women profiled here, their relative invisibility as a group is probably due to the very nature of their activism, which was directly linked to the patriarchal nature of the society in which they lived. In particular, their predilection for grassroots work and their emphasis on networking made their action inherently unspectacular so that they did not draw the attention of historians until women themselves started to show some interest in the issue. As Browning notes, "The feminine roles of building consensus, sustaining community, and nurturing 'freedom' for individuals, organizations, and the nation cannot be described in win/loss records or accounts of conflicts," which points out the specificity of this group's activism.[3]

The older generation based its very strategy on a nonconfrontational, quiet approach, and avoided publicity by all possible means. It is understandable that researchers focused first of all on the most visible actors of the struggle for civil rights and on the most accessible sources of documentation. The few women who were recognized were the most outspoken ones, notably Lillian Smith, Anne Braden, and Virginia Durr. As for the members of the younger generation, they also remained long in the shadows of history because of their peculiar status in the 1960s movement. Their sense of belonging to the racial group that had oppressed the black community for centuries, added to their awareness of being responsible, as white women, for the violence exerted against black men, led them to withdraw from the front lines and to shun positions of leadership as an expression of their antiracist creed. As a consequence of these strategic and moral choices, most of the women studied here have remained unknown to the general public and to historians alike.

Starting in the 1980s, however, historiographical trends began to change when a wave of autobiographical narratives signaled a desire on the part of former freedom activists to set the record straight by offering their own version of history. This was true of several "forgotten" groups and individuals, of which white southern women were a part. Scholarship finally came to focus on the role of minority groups and grassroots actors in the struggle for racial justice prior to the 1960s, placing a particular emphasis on African Americans and women. Although the new generation of historians has included white women in a number of important monographs, contemporary scholars have only marginally singled out white southern women as a distinctive subgroup. These women definitely deserve recognition for their contribution to the fight against racism. Since they constituted a minority in the civil rights movement at large, the risk is real of overestimating their role and influence. However, the wealth of private documentation scattered across southern and nonsouthern archives pleads for their recognition as it testifies to their significant, if scarcely visible, achievement. This book demonstrates that the white South of the segregation era, far from being the solid block of racism and resistance it seemed to be, was a complex web of radical, progressive, conservative, and reactionary forces trying to cope with the burden of southern history.

Appendix

Selected Biographical Sketches

(Compiled from the sources cited in the bibliography)

Ames, Jessie Daniel. 1883–1972. Born in Texas.

Education: Southwestern University, Georgetown, Texas (1897–1902). Progressive reformer and woman's suffrage activist in the 1910s. League of Women Voters. Director of Woman's Work for the Commission on Interracial Cooperation; founder and leader of Association of Southern Women for the Prevention of Lynching. Later worked for the Western North Carolina Conference of the Methodist Church.

Boyle, Sarah Patton. 1906–1994. Born in Virginia.

Renowned Virginian family. Education: Corcoran School of Art, Washington, D.C. (1926–1932). Freelance writer. Active with the Virginia Council on Human Relations until 1960. Active in the civil rights movement until 1967: participated in marches, was arrested several times, worked with the National Association for the Advancement of Colored People, was appointed to the Virginia advisory committee of the U.S. Commission on Civil Rights. Author of *The Desegregated Heart* (1962), *For Human Beings Only* (1964), and *The Desert Blooms: A Personal Adventure in Growing Old Creatively* (1983).

Braden, Anne McCarty. 1924–2006. Born in Kentucky, raised in Alabama and Mississippi.

Descendant of slaveholders. Old Kentuckian family. Education: Stratford College (1941–1943); Randolph-Macon Woman's College (1943–1945). Became a journalist. Worked at newspapers in Anniston and Birmingham, Alabama. Worked for left-wing labor unions before becoming field executive for the Southern Conference Educational Fund. Editor of its publication, the *Southern*

Patriot. Worked with Student Nonviolent Coordinating Committee and helped the foundation of Southern Student Organizing Committee in the 1960s. From 1975 on, worked with the Southern Organizing Committee for Economic and Social Justice. Was involved in Jesse Jackson's presidential campaign during the 1984 and 1988 elections. Author of articles, pamphlets, and a memoir, *The Wall Between* (1958).

Browning, Joan C. Born 1942, rural Georgia.

Education: Georgia State College for Women (1960–1961). Became involved in the civil rights movement by attending a black church off-campus in 1961. Participated in a Freedom Ride (jailed in Albany, 1961), in sit-ins, and in other nonviolent actions. Volunteered for Student Nonviolent Coordinating Committee. Vice-chair and chair of Student Council on Human Relations in Atlanta (1961–1963). Since the 1960s: human relations, antipoverty and community work. Earned a Regents B.A. from West Virginia State College. Author of "Shiloh Witness," in *Deep in Our Hearts: Nine White Women in the Freedom Movement* (2000), and "Invisible Revolutionaries," in *Journal of Women's History* (Fall 1996). Now a freelance writer and lecturer in West Virginia.

Burlage, Dorothy Dawson. Born 1937, Texas.

Old southern roots (back to early 1700s). Education: University of Texas (1956–1959); Harvard Divinity School (1960–1962); and Harvard University (1971–1978). Earned a Ph.D. in clinical psychology. Became involved in the struggle against segregation at the University of Texas. Worked with the Young Women's Christian Association. Helped create Students for a Democratic Society and the Northern Student Movement. In 1962–1963, worked for the National Student Association Southern Project. Also involved with Student Nonviolent Coordinating Committee. In 1964, helped found Southern Student Organizing Committee. 1965–1968: community organizer in Washington, D.C. Later became a child psychologist. Author of "Truths of the Heart," in *Deep in Our Hearts: Nine White Women in the Freedom Movement* (2000). Lives in Massachusetts.

Curry, Constance "Connie." Born 1933, Paterson, New Jersey, to Irish immigrant parents, raised in North Carolina.

Education: Agnes Scott College, Decatur, Georgia (graduated 1955). Fulbright scholar to France (1955–1956). Worked at Collegiate Council for the United Nations. Worked with the United States National Student Association Southern Project and on the Student Nonviolent Coordinating Committee executive committee (1959–1964), with the American Friends Service Committee in

Mississippi for school desegregation (1964–1975). Director of human services for the city of Atlanta (1975–1990). Earned a law degree (Woodrow Wilson College of Law) in 1984. Author of *Silver Rights* (1995); "Wild Geese of the Past," in *Deep in Our Hearts: Nine White Women in the Freedom Movement* (2000); and "An Official Observer," in *Hands on the Freedom Plow: Personal Accounts by Women in SNCC* (2010). Author, with Aaron Henry, *Aaron Henry: The Fire Ever Burning* (2000); with Winston Hudson, *Mississippi Harmony: Memories of a Freedom Fighter* (2002); with Robert Zellner, *The Wrong Side of Murder Creek: A White Southerner in the Freedom Movement* (2008). Lives in Atlanta.

Dabbs, Edith M. 1906–1991. Born in South Carolina.

White southern middle-class family. Father minister. Education: Coker College (graduated in 1927). Became a high school teacher. Became a civil rights activist after marrying James McBride Dabbs (1935) and moving to the antebellum plantation house he had inherited from his family. The two struggled together for racial equality. Among other activities, she was a leader of United Church Women in South Carolina. Author of an unpublished memoir.

Durr, Virginia Foster. 1903–1999. Born in Alabama.

Descendant of slaveholders. Father minister. Education: Wellesley College (1921–1923). Moved to Alexandria, Virginia, in 1933, when her husband, Cliff Durr, was appointed to the Reconstruction Finance Corporation. Founding member of Southern Conference for Human Welfare (1938), vice-chair of National Committee to Abolish the Poll Tax (1941), board member of Southern Conference Educational Fund. In 1948, ran for the U.S. Senate on a Progressive Party ticket. Returned to Montgomery, Alabama, in 1951. Worked as a secretary for her husband, who ran a private law practice. Both were active in the Montgomery civil rights struggle. Both worked with the National Association for the Advancement of Colored People and with Montgomery Bus Boycott members and leaders. She also worked with churchwomen's groups and the Alabama Council on Human Relations. Supported the 1960s civil rights movement. Remained active in local and national progressive political causes until her death. Author of *Outside the Magic Circle*, edited by Hollinger Barnard (1985).

Gladney, Margaret Rose. Born 1945, Louisiana.

Education: Southwestern at Memphis (now Rhodes College) (1963–1967); University of Michigan (1967–1968); University of New Mexico (1970–1974). Ph.D. American studies. Entered the civil rights movement in 1968–1969 through her teaching experience at a desegregated school in Memphis. Worked with the Southern Christian Leadership Conference, Memphis, Tennessee, 1969–1970. Cochair of American Federation of Teachers Organizing Committee, Memphis, 1969–1970. Member of American Civil Liberties Union since 1968. Member of National Organization for Women, Tuscaloosa, Alabama, 1974–1975; cofounder of Tuscaloosa Lesbian Coalition, 1986–1996. Became an associate professor, University of Alabama, Tuscaloosa. As a scholar, worked on issues of justice and social change, specializing in African American and women's liberation movements in the American South. Author of *How Am I to Be Heard? Letters of Lillian Smith* (1993). Now retired (Emeritus). Lives in Florida.

Hayden, Sandra "Casey" Cason. Born 1937, Texas.

Fourth generation, white, roots back to Mayflower and Virginia. Raised by her divorced, working mother. Education: Victoria Junior College, Victoria, Texas (1955–1957); University of Texas, Austin (1957–1961); national Young Women's Christian Association leader, first interracial experiences, beginning of antiracist activism. Early member of Students for a Democratic Society (1960). Worked for Student Nonviolent Coordinating Committee, National Student Young Women's Christian Association, Students for a Democratic Society, between 1960 and 1966. Moved to New York City, winter 1965–1966. Worked with New York Department of Welfare and Mobilization for Youth, Huggs Family Farm Commune in Vermont, and Integral Yoga Institute, San Francisco. Since 1971: grassroots social change, countercultural, religious, and permaculture activities. Coauthor of "Sex and Caste: A Kind of Memo" (1965) with Mary King; author of "The Movement" in *WITNESS* 2, no. 3 (Summer–Fall 1988) *The Sixties*; "Body on the Line," in *Being Bodies, Buddhist Women on the Paradox of Embodiment* (1997); "Fields of Blue," in *Deep in Our Hearts: Nine White Women in the Freedom Movement* (2000), which she initiated; "Onto Open Ground" and "In the Attics of My Mind," in *Hands on the Freedom Plow: Personal Accounts by Women in SNCC* (2010); and "Casey Hayden," in *Women in the Civil Rights Movement, 1954–1965* (2009), a collection of women's oratory. Lives in Arizona.

Johnson, Frances Guion Griffis. 1900–1989. Born in Texas.

Education: Baylor College for Women; University of Missouri (journalism); University of North Carolina (UNC) at Chapel Hill (1924–1927). Ph.D. in history and sociology (1927). From 1924 on, worked with her husband, Guy B. Johnson, a sociology professor, and Howard Odum, at Odum's Institute for Research in the Social Sciences, UNC. Became a teacher and scholar but did not obtain any teaching position at UNC. Career in research and volunteer community service. From 1947 on, worked with women's organizations and other civic groups, including North Carolina Council of Women's Organizations (founder), American Association of University Women (board member), North Carolina Federation of Women's Clubs (board member and vice president), North Carolina Council on World Affairs, League of Women Voters, and Church Women United. Active work with Methodist churchwomen and Young Women's Christian Association. Author of three books, including *Antebellum North Carolina* (1937).

King, Jeannette. Born 1935, Mississippi.

Education: Millsaps College (1954–1958); Florida State University (1958–1959); Boston University (1961). First interracial experience in college. In 1962, moved on the campus of Tougaloo Southern Christian College (Jackson, Mississippi) with her husband, Ed King, who took the job of chaplain there. Participated in the Jackson Movement, with the Jackson National Association for the Advancement of Colored People Youth Group (1962–1963). Was involved in Freedom Schools in 1964, and went to the Democratic National Convention at Atlantic City as an alternate Mississippi Freedom Democratic Party delegate. She and her family left Jackson for New Orleans in 1967. From 1970 on, after returning to Jackson, she worked as a psychiatric social worker. Author of "Inside and Outside of Two Worlds," in *Hands on the Freedom Plow: Personal Accounts by Women in SNCC* (2010). Lives in the state of Washington.

King, Mary Elizabeth. Born 1940, New York City.

Descendant of old Virginian and North Carolinian families (going back to the 1600s). Father Methodist minister (the eighth in six generations). Father left the South because did not wish to serve segregated churches. Mother teacher of nursing and artist. Education: Ohio Wesleyan University (1958–1962). Worked with Student Nonviolent Coordinating Committee (1963–1965), National Young Women's Christian Association, Southern Region (1962–1963). Coauthor of "Sex and Caste: A Kind of Memo" (1965), with Casey Hayden. After her experience within the U.S. civil rights movement, became a scholar-practitioner of international relations. Earned a doctorate in international politics from Aberystwyth University in Wales (1999). Specialized in peace and conflict studies, gender, and peace-building. Recognized authority on nonviolent civil resistance. Today professor of peace and conflict studies, University of Peace (affiliate of the United Nations), distinguished scholar-in-residence, American University's Center for Peacebuilding and Development, School of International Service, Washington, D.C., and a Distinguished Rothermere American Institute Fellow at the University of Oxford in Britain. Author of *Freedom Song* (1987) (Robert F. Kennedy Memorial Book Award), *The* New York Times *on Emerging Democracies in Eastern Europe* (2009), *A Quiet Revolution: The First Palestinian Intifada and Nonviolent Resistance* (2007), *Mahatma Gandhi and Martin Luther King, Jr.: The Power of Nonviolent Action* (1999, 2002), *Gandhian Nonviolent Struggle and Untouchability in South India: The 1924–25 Vykom* Satyagraha, *and the Mechanisms of Change* (2014). In 2011, her alma mater, Ohio Wesleyan University, awarded her a doctor of laws (honorary) degree; she received a James M. Lawson Award for Nonviolent Achievement, and Aberystwyth University elected her a Fellow, its equivalent of the honorary degrees bestowed elsewhere. King received the 2009 El-Hibri Peace Education Prize, and in 2003 in Mumbai the Jamnalal Bajaj International Prize, named for Gandhi's silent financial backer.

Leonard, Margaret Burr. Born 1942, Kentucky.

Grew up in Macon, Georgia. Daughter of Margaret Long Leonard and Howard Burr Leonard. Descended from writers, clergy, plantation owners, and merchants. Education: Newcomb College at Tulane University (1959–1963). Held no official position in the civil rights movement but joined civil rights groups for demonstrations. Became involved in the movement through Congress of Racial Equality (New Orleans). Notably participated in sit-ins in New Orleans, civil rights demonstrations in Atlanta, and a Freedom Ride from Atlanta to Mississippi (was arrested in Jackson) in 1961. Became a journalist. Now lives in Florida.

Leonard, Margaret Long. 1911–1989. Born and raised in Macon, Georgia.

Education: Lanier High School and Mercer University. Journalist and writer. Editorial page column for *Atlanta Journal*, for which she won the Florina Lasker Award of the American Civil Liberties Union. Author of two novels, *Louisville Saturday* (1950) and *Affair of the Heart* (1953). Married in 1931, divorced in 1951. Not an activist, but openly opposed segregation and supported 1960s civil rights groups. Editor from 1961–1966 of *New South*, the Southern Regional Council publication, in which she wrote a regular column, "Strictly Subjective."

Lumpkin, Katharine Du Pre. 1897–1988. Born in Georgia.

Descendant of a prominent slaveholding family. Father Confederate veteran and traveling salesman. Education: Brenau College in Gainsville (1912–1915); Columbia University (1918–1920); University of Wisconsin (1925–1928), where earned a Ph.D. in sociology. Became a sociologist, activist, teacher, and writer.

After a career outside of the South, returned to the region in 1967. Was a student Young Women's Christian Association leader (1920–1925). Her extensive scholarly work includes *The South in Progress* (1940). Also author of an autobiography, *The Making of a Southerner* (1947). After retiring, was also active in the League of Women Voters.

Mason, Lucy Randolph. 1882–1959. Born in Virginia.

Descendant of George Mason, author of the Virginia Declaration of Rights. A distant cousin of General Robert E. Lee. Woman's suffrage activist in the 1910s. League of Women Voters in the 1920s. Worked for the industrial Young Women's Christian Association and with the National Consumer's League (became general secretary in 1932), lobbying for labor rights legislation. From 1937 on, worked with the Congress of Industrial Organizations in the South. Served as a bridge between organized labor and religious institutions, and struggled against segregation in southern life. Author of essays, pamphlets, and a memoir, *To Win These Rights* (1952).

Morgan, Juliette Hampton. 1914–1957. Born in Alabama.

Aristocratic southern family. Education: University of Alabama, Tuscaloosa (1930–1935). Public school teacher, librarian, and director of research, Montgomery Public Library. Member of the local Democratic Club and of the Women's International League for Peace and Freedom. Attended founding meeting of the Southern Conference for Human Welfare (1938). Joined United Church Women in 1941 and Fellowship of the Concerned in 1951. Publicly supported the Montgomery Bus Boycott and the *Brown* decision.

Mulholland, Joan Trumpauer. Born 1941, Washington, D.C.

Mother of rural Georgia, Pentecostal background. Father's family from Iowa. Education: Duke University (1959–1960); Tougaloo Southern Christian College, Jackson, Mississippi (1964). Became involved in the civil rights movement when black students invited Duke students to join sit-ins. Participated in a Freedom Ride from New Orleans to Mississippi with Stokely Carmichael. Jailed at Parchman Penitentiary. Enrolled at black Tougaloo College (graduated in 1964). Participated in the Jackson Movement (Student Nonviolent Coordinating Committee and Congress of Racial Equality). Later became a public school teacher's aide in Washington, D.C. Author of "Diary of a Freedom Rider," in *Hands on the Freedom Plow: Personal Accounts by Women in SNCC* (2010).

Parsons, Sara Mitchell. 1912–2011. Born in Georgia.

Old southern family. Moved at thirteen with her mother to her grandmother's house after parents divorced. No college education. Married in 1933. Became involved in the desegregation movement in the 1950s through the Atlanta League of Women Voters (president, 1958–1963). Elected member of Atlanta Board of Education (1961–1968). Became a friend of Coretta Scott King. Moved to California with her second husband in 1968. Continued her career in social activism and progressive politics. Returned to Atlanta in 1986. Author of *From Southern Wrongs to Civil Rights* (2000).

Paschall, Eliza King. 1917–1990. Born in South Carolina.

Education: Agnes Scott College, Decatur, Georgia (1934–1938); Emory University; independent study in England. Worked with the American Red Cross during World War II. Involved in many organizations, including Greater Atlanta Council on Human Relations (executive director 1961–1967), Georgia League of Women Voters (president 1955–1957), and National Organization for Women. Member of U.S. Equal Employment Opportunity Commission (1966–1984) and Georgia Commission on the Status of Women. Also worked for the Reagan administration (1984–1985). Author of *It Must Have Rained* (1974), and coauthor of *Because of Sex* (1975).

Pauley, Frances Newborn. 1905–2003. Born in Ohio, raised in Georgia.

Education: Agnes Scott College, Decatur, Georgia (graduated in 1927). Devoted her life to social reform, racial equality, and the struggle against poverty. Worked with many organizations, including League of Women Voters (president of the Georgia League 1952–1955), Help Our Public Education, the Georgia Council on Human Relations (executive director 1961–1967). After the civil rights movement, worked for U.S. Department of Health, Education, and Welfare (1968–1973). Founder of the Georgia Poverty Rights Organization (1975).

Pendergrast, Nan. Born 1920, Georgia.

Prominent southern family. Education: Vassar College (1938–1941). Became a writer and botanist. During the segregation and desegregation eras: Help Our Public Education (cofounder and director of public relations, 1959–1960), National Association for the Advancement of Colored People (board member), National Urban League (board member), Georgia Council on Human Relations (executive committee 1967–1970), Georgia League of Women Voters (board member and officer), American Friends Service Committee. One of the most important causes for her has always been pacifism. Has served on the National Council of the Fellowship of Reconciliation. Lives in Atlanta.

Powell, Faye. Born 1940, Georgia.

Father a pharmacist and mother a social worker. Education: Georgia State College for Women (1958–1961); Mercer University (1961–1962; B.A. sociology); San Francisco State University (1973–1974, 1977, 1982; M.A. anthropology); University of British Columbia (1975–1977; M.L.S. library science). Became involved in the civil rights movement by attending a black church off-campus in 1961. Participated in a sit-in, mass meetings, demonstrations, and bus boycotts. Worked for the antipoverty program in Georgia. This experience impacted all her subsequent work. Later worked as a social science librarian, Portland State University. Now retired. Lives in Oregon.

Smith, Lillian E. 1897–1966. Born in Florida.

Moved to Georgia in 1915 after her parents lost their business and established the Laurel Falls Girls Camp in Clayton. Education: Piedmont College in Demorest (1915–1916); Peabody Conservatory in Baltimore (1917, 1919). After three years in China as a Methodist missionary teacher, became the director of the Girls Camp. Ran it with her partner, Paula Snelling, until 1948. Became a writer, editor, and integrationist activist in the 1930s. Coeditor of *South Today* (formerly named *Pseudopodia* and *North Georgia Review*). Actively supported the nonviolent civil rights movement from the *Brown* decision on. Died of cancer in 1966. Author of many articles, essays, and novels, including *Strange Fruit* (1944), *Killers of the Dream* (1949), and *Now Is the Time* (1954).

Stembridge, Jane. Born 1937, Virginia, father's home state; mother from South Carolina.

Grew up in Georgia. Father Baptist minister who opposed segregation. Education: Meredith College, Raleigh, North Carolina (1958); Union Theological Seminary (1959–1960). Became a poet. Recruited by Ella Baker to attend the April 1960 conference at Shaw University, Raleigh, North Carolina, where the Student Nonviolent Coordinating Committee was founded. Became Student Nonviolent Coordinating Committee's first staff person. Recruited by Ella Baker to open an "office" for Student Nonviolent Coordinating Committee in the Southern Christian Leadership Conference headquarters in Atlanta. Wrote the first issue and named Student Nonviolent Coordinating Committee's publication *Student Voice*. Left after a few months, but returned to work for Student

Nonviolent Coordinating Committee in Mississippi in 1963. Published a collection of poems on the movement, *I Play Flute* (1968). Lives in North Carolina.

Stevens, Thelma. 1902–1990. Born in Mississippi.

Lived with her older sister after her parents' death in 1912. Education: State Teachers College (now University of Southern Mississippi at Hattiesburg); Scarritt College, Nashville, Tennessee (1926–1928). Methodist leader. First worked as a teacher. From 1928 to 1940, director of the Bethlehem Center in Augusta, Georgia. Then became a leader of the Women's Division of the Methodist Church (1940–1968). Devoted her life to racial equality and social justice.

Terry, Adolphine Fletcher. 1882–1976. Born in Arkansas.

Descendant of a prominent Little Rock family. Father businessman, Confederate veteran. Education: Vassar College (graduated in 1902). Participated in the woman's suffrage movement in the 1910s. Became involved in civic action, social reform, and the struggle for racial equality in Little Rock, Arkansas. Founding member of Women's Emergency Committee. As a trustee of the city public library, worked for the desegregation of the library in the 1950s. Wrote several books, including an unpublished autobiography.

Thrasher, Martha Sue. Born 1941, Tennessee.

Farming/working-class background. Childhood in Savannah, Tennessee. Education: Methodist Student Movement (first interracial experience) (1959–1961); Scarritt College, Nashville, Tennessee (1961–1963). Gradual involvement in the Nashville movement through local Student Nonviolent Coordinating Committee and Southern Christian Leadership Conference people. Founder and executive director of Southern Student Organizing Committee (1964–1966). Founder and codirector of Institute for Southern Studies. Worked with Highlander Research and Education Center, Knoxville, Tennessee. Later earned a doctorate in educational policy and research, University of Massachusetts, Amherst. Worked with the Five Colleges Consortium in Amherst until 2013. Author of "Circle of Trust," in *Deep in Our Hearts: Nine White Women in the Freedom Movement* (2000).

Tilly, Dorothy Rogers. 1883–1970. Born in Georgia.

Father minister. Education: Reinhardt College (graduated in 1899); Wesleyan College in Macon (graduated in 1901). Became a prominent Methodist leader. Supported and encouraged by her husband, she devoted her life to social and racial reform. Leadership positions in many organizations, including Commission on Interracial Cooperation, Association of Southern Women for the Prevention of Lynching, and Southern Regional Council. Member of President Truman's Committee on Civil Rights. Founder of Fellowship of the Concerned.

Wilkins, Mathewson Josephine. 1893–1977. Born in Georgia.

Prominent Athens family. Education: Lucy Cobb Institute; University of Georgia; New York School of Fine and Applied Arts. Became a civic leader and social reformer. Used her wealth to support progressive causes. Worked for Georgia Children's Code Commission. Active in Georgia League of Women Voters (president 1934–1940) and in Citizens' Fact-Finding Movement of Georgia. Involved in Southern Conference for Human Welfare and Commission on Interracial Cooperation. Worked for the Southern Regional Council (executive board member and vice president) until her death. Also worked closely with Southern Conference Educational Fund and Student Nonviolent Coordinating Committee. From the 1950s on, her activities were limited by ill health and an accident.

Wright, Alice Norwood Spearman. 1902–1989. Born in South Carolina.

Prominent banking and business family. Education: Converse College (1919–1923); Young Women's Christian Association National Training School, New York City; Columbia Teachers College, New York City (1926). Traveled around the world between 1930 and 1933. Involved in workers' education in the 1930s. Worked for the Work's Progress Administration. Early interest in women's rights. Active member of Young Women's Christian Association, South Carolina Federation of Women's Clubs (executive secretary), League of Women Voters, South Carolina Council on Human Relations (executive director 1954–1967), United Church Women, Women's International League for Peace and Freedom. Supported the 1960s movement. Worked with the National Student Young Women's Christian Association and Ella Baker. Involved in Great Society programs with the South Carolina Council on Human Relations.

Young, Louise. 1892–1973. Born in Memphis, Tennessee.

Education: Vanderbilt University (B.A. 1912); University of Wisconsin (M.A. 1915); Bryn Mawr College (1916–1917). Became a professor of sociology. Taught at Paine College, Augusta, Georgia, a Central Methodist Episcopal (black) college (1919–1922). Dean of women at Hampton Institute in Virginia. From 1925 to 1957, chair of the Department of Sociology and Social Work, and director of the Department of Home Missions, Scarritt College, Nashville, Tennessee. Involved with Young Women's Christian Association (national board), Association of Southern Women for the Prevention of Lynching, Highlander Folk School, League of Women Voters, United Church Women, American Association of University Women, Tennessee Council on Human Relations. Also on the board of directors of the Nashville Bethlehem House.

Notes

Introduction

1. Casey Hayden, "Fields of Blue," in Curry et al., *Deep in Our Hearts*, 333–75, 347.
2. See Clinton, *Plantation Mistress*; Friedman, *Enclosed Garden*, on whites; see Jones, *Labor of Love*, and White, *Ar'n't I a Woman?*, on blacks.
3. Scott, "Most Invisible of All," 3; Hall, *Revolt against Chivalry*, xxiv.
4. The publication, in 1990, of *Women in the Civil Rights Movement*, edited by Vicki Crawford, Jacqueline Anne Rouse, and Barbara Woods, testifies to this new interest.
5. See, for instance, Fosl, *Subversive Southerner*, on Anne McCarty Braden; Sullivan, *Freedom Writer*, on Virginia Foster Durr; Stanton, *Journey toward Justice*, on Juliette Hampton Morgan; Little, *You Must Be from the North*, on Memphis; Greene, *Our Separate Ways*, on Durham, N.C.
6. See Hall, "Long Civil Rights Movement."
7. See, for instance, Egerton, *Speak Now*; Fairclough, *Race and Democracy*; Frystak, *Our Minds*; Gilmore, *Defying Dixie*; Payne, *I've Got the Light*; Ransby, *Ella Baker*; Reed, *Simple Decency*; Robertson, *Christian Sisterhood*; Sullivan, *Days of Hope*; Sullivan, *Lift Every Voice*.
8. Hall, "Long Civil Rights Movement," 1235.
9. Nasstrom, "Between Memory and History," 339. See also Rogers, *Righteous Lives*, 9–16. Rogers discusses at length the interest of using oral history narratives as privileged sources to connect collective and individual experiences.

Chapter 1. Profiles: Two Generations, One Identity

1. The following biographical and autobiographical documents constitute the main source of information for the present chapter:
Books: Bayless, *Obliged to Help*; Boyle, *Desegregated Heart*; Braden, *Wall Between*; Curry et al., *Deep in Our Hearts*; Durr, *Outside the Magic Circle*; Evans, *Journeys*; Fosl, *Subversive Southerner*; Hall, *Revolt against Chivalry*; Lumpkin, *Making of a Southerner*; Murphy, *Breaking the Silence*; Nasstrom, *Everybody's Grandmother*; Parsons, *From Southern Wrongs to Civil Rights*; Smith, *Killers of the Dream*; Stanton, *Journey toward Justice*.

Interviews with author: Joan C. Browning, Dorothy Dawson Burlage, Constance Curry, Virginia "Tilla" Foster Durr; Patricia Jarvis. Answers to author's questionnaire: Joan C. Browning, Virginia "Tilla" Foster Durr, Margaret Rose Gladney, Margaret Burr Leonard, Sheila Michaels, Faye Powell. Other interviews: Thelma Stevens, Interview with Thelma Stevens by Jacquelyn and Bob Hall, February 13, 1972 (G-0058), Southern Oral History Program Collection (#4007), Southern Historical Collection, Wilson Library, University of North Carolina at Chapel Hill; Winifred Green, "An Oral History with Winifred A. Green," interviewer Charles Bolton, vol. 704, November 12, 1997, Mississippi Oral History Program, University of Southern Mississippi Center for Oral History and Cultural Heritage, University of Mississippi Digital Collections.

2. Litwack, *Trouble*, 102–5, 381–82.
3. Joan Browning, "Shiloh Witness," in Curry et al., *Deep in Our Hearts*, 37–83, 51.
4. For more information, see, for instance, Bartley, *New South*, 271–73.
5. Dorothy Dawson Burlage, "Truths of the Heart," in Curry et al., *Deep in Our Hearts*, 85–130, 91.
6. Parsons, *Southern Wrongs*, 7, 9.
7. Braden, *Wall Between*, 22. For concurring testimonies about segregated life, see Green interview, 1–8 (about Mississippi) and Jarvis interview (about West Virginia).
8. Smith, *Killers of the Dream*, 29.
9. Smith, *Killers of the Dream*, 27.
10. Boyle, *Desegregated Heart*, 20; Burlage, "Truths," 88. See also Durr, *Outside the Magic Circle*, 19; Smith, *Killers of the Dream*, 28, 96–97.
11. Boyle, *Desegregated Heart*, 13.
12. See, for instance, Williamson, *Crucible of Race*, 50–51, 460.
13. Durr, *Outside the Magic Circle*, 253; Boyle, *Desegregated Heart*, 13.
14. Parsons, *Southern Wrongs*, 41; Boyle, *Desegregated Heart*, 107; Fosl, *Subversive Southerner*, 87; Nasstrom, *Everybody's Grandmother*, 51.
15. Williamson, *Crucible of Race*, 498; Boyle, *Desegregated Heart*, 16.
16. Boyle, *Desegregated Heart*, 14, 63, 104.
17. Nasstrom, *Everybody's Grandmother*, 51; Fosl, *Subversive Southerner*, 87.
18. Boyle, *Desegregated Heart*, 82; Nasstrom, *Everybody's Grandmother*, 70.
19. Braden, *Wall Between*, 299.
20. Boyle, *Desegregated Heart*, 34.
21. Braden, *Wall Between*, 20.
22. See Wolfe, *Daughters*, 7–9.
23. V. Durr to Jessica Mitford, March 24, 1961, in Sullivan, *Freedom Writer*, 243.
24. See Foster, *Ghosts*, 124.
25. Durr, *Outside the Magic Circle*, 44, 45.
26. Lumpkin, *Making of a Southerner*, 115, 118.
27. Quoted in Foster, *Ghosts*, 137, 136.

28. Boyle, *Desegregated Heart*, 29.

29. For full definitions of "belle" and "lady," see Anne Goodwyn Jones, "Belles and Ladies," in Bercaw and Ownby, *Gender*, 42. See also Clinton, *Plantation Mistress*, and Faust, *Mothers of Invention*, for in-depth studies of white southern elite women in the slaveholding South.

30. Smith, *Killers of the Dream*, 141; Foster, "Emancipation," 51.

31. Foster, "Emancipation," 50.

32. Among numerous examples, Durr attended Wellesley College; Katharine Lumpkin earned a master's degree in sociology from Columbia and a doctorate in economics from the University of Wisconsin; Lillian Smith studied music in Baltimore; Sarah Boyle studied painting in Washington, D.C.; Thelma Stevens earned a master's degree from Scarrit College in Nashville; and Juliette Morgan went to Northwestern University in Chicago after earning a master's degree in English from the University of Alabama. See Durr, *Outside the Magic Circle*, 51–65; Darlene Hine, "Foreword," in Lumpkin, *Making of a Southerner*, vii–viii; Margaret Gladney, "Smith, Lillian," in Bercaw and Ownby, *Gender*, 348; Houck and Dixon, *Women and the Civil Rights Movement*, 10; Knotts, *Fellowship*, 105; Stanton, *Journey toward Justice*, 41–42.

33. This is reflected, for instance, by Juliette Morgan's experience. This native Alabamian's academic achievements would have opened for her the doors of any prestigious women's college, "but leaving Alabama for an undergraduate degree was something few Montgomery women did.... While ambitious young men were expected to graduate from college, the recommended course of study for a genteel young woman was two years at a Virginia or South Carolina finishing school and another year or two at Tuscaloosa." Stanton, *Journey toward Justice*, 25, 42–43. So, Morgan went to the University of Alabama. In 1936, she was admitted to the Ph.D. program at Columbia University, but she had to decline the offer to care for her grandparents at her mother's demand. For further historical analysis of the issue, see Censer, *Reconstruction*, 16.

34. Fosl, *Subversive Southerner*, 29, 35.

35. Durr, *Outside the Magic Circle*, 47–49, 66–67, 70.

36. Quoted in Hall, *Revolt against Chivalry*, 9–10.

37. Durr, *Outside the Magic Circle*, 47.

38. Hall, *Revolt against Chivalry*, 13.

39. Quoted in Hall, *Revolt against Chivalry*, 13.

40. Scott, *Southern Lady*, 184; A. Elizabeth Taylor, "Suffrage and Antisuffrage," in Bercaw and Ownby, *Gender*, 276–79.

41. Durr, *Outside the Magic Circle*, 47.

42. Politicians actually held on to the image of the southern lady as a powerful electoral tool. Lillian Smith recollects that as late as 1948, a Mississippian politician used the following words in a speech: "When God made the Southern woman he summoned His angel messengers and He commanded them to go through all the star-strewn vicissitudes of space and gather all there was of beauty, of brightness and

sweetness, of enchantment and glamour, and when they returned and laid the golden harvest at His feet He began in their wondering presence the work of fashioning the Southern girl." Smith, *Killers of the Dream*, 169. Such rhetoric remained common in the South until the civil rights movement.

43. Burlage, "Truths," 117; Powell, answers to author's questionnaire; Leonard, answers to author's questionnaire.

44. Browning, answers to author's questionnaire; Leonard, answers to author's questionnaire; Burlage, "Truths," 95; Durr, answers to author's questionnaire.

45. Smith, *Killers of the Dream*, 121. Commenting on the white man's illicit sexual attraction to black women, Wilbur Cash had written in 1941: "On the one hand, the convention must be set up that the thing simply did not exist, and enforced under penalty of being shot; and on the other, the woman must be compensated, the revolting suspicion in the male that he might be slipping into bestiality got rid of, by glorifying her." Cash, *Mind of the South*, 86. Thus, if white women suffered in no way the physical and mental oppression that rape represented for black women, they were nevertheless the victims of white men. On the dichotomy between representations of black and white women, see, for instance, Goldfield, *Still Fighting*, 108–9; Olson, *Freedom's Daughters*, 25; Williamson, *Crucible of Race*, 307.

46. On black women, white women, and slavery, see, for instance, Higginbotham, "African-American Women's History," 258; Clinton, *Plantation Mistress*.

47. Higginbotham, "African-American Women's History," 261.

48. Durr, *Outside the Magic Circle*, 252, 19; Braden, *Wall Between*, 21. Dorothy Burlage, of the younger generation, learned the same distinction between black "women" and white "ladies" (Burlage interview).

49. Because segregation denied blacks access to all high-profile jobs, a majority of black women were employed in domestic service as cooks, maids, or nurses. Nine out of ten servants working in southern cities in 1900 were black women. While the black woman was expected to sacrifice her entire family life to the wishes of the white woman for whom she worked, she could not but be reminded every day of the legacy of slavery. See Jones, *Labor of Love*, 128, 127.

50. Boyle, *Desegregated Heart*, 44, 45.

51. Jones, *Labor of Love*, 127. According to Jones, "Caught up in a patriarchal world of their own, deprived of formal economic or political power, and convinced of their own racial superiority, [white women] fiercely tried to maintain the upper hand in governing sullen, recalcitrant servants" (130).

52. Quoted in Olson, *Freedom's Daughters*, 16. Olson rightly points out that "the pitting of black women against white women produced suspicions and rivalries that affected the nineteenth-century abolitionist movement, the civil rights movement of the 1950s and 1960s, and the women's movement." Olson, *Freedom's Daughters*, 26. For instance, black civil rights activists in the 1960s commonly depicted white women as lazy. "That was why all white women had colored women working for them," remarked Anne Moody (quoted in Jones, *Labor of Love*, 300).

53. On the symbolic function of the mammy in segregationist culture, see K. Sue Jewell, "Mammy," in Bercaw and Ownby, *Gender*, 171; Hale, *Making Whiteness*, 100, 101.

54. Smith, *Killers of the Dream*, 130; Smith, *Strange Fruit*, 107.

55. Lynching reached its height in the early 1890s, with a climax of 705 occurrences for the southern region in the five years between 1889 and 1893 (Hall, *Revolt against Chivalry*, 134). For an analysis of the racial fears that grew up among whites in the late nineteenth century, see, for instance, Litwack, *Trouble*, 197–216; Foner, *Reconstruction*, 122–23. Historians have shown that the phenomenon and its rationalization through the concomitant spread of the rape myth occurred at a time when southern black men had reached a position of relative economic and political influence in the region while white men, on the contrary, felt diminished in their manhood by the Civil War and its multiple consequences. With post-Reconstruction southern society being riddled with tensions of all sorts, from economic to gender relations, the major function of lynching thus was to reassert the social inferiority of black males by submitting them physically to the brutal force of white men. See Hale, *Making Whiteness*, 233; White, *Dark Continent*, 31.

56. Smith, *Killers of the Dream*, 162–63. A total of 114 lynchings were reported in the United States between 1931 and 1940 (with an average of 11.4 a year). Between 1941 and 1950 the average had dropped to 3 per year. Between 1951 and 1985, 10 lynchings were officially reported in the country. William Hair, "Lynching," in Bercaw and Ownby, *Gender*, 165.

57. For instance, speaking on the CBS program *Face the Nation*, Martin Luther King Jr. once said, "The Negro man in this country . . . has never been able to be a man. He has been robbed of his manhood because of the legacy of slavery and segregation and discrimination, and we have had in the Negro community a matriarchal family . . . in the midst of a patriarchal society." Quoted in Olson, *Freedom's Daughters*, 142. King's association of black men's victimization with the notion of black matriarchy proved a highly controversial subject, especially when Daniel Patrick Moynihan's report on the black family, published in 1965, expanded on the theme at length—and rightly provoked black women's anger—by arguing that black men had suffered more than black women from segregation. In any case, without engaging in the controversy, it seems reasonable to observe that lynching did deny black men their masculinity. For more information on the controversy over black matriarchy and the Moynihan report, see, for instance, Olson, *Freedom's Daughters*, 374–76; Erin Chapman, "Matriarchy, Myth of," in Bercaw and Ownby, *Gender*, 178–83.

58. See, for instance, J. Hall, quoted in Hale, *Making Whiteness*, 234. See also Goldfield's interpretation: "The white version of southern history created a new enemy, the black male, who enabled white men to fulfill their role as protector of white women, a role they had forfeited during the war and now could redeem." The historian explicitly accuses white men of consciously resorting to the rape myth in order to prevent women from entering the public sphere at the turn of the twentieth century: "After

Reconstruction, when white women looked to transfer their enhanced domestic roles into more public forums, supporting issues such as suffrage, child labor reform, and prohibition, white men joined sex and politics to banish women and their causes from the public arena." Goldfield, *Still Fighting*, 102.

59. Although the ideology of white supremacy stressed passivity as a major trait of white womanhood, many white women actively participated in the celebration of the Lost Cause and the restoration of white supremacy that logically coincided with the spread of lynching across the region. Hence Grace Elizabeth Hale's use of the phrase "willed passivity" when referring to the role played by white women of the middle class in the creation of a new southern order—of which lynching was a central constitutive feature. Hale shows that these women, empowered by the evolution of society in the late nineteenth century, were more active than passive in the overall transformation of the New South. Hale, *Making Whiteness*, 92–93. See also Gilmore, *Gender*, 96.

60. Murphy, *Breaking the Silence*, 29; Foster, "Emancipation," 51–52.

61. See Hall, *Revolt against Chivalry*, xx; Lisa Lindquist Dorr, "Rape," in Bercaw and Ownby, *Gender*, 230; Dorr, *White Women*.

62. Gladney, answers to author's questionnaire.

63. Boyle, *Desegregated Heart*, 78, 79, 80.

64. Durr, *Outside the Magic Circle*, 252–53.

65. Durr, *Outside the Magic Circle*, 295. See note 57.

66. Olson, *Freedom's Daughters*, 307, 308.

67. Ultimately, the issue of interracial sex in the movement stirred up much controversy in the following decades, and the suggestion that this was a central aspect of the activists' lives exasperated many of them. As the sociologist Belinda Robnett has shown in her own research, "While young people at the peak of the sexual revolution certainly engaged in intimate relations, they had little time to do so. . . . Certainly, for all of the Black and White interviewees, sexual relations were peripheral at best." Robnett quotes Bernice Johnson Reagon saying, "You were dealing with teenagers and young adults who were sexually active. So you had partnering going every way you can imagine between people who were risking their lives every day. And I don't know if I have much more than that to say about sexual activity in the movement." Robnett, *How Long?*, 131.

68. Hobson, *But Now*, 2. For examples of white southern men's rejection of racism, see, among others, Cash, *Mind of the South*; Dabbs, *Southern Heritage*; East, *Magnolia Jungle*; King, *Confessions*; Morris, *North*; McLaurin, *Separate Pasts*; Zellner, *Wrong Side*.

69. Braden, *Wall Between*, 25.

70. Lumpkin, *Making of a Southerner*, 132, 133.

71. Braden, *Wall Between*, 25, 31.

72. Quoted in Bayless, *Obliged to Help*, 29. The incident is also mentioned in Murphy, *Breaking the Silence*, 7.

73. Murphy, *Breaking the Silence*, 12.

74. Stevens interview, 9. For an in-depth analysis of spectacle lynchings, see Hale, *Making Whiteness*, 199–239. The enthusiasm of the schoolgirls who wanted to attend the lynching can be understood by the organization of some lynchings as real shows, advertised in the local media.

75. Smith, *Killers of the Dream*, 128.

76. Boyle, *Desegregated Heart*, 15; Smith, *Killers of the Dream*, 134.

77. Durr, *Outside the Magic Circle*, 16, 17.

78. Smith, *Killers of the Dream*, 28–29.

79. See Hale, *Making Whiteness*, 118, for further discussion of this point.

80. Lumpkin, *Making of a Southerner*, 192, 193.

81. Lumpkin, *Making of a Southerner*, 206.

82. Braden, *Wall Between*, 27. See also Sara Murphy's account of her own awakening at Columbia University. She had become friends with a black student from the West Indies who pointed out to her one day that their walking together down the street in New York City would be impossible in Nashville, where Murphy came from, because they would be identified as an interracial couple and could be arrested. She commented: "It was a sudden, big mindshift for me." Murphy, *Breaking the Silence*, 31.

83. Boyle, *Desegregated Heart*, 51.

84. Durr, *Outside the Magic Circle*, 59.

85. Frystak, *Our Minds*, 123; Rebecca Owen, in Evans, *Journeys*, 68; Sue Thrasher, "Circle of Trust," in Curry et al., *Deep in Our Hearts*, 207–51, 218.

86. Curry interview.

87. To Sara Evans, the stories of these women "underlined the importance of a subversive thread within mainstream Protestantism that nourished activism and leadership—for some from early childhood, for all in college, and for a few throughout their lives." Evans, *Journeys*, 9. Kimberly Little, who has studied white women's participation in the Memphis civil rights movement, has observed the same connection between activism and religion among Catholics and Jews. She notes that "women coming from both Jewish and Christian backgrounds echoed the claim that since all human beings belonged to a universal brotherhood, the unjust treatment of one of God's children constituted a sin against God." Little, *You Must Be from the North*, 50. See also Hobson, *But Now*, 7. One of the women consulted for this study, Sheila Michaels, is Jewish. She was born in St. Louis in 1939, and grew up in the same white supremacist environment as her Christian counterparts. She worked with CORE and SNCC in Mississippi and Atlanta between 1961 and 1964 (Michaels, answers to author's questionnaire). For a Catholic example, see Little, *You Must Be from the North*, 56–58. For a full-length study of Jewish female antiracist activism, see Schultz, *Going South*, an oral history focusing on northern Jewish women involved in the 1960s southern civil rights movement.

88. Smith, *Killers of the Dream*, 99; Thrasher, "Circle," 217; Nasstrom, *Everybody's Grandmother*, 13; Browning, "Shiloh," 39.

89. On the influence of religious tradition on the civil rights movement, see Chappell, *Stone*.

90. McCurdy, in Evans, *Journeys*, 158.

91. Braden, *Wall Between*, 22; Thrasher, "Circle," 217–18. See also Gladney, answers to author's questionnaire.

92. Braden, *Wall Between*, 275; Smith, *Killers of the Dream*, 39. Virginia Durr also refers to schizophrenia when evoking the effects of segregationist education on white southerners: "if you have kissed and hugged and sat on [Negroes'] laps and have loved them so much and have been so close to them, and all of a sudden you are told by your mother and your father and your aunts and your uncles and the whole white society that they are inferior people and they should not be treated like other people . . . it makes you feel that there is something wrong with *you*. I think it sets up a terrible conflict in people and I think they get to be schizophrenic." Quoted in Olson, *Freedom's Daughters*, 101.

93. If this is true of the white southern women considered here, it also seems to apply to all American women, black as well as white, who became involved in social reform movements after World War II. In her study of women reformers between 1945 and the 1960s, Susan Lynn notes that "the single characteristic most common to the women in this study, aside from their Protestant heritage, was their access to college education." Lynn, *Progressive Women*, 28. Interestingly enough, Lynn also finds Protestantism and a middle- to upper-class background common features of the women she examines—which incidentally tends to confirm that the real specificity of southern women reformers was their segregationist education.

94. Lumpkin, *Making of a Southerner*, 201.

95. Durr, *Outside the Magic Circle*, 63. Durr actually went to Wellesley College in Boston, but her words also apply to southern colleges.

96. Braden, *Wall Between*, 26; folder 6, box 4, Curry Papers.

97. Quoted in Hall, *Revolt against Chivalry*, 68. Hall adds that the other institution was the University of North Carolina.

98. Stevens interview, 20, 26; Knotts, *Fellowship*, 105.

99. Stevens interview, 30. See also Anne Braden's experience in Fosl, *Subversive Southerner*, 40.

100. Evans, *Journeys*, 4. For several testimonies about female mentoring, see Tamela Hultman, in Evans, *Journeys*, 150; Evans, *Journeys*, 9; Owen, in Evans, *Journeys*, 73, 74; Hayden, "Fields," 338.

101. Durr, *Outside the Magic Circle*, xi. Studs Terkel, who wrote the foreword, actually explains on the same page that Durr's original choice for the title had been "The Emancipation of Pure White Southern Womanhood."

102. Parsons, *Southern Wrongs*, xxv, 19.

103. Evans, *Personal Politics*, 57; Gladney, answers to author's questionnaire. Evans draws a parallel between southern white women in the 1960s civil rights movement

and the Grimké sisters, who articulated their critique of gender inequality while being involved in the abolitionist movement in the 1830s. "Unlike the Grimké sisters," she writes, "they did not leave the South; but like them, as they confronted the racial oppression of southern culture, they would be forced to challenge the most subtle assumptions behind their roles as southern whites who were also women.... Unlike their male companions, these young, driven, committed white women had also to challenge roles forced upon them by friends and enemies alike—assumptions about female behavior, goals, and responsibilities that were not only a part of the general culture, but naturally and painfully a part of themselves." Evans, *Personal Politics*, 57. This was especially true of Dorothy Burlage, Mary King, Jane Stembridge, and Casey Hayden. For an example of the Grimké sisters' reflection on gender inequality, see, for instance, Grimké, *Letters*.

104. Burlage, "Truths," 95, 104.

105. The "Waveland retreat" (in Waveland, Mississippi) was organized in November for this purpose. For further information on the event, see Carson, *In Struggle*, 133–52; King, *Freedom Song*, 437–43; Hayden, "Fields," 360–64.

106. "SNCC Position Paper, November 1964," in King, *Freedom Song*, 567–69. Also reprinted in Evans, *Personal Politics*, 233–35. King and Hayden submitted the paper unsigned at the Waveland conference, and it was later wrongly attributed to Ruby Doris Robinson, a black staff leader known for her self-assertiveness. See King's account of this incident in *Freedom Song*, 452.

107. King, *Freedom Song*, 471.

Chapter 2. Before *Brown*: Southern Lady Activism

1. For a short but well-documented synthesis of the evolution of southern society, politics, and culture between the Civil War and 1920, see Rabinowitz, *First New South*. See also Woodward, *Strange Career of Jim Crow*; Tindall, *Emergence of the New South*; Ayers, *Promise of a New South*.

2. Lynn, *Progressive Women*, 46–47. The charter declared: "Wherever there is injustice on the basis of race, whether in the community, the nation or the world, our protest must be clear and our labor for its removal, vigorous and steady. And what we urge on others we are constrained to practice ourselves. We shall be alert to opportunities to demonstrate the richness of life inherent in an organization unhampered by artificial barriers, in which all members have full status and all persons equal honor and respect as the children of one Father." In addition to the charter, the authors of the report recommended to local associations, "That the implications of the Purpose be recognized as involving the inclusion of Negro women and girls in the main stream of Association life, and that such inclusion be adopted as a conscious goal." Sabiston and Hiller, *Toward Better Race Relations*, 179, 181. The YWCA Purpose went as follows: "To build a fellowship of women and girls devoted to the task of realizing in our common life those ideals of personal and social living to which we are committed by our faith as Christians. In this endeavour, we seek to understand Jesus, to share his love

for all people, and to grow in the knowledge and love of God." Sabiston and Hiller, *Toward Better Race Relations*, 178.

3. Although the association lost some of its influence in the 1950s—probably due to the multiplication of competing denominational and civil rights groups—it continued to attract women, especially on southern campuses. Taylor, "On the Edge," 2; Robertson, *Christian Sisterhood*, 2, 8, 5. For a comprehensive study of the YWCA and race relations between 1906 and 1946, see Robertson, *Christian Sisterhood*.

4. The evolution from biracialism—based on separate black and white branches within the same organization—to full integration was due to the constant pressure exerted by black members on white leadership. As Lynn notes, "At each crucial juncture in the YWCA's progress toward racial integration, black women took the lead, pressing for an interracial conference in 1915, demanding that the southern Student YWCA integrate at the leadership level in the early 1920s, pushing for racial integration in community YWCAs during the years of World War II, and providing important leadership in the struggle to implement the Interracial Charter after the war." Student YWCAs were more advanced than community YWCAs, and they definitely influenced the national policy of the organization. The YWCA followed the trends initiated by the student associations, which were themselves influenced by their black members. Lynn, *Progressive Women*, 66, 65. In her study of the student YWCA in the South, Frances Taylor identifies the early 1920s as a turning point in blacks' attitudes when black staff members rejected accommodation to segregation as a necessary concession to racial progress. They asked in particular for integrated conferences. To Taylor, these demands "demonstrate that the black staff members of the early 1920s differed from their predecessors who operated on the philosophy 'that this ... attitude [discrimination through segregation] has to be borne for the sake of the cause; that the end justifies the means.'" Taylor, "On the Edge," 34.

5. Alice G. Knotts, "Methodist Women Integrate Schools and Housing, 1952–1959," in Crawford, Rouse, and Woods, *Women in the Civil Rights Movement*, 251–58, 251.

6. The first step in the organization of Methodist women came with the creation in 1878 of the Methodist Woman's Foreign Mission Society. It was followed in 1898 by the formation of the Home Mission Society, which enabled women to engage in local reform work in an autonomous and respectable way. Hall, *Revolt against Chivalry*, 67–69.

7. Knotts, *Fellowship*, 23.

8. For further information on the southern YWCA, see Marion W. Roydhouse, "Bridging Chasms," in Hewitt and Lebsock, *Visible Women*, 270–95.

9. Taylor, "On the Edge," 80–81, 41, 82. See also Robertson, *Christian Sisterhood*, 131.

10. In the interwar period, southern community YWCAs concentrated their efforts on social reform work, which included racial justice but did not challenge Jim Crow. They did not endorse federal measures against racial discrimination, preferring

to focus on general social issues that affected working women. For instance, between 1943 and 1952, the Atlanta YWCA successfully lobbied for the passage of the Georgia Child Labor Act. "Highlights in the History of Atlanta's YWCA," n.d., folder 1, box 50, YWCA of Greater Atlanta Records. On the Atlanta YWCA, see also folder 10, box 9, Barker Papers.

11. For a comprehensive study of the Social Gospel movement, see, for instance, White and Hopkins, *Social Gospel*. For an analysis specifically focused on racial reform, see White, *Liberty and Justice*. For a study of the movement in the South, see McDowell, *Social Gospel*.

12. Taylor, "On the Edge," 19–22, 26, 60, 47. On Lumpkin's discovery of the Social Gospel's interpretation of religion, see Lumpkin, *Making of a Southerner*, 187–88.

13. Taylor, "On the Edge," 12.

14. For a detailed analysis of these programs, see Taylor, "On the Edge," 89–106.

15. Webb, quoted in Taylor, "On the Edge," 93; Lumpkin, quoted in Taylor, "On the Edge," 100; Cuthbertson, quoted in Lynn, *Progressive Women*, 30; Lynn, *Progressive Women*, 32.

16. Taylor, "On the Edge," 70, 69–73. Lumpkin also became friends with Louise McLaren and Lois McDonald from the industrial YWCA.

17. Salmond, *Miss Lucy*, 15–19, 146–47.

18. Hall, *Revolt against Chivalry*, 83; "Summer School for Women in Industry," reprinted from General Federation News, June 1929 (folder 1, box 5, Barker Papers); Louise McLaren to "Members of the Executive Committee," March 15, 1933 (folder 1, box 5, Barker Papers); Lucy Mason to Mary Barker, April 26, 1933 (folder 1, box 5, Barker Papers); Louise McLaren to Members of Central and Advisory Committees who are also Members of Trade Unions, June 17, 1936 (folder 4, box 5, Barker Papers); Louise McLaren to Mary Barker, April 6, 1939 (folder 4, box 5, Barker Papers); Louise McLaren to James Dombrowski and Myles Horton, February 2, 1940 (folder 5, box 5, Barker Papers); "Report of Director Southern Summer School for Workers," May 1, 1940 (folder 5, box 5, Barker Papers); Mason, *To Win These Rights*, 8. For an in-depth analysis of the Summer School for Women, see Frederickson, "'Place to Speak Our Minds.'"

19. Quoted in Hall, *Revolt against Chivalry*, 73. For further information on Methodist white women's settlement work among blacks, see Hall, *Revolt against Chivalry*, 71–73; McDowell, *Social Gospel*, 84–87. For a personal account of interracial work at the Nashville Bethlehem House, see interview with Louise Young by Jacquelyn and Bob Hall, February 14, 1972 (G-0066), Southern Oral History Program Collection (#4007), Southern Historical Collection, Wilson Library, University of North Carolina at Chapel Hill.

20. McDonough, "Men and Women," 52–56, 99–100, 119; McDowell, *Social Gospel*, 93. The CIC did not question the legitimacy of segregation as the southern way of life. Although its executive director, Will Alexander, did express his wish to see segregation

laws repealed, thus aligning himself with the position of black members, the men who represented the majority in the organization were "not warriors or crusaders," as Josiah Morse put it, but tried to stir up "good will and love of fair play in the minds and hearts of all human beings" (McDonough, "Men and Women," 87). As for Baptist women in the CIC, Alice Norwood Spearman, who joined the South Carolina CIC in the 1930s, provides a good example. See Marcia G. Synnott, "Alice Norwood Spearman Wright: Civil Rights Apostle to South Carolinians," in Coryell et al., *Beyond Image*, 184–207; Marcia G. Synnott, "Alice Buck Norwood Spearman Wright: A Civil Rights Activist," in Spruill, Littlefield, and Johnson, *South Carolina Women*, 200–220.

21. Jessie Daniel Ames and Bertha Payne Newell, *"Repairers of the Breach": A Story of Interracial Cooperation Between Southern Women, 1935–1940* (Atlanta: Commission on Interracial Cooperation, December 1940), 14, reel 29, Commission on Interracial Cooperation Papers (hereafter cited as CIC Papers).

22. Ames and Newell, *"Repairers,"* 13.

23. McDonough, "Men and Women," 26, 46–47; McDowell, *Social Gospel*, 91. The daughter of a Methodist preacher, Johnson was endowed, according to Jacquelyn Hall, with the following qualities: "a combination of the aristocratic benevolence of her slave-owning grandparents and the religious fervor of her missionary father; the ability to translate social issues into the language of the southern Methodist pulpit; and a strong identification with the problems of women as a group." Hall, *Revolt against Chivalry*, 95.

24. Hall, *Revolt against Chivalry*, 101, 93.

25. Hall, *Revolt against Chivalry*, 95–98. For the differences between the black women's and white women's position statements regarding suffrage, see "Southern Women and Race Cooperation," [1921], published by Woman's Missionary Council, Methodist Episcopal Church, South, reel 14, CIC Papers.

26. H. L. Hammond, *Southern Women and Racial Adjustment* (1917; reprint, Atlanta: Commission on Interracial Cooperation, 1920), 32, 34, 33, reel 14, CIC Papers.

27. Hammond, *Southern Women*, 5. In contrast to Hammond, Thelma Stevens, who held a key position as secretary of the Department of Christian Social Relations and Local Church Activities (CSR/LCA) between 1940 and 1968, was not paternalistic in her outlook, which can certainly be accounted for by her poor rural Mississippi background. She dedicated her life to building "strong team leadership and volunteer support by down-playing her own role and giving credit to group efforts." Knotts, *Fellowship*, 10. Nevertheless, in the first half of the twentieth century, many churchwomen expressed the same sense of moral superiority as Hammond had in 1917. For a discussion of paternalism by Thelma Stevens, see Stevens interview, 29, 73–77.

28. Women first facilitated the creation of local and state interracial committees. Rather than being interracial in the literal sense of the word, these usually consisted of parallel committees of blacks and whites who met regularly to share views and skills on how to improve the condition of blacks. By 1924, eleven state committees had been

organized. The effectiveness of women's committees depended on local conditions and the CIC was not very successful in the grassroots work. Some women, however, made a difference in a few areas. Hall, *Revolt against Chivalry*, 102–3.

29. McDowell, *Social Gospel*, 100–101; Hall, *Revolt against Chivalry*, 102; Interview with Jessie Daniel Ames by Pat Watters, 1965, 1966 (G-003), Southern Oral History Program Collection (#4007), Southern Historical Collection, Wilson Library, University of North Carolina at Chapel Hill, 5–7.

30. The papers of Alice Spearman (who later became Alice Spearman Wright), from South Carolina, provide an illuminating illustration of churchwomen's interracial work in the pre-*Brown* era and after. See, for instance, J. E. Blanton to A. Spearman, March 20, 1947, folder 637, box 24, South Carolina Council on Human Relations Records (hereafter cited as SCCHR Records).

31. D. Tilly to Mrs. Elmer Clark, August 14, 1944 (folder 6, box 1, Tilly Papers); Ruth Mougey Worrell to D. Tilly, November 7, 1947 (folder 6, box 1, Tilly Papers).

32. Mrs. Gene Berkey to Mrs. Tilly, March 6, 1948 (folder 7, box 1, Tilly Papers); anonymous letter to D. Tilly, marked February 8, 1948, Atlanta (folder 7, box 1, Tilly Papers). About Tilly's radicalism, see also Jane McDonald to Alice Spearman, April 6, 1948 (folder 8, box 1, Wright Papers).

33. Lynn, *Progressive Women*, 55. For a personal account of the resistance the Interracial Charter met in the South, see Height, *Open Wide*, 117–24.

34. See Sabiston and Hiller, *Toward Better Race Relations*, 17, 21; Lynn, *Progressive Women*, 50; Robertson, *Christian Sisterhood*, 165–69.

35. Sabiston and Hiller, *Toward Better Race Relations*, 67, 42.

36. Shannon, *Just Because*, 33; Knotts, *Fellowship*, 198.

37. See Young interview, 35–36, 48, 52–53.

38. For a discussion of the tensions between Methodist women and Methodist male leaders in the 1910s, see Knotts, *Fellowship*, 34. See also Hall, *Revolt against Chivalry*, about female solidarity. Hall writes that "for most middle-class southern women, it was the institutional structure of the church that provided a basis for female solidarity, and evangelical religion that created a rationale for seeking a female alliance across racial lines." The female solidarity Hall alludes to emerged after 1906 out of the decision by the General Conference of the Methodist Episcopal Church, South to merge the Home Mission Society—created in 1898—with the Foreign Mission Society—created in 1878—and to place the new Woman's Missionary Council under the authority of the male-controlled Board of Missions. Such a move to subordinate women to male leadership triggered off a movement for women's voting rights within the church. Women won the battle for laity rights in 1918. Significantly, along with struggling for gender equality within the church, Methodist women had also engaged in interracial mission work in the 1910s. As a result, writes Hall, "By 1920, Methodist women leaders implicitly saw themselves as a sisterhood within an alien institution." Hall, *Revolt against Chivalry*, 66, 74–76, 77.

39. Quoted in Taylor, "On the Edge," 195.

40. Giddings, *When and Where*, 177. The pioneer in the antilynching fight was the black journalist Ida B. Wells, born a slave in 1862, who first denounced lynching in her journal, the Memphis *Free Speech*, in 1892. She then played a key role in the mobilization of educated black women against racial violence and discrimination. See Wells, *Crusade*; Wells-Barnett, *On Lynchings*; Giddings, *When and Where*, 17–32; Hall, *Revolt against Chivalry*, 78–80.

41. For biographical and other information on Mary McLeod Bethune, see Giddings, *When and Where*, 199–230.

42. Hall, *Revolt against Chivalry*, 160–62.

43. Ducey, *Commission on Interracial Cooperation Papers*, 4.

44. McDonough, "Men and Women," 130; Hall, *Revolt against Chivalry*, 180, 236.

45. Hall, *Revolt against Chivalry*, 190.

46. Hall, *Revolt against Chivalry*, 196, 194; Smith, *Killers of the Dream*, 145, 147.

47. Hall, "Women and Lynching," 54.

48. Hall, *Revolt against Chivalry*, 256.

49. Ames interview, 7. The Dyer Bill and the Costigan-Wagner Bill were two federal antilynching bills that made lynching a federal crime and allowed for punishment of local and state officers who did not use their powers to protect potential victims and/or to prosecute the people involved in a lynching. The Dyer Bill was introduced in Congress twice, in 1918 and 1923. Although it passed the House in 1922, it was defeated several times in the Senate. The Costigan-Wagner Bill, introduced in 1934, was defeated several times between 1934 and 1940. For further information on the Dyer Bill, the Costigan-Wagner Bill, and the fight for federal antilynching legislation, see Hall, *Revolt against Chivalry*, 165–66, 237–48; Sullivan, *Lift Every Voice*, 105–11, 194–97, 203–4.

50. Durr, *Outside the Magic Circle*, xi.

51. Quoted in Hall, *Revolt against Chivalry*, 194, 195.

52. Smith, *Killers of the Dream*, 145.

53. For more information on the South during the Great Depression, see, for instance, Biles, *South and the New Deal*; Sosna, *In Search*; Tindall, *Emergence of the New South*; Grantham, *South in Modern America*; Sullivan, *Days of Hope*.

54. Sullivan, *Days of Hope*, 3.

55. Eleanor Roosevelt's grandmother (Martha "Mittie" Bullock) and great-grandmother (Martha Stewart Elliott Bullock) belonged to a Georgia slaveholding family. See Cook, *Eleanor Roosevelt*, 1:27–28.

56. Olson, *Freedom's Daughters*, 62, 56–64.

57. Up to World War II, the association had mainly fought on the front of lynching and various forms of discrimination across the nation. It had been present in the South since the first membership drives organized during World War I, but the repressive policy of segregationist forces in the 1920s and 1930s had made progress difficult

in the region. Some state chapters had made significant gains in the fields of voting registration and black education during the interwar years, but the real turning point occurred in the 1940s when the organization led successful membership drives that raised its membership from 50,000 in 1940 to almost 450,000 in 1945. Ella Baker, who became national director of branches in 1943, focused her efforts on the South. She played a crucial part in the proliferation of local and state southern branches during the latter years of the war. Sullivan, *Lift Every Voice*, xv–viii, 61–100, 304–8; Ransby, *Ella Baker*, 107–18.

58. Reed, *Simple Decency*, 4–8. The report had actually been written by a group of southern New Dealers working for FDR's administration, which included Virginia Durr and Lucy Mason, among others.

59. Reed, *Simple Decency*, 15–19.

60. Although it did not make segregation its official target, the SCHW practiced racial integration within its ranks and challenged the major forms of discrimination that were directly connected to segregation. As Linda Reed has noted, "People in SCHW were willing to accept criticism from outside sources such as the NEC [National Emergency Council] and to challenge the status quo concerning the status of blacks. Indeed, the SCHW based its reason for being on the principle of equality for all." Reed, *Simple Decency*, 19.

61. Mason, *To Win These Rights*, 29. Before committing herself to labor organizing, she was appointed general secretary of the National Consumers' League in 1932 and went to live in New York, where she worked for the betterment of national working conditions. Mason, *To Win These Rights*, 13–17.

62. Mason, *To Win These Rights*, 32, 30; Patton, "Southern Liberals," 38–39. See also Mason, "CIO and the Negro in the South."

63. Mason, *To Win These Rights*, 19, 181.

64. Mason, *To Win These Rights*, 24, 39–40; Durr, *Outside the Magic Circle*, 118.

65. "Georgia Inventory, 1937–1938" (folder 9, box 13, Wilkins Papers); "Proposed Plan for a Twelve Month's Cooperative Program" (folder 1, box 12, Wilkins Papers); "Memorial Friday for Miss Wilkins," *Atlanta Constitution*, June 2, 1977, clipping (folder 2, box 5, Wilkins Papers); William Ivey to J. Wilkins, November 28, 1938 (folder 5, box 14, Wilkins Papers). On Spearman, see folder 4, box 1, and "Biographical information," box 2, Wright Papers.

66. Nasstrom, *Everybody's Grandmother*, 25, 26.

67. Durr, *Outside the Magic Circle*, 78–79, 99–115.

68. Folder 12, box 3, Wilkins Papers; J. Wilkins to Members of the Coordinating Committee, April 19, 1938 (folder 4, box 13, Wilkins Papers); Hall, *Revolt against Chivalry*, 44–56; Salmond, *Miss Lucy*, 23–29; "Biographical information," box 2, Wright Papers.

69. "Biographical note," finding aid, Pauley Papers.

70. Nasstrom, *Everybody's Grandmother*, 36, 40, 44–45; Mason, *To Win These Rights*, 12.

71. Sullivan, *Days of Hope*, 110–18, 108; J. Wilkins to V. Durr, January 29, 1943 (folder 1, box 22, Wilkins Papers). See also Virginia Durr's personal account of the poll tax fight, Durr, *Outside the Magic Circle*, 126–31, 152–70.

72. *Report of Proceedings of the Southern Conference for Human Welfare*, Birmingham, Ala., November 20–23, 1938 (folder 6, box 9, Barker Papers); Sullivan, *Days of Hope*, 202–7, 206; Greene, *Our Separate Ways*, 36. The other groups involved in the campaign were the NAACP, the CIO Political Action Committee, and the Southern Negro Youth Congress.

73. Edith Holbrook Riehm, "Dorothy Tilly and the Fellowship of the Concerned," in Murray, *Throwing Off the Cloak*, 23–48, 29–30; Knotts, *Fellowship*, 164.

74. President's Committee on Civil Rights, *To Secure These Rights*; Reed, *Simple Decency*, 138.

75. See, for example, President's Committee on Civil Rights, transcript of proceedings, March 20, 1947, Washington D.C., 100–102 (folder 2, box 4, Tilly Papers); May 14, 1947, Washington, D.C., 366 (folder 4, box 4, Tilly Papers).

76. Black- and Red-baiting, as it came to be called, plagued the southern civil rights movement from the late 1940s on, reaching a peak in the immediate post-*Brown* years. Virginia Durr was one of its victims, as will be seen later in this book. She was among the very few who considered Communists less dangerous for democracy than white supremacists. Thus she supported Henry Wallace's candidacy in the 1948 presidential election, based on a popular-front platform, and even ran for the U.S. Senate as Progressive candidate for Virginia. Durr, *Outside the Magic Circle*, 195–201; Sullivan, *Days of Hope*, 253–57.

77. The House Committee issued a report accusing the SCHW of serving the Communists' interests (see House Committee on Un-American Activities, *Report on Southern Conference for Human Welfare*). Krueger, *Promises*, 167–81; Reed, *Simple Decency*, 127; Dunbar, *Against the Grain*, 217.

78. For more information on the Southern Regional Council, see Sosna, *In Search*, 152–66; Egerton, *Speak Now*, 311–16, 432–37, 446–48, 481–83, 564–68; McDonough, "Men and Women."

79. Interview with Guion B. Johnson by Mary Frederickson, July 1, 1974 (G-0029-4), Southern Oral History Program Collection (#4007), Southern Historical Collection, Wilson Library, University of North Carolina at Chapel Hill, 26, 4. For a reflection on women's organizing role in the civil rights movement, see Charles M. Payne, "Men Led, but Women Organized: Movement Participation of Women in the Mississippi Delta," in Crawford, Rouse, and Woods, *Women in the Civil Rights Movement*, 1–11.

80. *Atlanta Journal*, June 2, 1977, folder 2, box 5, Wilkins Papers.

81. "In Joyful Memory of Josephine Mathewson Wilkins," Sheraton-Biltmore Hotel in Atlanta, Georgia, June 3, 1977, 11, 9, 8 (folder 3, box 5, Wilkins Papers). Since the 1930s, Wilkins had mobilized thousands of Georgians to participate in civic, social,

and racial reform, her major asset being her network of women friends and coworkers from religious and civic associations. Her private correspondence testifies to her influential role over decades. Before devoting her time to fundraising and campaign-organizing for the SRC, she had proved her organizing and mobilizing skills by committing the Georgia LWV to ever more militant action and by creating the Georgia Citizens Fact Finding Movement, which the *Atlanta Journal* described as "a pioneer effort at citizen participation in public policy discussion," adding that Governor Ellis Arnall [1943–47] had once said that "without this network of community activities his election would have been impossible." *Atlanta Journal*, June 2, 1977.

82. "In Joyful Memory," 13. As an illustration, in 1958, Alice Spearman sent a letter to Wilkins as executive director of the South Carolina Council on Human Relations. Spearman was writing to complain about the attitude of the national LWV during the school desegregation crisis. A national staff person had actually advised local league members not to work with the SCCHR. Spearman asked Wilkins to use her personal influence to talk the national LWV into supporting integrationists rather than avoiding them: "I hope you will not quote me in this matter, but do what you can, with your usual skill, to secure for us encouragement rather than discouragement from the national level." A. Spearman to J. Wilkins, March 11, 1958 (folder 3, box 1, Wilkins Papers). In 1962, Jim Dombrowski wrote Wilkins to thank her for a $1,000 check she had contributed to a bail fund that had been set up to free jailed student activists (James Dombrowski to J. Wilkins, March 2, 1962, folder 17, box 2, Wilkins Papers). For other examples of correspondence with women friends, see in Wilkins Papers: Eliza Paschall to J. Wilkins, August 7 [1960] (folder 9, box 1); Jessie Daniel Ames to J. Wilkins, August 21 [1960] (folder 11, box 1); Jessie Daniel Ames to J. Wilkins, December, 26, 1960 (folder 19, box 1); Virginia Durr to J. Wilkins, [1960] (folder 4, box 2); J. Wilkins to Lucy Mason, May 17, 1939 (folder 3, box 15). On Grace T. Hamilton, see Mullis, "Public Career of Grace Towns Hamilton."

83. Smith, "Growing into Freedom;" Patton, "Southern Liberals," 158–59; "Lillian Smith Chronology," folder 1:1, box 1, Smith Papers.

84. Lillian Smith and Paula Snelling, "Man Born of Woman," in White and Sugg, *From the Mountain*, 236–48, 245, 246.

85. Smith, quoted in Gladney, *How?*, 63. On Smith's loss of security after abandoning her "acceptable gender role," see Gladney, *How?*, 14–15.

86. L. Smith to Jerry Bick, October 27, 1961, in Gladney, *How?*, 287–89; Smith, "Southern Liberalism;" Smith, "Southerner Talking," October 23, 1948. For an example of her early calls to action, see "Addressed to Intelligent White Southerners," [Winter 1942–43], in White and Sugg, *From the Mountain*, 116–30. For an illustration of southern liberals' argumentation against federal intervention, see Hodding Carter, "A Southern Liberal Looks at Civil Rights," *New York Times Magazine*, August 8, 1948, 10, 20, 25; Ralph McGill, "The Uncomfortable Southern Dilemma," *Atlanta Constitution*, March 1, 1948.

Chapter 3. After *Brown*, Part One: The Tactics of Respectability

1. Smith, *Now Is the Time*; *Brown v. Board of Education*: *Brown* I 347 U.S. 483 (1954), *Brown* II 349 U.S. 294 (1955).

2. See *Smith v. Allwright*, 321 U.S. 649 (1944); *Missouri ex rel. Gaines v. Canada*, 305 U.S. 337 (1938); *Sweatt v. Painter*, 339 U.S. 629 (1950).

3. On interposition measures, see Bartley, *New South*, 221, 187–222. See also Lewis, *Massive Resistance*, 32–33 and 50–61 (on southern states' legislative response to *Brown*), 39–47 (on white citizens' councils), 62–63 (on interposition measures), 90–99 (on anti-NAACP measures); and McMillen, *Citizens' Council*. For typical examples of antidesegregation pamphlets, see, for instance, Talmadge, *You and Segregation*; Brady, *Black Monday*.

4. Encouraged by a few leaders who had played key roles in the national witch hunt, such as Mississippi senator James Eastland, southern legislatures passed antisubversive laws and set up investigative committees whose official targets were Communists but whose real ones were integrationists. Most of the committees, notes Bartley, "searched for Communists and inevitably found integrationists." Bartley, *New South*, 221. As Jeff Woods has shown, McCarthyism provided southerners with ready-made instruments of repression against racial dissenters. "Indeed," Woods writes, "when the regional issue of race came to the fore in the late 1950s and the 1960s, southerners already had the tools of anti-Communism at hand. Loyalty oaths, public hearings, covert investigations, and Communist-control laws were easily converted into instruments capable of harassing civil rights organizations and activists." Woods, *Black Struggle*, 6.

5. McGill, *Atlanta Constitution*, September 18, 1963.

6. For illuminating studies of the white southern response to the *Brown* decision, see, for instance, Bartley, *Rise of Massive Resistance*; Egerton, *Speak Now*; Newberry, "Without Urgency or Ardor."

7. Some of the materials and ideas featured in this chapter were used in a previously published article. See Anne Stefani, "Image, Discourse, Facts: Southern White Women in the Fight for Desegregation, 1954–1965," *Miranda* [online], 5 (2011), http://miranda.revues.org/2262.

8. Shannon, *Just Because*, 107, 111, 112. For an example of UCW's preparation of the *Brown* decision in South Carolina, see Myrta Ross, "Report of Field Trip to South Carolina on Leadership Training Institutes, April 14–19, 1952" (folder "South Carolina Council of Church Women [SCCCW], 1950–52," box 4, Dabbs Papers); E. Dabbs to "Maude," January 23, 1954 (folder 9, box 4, Dabbs Papers).

9. Knotts, *Fellowship*, 198; Knotts, "Methodist Women," 252, 253, 257.

10. The Dixiecrats were the southern Democrats who challenged the national Democratic Party in 1948 after it nominated Truman as its presidential candidate and adopted a strong civil rights plank. They created the States' Rights Democratic Party and nominated their own candidate for president, Strom Thurmond, governor of South Carolina. They based their platform on the preservation of states' rights and

segregation. Thurmond carried four states in the election. See Key, *Southern Politics*, 317–44; Heard, *Two-Party South?*, 251–79; Bartley, *New South*, 74–103.

11. "Fellowship of the Concerned" (folder 4, box 2, Tilly Papers); Riehm, "Dorothy Tilly," 24.

12. "Fellowship of the Concerned" (folder 4, box 2, Tilly Papers).

13. "Report of Mrs. M. E. Tilly, First Quarter 1956" (folder 6, box 2, Tilly Papers). For a typical example of Tilly's rationale, see "Workshop on the Supreme Court Decision," New Orleans, reel 196, Southern Regional Council Papers (hereafter cited as SRC Papers). For numerous examples of correspondence between Tilly and other churchwomen between 1954 and 1960, see reel 196, SRC Papers.

14. See, for instance, Frystak, *Our Minds*, 84.

15. Lynn, *Progressive Women*, 78.

16. "Mrs. M. E. Tilly," n.d. (folder 4, box 1, Tilly Papers); Mary McLeod Bethune to D. Tilly, March 29, 1955 (folder 8, box 1, Tilly Papers); Dorothy Tilly, "Dr. Mary McLeod Bethune, Great Christian," n.d. (folder 6, box 2, Tilly Papers); A. Spearman to Mrs. J. E. Blanton, March 23, 1957 (folder 30, box 1, SCCHR Records); Alestis Coleman to Mrs. T. J. Ledeen, June 15, 1962 (folder 652c, box 24, SCCHR Records); Summary of "Interracial Conference of Women," 21st annual convention, National Council of Negro Women, Washington, D.C., 16–17 November, 1956 (folder 943, box 34, SCCHR Records).

17. M. McLeod Bethune to D. Tilly, March 29, 1955 (folder 8, box 1, Tilly Papers).

18. Paschall, *It Must Have Rained*, 7; "The Purpose and Philosophy of a Council on Human Relations" (folder 3, box 9, Pauley Papers).

19. Pauley Papers; Paschall Papers; Wright Papers; Durr, *Outside the Magic Circle*, 63; Murphy, *Breaking the Silence*, 71, 77; Frystak, *Our Minds*, 55–56; Lassiter and Lewis, *Moderates' Dilemma*, 40. For more information on Alice Spearman's work with the South Carolina CHR, see Daniel, *Lost Revolutions*, 229–50.

20. "Georgia's Schools—Public or Private?," *Georgia Voter* Vol. 24, no. 6, February 1954 Revised (folder 1, box 5, Pauley Papers); telegram to Honorable Herman Talmadge, June 8, 1954 (folder 1, box 5, Pauley Papers); Nasstrom, *Everybody's Grandmother*, 47, 45.

21. Cited in Frystak, *Our Minds*, 42.

22. Whitney, *League of Women Voters*, 51, 53; Parsons, *Southern Wrongs*, 27, 73–90, 100–140.

23. Frystak, *Our Minds*, 44, 45, 46–54.

24. Interview with Frances Pauley by Paul Mertz, August 1, 1983, box 95, Pauley Papers, 2; Frystak, *Our Minds*, 82.

25. Greene, *Our Separate Ways*, 51.

26. Mars, *Witness*, 52–53. For another illustration of white women's antiracist activities in Mississippi and the hostility they met, see "An oral history with Mrs Jane Schutt," October 3 and 10, 1994, interviewer Leesha Faulkner, Mississippi Oral History

Program, University of Southern Mississippi Center for Oral History and Cultural Heritage, University of Mississippi Digital Collections. Jane Schutt was an active member of Church Women United in Mississippi, serving as state president between 1960 and 1963. She also worked with the Mississippi Council on Human Relations.

27. Clark, "Analysis of the Relationship," 79, 80, 84–87.

28. Elizabeth Noble to D. Tilly, January 14, 1955 (reel 196, SRC Papers); "Report of Mrs. M. E. Tilly," First Quarter 1956 (folder 6, box 2, Tilly Papers); Alice Spearman to Camille Levy, January 21, 1960 (folder 652 c, box 24, SCCHR Records); "What Human Relations?" *Rock Hill (S.C.) Evening Herald*, February 15, 1957 (folder 29, box 1, SCCHR Records); Isabel Goldthwait to D. Tilly, March 4, 1956 (reel 196, SRC Papers); Durr, *Outside the Magic Circle*, 245.

29. Knotts, *Fellowship*, 263; Pauley, Mertz interview, 20. See also Pauley's diary, 1961–67 (folder 10, box 94, Pauley Papers).

30. Paschall, *It Must Have Rained*, 7; Parsons, *Southern Wrongs*, 38, 46; Murphy, *Breaking the Silence*, 62, 63, 72–73, 78, 113.

31. Frystak, *Our Minds*, 50; Muriel Ferris to F. Pauley, April 4, 1956 (folder 1, box 5, Pauley Papers); Elizabeth Noble to D. Tilly, January 14, 1955 (reel 196, SRC Papers); Isabel Goldthwait to D. Tilly, March 4, 1956 (reel 196, SRC Papers).

32. Edith Dabbs, "Through the Years with Church Women United in South Carolina," unpublished manuscript, folder "South Carolina Council of Church Women, 1955–75," 11, box 4, Dabbs Papers.

33. For an illustration of how the same groups allied themselves in 1964 with national women's organizations such as the National Council of Negro Women, the National Council of Catholic Women, and the National Council of Jewish Women, to promote desegregation in the South—including Mississippi—see Height, *Open Wide*, 162–99.

34. "Margaret" to E. Dabbs, February 3, 1954 (folder "SCCCW, 1953–54," box 4, Dabbs Papers); Isabel Goldthwait to D. Tilly, February 27, 1955 (reel 196, SRC Papers); Mrs. John Shields to F. Pauley, July 11, 1963 (folder 8, box 9, Pauley Papers); Murphy, *Breaking the Silence*, 114; Knotts, *Fellowship*, 107.

35. On the leadership of the VCPS, see Lassiter and Lewis, *Moderates' Dilemma*, 107–9.

36. Bartley, *New South*, 167–68. For a detailed history of the school cases that ended up in the *Brown* decision, see Hall, *Oxford Companion*, 111–12.

37. In 1954, after obtaining the population's approval by referendum, the Georgia legislature adopted what the League of Women Voters and other opponents dubbed the "private school amendment," a state constitutional amendment that allowed state and local governments to grant tuition fees for private education while it relieved the state of the obligation to maintain a public school system. In 1956, the Georgia General Assembly passed a law allowing the governor to close all public schools if only one was desegregated as a result of the *Brown* decision. In the same spirit as Georgia's leaders,

Virginians altered their state constitution in March 1956 to allow provision of tuition grants by the state while the General Assembly adopted an interposition resolution against the implementation of *Brown*. Interposition resolutions were concomitantly adopted in early 1956 by the legislative assemblies of Alabama, Georgia, Louisiana, Mississippi, and South Carolina. In November of that year, the people of Arkansas approved an interposition amendment to the state's constitution. Dartt, *Women Activists*, 9, 14; Bartley, *New South*, 160–61, 194–95; *Georgia Voter*, February 1954. As for Louisiana, according to Shannon Frystak, it "had the distinction of passing the first constitutional amendment mandating segregation in the public schools by placing them under state 'police powers'" in 1954. In a sweeping rejection of the first *Brown* decision, the Louisiana state legislature "prohibited the state's colleges and universities from accepting graduation certificates from students from integrated schools, cut supplies and funds to integrated schools, and gave broad powers to superintendents in pupil assignment." After *Brown* II, "it also repealed compulsory school attendance laws, dismissed teachers and school employees who advocated integration, and banned all interracial sports and social activities." Frystak, *Our Minds*, 78–79. On the Georgia referendum, see also Lewis, *Massive Resistance*, 33–35.

38. Bartley, *New South*, 189, 191, 192, 194, 217–18. See also Lewis, *Massive Resistance*, 52–60, on the Virginia crisis.

39. Bartley, *New South*, 240–41. See also Lewis, *Massive Resistance*, 81–90, on massive resistance in Little Rock. For a recent study of the Little Rock crisis analyzing the interconnected influences of race, sex, gender, and class on the events, see Anderson, *Little Rock*.

40. Bartley, *New South*, 223–30, 241, 242, 244, 247–48. On the role of the WEC in the Little Rock crisis, see Anderson, *Little Rock*, 138–39, 150–65, 185–88, 197–99, 218–20, 223–25. See also Brewer, *Embattled Ladies*.

41. Murphy, *Breaking the Silence*, 68, 77; Frystak, *Our Minds*, 86; Dartt, *Women Activists*, 10. See also Bayless, *Obliged to Help*, 113–32, about the WEC. On Rosa Keller's racial activism in New Orleans, see Fairclough, *Race and Democracy*, 165–66, 232, 236, 240, 262–63; Rogers, *Righteous Lives*, 26–30, 44–45, 97–101. On SOS, see Fairclough, *Race and Democracy*, 236–42; Rogers, *Righteous Lives*, 49–76.

42. Ducey, *Southern Regional Council Papers*, 188. On the defeat of interposition policy in Georgia, see Bartley, *Rise of Massive Resistance*, 332–35. The major battle was waged in 1960, when Governor Ernest Vandiver and the state legislature charged the Sibley Commission with gauging public opinion on the prospect of closing the schools. The commission held ten hearings across the state, where HOPE sent members to testify in favor of desegregated schools as better than closed schools. Although by the end of the hearings, 60 percent of the witnesses had expressed support for total segregation, the proportion of people ready to accept controlled integration had increased significantly between the first and the last hearings. In the end, the commission did not support closing the schools and recommended a "local option" policy that gave

local communities the power to devise their own plans. After an episode of resistance to the integration of the University of Georgia in January 1961, the Georgia legislature adopted the Sibley commission's recommendations. Bartley, *New South*, 250, 253; Dartt, *Women Activists*, 93–115.

43. Bartley, *New South*, 250–52; Frystak, *Our Minds*, 91, 87–103; Lewis, *Massive Resistance*, 114–20.

44. Murphy, *Breaking the Silence*, 211; Frystak, *Our Minds*, 86; Bartley, *Rise of Massive Resistance*, 333.

45. Murphy, *Breaking the Silence*, 211; Frystak, *Our Minds*, 86; Bartley, *New South*, 244. On the WEC's, HOPE's, and SOS's links with other women's groups, see, for instance, Murphy, *Breaking the Silence*, 98, 212; folders 4, 14, 23, box 7, Pauley Papers; Frystak, *Our Minds*, 86–87.

46. Rilling quoted in Frystak, *Our Minds*, 86; Nasstrom, *Everybody's Grandmother*, 50, 55; Murphy, *Breaking the Silence*, 73, 74; Brewer, *Embattled Ladies*, 6–7. See also Bayless, *Obliged to Help*, 123, about Daisy Bates and the WEC's all-white policy. For an analysis of the WEC's middle-class outlook and of its all-white policy, see Anderson, *Little Rock*, 179–83. The Virginia Committee for Public Schools, created in December 1958, also adopted an all-white policy on the same grounds. Lassiter and Lewis, *Moderates' Dilemma*, 108.

47. Dartt, *Women Activists*, 40; Pendergrast, "Integration or Ignorance," *Vassar Quarterly* [1960], clipping, scrapbook 2.3 (folder 9, box 1, Pendergrast Papers).

48. Dartt, *Women Activists*, 60; Murphy, *Breaking the Silence*, 1, 255–56.

49. Pauley to "Annamarie," August 4, 1960 (folder 7, box 7, Pauley Papers); Murphy, *Breaking the Silence*, 94; Frystak, *Our Minds*, 88, 86.

50. Murphy, *Breaking the Silence*, 75, 77, 80; Brewer, *Embattled Ladies*, 11–12; Dartt, *Women Activists*, 45; Frystak, *Our Minds*, 88; Lassiter and Lewis, *Moderates' Dilemma*, 108. For further illustration of the WEC's rhetoric, see Brewer, *Embattled Ladies*.

51. Murphy, *Breaking the Silence*, 232; Pauley to W. C. Henson, January 28, 1961 (folder 8, box 7, Pauley Papers); Murphy, *Breaking the Silence*, 214.

52. Murphy, *Breaking the Silence*, 209; Frystak, *Our Minds*, 105. Save-our-schools groups also inspired other women in other states, such as Mississippians for Public Education (1963–64). See Green interview, 11–13.

53. On Pauley, see folder 8, "correspondence 1962–1965," box 9, Pauley Papers, and Human Relations Council Diary, 1961–67, 1988 (folder 10, box 94, Pauley Papers); on Pendergrast, see folders 3–6, box 1, Pendergrast Papers; on Paschall, see folder "GA-CHR, Correspondence 1962, June-August," box 10, Paschall Papers; on Spearman, see folders 925, 929, 937, box 34, SCCHR records.

54. Murphy, *Breaking the Silence*, 226, 244. On Memphis, see Gail S. Murray, "White Privilege, Racial Justice: Women Activists in Memphis," in Murray, *Throwing Off the Cloak*, 204–30; on New Orleans, see Shannon L. Frystak, "Elite White Female Activism and Civil Rights in New Orleans," in Murray, *Throwing Off the Cloak*, 181–203.

55. Murphy, *Breaking the Silence*, 242. Among many episodes of the 1960s movement, Frances Pauley recalls how she took a SNCC member to the hospital in July 1965 after he was beaten up for trying to register to vote in Baker County, Georgia. Virginia Durr played a similar role, her house in Montgomery serving as a haven for SNCC activists between 1961 and 1964. It was in exactly the same spirit that Jane Schutt, a white churchwoman, accommodated Mississippi Freedom Summer activists in her house in 1964. See Nasstrom, *Everybody's Grandmother*, 90–95; Durr, *Outside the Magic Circle*, 322–24; Thrasher, "Circle," 234.

56. Murphy, *Breaking the Silence*, xvii.

57. Quoted in Riehm, "Dorothy Tilly," 35–36 (Tilly's original quote is from Nelson, "The Association of Southern Women for the Prevention of Lynching," 95). L. Smith to Dorothy Fisher, March 10, 1956, in Gladney, *How?*, 200. See also letters to Charles Johnson (June 10, 1955), and to Hallock Hoffman (July 28, 1955), in Gladney, *How?*, 169–72, 176–78.

58. Quoted in Frystak, *Our Minds*, 83.

59. Motherhood and a commitment to public education were also a unifying factor for the ten women who formed the Parents' Committee for Emergency Schooling in Charlottesville, Virginia, when it became clear that local schools would close in September 1958. Unlike the WEC, HOPE, and SOS, however, this group did not set up a large-scale campaign to lobby authorities into keeping public schools open but proposed temporary alternative schooling for the time of the crisis. The campaign for public schools was then taken over by the statewide Virginia Committee for Public Schools. See Lassiter and Lewis, *Moderates' Dilemma*, 80–92.

60. Dartt, *Women Activists*, 45; "Nan Is Still Fighting," *Atlanta Journal and Constitution*, October 18, 1979, clipping, 29, 39, and "Partners for Progress" (folder 6, box 1, Pendergrast Papers). For an illustration of the way Atlanta's newspapers conveyed the image of Pendergrast as a model mother, see clippings in Pendergrast Papers: "Babies Are Fun," *Atlanta Journal Magazine*, September 1, 1946 (folder 6, box 1); "We Are a Family of Sailors," *Atlanta Journal and Constitution Magazine*, July 28, 1957, 10–11, 30, 32 (folder 9, box 1); "'Most Belligerent Pacifist' Reveres Life," *This Week* May 4, 1977, 1, 14 (folder 6, box 1).

61. Riehm, "Dorothy Tilly," 26, 29; Pendergrast, answers to author's questionnaire.

62. Young interview, 35.

63. Dabbs, "Through the Years," 7, 8.

64. Murphy, *Breaking the Silence*, 67.

65. Dabbs, "Through the Years," 1, 2.

66. In her study of African American women's role in the civil rights struggle, the sociologist Belinda Robnett identifies women as "bridge leaders" as compared to men's position of "formal leaders" in the civil rights movement. Robnett argues that traditional cultural norms prevented women from occupying official positions of leadership in the main civil rights organizations but that they were leaders of another sort. Although the major thrust of her work concerns black women, since her perspective

is the black-led civil rights struggle from the 1920s on, Robnett includes white women in her study and shows that her findings apply to white and black women alike. Her analysis of women's role in the movement for racial justice hinges on the idea that women served as chain-links between the private and public spheres, or between communities and the formal organizations that led the fight against segregation. She argues that as "bridge leaders," women "were able to cross the boundaries between the public life of a movement organization and the private spheres of adherents and potential constituents." It is striking to note that all of the ten characteristics Robnett lists in her definition of bridge leaders fit most of the white women featured in this book, the following selection (Robnett, *How Long?*, 19–20) being sufficiently telling:

> 1. They become bridge leaders not because they lack leadership experience, but rather because of a social construct of exclusion....
> 3. They operate in the movement's or organization's free spaces, thus making connections that cannot be made by formal leaders.
> 4. They employ a one-to-one interactive style of leadership for mobilization and recruitment....
> 7. They are more closely bound to the wishes and desires of the constituency because, unlike formal leaders, they do not need legitimacy with the state.
> 8. They tend to advocate more radical or nontraditional tactics and strategies because, unlike formal leaders, they do not need legitimacy with the state....
> 10. They may be formal leaders at the local level, but within movement organizations or within the movement sector, they are excluded from the primary formal leadership tier.

From these standards, the women of the older generation who worked for mixed organizations were definitely bridge leaders. This definition also applies to the younger generation who participated in the more radical 1960s civil rights movement, notably represented by SNCC (see chapter 5).

67. Johnson interview, 4–5.

68. Pendergrast quoted in *Atlantic* 245, no. 6, June 1980, clipping (folder 6, box 1, Pendergrast Papers); Nasstrom, *Everybody's Grandmother*, 47–48, 57–58; Murphy, *Breaking the Silence*, 115, 117; Pauley, Mertz interview, August 1, 1983, 6.

69. Nasstrom, *Everybody's Grandmother*, 38; Dartt, *Women Activists*, 45.

70. Riehm, "Dorothy Tilly," 26.

71. Parsons, *Southern Wrongs*, 101, 73, 102.

72. Parsons, *Southern Wrongs*, 54, 68.

Chapter 4. After *Brown*, Part Two: Open Confrontation

1. For a historical account of the Montgomery Bus Boycott, see, for instance, Branch, *Parting the Waters*, 128–205.

2. On the role of the black church in African American history, see, for instance, Frazier and Lincoln, *Negro Church*; Lincoln and Mamiya, *Black Church*; Higginbotham, *Righteous Discontent*, 1–13.

3. Blumberg, *Civil Rights*, 79; Carson, *In Struggle*, 19–20; Ransby, *Ella Baker*, 241–47, 269–70.

4. Highlander Folk School, founded in 1932 by Don West and Myles Horton, was an institution first dedicated to worker education. It promoted interracialism as early as the 1930s. Its leaders were Protestant ministers whose vision was based on a combination of Christian and socialist principles. After World War II, it became a training school for black and white civil rights activists. Adams, *Unearthing*; Gilmore, *Defying Dixie*, 175–76; Reed, *Simple Decency*, 31; Dunbar, *Against the Grain*, 44–45; "Official Statement of Policy, Highlander Folk School, Monteagle, Tennessee," [1957] (folder 7, box 50, Braden Papers). The National Student Movement, represented by the United States National Student Association, was created in 1947. Its major goal as stated in its constitution was "to guarantee to all people because of their inherent dignity as individuals, equal rights and possibilities for primary, secondary, and higher education, regardless of sex, race, religion, political belief, or economic circumstance." "Introduction," finding aid, Records of the United States National Students Association Southern Project, 1957–1969 (hereafter cited as Southern Project Records).

5. On the Freedom Rides, see Carson, *In Struggle*, 31–44; Arsenault, *Freedom Riders*; on the Albany Movement, see Carson, *In Struggle*, 56–65. On Freedom Summer and the MFDP, see Carson, *In Struggle*, 111–17, 123–29. On Selma, see Blumberg, *Civil Rights*, 130–33. For an in-depth study of the movement in Mississippi, see Dittmer, *Local People*.

6. Some of the most publicized episodes of white extremism were the beatings of Freedom Riders and the destruction of their bus by fire in Anniston, Alabama, in May 1961; the use of fire hoses and dogs against marchers in Birmingham, Alabama, in May 1963; the murder of Medgar Evers—head of the Mississippi NAACP—and the killing of four girls in the bombing of Birmingham's Sixteenth Street Baptist Church in June and September of the same year; the murder of three Mississippi Freedom Summer volunteers by local white men in July 1964; and the killing of James Reeb and Viola Liuzzo in Selma in 1965. On Anniston, see Carson, *In Struggle*, 33–34; Arsenault, *Freedom Riders*, 140–49; on Birmingham, see Branch, *Parting the Waters*, 758–61, 889–92; on the Mississippi murders, see Carson, *In Struggle*, 114–15; on Selma, see Blumberg, *Civil Rights*, 131, 133.

7. See Chappell, *Inside Agitators*, for further information.

8. As an illustration, in January 1956, Grover Hall Jr., editor of the *Montgomery Advertiser*, who had been considered as a moderate until then, said that King was "a dangerous communist son of a bitch." Quoted in Stanton, *Journey toward Justice*, 172.

9. See, for instance, Ralph McGill, *Atlanta Constitution*, September 8, 1966, and May 22, 1967.

10. See Smith, "No Easy Way, Now"; Smith, "South's Moment of Truth."

11. Smith, "What Segregation Does," 71. On the notion of spiritual lynching, see Smith, "Mob and the Ghost."

12. McGill, *Atlanta Constitution*, February 9, 1950; Stanton, *Journey toward Justice*, 118.

13. Gladney, *How?*, 164, 184–87.

14. Smith, "No Easy Way, Now," 16; Smith, "The Right Way Is Not the Moderate Way," speech read at the Institute of Non-Violence and Social Change, December 5, 1956, in Cliff, *Winner Names the Age*, 67–75, 68; Stanton, *Journey toward Justice*, 190; Gladney, *How?*, 108.

15. *Now Is the Time* is by far the best illustration of Smith's Cold War rationale.

16. Biographical information on Morgan is taken from Stanton, *Journey toward Justice*, 41, 45–46, 50, 80–81, 75–76, 107, 99, 142, 150, 169–70, 176–78, 190; the letter published on December 13, 1955, is reproduced on 160–63.

17. Boyle, *Desegregated Heart*, 193–97.

18. James Meredith became famous when he entered the University of Mississippi in 1962, after the intervention of federal troops and two days of riots. In 1966, he started a one-man "March against Fear" from Memphis to Jackson, and was shot by a sniper. Several civil rights leaders took over the march, including Martin Luther King Jr., Floyd McKissick, and Stokely Carmichael. It was then that Carmichael publicly shouted the slogan "Black Power" for the first time. Blumberg, *Civil Rights*, 101–2, 135, 176.

19. Biographical information on Boyle is taken from Boyle, *Desegregated Heart*; Egerton, *Mind to Stay*, 128–45. See also Dierenfield, "One 'Desegregated Heart'"; Joanna Bowen Gillespie, "Sarah Patton Boyle's Desegregated Heart," in Coryell et al., *Beyond Image*, 158–83; Hobson, *But Now*, 61–71.

20. See King's praise for Boyle's autobiography, Boyle, *Desegregated Heart*, back flap.

21. Stanton, *Journey toward Justice*, 128; Boyle, *Desegregated Heart*, 108.

22. Stanton, *Journey toward Justice*, 149, 187; Boyle, *Desegregated Heart*, 193; Egerton, *Mind to Stay Here*, 141.

23. Braden, *Wall Between*, 275, 292. For a discussion of the word "crusader," see T. Stevens to D. Tilly, n.d. (reel 196, SRC Papers).

24. Braden, *Wall Between*, 294–95. Like Lillian Smith, Braden indicted white southern liberals for their silence or lack of support for the *Brown* decision in 1954 (282).

25. Sullivan, *Freedom Writer*, 19. For an analysis of Durr's dissenting position in Alabama during the desegregation crisis, see Stefani, "Dissenting Voice."

26. Braden, *Wall Between*, 33–34.

27. Sullivan, *Freedom Writer*, 66.

28. See "Program for Southern Conference Educational Fund," [1947] (folder 2, box 2, Braden Papers); "Policy Statement," adopted by Board of Directors, Atlanta, June 12, 1954 (folder 3, box 22, Braden Papers); Adams, *James A. Dombrowski*, 167–68, 182–83, 210–12.

29. Fosl, *Subversive Southerner*, 224, 218; A. Braden, "SCEF's Relations with SNCC and Highlander," prepared May 25, 1963 (folder 12, box 58, Braden Papers). For more information on SCEF, see also Klibaner, *Conscience*.

30. This was Durr's interpretation. See her letter to Esther Gelders, April 6, 1954, in Sullivan, *Freedom Writer*, 69–70.

31. Reed, *Simple Decency*, 170; Sullivan, *Freedom Writer*, 67; "Statement of Virginia Foster Durr Before the Senate Internal Security Commitee [*sic*] in New Orleans" (folder 179, carton 3, Durr Papers); Subcommittee to Investigate the Administration of the Internal Security Act and Other Internal Security Laws of the Committee on the Judiciary, Transcript of Hearings vol. 2, March 19, 1954, 202–16 (folder 7, box 25, Braden Papers); Durr, *Outside the Magic Circle*, 259–60. See also Woods, *Black Struggle*, 44–46.

32. Woods, *Black Struggle*, 47; Reed, *Simple Decency*, 171; Fried, *Nightmare*, 175–76.

33. Louisiana's Joint Legislative Committee on Un-American Activities had been created in 1954 under the name Joint Legislative Committee on Segregation (JLCS). It had been created by the Louisiana legislature as part of its massive resistance program to the implementation of the *Brown* decision. It was the equivalent of the Georgia Commission on Education, of the Johns Committee in Florida, and of Mississippi's and Alabama's State Sovereignty Commissions. See Woods, *Black Struggle*, 5–6, 98, 182–90.

34. "Fact Sheet on the Raid and Arrests," November 22, 1963 (folder 3, box 23, Braden Papers); State of Louisiana Joint Legislative Committee on Un-American Activities, Report no. 5, "Activities of the Southern Conference Educational Fund, Inc. in Louisiana," Part 2 (Baton Rouge, La.: April 13, 1964), 124–25 (folder 11, box 24, Braden Papers); Fosl, *Subversive Southerner*, 297–98. See also Reed, *Simple Decency*, 174–75.

35. For an analysis of the impact of anti-Communism on the integrationist movement in the South, see, for instance, Schrecker, *Many Are the Crimes*, 389–95; Caute, *Great Fear*, 70, 166–68.

36. Fosl, *Subversive Southerner*, 209.

37. Stanton, *Journey toward Justice*, 110.

38. "News from Field Secretaries' Office, SCEF," December 2, 1958 (folder 3, box 95, Braden Papers); Fosl, *Subversive Southerner*, 272–74.

39. V. Durr to Clark Foreman, in Sullivan, *Freedom Writer*, 187.

40. Fosl, *Subversive Southerner*, 203. For an example of the rift between the NAACP and SCEF, see Carl Braden to Jim Dombrowski, January 20, 1960 (folder 3, box 20, Braden Papers). On Durr's views of the NAACP, see, for example, her letter to Corliss Lamont, July 24, 1956 (folder 180, carton 3, Durr Papers). In a December 23, 1953, letter to Clark Foreman and other friends where she commented on McGill's anti-Communism, Durr wrote that he followed "the Lillian Smith line of making himself respectable by exchanging one prejudice for another" (folder 124, carton 2, Durr Papers). On the SRC, see, for instance, Fosl, *Subversive Southerner*, 288.

41. "Petition for Clemency," n.d. (folder 3, box 12, Braden Papers); *My Beliefs*, 1, 17 (folder 5, box 93, Braden Papers). See also Braden's pamphlet, *House Un-American Activities Committee*, published by the NCAHUAC.

42. The Emergency Civil Liberties Committee, created in the mid-1950s, aimed at the elimination of federal, state, and local internal-security bodies. It was listed by the U.S. attorney general as a Communist-front organization (Woods, *Black Struggle*, 137). On Durr's links with it, see Sullivan, *Freedom Writer*, 46–48, 131–34, 141–42.

43. Durr, *Outside the Magic Circle*, 245, 252–53, 275, 278–79, 295.

44. V. Durr to Clark and Mairi Foreman, May 1956, in Sullivan, *Freedom Writer*, 119.

45. Up to the late 1950s, Congress remained controlled by a powerful coalition of conservative Republicans and southern Democrats who systematically prevented the passage of civil rights legislation. From 1956 on, southern Democrats steadily lost ground. Two civil rights acts were passed in 1957 and 1960 but they were limited to watered-down legal protection and did not affect segregation. See Lawson, *Black Ballots*, xvi–xvii, 140–202.

46. V. Durr to Lyndon Johnson, December 13, 1960, in Sullivan, *Freedom Writer*, 229; V. Durr to Burke Marshall, May 15, 1961, in Sullivan, *Freedom Writer*, 249–50.

47. A. Braden to Rev. Albert J. Kissling, June 18, 1961 (folder 10, box 50, Braden Papers); V. Durr to Curtis MacDougall, August 17, 1953, in Sullivan, *Freedom Writer*, 56; Fosl *Subversive Southerner*, 291.

48. S. Boyle to V. Durr, October 30, 1956 (folder 127, carton 2, Durr Papers).

49. V. Durr to J. Wilkins, January 18, 1961 (folder 7, box 2, Wilkins Papers); V. Durr to J. Wilkins, [1960] (folder 4, box 2, Wilkins Papers).

50. V. Durr to Jim Dombrowski, May 14, 1968, in Sullivan, *Freedom Writer*, 398.

51. V. Durr to A. Braden, n.d. [Spring 1960], in Sullivan, *Freedom Writer*, 202, 203–4.

52. V. Durr to Anne Braden, n.d. [Spring 1960], in Sullivan, *Freedom Writer*, 202–3.

53. A. Braden to V. Durr, April 19, 1959, 3, 4, 5 (folder 103, carton 2, Durr Papers).

54. L. Smith to Michael Carter, September 21, 1943, in Gladney, *How?*, 76.

55. See Sullivan, *Freedom Writer*, 202, 203, 216.

56. A. Braden to George [Weissman], February 21, 1959, quoted in Greene, *Our Separate Ways*, 56; L. Smith to Margaret Long, October, 26, 1961, in Gladney, *How?*, 291.

57. Smith, "Southerner Talking," November 6, 1948. See also Smith, "What Segregation Does."

58. Durr, answers to author's questionnaire; Fosl, *Subversive Southerner*, 259, 124. See also LeeAnn Whites, "Rebecca Latimer Felton and the Problem of 'Protection' in the New South," in Hewitt and Lebsock, *Visible Women*, 41–61.

59. Durr, *Outside the Magic Circle*, 271.

60. Heard, "In the Name," 16, 18.

Chapter 5. The 1960s Movement: Modern Abolitionists

1. Smith quoted in Olson, *Freedom's Daughters*, 172. See also Loveland, *Lillian Smith*, 214.

2. "Student Nonviolent Coordinating Committee Statement of Purpose," 1960, reprinted in Carson et al., *Eyes on the Prize*, 119–20.

3. The Student Christian Movement, which attracted thousands of students in the 1950s and 1960s, was composed of denominational campus ministries, the student YMCA and YWCA, and international organizations like the World Student Christian Federation. See Evans, *Journeys*, 1–7.

4. Given the protean form of the 1960s movement, reliable statistics are difficult to find. As an indication of the extent of white involvement in SNCC, Howard Zinn has noted that in mid-1964—that is, at the height of the movement—whites made up approximately 20 percent of SNCC (Zinn, *SNCC*, 10).

5. Finding Aid to Southern Project Records, i; Constance Curry, "Wild Geese to the Past," in Curry et al., *Deep in Our Hearts*, 1–35, 8.

6. Constance Curry, "An Official Observer," in Holsaert et al., *Hands on Plow*, 45–48; see also *Silver Rights*, Curry's account of the experience of the Carter family, who sent their children to desegregate an all-white school in Mississippi in 1965. For more information about Winifred Green, see Green interview.

7. Hayden, "Fields," 340. Hayden's speech at the NSA Congress is reproduced in Holsaert et al., *Hands on Plow*, 49–51. For biographical information, see also Casey Hayden, "In the Attics of My Mind," in Holsaert et al., *Hands on Plow*, 381–87.

8. Burlage, "Truths," 95–102, 107–11; Burlage interview.

9. Hayden, "Fields," 341–60; Burlage, "Truths," 100–102. On Hayden's pivotal function as a workshop leader and as a bridge between the North and South, see Hogan, *Many Minds*, 95–100.

10. Thrasher, "Circle," 222, 227. Biographical information on Thrasher is taken from Thrasher, "Circle."

11. King, *Freedom Song*, 53, 33–69; King, "Getting Out the News," in Holsaert et al., *Hands on Plow*, 332–44.

12. Carson, *In Struggle*, 25.

13. Joan Trumpauer Mulholland, "Diary of a Freedom Rider," in Holsaert et al., *Hands on Plow*, 67–76, 67.

14. The function of observer was part of the planned structure of early SNCC demonstrations. As Connie Curry explains, each action relied on designated captains, monitors, and observers. "Captains kept the demonstrators organized. Monitors, usually the physically larger students or members of the community, provided a measure of security. In addition to watching and following each protest, observers alerted the SNCC office, the U.S. Justice Department, and the press when the demonstrators were arrested." Curry adds that "observers might also witness or testify at the subsequent trials." Curry, "Official Observer," 46.

15. Biographical information on Browning for this paragraph is taken from Browning, "Shiloh," and correspondence with author.

16. Biographical information is taken from Jeannette King, "Inside and Outside of Two Worlds," in Holsaert et al., *Hands on Plow*, 223–30. For more information on CDGM, see Payne, *I've Got the Light*, 328–30, 342–48, 377–78.

17. Frystak, *Our Minds*, 121–30; Leonard, answers to author's questionnaire.

18. Moses quoted in Zinn, *SNCC*, 35; Curry, "Wild Geese," 16. See also Mussatt, "Journey for Justice."

19. Burlage, "Truths," 102; Browning, "Shiloh," 72; Joan Browning, Application Form, 5th Southern Student Human Relations Seminar (folder 2, box 13, Southern Project Records); Carolyn Faye Powell, Application Form, 4th Southern Student Human Relations Seminar (folder 9, box 12, Southern Project Records). Powell recently confirmed that spirituality had been a major influence in her life (Powell, answers to author's questionnaire).

20. Hayden, "Attics," 385; Browning, "Shiloh," 73; Thrasher, "Circle," 221; Browning, Paine College Christian Student Conference notes, April 7–9, 1961 (folder 9, Browning Papers).

21. Olson, *Freedom's Daughters*, 169; Hayden, "Fields," 341–42; Casey Hayden, "Onto Open Ground," in Holsaert et al., *Hands on Plow*, 49–52, 51, 52. See also Hogan, *Many Minds*, 133–40, on the links between SDS and SNCC. Nonviolence was always a matter of debate within SNCC as some members saw in it a simple means to attain their goals whereas others defined it as a way of life, but it remained the driving force of the organization until the summer of 1964. After the murders of three Freedom Summer volunteers and the nonrecognition of the MFDP delegation at the Democratic National Convention, disillusionment grew along with an increasing questioning of nonviolence, until it was pushed into the background by the new leadership in late 1966. The Student Nonviolent Coordinating Committee was renamed "Student National Coordinating Committee" in June 1969. See Carson, *In Struggle*, 237–38, 295–96.

22. Olson, *Freedom's Daughters*, 166.

23. Thrasher, "Circle," 222; Michel, *Struggle*, 59.

24. For whites' firsthand testimonies about the redeeming power of the civil rights movement in their lives, see Sokol, *There Goes My Everything*, 309–25.

25. Thrasher, "Circle," 225; Browning, "Saturday Night Discussion," Worship Seminar, Lake Laurel, May 15, 1961 (folder 9, "Notebook-meetings-1961–62," Browning Papers). See also Browning's retrospective assessment of her experience in "Freedom and Unfreedom: Breaking Out of the Cage of Race," paper presented at Georgia Association of Historians, April 17, 1999, Savannah, Georgia, and "Religion Gave Me Power to Witness," paper presented at U.S. Senator Rush Holt History Conference, West Virginia University, Morgantown, September 18, 1999, in Browning's possession. J. Browning to F. Powell, December 13, 1961 (folder 1, Browning Papers); Mulholland,

"Diary," 68; King, "Inside and Outside," 223. See also Browning, "Shiloh," 60–62, on the teaching role of black students and nonviolent leaders.

26. Hayden, "Attics," 386; Burlage, "Truths," 103.

27. Robnett, *How Long?*, 129; Curry, quoted in Robnett, *How Long?*, 127; Burlage, "Truths," 106, 107; Burlage interview; Browning, "Shiloh," 70.

28. Hayden, "Fields," 355; Zinn, *SNCC*, 35; King, *Freedom Song*, 69. Other white women thought, like Hayden, that their being white women imposed specific constraints on their actions in the civil rights movement because it was taking place in the South. Penny Patch, a native of New York, understood from the start that "there were always some limitations because I was White and particularly [because] I was a White female. My participation in certain kinds of activities would put the Black community at a lot of risk." Quoted in Robnett, *How Long?*, 123.

29. Hayden, "Attics," 386.

30. Thrasher, "Circle," 228–29.

31. Thrasher, "Circle," 228–39.

32. Michel, *Struggle*, 54, 56–57, 58–59.

33. Thrasher and Grogan quoted in Michel, *Struggle*, 33, 39; King, *Freedom Song*, 67.

34. Michel, *Struggle*, 41–42; Burlage, "Truths," 120. For a summarizing report on the April founding meeting, see "Southern Student Organizing Committee," folder 3, box 61, Braden Papers.

35. Thrasher, "Circle," 232, 229; Thrasher, quoted in Michel, *Struggle*, 39; Michel, *Struggle*, 109. By 1966, SSOC had managed to mobilize a significant constituency of southern white college students across every southern state and was shifting to protests against the war in Vietnam. It had become, according to Gregg Michel, "a multi-issue group with a broader perspective and an interest in a wide array of issues." After this development, however, the group drifted into southern nationalism in 1968 and did not survive the decade. For a discussion of the relationship between SNCC and SSOC, see Michel, *Struggle*, 45–49.

36. Hayden, "Attics," 386; Burlage, "Truths," 120. For a discussion of white women's relation to leadership in a black-led movement, see Robnett, *How Long?*, 122–25.

37. Curry, "Report to the Marshall Field Foundation," March, 1961, 6–7 (folder 22, box 9, Southern Project Records).

38. Bond, quoted in Curry, "Wild Geese," 23–24; King, "Inside and Outside," 229. Browning, "Shiloh," 62.

39. Hayden, "Attics," 385.

40. Quoted in Michel, *Struggle*, 60. See Curry, "Wild Geese," 20, 26, 30, about harassment.

41. J. Browning to Lynne Strauss, January 10, 1963 (folder 13, Browning Papers), reprinted in Browning, "Shiloh," 76; J. Browning to Vincent Harding et al., June 18, 1962 (folder 13, Browning Papers); Browning, "Shiloh," 76.

42. Hayden, "Fields," 368, 371–72; Burlage, "Truths," 127; Browning, "Shiloh," 82; King, "Inside and Outside," 229.

43. Browning, "Shiloh," 82; Thrasher, "Circle," 251; Burlage, "Truths," 129.

44. Curry, "Wild Geese," 30–31. For an illustration of Braden's views on Black Power, see, for instance, "On Black Power," SCEF memo to Friends of SCEF, n.d. (folder 5, box 93, Braden Papers).

45. Hayden, "Attics," 385.

46. Stembridge, quoted in Zinn, *SNCC*, 7.

47. See Stefani, "From Southern Lady."

48. Hayden, "Fields," 341. On Curry and Stembridge, see Curry, "Wild Geese," 16; on Hayden and Mary King, see Hayden, "Fields," 351; King, *Freedom Song*, 73–78; on Burlage and Browning, see Burlage, "Truths," 104; Burlage interview; Browning, answers to author's questionnaire.

49. Burlage, "Truths," 118; Hayden, "Fields," 352. Burlage also recalled discussing other issues at length with Jane Stembridge, notably the centrality of religion in their experience, because they "both came out of very religious backgrounds." Burlage, quoted in Evans, *Personal Politics*, 58.

50. Stembridge quoted in King, *Freedom Song*, 123, 124.

51. J. Browning to F. Powell, December 12 and December 28, 1961 (folder 1, Browning Papers). Browning met Powell in 1960 during her sophomore year at Georgia State College for Women in Milledgeville (Browning, answers to author's questionnaire). The two students were united by a deep religious faith, which motivated their decision to attend a local black church off campus whereas they had been forbidden to do so by college authorities. Browning remembers, "I felt that Faye and I were facing serious decisions in an increasingly hostile place" (Browning, "Shiloh," 59). Their relationship deepened as they participated in direct action campaigns.

52. V. Brown to C. Curry, September 14, 1960 (folder 25, box 9, Southern Project Records); J. Carter to C. Curry, February 13, 1962 (folder 11, box 11, Southern Project Records); C. F. Powell to C. Curry, September 14, 1961 (folder 9, box 12, Southern Project Records). See also Sally Hobbes to C. Curry, September 1, 1961 (folder 14, box 11, Southern Project Records). Burlage, "Truths," 102. On Hayden's and Browning's participations in the seminar, see Hayden, "Fields," 340–41; folders 22, 23, box 9, folder 1, box 10, and folder 2, box 13, Southern Project Records; Browning, "Shiloh," 61, 75.

53. Burlage, "Truths," 96; Hayden, "Fields," 338. Oakes had been a member of the student YWCA between 1935 and 1939 and had served as student secretary for the Southern Region from 1946 to 1953 (Taylor, "On the Edge," 178). As another illustration, Rebecca Owen, who was a student at Randolph Macon Woman's College in Lynchburg when the first sit-ins occurred, describes an elderly YWCA leader in these terms: "The magic of Miss Hudgins for me was that she was truly of my local white tribe, her family living a few miles from my Saluda home. She knew me as no one else did, for she had lived in her own way what I was living." Owen, in Evans, *Journeys*, 74. See also Tamela Hultman's description of Nancy Richardson, YWCA adviser at Duke University, and Elmira Kendricks Nazombe's appreciation of Nelle Morton, her theology teacher at Drew Theological School in 1963, in Evans, *Journeys*, 150, 94.

54. Browning, answers to author's questionnaire; Browning, "Freedom and Unfreedom;" Browning, "Virginia Foster Durr, 1903–1999," *News from Papilion Lane Press*, February 25, 1999, in Browning's possession. For examples of Margaret Long's personal connections with the young generation, see, for instance: M. Long to Jane Stembridge, October 4, 1963; M. Long to Erin Simms, August 1965; M. Long to Dorothy Miller, August, 29, 1962; Peggy W. Minshall to M. Long, February 12, 1962; M. Long to Florence Robin, October 4, 1962; M. Long to Dorothy Swisshelm, March 21, 1966. Except where otherwise specified, all letters to and from Margaret Long are part of the SRC Papers, series II, reels 76–109. Copies were made available by Joan Browning.

55. Curry, "Wild Geese," 22; Burlage, "Truths," 118; Browning, email to author, December 26, 2010; L. Smith to J. Stembridge, October 22, 1960, in Gladney, *How?*, 258. Margaret Rose Gladney, who discovered Smith's life and work in 1970 when she was admitted to the Ph.D. program in American studies at the University of New Mexico, recalls that she found in Smith the role model she needed as a white, southern, upper-middle class, educated woman. Gladney, answers to author's questionnaire.

56. Evans, *Personal Politics*, 48–49; Fosl, *Subversive Southerner*, 253; J. Stembridge to A. Braden, November 30, 1960 (folder 2, box 62, Braden Papers); Thrasher, "Circle," 228, 246. On Braden's participation in the creation of SSOC, see, for instance, A. Braden to Jim Dombrowski (folder 7, box 22, Braden Papers). Joan Browning also remembers Braden as encouraging her to write, publishing her in the *Southern Patriot*, as well as encouraging her to apply for a SCEF-SNCC job in 1963 (Browning, answers to author's questionnaire).

57. Ransby, *Ella Baker*, 258.

58. Braden quoted in Olson, *Freedom's Daughters*, 223; Ransby, *Ella Baker*, 254; Fosl, *Subversive Southerner*, 296.

59. Burlage, "Truths," 105; Burlage interview.

60. Olson, *Freedom's Daughters*, 368. Durr was also a close friend of Rosa Parks (see Durr, answers to author's questionnaire). The relationship that Lillian Smith and Pauli Murray developed still provides another example of interracial friendship (Gladney, *How?*, 135).

61. Many examples are available apart from those developed in the above paragraphs. Among them, Sara Murphy, of the older generation, evokes her relationship with Gwen Riley, the main black member of her "Panel of American Women" in Little Rock. Murphy had recruited Riley without knowing her, and the two women soon became close. Riley was the first black person Murphy truly interacted with, and she literally taught her about blacks' human value, as Murphy explained: "As far as knowing any blacks as equals or knowing any Jews or Catholics at all, I did not as a child." Murphy, *Breaking the Silence*, 244.

62. Burlage, "Truths," 118, 119.

63. See chapter 1.

64. "SNCC Position Paper, November 1964," in King, *Freedom Song*, 567–69, 568, 569. Also reprinted in Evans, *Personal Politics*, 233–35.

65. Casey Hayden and Mary King, *A KIND OF MEMO FROM CASEY HAYDEN AND MARY KING TO A NUMBER OF OTHER WOMEN IN THE PEACE AND FREEDOM MOVEMENT*, as reprinted in *Liberation*, April 1966, November 18, 1965, in King, *Freedom Song*, 571–74, 573. Also reprinted in Evans, *Personal Politics*, 235–38. For Hayden's and King's accounts of the circumstances in which they wrote, see Hayden, "Fields," 370–71; King, *Freedom Song*, 456–59. The two texts of 1964 and 1965 are mentioned in many books dealing with women's history and feminism since the 1960s, which highlights their significance. See, for instance, Robnett, *How Long?*, 119–20; Olson, *Freedom's Daughters*, 350–54; Freeman, *Politics*, 57–58; Brownmiller, *In Our Time*, 13–15; Echols, *Daring*, 29–34.

66. King, *Freedom Song*, 459; Hayden, "Fields," 365. The historian who traced the roots of the women's movement back to the civil rights movement was Sara Evans in her now classic study, *Personal Politics*. Several SNCC veterans have reproached her with overemphasizing sexism in SNCC. Mary King recognizes Evans's "pathfinding" role in identifying King and Hayden's manifesto as a catalyst for the women's movement, but she adds that Evans misinterpreted it as the work of a wider group than what it actually was, and wrongly emphasized status as the "genesis" of their protest (King, *Freedom Song*, 467). For a compelling illustration of the controversy over the relationship between women and SNCC, see "SNCC Women and the Stirrings of Feminism," in Greenberg, *Circle of Trust*, an oral history volume based on the transcripts from a SNCC reunion conference held at Trinity College, Connecticut, in 1988.

67. Hayden, "Fields," 366; King, *Freedom Song*, 452, 445, 459; Burlage interview; Robnett, *How Long?*, 137.

Chapter 6. A Peculiar Brand of Feminism

1. This chapter examines the experience of white southern antiracist activists against the backdrop of second-wave feminism. It argues that, in the late 1960s and early 1970s, many of these women distinguished themselves from national feminists by being aware of the fundamental interconnection of race and sex in their identity. Due to their white supremacist education and their participation in the civil rights movement, they were acutely conscious of the differences separating black and white women. Consequently, when the new feminist movement emerged in the 1960s, even if many recognized themselves in several founding texts such as Simone de Beauvoir's *The Second Sex* and Betty Friedan's *The Feminine Mystique*, the women studied here did not share the rising feminist view that sexism was a more fundamental form of oppression than racism. The most popular feminist theorists of the early 1970s did not deny the reality of racial oppression, but argued that sexism was a more essential issue (see, for instance, Millett, *Sexual Politics*; Firestone, *Dialectic of Sex*). Although the feminist movement was characterized by a great variety of perspectives, it was predominantly white, and its main leaders—such as Sarah Amatniek Sarachild and Carol Hanish—emphasized the necessity of downplaying differences between women in order to build an effective national movement (see, for instance, Echols, *Daring*, 10, 104–7; Brownmiller, *In Our*

Time, 32–34). They insisted on the existence of a universal sisterhood transcending class and race differences. Understandably, women of color did not feel attracted to a movement that did not give priority to the fight against racism (see Freeman, *Politics*, 37–43; Evans, *Tidal Wave*, 115–19). Although a significant number of black women, such as Frances Beale and Cynthia Washington, embraced feminism while stressing the differences between white and black women (see Beale, "Double Jeopardy"; Washington, "We Started"), most of them rejected the women's liberation movement as an alien cause. The new feminist movement was also geographically concentrated in the Northeast, where the most vocal groups and individuals lived (see Echols, *Daring*, 10–11). The present chapter shows that the outlook of white southern women activists was, in many respects, closer to that of black women than to that of national feminists. In the 1980s, following the development of a black feminist movement and a renewed questioning of essentialism, the concept of universal sisterhood gave way to the idea of multiple female identities. Black feminists denounced the racism and classism of the dominant feminist movement (see, for instance, hooks, *Ain't I a Woman*, 119–58), while southern scholars denounced its regional chauvinism (see, for instance, Fox-Genovese, *Within the Plantation*, 42; Clinton, *Plantation Mistress*, xv). A new wave of feminist thought focused on the intersection of gender, race, class, and sexuality in the shaping of female identity, paving the way for the concept of intersectionality. This development actually corresponds much better to the experience of white southern antiracist activists because it does not prioritize one factor of oppression over others. For a brilliant discussion of gender, class, and race in feminist thought, see Spelman, *Inessential Woman*. For a comprehensive history of women's activism in the late twentieth century, see Evans, *Tidal Wave*.

2. Folder "Great Speckled Bird: Eliza Paschall Writings for (b)," box 19, Paschall Papers.

3. V. Durr to C. and M. Foreman, February 26, 1953, in Sullivan, *Freedom Writer*, 48.

4. V. Durr to C. Foreman, December 6, 1960, in Sullivan, *Freedom Writer*, 227; V. Durr to Clark and Mairi Foreman, June 25, 1959, in Sullivan, *Freedom Writer*, 188. On Durr's somber view of the South, see, for instance, her letter to Jessica Mitford, May 5, 1955, in Sullivan, *Freedom Writer*, 86–87, and her letter to Corliss Lamont, November 6, 1954 (folder 179, carton 3, Durr Papers).

5. Paschall, "A Southern Point of View," *Atlantic Monthly*, May 1960 (clipping, "Miscellaneous writings" [c], box 31, Paschall Papers).

6. See, for instance, E. Paschall to Harris Wofford, special assistant to the President, April 12 and April 24, 1962 (folder 3, box 1, Paschall Papers); E. Paschall to John Macy, chairman of the U.S. Civil Service Commission, April 18 and April 30, 1962 (folder 3, box 1, Paschall Papers).

7. V. Durr to Burke Marshall, May 15, 1961, in Sullivan, *Freedom Writer*, 249–50; E. Paschall to Dean Rusk, December 11, 1962 (folder "Correspondence, 1962, Dec. and n.d.," box 2, Paschall Papers).

8. V. Durr to C. Foreman, December 6, 1960, in Sullivan, *Freedom Writer*, 227; E. Paschall to John Oakes, March 19, 1962 (folder "Greater Atlanta Council on Human Relations Correspondence, 1962, Jan-March," box 1, Paschall Papers); E. Paschall to Robert Hutchins, September 1961 (folder "Correspondence 1937–1962," box 29, Paschall Papers). See also E. Paschall to Oz Elliott, March 19, 1962 (folder "Greater Atlanta Council on Human Relations Correspondence, 1962, Jan-March," box 1, Paschall Papers).

9. Egerton, *Speak Now*, 313; Johnson interview, 34–35.

10. V. Durr to J. Wilkins, January 18, 1961 (folder 7, box 2, Wilkins Papers); V. Durr to J. Wilkins, [1960] (folder 4, box 2, Wilkins Papers).

11. Quoted in Hall, *Revolt against Chivalry*, 73, 90, 76.

12. Tilly quoted in Knotts, *Fellowship*, 169. Tilly was especially disturbed by some committee members' wish to call for the desegregation of schools and to recommend withdrawal of federal funds from schools that would not desegregate. She was convinced—and subsequent events proved her right—that southerners would rather close their schools than desegregate them. Arguing instead for federal help for education as a means to eradicate racism at its roots, she declared that such help would contribute to accelerating the desegregation process by bettering southern educational standards and leading southerners to accept desegregated schools as a result. President's Committee on Civil Rights, transcript of meeting, June 30, 1947, Hanover, NH, 898 (folder 9, box 4, Tilly Papers). For further analysis of Tilly's stance within the PCCR, see Knotts, *Fellowship*, 165–69.

13. Rachelle McLure to D. Tilly, November 11, 1947 (folder 6, box 1, Tilly Papers).

14. Lillian Smith, "Autobiography as a Dialogue between King and Corpse," in Cliff, *Winner Names the Age*, 187–97, 197–98. For a discussion of southern women's predilection for autobiography as a genre, see Brantley, *Feminine Sense*.

15. Fox-Genovese, "Between Individualism and Community," 25.

16. Hall, "You Must Remember This," 463.

17. See chapter 1.

18. Lumpkin, *Making of a Southerner*, 132–33; Fox-Genovese, "Between Individualism and Community," 32; Smith, *Killers of the Dream*, 27; Boyle, *Desegregated Heart*, xi.

19. The phrase "models of the possible" is borrowed from Frances Taylor, who applies it to the seven YWCA student secretaries—including Lumpkin—on whom she focuses her study. The historian states, "These women and the few students who adopted the vision as their own belong to that small band of southern dissidents whom historians have found scattered across the pages of southern history. . . . Serving as models of the possible, the seven southern-born secretaries were living proof that southern white women could embrace new ways of thinking and acting." Taylor, "On the Edge," 12, 46. See also Jennifer Ritterhouse's study, in which she writes: "Like black autobiography, white southern autobiography has often had an explicit political intent. For white southerners who went on to challenge all or part of the Jim Crow

system as adults, usually as a result of some moral or political transformation, an account of their 'typical' southern upbringing served not only to show how much their own racial attitudes had changed but also to suggest that if *they* could change, so could other white southerners, and so, ultimately, could the South." Ritterhouse, *Growing Up Jim Crow*, 129.

20. Lumpkin, *Making of a Southerner*, 238, 239. See also Hall, "You Must Remember This," 458.

21. Smith, *Killers of the Dream*, 57, 73.

22. Braden, *Wall Between*, 275, 276, 277.

23. Boyle, *Desegregated Heart*, 8–9, 5.

24. Taylor, "On the Edge," 77.

25. Murphy, *Breaking the Silence*, 255; Browning quoted in Olson, *Freedom's Daughters*, 249.

26. Stanton, *Journey toward Justice*, 47.

27. V. Durr to Nat Hentoff, July 20, 1960, in Sullivan, *Freedom Writer*, 215 (see also Durr's letter to Lyndon Johnson, May 4, 1960, in Sullivan, *Freedom Writer*, 208–9); V. Durr to Glenn and Vann Woodward, June 9, 1967, in Sullivan, *Freedom Writer*, 388; Woodward, *Burden of Southern History*; Durr, answers to author's questionnaire.

28. Mulholland, "Diary," 73.

29. J. Browning to Vincent Harding et al., June 18, 1962 (folder 13, Browning Papers); Browning, "Shiloh," 81.

30. Curry quoted in Robnett, *How Long?*, 127; Robnett, *How Long?*, 138; Burlage interview.

31. Hall, *Revolt against Chivalry*, 26–45; Bayless, *Obliged to Help*, 81–83; Murphy, *Breaking the Silence*, 10; Durr, *Outside the Magic Circle*, 101, 102.

32. Durr, *Outside the Magic Circle*, 103.

33. See Smith, "Autobiography as a Dialogue" (1962); Lillian Smith, "Woman Born of Man" (1963), in Cliff, *Winner Names the Age*, 201–11.

34. V. Durr to Jessica Mitford, October 11, 1960, in Sullivan, *Freedom Writer*, 224.

35. Lumpkin, *Making of a Southerner*, 185–86.

36. Quoted in Olson, *Freedom's Daughters*, 271; Fosl, *Subversive Southerner*, 260.

37. For more information on Robert Zellner, a white Alabamian committed to the antiracist cause, see his memoir, *Wrong Side*.

38. A. Braden to J. Browning, March 13, 1963 (folder 4, box 40, Braden Papers).

39. Sullivan, *Freedom Writer*, 418; Parsons, *Southern Wrongs*, xxv.

40. Parsons, *Southern Wrongs*, 80, 81–82.

41. V. Durr to Jessica Mitford, Spring 1961, in Sullivan, *Freedom Writer*, 244.

42. Heard, "In the Name"; Foster, "Emancipation"; Durr, *Outside the Magic Circle*.

43. A. Braden to Kathie Amatniek, n.d. (folder 5, box 82, Braden Papers).

44. Olson, *Freedom's Daughters*, 351.

45. Greene, "'We'll Take Our Stand,'" 196, 199.

46. Thrasher, "Circle," 251; "Biographical information—Eliza Paschall," box 62, Paschall Papers; "Biographical note," finding aid, Paschall Papers; Evans, *Tidal Wave*, 26, 63–64; King, answers to author's questionnaire. The President's Commission on the Status of Women, established by Kennedy, was meant to conduct extensive research on all forms of discrimination against women. It issued its report in 1963. State commissions were then established on the same pattern, contributing to the emergence of the women's movement. Freeman, *Politics*, 52–53.

47. Washington, "We Started," 239; Hayden, "Fields," 371; A. Braden to Kathie Amatniek, n.d. (folder 5, box 82, Braden Papers). For a discussion of this point by a radical feminist who disapproved of SCEF's views, see Brownmiller, *In Our Time*, 47–48.

48. Burlage interview; Burlage, "Truths," 125; Browning, answers to author's questionnaire.

49. For a denunciation of white feminists' racism, see Caraway, *Segregated Sisterhood*.

50. Thrasher, "Circle," 251; King, *Freedom Song*, 78, 473.

51. hooks, "Black Women," 134, 140–41.

52. Braden sympathized with feminist organizations such as the National Women's Political Caucus (NWPC), for which sexism only constituted one front among others, and she continued to favor the fight against racism and poverty through social and political activism. She was, for instance, a founder of the Southern Organizing Committee for Economic and Social Justice in 1975 (Fosl, *Subversive Southerner*, 322–24). Durr worked with the national Democratic Party, and continued to support all people and groups struggling for economic justice (Sullivan, *Freedom Writer*, 414–15, 419–21). Parsons continued her social activism through public service and political activities in California (Biographical Note, Finding Aid, Parsons Papers). Pauley worked for the U.S. Department of Health, Education, and Welfare from 1968 to 1973, after which she founded the Georgia Poverty Rights Organization (Nasstrom, *Everybody's Grandmother*, 105–34). In the early 1970s, Dorothy Burlage started doctoral work in psychology at Harvard. While she focused her research on single mothers, she realized that women were critical to the overall economic and political structure of any given society, and that women's issues could not be dissociated from economic considerations. Thus, in the aftermath of the civil rights movement, her various experiences coalesced, bringing to the fore the interconnection of race, gender, and class. Her general outlook came to resemble that of black women, who had always known this for a fact (Burlage interview). Connie Curry continued her work with the American Friends Service Committee until 1975, when she became director of human services for the city of Atlanta. She held that position until 1990 (Curry et al., *Deep in Our Hearts*, 383). Joan Browning concentrated on human relations and antipoverty programs throughout the 1970s, and is still involved in community work and public service to this day (Browning, correspondence with author). Casey Hayden has dedicated her life to grassroots and countercultural activities (Hayden, "Fields," 372–74). Sue Thrasher became involved in a variety of social-change and social-policy organizations, and finally earned

a doctorate in education from the University of Massachusetts (Thrasher, "Circle," 242–50).

53. Brownmiller, *In Our Time*, 194; Brownmiller, *Against Our Will*, 247.

54. Braden, "Second Open Letter," 52.

55. Burlage interview; Braden, "Free Thomas Wansley;" V. Durr to Jessica Mitford, n.d. [ca. July/August 1958], in Sullivan, *Freedom Writer*, 165.

56. Braden, "Second Open Letter," 51.

57. Jane Cahill to "all commission members," April 5, 1974, draft of rape publication, 7 (folder "January–June, 1974," box 27, Paschall Papers); Georgia Commission on the Status of Women, "Rape and the Treatment of Rape Victims in Georgia," 3 (folder 4, box 28, Paschall Papers).

58. King, answers to author's questionnaire; Hayden, "Attics," 385; Smith, "Woman Born of Man," 210.

Conclusion

1. It is not the object of this book to discuss the limitations of the antiracist struggle, an issue of far greater scope than the experience of white southern women reformers.

2. Browning, "Invisible Revolutionaries," 186. Browning based her statement on an article published by Steven Lawson. See Lawson, "Freedom Then, Freedom Now."

3. Browning, "Invisible Revolutionaries," 186.

Bibliography

PRIMARY SOURCES

Manuscript Collections

Ames, Jessie Daniel. Papers. Southern Historical Collection, Wilson Special Collections Library, University of North Carolina at Chapel Hill.
Association of Southern Women for the Prevention of Lynching. Papers (microfilm). Archives and Special Collections, Robert W. Woodruff Library, Atlanta University Center, Atlanta.
Barker, Mary Cornelia. Papers. Manuscript, Archives, and Rare Book Library, Emory University, Atlanta
Braden, Carl and Anne. Papers. Wisconsin Historical Society, Madison.
Browning, Joan C. Papers. Manuscript, Archives, and Rare Book Library, Emory University, Atlanta.
Bullard, Helen. Papers. Manuscript, Archives, and Rare Book Library, Emory University, Atlanta.
Commission on Interracial Cooperation. Papers (microfilm). Archives and Special Collections, Robert W. Woodruff Library, Atlanta University Center, Atlanta.
Curry, Constance. Papers. Manuscript, Archives, and Rare Book Library, Emory University, Atlanta.
Dabbs, Edith M. Papers. Caroliniana Library Archives, University of South Carolina, Columbia.
Durr, Virginia Foster. Papers. Schlesinger Library, Radcliffe Institute for Advanced Studies, Harvard University, Cambridge, Mass.
Georgia Government Documentation Project. Special Collections and Archives, Georgia State University, Atlanta.
Georgia Women's Movement Oral History Project. Special Collections and Archives, Georgia State University, Atlanta.
Johnson, Guion Griffis. Papers. Southern Historical Collection, Wilson Special Collections Library, University of North Carolina at Chapel Hill.

League of Women Voters of DeKalb County. Papers. Manuscript, Archives, and Rare Book Library, Emory University, Atlanta.

Lumpkin, Katharine Du Pre. Papers. Southern Historical Collection, Wilson Special Collections Library, University of North Carolina at Chapel Hill.

Mississippi Oral History Program of the University of Southern Mississippi. University of Southern Mississippi Center for Oral History and Cultural Heritage, University of Mississippi Digital Collections.

Parsons, Sara Mitchell. Papers. Manuscript, Archives, and Rare Book Library, Emory University, Atlanta.

Paschall, Eliza King. Papers. Manuscript, Archives, and Rare Book Library, Emory University, Atlanta.

Pauley, Frances Freeborn. Papers. Manuscript, Archives, and Rare Book Library, Emory University, Atlanta.

Pendergrast, Nan. Papers. Manuscript, Archives, and Rare Book Library, Emory University, Atlanta.

Smith, Lillian E. Papers. Hargrett Rare Book and Manuscript Library, University of Georgia Libraries, Athens.

South Carolina Council on Human Relations Records. Caroliniana Library Archives, University of South Carolina, Columbia.

Southern Oral History Program. Southern Historical Collection, Wilson Special Collections Library, University of North Carolina at Chapel Hill.

Southern Regional Council. Papers (microfilm). Archives and Special Collections, Robert W. Woodruff Library, Atlanta University Center, Atlanta.

Student Nonviolent Coordinating Committee. Papers. King Library and Archives, Martin Luther King, Jr. Center for Nonviolent Social Change, Atlanta.

Tilly, Dorothy Rogers. Papers. Manuscript, Archives, and Rare Book Library, Emory University, Atlanta.

United States National Student Association Southern Project, 1957–69. Records. King Library and Archives, Martin Luther King, Jr. Center for Nonviolent Social Change, Atlanta.

Wilkins, Josephine Mathewson. Papers. Manuscript, Archives, and Rare Book Library, Emory University, Atlanta.

Woodward, Emily. Papers. Manuscript, Archives, and Rare Book Library, Emory University, Atlanta.

Wright, Alice Norwood Spearman. Papers. Caroliniana Library Archives, University of South Carolina, Columbia.

YWCA of Greater Atlanta Records. Manuscript, Archives, and Rare Book Library, Emory University, Atlanta.

Interviews

Ames, Jessie Daniel. Interviewed by Pat Watters, 1965, 1966 (G-003). Southern Oral History Program Collection (#4007), Southern Historical Collection, Wilson Library, University of North Carolina at Chapel Hill.
Browning, Joan C. Interview with author. Toulouse, France. October 11, 2012.
Burlage, Dorothy Dawson. Interview with author. Online. August 25, 2013.
Curry, Constance. Interview with author. Atlanta. October 16, 2010.
Derby, Doris A. Interview with author. Atlanta. November 12, 2010.
Durr, Virginia "Tilla" Foster, and Patricia Sullivan. Interview with author. Cambridge, Mass. August 17, 2006.
Green, Winifred. "An Oral History with Winifred A. Green." Interviewed by Charles Bolton, November 12, 1997. Mississippi Oral History Program, University of Southern Mississippi Center for Oral History and Cultural Heritage, University of Mississippi Digital Collections.
Jarvis, Patricia. Interview with author. Toulouse, France. October 11, 2012.
Johnson, Guion G. Interviewed by Mary Frederickson, July 1, 1974 (G-0029-4). Southern Oral History Program Collection (#4007), Southern Historical Collection, Wilson Library, University of North Carolina at Chapel Hill.
Pauley, Frances. Interviewed by Paul Mertz, August 1, 1983. Box 95, Pauley Papers, Manuscript, Archives, and Rare Book Library, Emory University, Atlanta.
Schutt, Jane. "An Oral History with Mrs Jane Schutt." Interviewed by Leesha Faulkner, October 3 and 10, 1994. Mississippi Oral History Program, University of Southern Mississippi Center for Oral History and Cultural Heritage, University of Mississippi Digital Collections.
Stevens, Thelma. Interviewed by Jacquelyn and Bob Hall, February 13, 1972 (G-0058). Southern Oral History Program Collection (#4007), Southern Historical Collection, Wilson Library, University of North Carolina at Chapel Hill.
Young, Louise. Interviewed by Jacquelyn and Bob Hall, February 14, 1972 (G-0066). Southern Oral History Program Collection (#4007), Southern Historical Collection, Wilson Library, University of North Carolina at Chapel Hill.

Answers to Questionnaire/Correspondence with Author

Browning, Joan C.; Curry, Constance; Durr, Virginia "Tilla" Foster; Gladney, Margaret Rose; Hayden, Casey; King, Mary E.; Leonard, Margaret Burr; Michaels, Sheila; Pendergrast, Nan; Powell, Faye; Thrasher, Sue; Walbert, Eileen.

Published Primary Sources

Beale, Frances. "Double Jeopardy: To Be Black and Female." In *The Black Woman: An Anthology*, edited by Toni Cade Bambara, 109–22. New York: Washington Square Press, 1970.
Beauvoir, Simone de. *The Second Sex*. Translated and edited by H. M. Parshley. New York: Knopf, 1953.

Boyle, Sarah Patton. *The Desegregated Heart: A Virginian's Stand in Time of Transition.* New York: Morrow, 1962.
———. *For Human Beings Only: A Primer of Human Understanding.* New York: Seabury Press, 1964.
———. "Southerners Will *Like* Integration." *Saturday Evening Post* 19 (February 1955), 25, 133–34.
Braden, Anne. "Free Thomas Wansley: A Letter to White Southern Women." Louisville, Ky.: SCEF Press, December 1972.
———. *House Un-American Activities Committee: Bulwark of Segregation.* Los Angeles: National Committee to Abolish the House Un-American Activities Committee, 1963.
———. "A Second Open Letter to Southern White Women." *Southern Exposure* 4, no. 4 (July 1977): 50–54.
———. *The Wall Between.* New York: Monthly Review Press, 1958.
Brady, Tom P. *Black Monday: Segregation or Amalgamation . . . America Has Its Choice.* Winona, Miss.: Association of Citizens' Councils, 1955.
Brewer, Vivion L. *The Embattled Ladies of Little Rock: 1958–1963, The Struggle to Save Public Education at Central High.* Fort Bragg, Calif.: Lost Coast Press, 1999.
Brownmiller, Susan. *Against Our Will: Men, Women and Rape.* 1975. Reprint, New York: Fawcett Books, 1993.
———. *In Our Time: Memoir of a Revolution.* New York: Dell, 1999.
Carson, Clayborne, David J. Garrow, Gerald Gill, Vincent Harding, and Darlene Clark Hine, eds. *The Eyes on the Prize Civil Rights Reader: Documents, Speeches, and Firsthand Accounts from the Black Freedom Struggle.* New York: Penguin Books, 1991.
Carter, Hodding. "A Southern Liberal Looks at Civil Rights." *New York Times Magazine*, August 8, 1948, 10, 20, 25.
Cash, Wilbur. *The Mind of the South.* 1941. Reprint, New York: Vintage, 1991.
Cliff, Michelle, ed. *The Winner Names the Age: A Collection of Writings by Lillian Smith.* New York: Norton, 1978.
Curry, Constance. *Silver Rights.* Chapel Hill, N.C.: Algonquin Books of Chapel Hill, 1995.
Curry, Constance, Joan C. Browning, Dorothy Dawson Burlage, Penny Patch, Theresa Del Pozzo, Sue Thrasher, Elaine DeLott Baker, Emmie Schrader Adams, and Casey Hayden. *Deep in Our Hearts: Nine White Women in the Freedom Movement.* Athens: University of Georgia Press, 2000.
Dabbs, James McBride. *The Southern Heritage.* New York: Knopf, 1958.
Durr, Virginia Foster. *Outside the Magic Circle: The Autobiography of Virginia Foster Durr.* Edited by Hollinger F. Barnard. Tuscaloosa: University of Alabama Press, 1985.
East, P. D. *The Magnolia Jungle.* New York: Simon and Schuster, 1960.
Evans, Sara M., ed. *Journeys That Opened Up the World: Women, Student Christian*

Movements, and Social Justice, 1955–1975. New Brunswick, N.J.: Rutgers University Press, 2003.

Firestone, Shulamith. *The Dialectic of Sex: The Case for Feminist Revolution*. New York: Morrow, 1970.

Foster, Virginia. "The Emancipation of Pure, White, Southern Womanhood." *New South* 26 (Winter 1971): 46–54.

Friedan, Betty. *The Feminine Mystique*. New York: Dell, 1963.

Gladney, Margaret Rose, ed. *How Am I to Be Heard? Letters of Lillian Smith*. Chapel Hill: University of North Carolina Press, 1993.

Glasgow, Ellen. *Virginia*. Garden City, N.Y.: Doubleday, Page, 1913.

Greenberg, Cheryl Lynn, ed. *A Circle of Trust: Remembering SNCC*. New Brunswick, N.J.: Rutgers University Press, 1998.

Grimké, Sarah. *Letters on the Equality of the Sexes and Other Essays*. Edited by Elizabeth Ann Bartlett. New Haven, Conn.: Yale University Press, 1988.

Heard, Eliza. "In the Name of Southern Womanhood." *New South* (November–December 1962): 16–18.

Height, Dorothy. *Open Wide the Freedom Gates: A Memoir*. New York: PublicAffairs, 2003.

Holsaert, Faith S., Martha Prescod Norman Noonan, Judy Richardson, Betty Garman Robinson, Jean Smith Young, and Dorothy M. Zellner, eds. *Hands on the Freedom Plow: Personal Accounts by Women in SNCC*. Urbana: University of Illinois Press, 2010.

Houck, Davis W., and David E. Dixon. *Women and the Civil Rights Movement, 1954–1965*. Jackson: University Press of Mississippi, 2009.

House Committee on Un-American Activities. *Report on Southern Conference for Human Welfare*. 80th Congress, 1st Session. Washington, D.C.: Government Printing Office, 1947.

King, Florence. *Southern Ladies and Gentlemen*. 1975. Reprint, New York: St. Martin's Griffin, 1993.

King, Larry. *Confessions of a White Racist*. New York: Viking, 1971.

King, Mary. *Freedom Song: A Personal Story of the 1960s Civil Rights Movement*. New York: Morrow, 1987.

Lumpkin, Katharine Du Pre. *The Making of a Southerner*. 1947. Reprint, Athens: University of Georgia Press, 1991.

Mars, Florence, with the assistance of Lynn Eden. *Witness in Philadelphia*. Baton Rouge: Louisiana State University Press, 1977.

Mason, Lucy Randolph. "The CIO and the Negro in the South." *Journal of Negro Education* 14, no. 4 (Autumn 1945): 552–61.

———. *To Win These Rights: A Personal Story of the CIO in the South*. New York: Harper, 1952.

McGill, Ralph. *Atlanta Constitution*. Daily Editorial Column, 1938–1969.

McLaurin, Melton A. *Separate Pasts: Growing Up White in the Segregated South*. 2nd ed. Athens: University of Georgia Press, 1998.
Millett, Kate. *Sexual Politics*. Garden City, N.Y.: Doubleday, 1970.
Morris, Willie. *North toward Home*. Boston: Houghton Mifflin, 1967.
Murphy, Sara Alderman. *Breaking the Silence: Little Rock's Women's Emergency Committee to Open Our Schools, 1958–1963*. Edited by Patrick C. Murphy II. Fayetteville: University of Arkansas Press, 1997.
Murray, Pauli. *Proud Shoes: The Story of an American Family*. 1956. Reprint, Boston: Beacon Press, 1999.
My Beliefs and My Associations Are None of the Business of This Committee. Southern Conference Educational Fund, n.d.
Nasstrom, Kathryn L., ed. *Everybody's Grandmother and Nobody's Fool: Frances Freeborn Pauley and the Struggle for Social Justice*. Ithaca, N.Y.: Cornell University Press, 2000.
Parsons, Sara Mitchell. *From Southern Wrongs to Civil Rights: The Memoir of a White Civil Rights Activist*. Tuscaloosa: University of Alabama Press, 2000.
Paschall, Eliza. *It Must Have Rained*. Atlanta: Center for Research in Social Change, Emory University, 1975.
President's Committee on Civil Rights. *To Secure These Rights: The Report of the President's Committee on Civil Rights*. New York: Simon and Schuster, 1947.
Sabiston, Dothory, and Margaret Hiller. *Toward Better Race Relations*. New York: Woman's Press, 1949.
Shannon, Margaret. *Just Because: The Story of the National Movement of Church Women United in the U.S.A., 1941 through 1975*. Corte Madera, Calif.: Omega Books, 1977.
Smith, Lillian. "Growing into Freedom." *Common Ground* 4 (Autumn 1943): 47–52.
———. *Killers of the Dream*. Rev. and enl. ed. New York: Norton, 1961.
———. "The Mob and the Ghost." *Progressive* (December 1962). Reprinted in Bradford Daniel, *Black, White and Gray*, 266–77 (New York: Sheed and Ward, 1964).
———. "No Easy Way, Now." *New Republic*, December 16, 1957, 12–16.
———. *Now Is the Time*. New York: Viking, 1955.
———. "Southern Liberalism." *New York Times*, April 4, 1948, E7.
———. "A Southerner Talking." *Chicago Defender*, October 1948–September 1949.
———. "The South's Moment of Truth." *Progressive* 24 (September 1960): 32–35.
———. *Strange Fruit*. 1944. Reprint, New York: Harvest-Harcourt, Brace, Jovanovitch, 1992.
———. "What Segregation Does to Our Children." *Child Study* 22 (Spring 1945): 71–72, 90.
Sullivan, Patricia, ed. *Freedom Writer: Virginia Foster Durr, Letters from the Civil Rights Years*. New York: Routledge, 2003.
Talmadge, Herman. *You and Segregation*. Birmingham, Ala.: Vulcan Press, 1955.

United States Congress. "Declaration of Constitutional Principles." *U.S. Congressional Record*, 4515–16, 84th Congress, 2nd sess. Washington, D.C.: Government Printing Office, 1956.

Washington, Cynthia. "We Started from Different Ends of the Spectrum." *Southern Exposure* 4, no 4 (July 1977): 14–19. Reprinted in Sara M. Evans, *Personal Politics: The Roots of Women's Liberation in the Civil Rights Movement and the New Left*, 238–40. New York: Knopf, 1979.

Wells, Ida B. *Crusade for Justice: The Autobiography of Ida B. Wells*. Edited by Alfreda Duster. Chicago: University of Chicago Press, 1970.

Wells-Barnett, Ida B. *On Lynchings: Southern Horrors; A Red Record; Mob Rule in New Orleans*. New York: Arno Press, 1969. First published in 3 vols., 1892, 1895, and 1900.

White, Helen, and Redding S. Sugg, eds. *From the Mountain: An Anthology of the Magazine Successively Titled* Pseudopodia, *the* North Georgia Review, *and* South Today. Memphis, Tenn.: Memphis State University Press, 1972.

Whitney, Susan E. *The League of Women Voters: Seventy-Five Years Rich: A Perspective on the Woman's Suffrage Movement and the League of Women Voters in Georgia*. Atlanta: League of Women Voters of Georgia, 1995.

Zellner, Robert, with Constance Curry. *The Wrong Side of Murder Creek: A White Southerner in the Freedom Movement*. Montgomery, Ala., and Louisville, Ky.: New-South Books, 2008.

Secondary Sources

Adams, Frank, with Myles Horton. *Unearthing Seeds of Fire: The Idea of Highlander*. Winston-Salem, N.C.: John F. Blair, 1975.

Adams, Frank T. *James A. Dombrowski: An American Heretic, 1897–1983*. Knoxville: University of Tennessee Press, 1992.

Anderson, Karen. *Little Rock: Race and Resistance at Central High School*. Princeton, N.J.: Princeton University Press, 2010.

Arsenault, Raymond. *Freedom Riders: 1961 and the Struggle for Racial Justice*. New York: Oxford University Press, 2006.

Ayers, Edward L. *The Promise of the New South, Life After Reconstruction*. New York: Oxford University Press, 1992.

Bartley, Numan V. *The New South: 1945–1980*. Baton Rouge: Louisiana State University Press and Littlefield Fund for Southern History of the University of Texas, 1995.

———. *The Rise of Massive Resistance: Race and Politics in the South during the 1950s*. 1969. Reprint, Baton Rouge: Louisiana State University Press, 1999.

Bayless, Stephanie. *Obliged to Help: Adolphine Fletcher Terry and the Progressive South*. Little Rock, Ark.: Butler Center for Arkansas Studies, Central Arkansas Library System, 2011.

Bercaw, Nancy, and Ted Ownby, eds. *Gender*. Vol. 13 of *The New Encyclopedia of South-*

ern Culture, edited by Charles Reagan Wilson. Chapel Hill: University of North Carolina Press, 2009.

Biles, Roger. *The South and the New Deal*. Lexington: University Press of Kentucky, 1994.

Blumberg, Rhoda Lois. *Civil Rights: The 1960s Freedom Struggle*. Rev. ed. New York: Twayne and Hall, 1991.

Boswell, Angela, and Judith N. McArthur, eds. *Women Shaping the South: Creating and Confronting Change*. Columbia: University of Missouri Press, 2006.

Branch, Taylor. *Parting the Waters: Martin Luther King and the Civil Rights Movement, 1954–63*. 1988. Reprint, London: Papermac, 1990.

Brantley, Will. *Feminine Sense in Southern Memoir: Smith, Glasgow, Welty, Hellman, Porter, and Hurston*. Jackson: University Press of Mississippi, 1993.

Browning, Joan. "Invisible Revolutionaries: White Women in Civil Rights Historiography." *Journal of Women's History* 8, no. 3 (Fall 1996): 186–204.

Brundage, Fitzhugh. "White Women and the Politics of Historical Memory in the New South, 1880–1920." In *Jumpin' Jim Crow: Southern Politics from Civil War to Civil Rights*, edited by Jane Dailey, Glenda Elizabeth Gilmore, and Bryant Simon, 115–39. Princeton, N.J.: Princeton University Press, 2000.

Caraway, Nancie. *Segregated Sisterhood: Racism and the Politics of American Feminism*. Knoxville: University of Tennessee Press, 1991.

Carson, Clayborne. *In Struggle: SNCC and the Black Awakening of the 1960s*. 1981. Reprint, Cambridge, Mass.: Harvard University Press, 1995.

Caute, David. *The Great Fear: The Anti-Communist Purge Under Truman and Eisenhower*. New York: Simon and Schuster, 1978.

Censer, Jane Turner. *The Reconstruction of White Southern Womanhood, 1865–1895*. Baton Rouge: Louisiana State University Press, 2003.

Chappell, David L. *Inside Agitators: White Southerners in the Civil Rights Movement*. Baltimore: Johns Hopkins University Press, 1994.

———. *A Stone of Hope: Prophetic Religion and the Death of Jim Crow*. Chapel Hill: University of North Carolina Press, 2004.

Clark, Wayne Addison. "An Analysis of the Relationship between Anti-Communism and Segregationist Thought in the Deep South, 1948–1964." Ph.D. diss., University of North Carolina at Chapel Hill, 1976.

Clinton, Catherine. *The Plantation Mistress: Woman's World in the Old South*. New York: Pantheon, 1982.

Cook, Blanche Wiesen. *Eleanor Roosevelt*. Vol. 1, *1884–1933*. New York: Penguin, 1992.

———. *Eleanor Roosevelt*. Vol. 2, *1933–1938*. New York: Penguin, 1999.

Coryell, Janet L., Martha H. Swain, Sandra Gioia Treadway, and Elizabeth Hayes Turner, eds. *Beyond Image and Convention: Explorations in Southern Women's History*. Columbia: University of Missouri Press, 1998.

Cox, Karen L. *Dixie's Daughters: The United Daughters of the Confederacy and the Preservation of Confederate Culture.* Gainesville: University Press of Florida, 2003.
Crawford, Vicki L., Jacqueline Anne Rouse, and Barbara Woods, eds. *Women in the Civil Rights Movement: Trailblazers and Torchbearers, 1941–1965.* 1990. Reprint, Bloomington: Indiana University Press, 1993.
Daniel, Pete. *Lost Revolutions: The South in the 1950s.* Chapel Hill: University of North Carolina Press, 2000.
Dartt, Rebecca. *Women Activists in the Fight for Georgia School Desegregation, 1958–1961.* Jefferson, N.C.: McFarland, 2008.
Dierenfield, Kathleen Murphy. "One 'Desegregated Heart': Sarah Patton Boyle and the Crusade for Civil Rights in Virginia." *Virginia Magazine of History and Biography* 104, no. 2 (Spring 1996): 251–84.
Dittmer, John. *Local People: The Struggle for Civil Rights in Mississippi.* Urbana: University of Illinois Press, 1994.
Dorr, Lisa Lindquist. *White Women, Rape, and the Power of Race in Virginia, 1900–1960.* Chapel Hill: University of North Carolina Press, 2004.
Ducey, Mitchell F., ed. *The Commission on Interracial Cooperation Papers, 1919–1944, and the Association of Southern Women for the Prevention of Lynching Papers, 1930–1942: A Guide to the Microfilm Edition.* Ann Arbor: University Microfilms International, 1984.
———. *The Southern Regional Council Papers, 1944–1968: A Guide to the Microfilm Edition.* Ann Arbor: University Microfilms International, 1984.
Dunbar, Anthony P. *Against the Grain: Southern Radicals and Prophets, 1929–1959.* Charlottesville: University Press of Virginia, 1981.
Echols, Alice. *Daring to Be Bad: Radical Feminism in America, 1967–1975.* Minneapolis: University of Minnesota Press, 1989.
Edwards, Laura F. *Gendered Strife and Confusion: The Political Culture of Reconstruction.* Urbana: University of Illinois Press, 1997.
Egerton, John. *A Mind to Stay Here: Profiles from the South.* New York: McMillan, 1970.
———. *Speak Now Against the Day: The Generation Before the Civil Rights Movement in the South.* 1994. Reprint, Chapel Hill: University of North Carolina Press, 1995.
Evans, Sara M. *Personal Politics: The Roots of Women's Liberation in the Civil Rights Movement and the New Left.* New York: Knopf, 1979.
———. *Tidal Wave: How Women Changed America at Century's End.* New York: Free Press, 2003.
Fairclough, Adam. *Race and Democracy: The Civil Rights Struggle in Louisiana, 1915–1972.* Athens: University of Georgia Press, 1995.
Faust, Drew Gilpin. *Mothers of Invention: Women of the Slaveholding South in the American Civil War.* Chapel Hill: University of North Carolina Press, 1996.

Foner, Eric. *Reconstruction: America's Unfinished Revolution, 1863–1877*. New York: Harper and Row, 1988.
Fosl, Catherine. *Subversive Southerner: Anne Braden and the Struggle for Racial Justice in the Cold War South*. New York: Palgrave Macmillan, 2002.
Foster, Gaines M. *Ghosts of the Confederacy: Defeat, the Lost Cause, and the Emergence of the New South (1865 to 1913)*. New York: Oxford University Press, 1985.
Fox-Genovese, Elizabeth. "Between Individualism and Community: Autobiographies of Southern Women." In *Located Lives: Place and Idea in Southern Autobiography*, edited by J. Bill Berry, 20–38. Athens: University of Georgia Press, 1990.
———. *Within the Plantation Household: Black and White Women of the Old South*. Chapel Hill: University of North Carolina Press, 1988.
Frazier, E. Franklin, and C. Eric Lincoln. *The Negro Church in America/The Black Church since Frazier*. New York: Schocken, 1974.
Frederickson, Mary E. "'A Place to Speak Our Minds': The Southern School for Women Workers." Ph.D. diss., University of North Carolina, 1981.
Freeman, Jo. *The Politics of Women's Liberation: A Case Study of an Emerging Social Movement and Its Relation to the Policy Process*. 1975. Reprint, Lincoln, Neb.: Authors Guild Backinprint.com, 2000.
Fried, Richard. *Nightmare in Red: The McCarthy Era in Perspective*. Oxford: Oxford University Press, 1990.
Friedman, Jean E. *The Enclosed Garden: Women and Community in the Evangelical South, 1830-1900*. Chapel Hill: University of North Carolina Press, 1985.
Frystak, Shannon. *Our Minds on Freedom: Women and the Struggle for Black Equality in Louisiana, 1924–1967*. Baton Rouge: Louisiana State University Press, 2009.
Giddings, Paula. *When and Where I Enter: The Impact of Black Women on Race and Sex in America*. 1984. Reprint, New York: HarperCollins, 2001.
Gilmore, Glenda Elizabeth. *Defying Dixie: The Radical Roots of Civil Rights, 1919–1950*. New York: Norton, 2008.
———. *Gender and Jim Crow: Women and the Politics of White Supremacy in North Carolina, 1896–1920*. Chapel Hill: University of North Carolina Press, 1996.
Goldfield, David. *Still Fighting the Civil War: The American South and Southern History*. Baton Rouge: Louisiana State University Press, 2002.
Grantham, Dewey. *The South in Modern America*. New York: Harper-Perennial, 1995.
Greene, Christina. *Our Separate Ways: Women and the Black Freedom Movement in Durham, North Carolina*. Chapel Hill: University of North Carolina Press, 2005.
———. "'We'll Take Our Stand': Race, Class, and Gender in the Southern Student Organizing Committee, 1964–1969." In *Hidden Stories of Women in the New South*, edited by Virginia Bernhard, Betty Brandon, Elizabeth Fox-Genovese, Theda Perdue, and Elizabeth H. Turner, 173–203. Columbia: University of Missouri Press, 1994.

Hale, Grace Elizabeth. *Making Whiteness: The Culture of Segregation in the South, 1890–1940*. New York: Vintage, 1998.

Hall, Jacquelyn Dowd. "The Long Civil Rights Movement and the Political Uses of the Past." *Journal of American History* 91, no. 4 (March 2005): 1233–63.

———. *Revolt against Chivalry: Jessie Daniel Ames and the Women's Campaign against Lynching*. Rev. ed. New York: Columbia University Press, 1993.

———. "Women and Lynching." *Southern Exposure* 4, no. 4 (July 1977): 53–54.

———. "'You Must Remember This': Autobiography as Social Critique." *Journal of American History* 85, no. 2 (September 1998): 439–65.

Hall, Kermit L., ed. *The Oxford Companion to the Supreme Court of the United States*. 2nd ed. New York: Oxford University Press, 2005.

Heard, Alexander. *A Two-Party South?* Chapel Hill: University of North Carolina Press, 1952.

Hewitt, Nancy, and Suzanne Lebsock, eds. *Visible Women: New Essays on American Activism*. Urbana: University of Illinois Press, 1993.

Higginbotham, Evelyn Brooks. "African-American Women's History and the Metalanguage of Race." *Signs* 17, no. 2 (Winter 1992): 251–74.

———. *Righteous Discontent: The Women's Movement in the Black Baptist Church, 1880–1920*. Cambridge, Mass.: Harvard University Press, 1993.

Hobson, Fred. *But Now I See: The White Southern Racial Conversion Narrative*. Baton Rouge: Louisiana State University Press, 1999.

Hogan, Wesley C. *Many Minds, One Heart: SNCC's Dream for a New America*. Chapel Hill: University of North Carolina Press, 2007.

hooks, bell. *Ain't I a Woman: Black Women and Feminism*. Boston: South End Press, 1981.

———. "Black Women: Shaping Feminist Theory." In *The Black Feminist Reader*, edited by Joy James and T. Denean Sharpley-Whiting, 131–45. Malden, Mass.: Blackwell, 2000.

James, Joy, and T. Denean Sharpley-Whiting, eds. *The Black Feminist Reader*. Malden, Mass.: Blackwell, 2000.

Johnson, Joan Marie. *Southern Ladies, New Women: New Perspectives on the History of the South*. Gainesville: University Press of Florida, 2004.

Jones, Cherisse Renee. "'Repairers of the Breach': Black and White Women and Racial Activism in South Carolina, 1940s–1960s." Ph.D. diss., Ohio State University, 2003.

Jones, Jacqueline. *Labor of Love, Labor of Sorrow: Black Women, Work, and the Family from Slavery to the Present*. 1985. New York: Vintage, 1986.

Key, V. O. *Southern Politics in State and Nation*. New York: Knopf, 1949.

Klibaner, Irwin. *Conscience of a Troubled South: The Southern Conference Educational Fund, 1946–1966*. Brooklyn, N.Y.: Carlson, 1989.

Knotts, Alice G. *Fellowship of Love: Methodist Women Changing American Racial Attitudes, 1920–1968.* Nashville, Tenn.: Abingdon Press, 1996.

Krueger, Thomas A. *And Promises to Keep: The Southern Conference for Human Welfare, 1938–1948.* Nashville, Tenn.: Vanderbilt University Press, 1967.

Lassiter, Matthew D., and Andrew B. Lewis, eds. *The Moderates' Dilemma: Massive Resistance to School Desegregation in Virginia.* Charlottesville: University Press of Virginia, 1998.

Lawson, Steven F. *Black Ballots: Voting Rights in the South, 1944–1969.* 1976. Reprint, Lanham, Md.: Lexington Books, 1999.

———. "Freedom Then, Freedom Now: The Historiography of the Civil Rights Movement." *American Historiographical Review* 96, no. 2 (April 1991): 456–71.

Lewis, George. *Massive Resistance: The White Response to the Civil Rights Movement.* London: Hodder Education, 2006.

Lincoln, C. Eric, and Lawrence H. Mamiya. *The Black Church in the African American Experience.* Durham, N.C.: Duke University Press, 1990.

Little, Kimberly K. *You Must Be from the North: Southern White Women in the Memphis Civil Rights Movement.* Jackson: University Press of Mississippi, 2009.

Litwack, Leon F. *Trouble in Mind: Black Southerners in the Age of Jim Crow.* 1998. Reprint, New York: Vintage, 1999.

Loveland, Anne C. *Lillian Smith: A Southerner Confronting the South. A Biography.* Baton Rouge: Louisiana State University Press, 1986.

Lynn, Susan. *Progressive Women in Conservative Times: Racial Justice, Peace, and Feminism, 1945 to the 1960s.* New Brunswick, N.J.: Rutgers University Press, 1992.

McDonough, Julia Anne. "Men and Women of Good Will: A History of the Commission on Interracial Cooperation and the Southern Regional Council, 1919–1954." Ph.D. diss., University of Virginia, 1993.

McDowell, John Patrick. *The Social Gospel in the South: The Woman's Home Mission Movement in the Methodist Episcopal Church, South, 1886–1939.* Baton Rouge: Louisiana State University Press, 1982.

McMillen Neil R. *The Citizens' Council: Organized Resistance to the Second Reconstruction, 1954–1964* [Illini Book Edition]. 1971. Reprint, Urbana: University of Illinois Press, 1994.

———. *Dark Journey: Black Mississippians in the Age of Jim Crow.* Urbana: University of Illinois Press, 1989.

Michel, Gregg L. *Struggle for a Better South: The Southern Student Organizing Committee, 1964–1969.* New York: Palgrave MacMillan, 2004.

Mullis, Sharon Mitchell. "The Public Career of Grace Towns Hamilton: A Citizen Too Busy to Hate." Ph.D. diss., Emory University, 1976.

Murray, Gail S., ed. *Throwing Off the Cloak of Privilege: White Southern Women Activists in the Civil Rights Era.* Gainesville: University Press of Florida, 2004.

Mussatt, David J. "Journey for Justice: A Religious Analysis of the Ethics of the 1961 Albany Freedom Ride." Ph.D. diss., Temple University School of Religion, 2001.

Nasstrom, Kathryn L. "Between Memory and History: Autobiographies of the Civil Rights Movement and the Writing of Civil Rights History." *Journal of Southern History* 74, no. 2 (May 2008): 325–64.

Nelson, Susan McGrath. "The Association of Southern Women for the Prevention of Lynching and the Fellowship of the Concerned and Racial Politics." Master's thesis, Emory University, 1982.

Newberry, Anthony Lake. "Without Urgency or Ardor: The South's Middle-of-the-Road Liberals and Civil Rights, 1945–1960." Ph.D. diss., Ohio University, 1982.

O'Dell, Darlene. *Sites of Southern Memory: The Autobiographies of Katharine Du Pre Lumpkin, Lillian Smith, and Pauli Murray*. Charlottesville: University Press of Virginia, 2001.

Olson, Lynne. *Freedom's Daughters: The Unsung Heroines of the Civil Rights Movement from 1830 to 1970*. New York: Simon and Schuster, 2001.

Patton, Randall Lee. "Southern Liberals and the Emergence of a 'New South,' 1938–1950." Ph.D. diss., University of Georgia, 1990.

Payne, Charles M. *I've Got the Light of Freedom: The Organizing Tradition and the Mississippi Freedom Struggle*. Berkeley: University of California Press, 1995.

Rabinowitz, Howard N. *The First New South, 1865–1920*. Arlington Heights, Ill.: Harlan Davidson, 1992.

Ransby, Barbara. *Ella Baker and the Black Freedom Movement: A Radical Democratic Vision*. Chapel Hill: University of North Carolina Press, 2003.

Reed, Linda. *Simple Decency and Common Sense: The Southern Conference Movement, 1938–1963*. Bloomington: Indiana University Press, 1991.

Ritterhouse, Jennifer. *Growing Up Jim Crow: How Black and White Southern Children Learned Race*. Chapel Hill: University of North Carolina Press, 2006.

Robertson, Nancy Marie. *Christian Sisterhood, Race Relations, and the YWCA, 1906–1946*. Urbana: University of Illinois Press, 2007.

Robnett, Belinda. *How Long? How Long? African-American Women in the Struggle for Civil Rights*. New York: Oxford University Press, 1997.

Rogers, Kim Lacy. *Righteous Lives: Narratives of the New Orleans Civil Rights Movement*. New York: New York University Press, 1993.

Salmond, John A. *Miss Lucy of the CIO: The Life and Times of Lucy Randolph Mason, 1882–1959*. Athens: University of Georgia Press, 1988.

Schrecker, Ellen. *Many Are the Crimes: McCarthyism in America*. Princeton, N.J.: Princeton University Press, 1998.

Schultz, Debra L. *Going South: Jewish Women in the Civil Rights Movement*. New York: New York University Press, 2001.

Scott, Anne Firor. "After Suffrage: Southern Women in the Twenties." *Journal of Southern History* 30, no. 3 (August 1964): 298–318.

———. "Most Invisible of All: Black Women's Voluntary Associations." *Journal of Southern History* 56, no. 1 (February 1990): 3–22.

———. *The Southern Lady: From Pedestal to Politics (1830–1930)*. 1970. Reprint, Charlottesville: University Press of Virginia, 1995.

Sokol, Jason. *There Goes My Everything: White Southerners in the Age of Civil Rights, 1945–1975*. 2006. Reprint, New York: Vintage, 2007.

Sosna, Morton. *In Search of the Silent South: Southern Liberals and the Race Issue*. New York: Columbia University Press, 1977.

Spelman, Elizabeth V. *Inessential Woman: Problems of Exclusion in Feminist Thought*. Boston: Beacon Press, 1988.

Spruill, Marjorie Julian, Valinda W. Littlefield, and Joan Marie Johnson, eds. *South Carolina Women: Their Lives and Times*. Vol. 3. Athens: University of Georgia Press, 2012.

Stanton, Mary. *Journey toward Justice: Juliette Hampton Morgan and the Montgomery Bus Boycott*. Athens: University of Georgia Press, 2006.

Stefani, Anne. "A Dissenting Voice in Alabama: Virginia Foster Durr's Correspondence (1951–68)." *Revue Française d'Etudes Américaines* 120 (2nd quarter 2009): 65–78.

———. "From Southern Lady to Southern Activist: Integrationist White Women in the American South (1920–1970)." In *Exchanges and Correspondence: The Construction of Feminism*, edited by Claudette Fillard and Françoise Orazi, 250–63. Newcastle upon Tyne, U.K.: Cambridge Scholars, 2010.

Sullivan, Patricia. *Days of Hope: Race and Democracy in the New Deal Era*. Chapel Hill: University of North Carolina Press, 1996.

———. *Lift Every Voice: The NAACP and the Making of the Civil Rights Movement*. New York: New Press, 2009.

Taylor, Frances Sanders. "'On the Edge of Tomorrow': Southern Women, the Student YWCA, and Race, 1920–1944." Ph.D. diss., Stanford University, 1984.

Tindall, George B. *The Emergence of the New South, 1913–1945*. Baton Rouge: Louisiana State University Press and Littlefield Fund for Southern History of University of Texas, 1967.

White, Deborah Gray. *Ar'n't I a Woman?: Female Slaves in the Plantation South*. New York: Norton, 1985.

White, E. Frances. *Dark Continent of Our Bodies: Black Feminism and the Politics of Respectability*. Philadelphia: Temple University Press, 2001.

White, Ronald C., Jr. *Liberty and Justice for All: Racial Reform and the Social Gospel (1877–1925)*. San Francisco: Harper and Row, 1990.

White, Ronald C., Jr., and Charles Howard Hopkins. *The Social Gospel: Religion and Reform in Changing America*. Philadelphia: Temple University Press, 1976.

Whites, LeeAnn. *Gender Matters: Civil War, Reconstruction, and the Making of the New South*. New York: Palgrave, 2005.

Williamson, Joel. *The Crucible of Race: Black-White Relations in the American South Since Emancipation*. New York: Oxford University Press, 1984.

Wolfe, Margaret Ripley. *Daughters of Canaan: A Saga of Southern Women*. Lexington: University Press of Kentucky, 1995.

Woods, Jeff. *Black Struggle, Red Scare: Segregation and Anti-Communism in the South, 1948–1968*. Baton Rouge: Louisiana State University Press, 2004.

Woodward, C. Vann. *The Burden of Southern History*. Enl. ed. 1960. Reprint, Baton Rouge: Louisiana State University Press, 1970.

———. *The Strange Career of Jim Crow*. 2nd rev. ed. New York: Oxford University Press, 1966.

Zinn, Howard. *SNCC: The New Abolitionists*. 1964. Reprint, Cambridge, Mass.: South End Press, 2002.

Index

Page numbers in *italics* refer to illustrations.

Abernathy, Juanita, 141, 155
Abernathy, Ralph, 37, 155
Agricultural Adjustment Administration, 81
Albany Movement, 1–2, 47, 135, 186, 193, 206, 208, 256, 291n5
Alexander, Will, 65, 75, 86, 224, 277n20
Almond, Lindsay, 114
Amatniek, Sarah. *See* Sarachild, Sarah Amatniek
American Association of University Women (AAUW), 117, 153, 259, 266
American Friends Service Committee (AFSC), 102, 135, 182, 202, 256, 262, 304n52
Ames, Jessie Daniel, 5, 87, 92, 118, 234; and Association of Southern Women for the Prevention of Lynching, 74–80; biographical sketch of, 255; and Commission on Interracial Cooperation, 66–67, 70, 75; and womanhood, 25–26, 79
Anti-Communism, 78, 90–91, 140, 149, 158, 291n8, 293n35, 294n42. *See also* Black- and Red-baiting; McCarthyism
Anti-Lynching Crusaders, 75
Arnall, Ellis, 86, 282–83n81
Ashmore, Harry, 127
Association of Southern Women for the Prevention of Lynching (ASWPL), 5, 74–80, 96, 101, 141, 255, 264, 266; and chivalry rhetoric, 75–77, 79–80, 235; founding of, 75–76; and gender, 78–80; as inspiration for female activists, 118, 165. *See also* Lynching
Autobiography, 8–10, 254; as southern catharsis, 13–14, 39–40, 51–53, 138, 143–44, 146, 225–27, 235–40, 302nn14,19

Baker, Ella, 55, 135, *170*, 210–11, 281n57; and 1960s civil rights movement, 182, 184–85, 197, 208, 263, 265
Barker, Mary, 64, 89
Bates, Daisy, 117–18, 288n46
Beale, Frances, 301n1
Beauvoir, Simone de, 205, 300n1
Beloved Community, 38, 180, 189, 191, 201–4
Berkey, Mrs. Gene, 71
Bethlehem House (Nashville), 65, 224, 266, 277n19
Bethune, Mary McLeod, 75, 81, 87, 103, 280n41
Bickett, Mrs. T. W. (Fanny Yarborough), 68
Biracialism, 5, 7, 65–68, 100, 276n4, 278–79n28
Black, Hugo, 25, 149–50
Black, Josephine, 25–26
Black- and Red-baiting, 97–99, 108, 110, 118, 146, 149–55, 282n76, 284n4
Black men, 3, 4, 17, 33–38, 97, 245–48, 271nn55,58
Black Power, 136, 140, 200–203, 292n18, 298n44
Blacks. *See* Black men; Black women

Black women, 3–4, 42–43, 241, 270n49, 271n57, 301n1; prejudice against, 26, 30–33, 69, 271n53; racial and social activism of, 66–68, 75, 77, 79, 103, 188, 278n25, 280n40, 289–90n66; relationships between white women and, 29–33, 38, 68, 102–3, 243–44, 270nn46,51; sexual abuse of, 29, 31, 270n45
Blanchard, Emily, 106
Blanchard, Leslie, 64
Blease, Cole, 80
Bond, Julian, 185, 195, 199
Boone, Buford, 142
Boothe, Armistead, 104
Boyle, Sarah Patton, 47, 157–58, 163, 269n32; autobiography of, 13, 143, 146, 225–28, 235–36, 292nn19,20; biographical sketch of, 255; as moral radical, 137–45; paternalism of, 19–21, 31; white supremacist education of, 16–20, 23–24, 35–36, 43, 45, 142
Braden, Anne, *170*, 221, 253, 267n5; autobiographical memoir of, 13, 146, 153, 209, 225–27, 235–36; biographical sketch of, 255–56; and Communism, 137, 152–57; friendships between black women and, 210–11; and 1960s civil rights movement, 179, 203, 196–97, 298n44; as political radical, 145–66, 248, 292n24; Red-baiting, target of, 152–55; as role model, 209–10, 299n56; as southerner, 219, 229; and white southern womanhood, 25, 159–64; white supremacist education of, 15, 18, 20–21, 31, 40–41; white supremacist education, emancipation from, 45–49, 274n99; and women's liberation issue, 237, 240–42, 245–48, 304n52
Braden, Carl, 146, 148, 152, 154, 156–57, 196
Bradford, Connie, 46, 188
Breeden, Fran, 118
Brewer, Vivion, 114, 119–21, *169*
Brown, Charlotte Hawkins, 68, 91
Brown, Valerie, 207
Browning, Joan C., 13–14, 47, *171*, *173*, *176*–77, 223, 236, 304n52; biographical sketch of, 256; on Anne Braden, 229, 299n56; civil rights movement, involvement with, 183, 185–87, 189–90, 193, 195, 199–202, 205–9, 296n25, 298nn48,51,52; and gender issue, 28, 237, 242, 245, 253, 305n2; on southern identity, 231–32
Brownmiller, Susan, 245–48
Bryant, Carolyn, 246
Bullard, Helen, 110
Burlage, Dorothy Dawson, 13, *173*, 232, 236–37, 304n52; biographical sketch of, 256; civil rights movement, involvement with, 183–84, 189, 194–95, 197–202, 298nn48,49; and gender issue, 28–29, 54, 205, 207–9, 211–13, 215, 242–43, 245–46, 275n103; white supremacist education of, 15–16, 270n48
Burlage, Robb, 183, 197, 212
Burt, Martha, 102

Cahn, Gladys, 115
Camus, Albert, 191
Carmichael, Stokely, 186, 197, 202, 215, 261, 292n18
Carr, Johnnie, 155
Carter, Hodding, II, 95, 283n86
Carter, Judy, 207
Cash, Wilbur C., 30, 50, 270n45
Charlton, Louise, 89
Chivalry rhetoric, 34, 42, 75–77, 79–80, 96, 235, 239, 251–52
Christianity, 15, 291n4; as major influence for white female racial activists, 7, 46–51, 62–63, 145–46, 189, 298n49; in 1960s civil rights movement, 134–35, 179, 188–93, 274n89; as progressive force, 60–61, 65–66, 73, 101–2, 109, 183, 229, 273n87, 274n93, 275n2, 279n38
Church, Roberta, 124
Churchwomen, 59–61, 86, 90, 96, 132, 257, 259, 279n30, 285nn13,26; in Commission on Interracial Cooperation, 65–74; and desegregation crisis, 99–105, 108–12, 117, 129, 142–43; paternalism of, 66–70, 278n27; rejection of chivalry rhetoric, 78–80; and Social Gospel, 65–67, 69; and

women's activism, 123–24, 127–28. *See also* Methodist Women; United Church Women
Civil Rights Act (1964), 14, 98, 136, 201
Civil rights movement, 3–4, 47, 133–36, 188–92, 272n7, 274n89, 295n4; as a black-led movement, 98, 112, 134–35, 192–200, 297n36; as liberating experience for white women, 54–56, 181, 202–16, 239–40, 249, 274–75n103, 300n66; long, 5–6, 9, 13, 52, 56, 251; male leadership of, 210, 214, 237, 253; older white women's support of, 37–38, 122–23, 143, 210–12, 255–57, 260–66; and sexism, 54–55, 213–16, 237, 275n106, 300n66; women's role in, 213–15, 238, 282n79, 289–90n66; young white women's involvement with, 180–88, 192–200, 256–61, 263–64, 270n52
Clark, Septima, 195, 210–11
Class, 43, 180; interconnection between race and, 67, 83, 240; prejudice, 21, 30–31, 34, 42, 67, 70
Cold War, 51, 90, 140, 147, 292n15
Commission on Interracial Cooperation (CIC), 65–70, 79, 85–86, 91–92, 224, 277–78n20; and Association of Southern Women for the Prevention of Lynching, 74–75; Committee on Woman's Work, 66–68, 75; paternalism of, 66–68; white male leadership of, 65–66; white women's involvement with, 255, 264–65, 278–79n28
Communism, 81–82, 97, 102, 110, 122, 137, 140, 157, 282n76
Communist Party, 150–51, 156, 164, 245
Congress of Industrial Organizations (CIO), 83–85, 88, 261
Congress of Racial Equality (CORE), 134–36, 191; white women's involvement with, 46, 140, 181, 184, 186, 188, 208, 260–61, 273n87
Connor, Eugene "Bull," 52
Costigan-Wagner bill, 79, 280n49
Cotton, Dorothy, 195
Council on Human Relations (CHR), 48, 103–4, 122, 141, 143, 153, 158, 186, 223; and massive resistance, 108–12, 153; and 1960s civil rights movement, 135, 181, 186–87, 208, 286n26; white women's involvement with, 255–57, 262, 265–66, 283n82
Crouch, Paul, 150–51
Cunningham, Anne, 102
Curry, Constance (Connie), 13, 16, 47, 49, *174*, 236, 245, 304n52; biographical sketch of, 256; civil rights movement, involvement with, 181–83, 185–86, 189, 194–200, 202, 203, 232, 295nn6,14; and southern sisterhood, 205, 207–9, 211, 298n48
Cuthbertson, Mary (Polly), 63

Dabbs, Edith M., 47, 102, 109, 111, 127–28; biographical sketch of, *257*
Dabbs, James McBride, 257
Davis, James (Jimmy), 116
Davis, Kate T. (Mrs. George E.), 80
Davis, Mrs. A.J.E., 142
Democratic National Convention, 184, 187, 259, 296n21
Democratic Party, 57, 144, 284n10, 304n52
Desegregated Heart, The, 143, 226, 236, 255
Didley, Bill, 199
Direct action, 180, 183, 185–88, 193–94, 198–99, 298n51
Dixiecrats, 100, 284–85n10
Dombrowski, James, 148–52, 159, 223, 283n82
Dowd, J. E., 85
Dowd, Mollie, 89
Dreyfous, Mathilde, 107
Durr, Clifford, 25, 37, 86, 141, 147, 151, 155, 159, 257
Durr, Virginia, 47, 81, 92, 141, *178*, 253, 267n5, 269n32, 292n25, 304n52; autobiography of, 13, 30, 234–35, 238, 274n101; biographical sketch of, 257; and Communism, 137, 152–57, 282n76, 293n40; and desegregation crisis, 104, 109, 219–23, 301n4; friendships between black women and, 155, 211–12, 299n60; gender consciousness and personal emancipation of, 52–53, 234–40, 245; on ladyhood and white

Durr, Virginia—*continued*
  southern womanhood, 22–27, 30, 79, 85, 154, 159–66, 247; and 1960s civil rights movement, 157, 289n55; as political radical, 145–59, 294n42; politics, early involvement in, 86–88, 281n58; Red-baiting, target of, 149–51, 282n76, 293n30; as role model, 208–9; and Southern Conference for Human Welfare, 83, 89, 148, 282n71; as southerner, 230–31; white supremacist education of, 17, 22, 35–37, 43, 45–46, 49, 274n92
Durr, Virginia Foster (Tilla), 29, *178*
Dyer bill, 79, 280n49

Eastland, James, 108, 149–51, 157, 164, 284n4
Eisenhower, Dwight, 114
Ellison, Diana, 207
Emergency Civil Liberties Committee, 155, 294n42
Emerson, Ralph Waldo, 191
Equal Employment Opportunity Commission, 241, 262
Evans, Sara, 51, 54, 209, 300n66
Evers, Medgar, 291n6

Faubus, Orville, 113–14
Fellowship of the Concerned (FOC), 48, 71, 100–102, 111, 124, 139, 141, 261, 264
Feminine Mystique, The, 243–44, 300n1
Feminism, 205, 211–12; feminist consciousness, 54, 166, 236–37, 239; southern women and, 8, 201, 213–15, 217–18, 233–34, 238–45, 248–50, 300–301n1; women's movement (second wave), 11, 233, 236, 244, 249, 253, 300n65,66, 304nn46,47,49; woman's suffrage movement, 27, 234, 255, 261, 264
Finsten, Jill, 188
Fischer, Margaret, 89, 92
Folsom, James (Jim), 144
Foreman, Clark, 86–87, 153, 219–20, 222–23, 293n40
Foreman, Mairi, 219–20

Forman, James, 122, 185
Freedom Rides, 1, 135, 184, 187, 208, 291nn5,6; white women's participation in, 47, *172*, 186, 188, 193, 195, 206, 231, 256, 260–61
Friedan, Betty, 243, 300n1
Friedman, Maxine, 115

Gandhi, Mohandas, 141, 191
Gelders, Joseph, 87
Gender, 6–8, 217, 251; consciousness, 54–55, 137, 159, 162, 205–6, 212, 235–39, 251–52; discrimination, 54–56, 213–15, 237–38, 304n46; emancipation, 10, 51–56, 74, 123, 128–33, 137, 159–66, 181, 204–15, 239; norms, 7, 11, 13, 28–30, 35, 38–39, 49, 79, 96, 157, 164–65, 233; oppression, 33, 52, 159, 162, 218, 240, 243; roles, 16, 29, 56, 59, 78–80, 163, 253; solidarity, 73–75, 279n38 (*see also* Sisterhood)
Georgia Commission on the Status of Women, 241, 248–49, 262
Georgia Education Commission, 105, 129, 293n33
Geyers, Lee, 88
Gladney, Margaret Rose, 35, 54, 299n55; biographical sketch of, 257
Goldthwait, Isabel, 102, 111
Graham, Frank Porter, 90
Gray, Fred, 155
Gray, Garland, 113
Gray Commission, 113, 142
Great Depression, 31, 58, 64, 80–88, 280n53
Great Speckled Bird, 218, 241
Green, Winifred, 182, 295n6
Griffin, John, 92
Grimké sisters, 275n103
Grogan, Nan, 192, 196–97, 200

Hall, Grover, Jr., 291n8
Hamilton, Grace T., 91–93, 283n82
Hamlett, Ed, 197
Hammond, Lily H., 68–70, 278n27
Hanish, Carol, 300n1
Harding, Vincent, 201, 231

Harris, Betty, 118
Hartsfield, William, 115
Haskin, Sara Estelle, 67
Hayden, Casey, *175*, 236, 259, 304n52; biographical sketch of, 258; civil rights movement, involvement with, 1–2, 182–86, 189–92, 194–96, 198–201, 203, 295nn7,9, 297n28, 298nn48,52; and gender issue, 54–56, 106, 205–15, 232, 240–43, 245, 249, 275nn103,106, 300n65,66
Hayden, Tom, 1, 183
Help Our Public Education (HOPE), 115–21, 125, 129–31, 182, 262, 287n42, 288n45, 289n59
Highlander Folk School, 65, 135, 149, *170*, 266, 291n4
Hillman, Sydney, 83–84
hooks, bell, 244
Hope, John, 67
Hope, Lugenia, 76
House Committee on Un-American Activities (HUAC), 91, 151, 153–56, 282n77
Hultman, Tamela, 298n53
Hutchins, Robert, 222

Interracialism, 59–66, 83, 119, 186–90, 194–96, 201, 291n4; interracial contact, 45–46, 51, 63, 66, 71–73, 121–22, 211; interracial friendships, 102–3, 202, 210–12, 299nn60,61; interracial movement, 82, 180, 183–84, 202, 281n60; interracial sex, 35–38, 165, 272n67, 273n82; interracial work, 19–20, 68–75, 85–86, 102–9, 132, 141, 276n4, 277n19, 279n30

Jackson, Jesse, 256
Jackson movement, *172*, 186–87, 193, 259, 261
Jewish women, 47, 102, 117, 119, 188, 273n87, 286n33, 299n61
Johns Committee, 293n33
Johnson, Carrie Parks, 67–68, 278n23
Johnson, Charles, 50
Johnson, Guion, 91, 128–29, 222–23; biographical sketch of, 258–59

Johnson, Guy, 91, 129, 222–23, 258
Johnson, Lady Bird, 156
Johnson, Lyndon, 156
Jones, Susie, 100

Keller, Rosa, 104, 106–7, 115, 117, 287n41
Kennedy, John F., 154, 221, 304n46
Kennedy, Robert F., 187, 221
Killers of the Dream, 78, 94, 146, 160, 226, 235–36, 263; influence of, on antiracist activism, 138–40, 209, 212, 218
King, Coretta Scott, 141, 155, 262
King, Ed, 187, 259
King, Jeannette, 187, 194, 199–200, 202; biographical sketch of, 259
King, Lonnie, 18
King, Martin Luther, Jr., 134–36, 189, 271n57, 291n8, 292n18; links between white women activists and, 37, 47, 122, 140, 143, 153, 292n20
King, Mary, 47, *175*, 232, 236, 258; biographical sketch of, 259–60; civil rights movement, involvement with, 185, 195–97, 298n48; and gender issue, 54–55, 106, 205–8, 211, 213–15, 240–41, 243, 249, 275nn103, 300nn65,66
Ku Klux Klan, 97

Ladyhood, 1, 28, 35, 37, 158, 229, 239, 269n29; lady activism, 58, 78–80, 84–85, 96, 98–99, 112, 123–33, 136, 157, 163–64; lady ideal, 2, 6–7, 22–31, 52–57, 154, 162–66, 212–13, 215, 251–52; southern belle, 24–25, 53, 82, 129, 140, 269n29
Leadership: black, 117, 184, 196, 198, 276n4, 297n36; white male, 67, 70, 74, 80, 91, 124, 127–28, 130, 279n38; women and, 53, 70, 92, 198, 233
League of Women Voters (LWV), 53, 96, 110, 123, 153, 234; and desegregation crisis, 104–8, 111–12, 116–17, 129, 132, 283n82, 286n37; Georgia, 86–87, 89, 92, 105, 282–83n81; members of, 255, 259, 261–62, 265–66; of New Orleans, 104, 106–7, 110

Lee, Robert E., 84, 261
Leonard, Margaret Burr, 28–28, *172*, *176*, 188, 208; biographical sketch of, 260
Leonard, Margaret Long, 28, 163, *168*, 207–8, 223, 299n54; biographical sketch of, 260
Lessing, Doris, 205
Lewis, John (CIO), 83, 85
Lewis, John (SNCC), 193
Little Rock's desegregation crisis, 89, 104, 110–20, 122–23, 125, 127, 130, 287nn39,40
Liuzzo, Viola, 291n6
Lobbying, 99–100, 114, 129–31, 155–56
Lokey, Muriel, 115
Long, Margaret. *See* Leonard, Margaret Long
Lost Cause, 22–23, 33, 219, 272n59
Louisiana Joint Legislative Committee on Un-American Activities (LUAC), 151, 293nn33,34
Lucy, Autherine, 142, 147
Lumpkin, Elizabeth, 23
Lumpkin, Katharine Du Pre, 40–41, 44–45, 49, 269n32, 277nn12,16; autobiography of, 13, 225–29; biographical sketch of, 260–61; on gender and womanhood, 23, 235–36; as student YWCA leader, 62–64, 302n19
Lynching, 2, 21, 41, 74–80, 88, 93–94, 165, 245, 248, 271nn55,56; as an act of chivalry, 34, 75, 80, 165, 217; black women's fight against, 68, 75, 77, 79, 280n40; federal legislation against, 75, 79–80, 90, 141, 280n49; impact on relationship between black men and white women, 33–39, 194–95; as means to control black men, 33, 57, 58, 245–48, 271nn55, 273n74; white women's ambivalence toward, 41–42, 75, 77, 272n59

MacDougall, Margaret, 129
Making of a Southerner, The, 226, 261
March on Washington, 135, 143, 192, 196
Mars, Florence, 108
Marshall, Burke, 156, 221

Mason, George, 84, 261
Mason, Lucy Randolph, 47, 64–65, 81–85, 87–89, 92, 148, 234, 281nn58,61; biographical sketch of, 261
Massive resistance, 97–98, 112–16, 284n3, 286n37, 287nn38,39,42, 293n33; and harassment of integrationists, 102, 104, 108–9, 142–43, 149–54, 157, 228; integrationists' response to, 146, 154–55, 165, 219–22
Mays, Sadie, 18
McCall, Gertrude, 102
McCarthy, Joseph, 108
McCarthyism, 98, 140, 154, 156, 284n4. *See also* Anti-Communism; Black- and Red-baiting
McCurdy, Sheila, 47, 273n87
McDew, Charles (Chuck), 237
McDonald, Lois, 64, 277n16
McGee, Willie, 245, 247–48
McGill, Ralph, 95, 98, 138, 154, 283n86, 293n40
McKissick, Floyd, 292n18
McLaren, Louise, 64, 277n16
Meares, Carrie, 64
Memphis movement, 35, 54, 122, 258, 267n5, 273n87, 288n54
Mentoring, 50–51, 54, 182–83, 204, 207–10, 274n100
Meredith, James, 143, 292n18
Methodist Student Movement, 46, 264
Methodist women, 50, 59–61, 71, 76, 259, 264–65, 276n6, 277n19; *Brown* decision, support of, 100–103, 111–12; in Commission on Interracial Cooperation, 65–74; opposition to male leaders, 73–74, 224, 279n38; work with federal government, 89–90. *See also* Churchwomen; Woman's Division of the Board of Missions of the Methodist Church (Woman's Division)
Michaels, Sheila, 273n87
Mind of the South, The, 50
Miscegenation, 35, 66, 77, 97, 165
Mississippians for Public Education, 182, 288n52

Mississippi Freedom Democratic Party (MFDP), 135, 184, 187, 259, 291n5, 296n21
Mississippi Freedom Summer, 135, 184, 244, 289n55, 291nn5,6, 296n21; white women's participation in, 187, 196, 200–201, 232, 258–59
Mitford, Jessica, 235, 239, 247, 301n4
Montgomery Advertiser, 141, 144, 230, 291n8
Montgomery Bus Boycott, 134–36, 139–42, 155, 159, 222, 257, 261, 290n1
Morgan, Juliette, 137–45, 152, 157, 160–62, *167*, 230, 267n5, 269nn32,33, 292n16; biographical sketch of, 261
Morgan, Paula, 144
Morton, Nelle, 298n53
Moses, Robert (Bob), 189, 197
Motherhood, 26–27, 32, 43, 94, 120, 124–25, 289n59
Moynihan, Daniel Patrick, 271n57
Mulholland, Joan Trumpauer, *172*, *176*, 185–86, 193, 199, 231; biographical sketch of, 261
Murison, Peggy, 119–20
Murphy, Sara Alderman, 34–35, 111, 115, 118–19, 121–23, 229, 273n82, 299n61
Murray, Pauli, 81, 299n60

Nance, Steve, 84–85
Nashville movement, 46, 184, 192–93, 197
National Association for the Advancement of Colored People (NAACP), 37, 79–80, 291n6; anti-Communism of, 154, 293n40; massive resistance, target of, 108, 155, 284n3; and modern civil rights movement, 97–98, 102, 112, 117, 134–36, 181, 187, 291n6; white women's involvement with, 20–21, 122–23, 143, 148, 255, 257, 259, 262; during World War II, 82, 88, 280–81n57, 282n72
National Association of Colored Women (NACW), 67, 75
National Committee to Abolish HUAC (NCAHUAC), 153–55, 294n41
National Committee to Abolish the Poll Tax (NCAPT), 88, 257

National Consumers' League, 83, 261, 281n61
National Council of Catholic Women, 286n33
National Council of Churches, 127
National Council of Jewish Women (NCJW), 102, 107, 117, 286n33
National Council of Negro Women, 103, 286n33
National Emergency Council (NEC), 82, 86, 281n60
National Negro Congress, 88
National Organization for Women (NOW), 211, 241, 258, 262
National Recovery Act, 83
National Student Association (NSA), 181–84, 189, 191, 195–99, 214, 256, 291n4
National Student Movement, 135, 183, 291n4
National Women's Political Caucus, 304n52
National Youth Administration, 85
Nazombe, Elmira Kendricks, 298n53
New Deal, 5, 58, 80–88, 156
Newell, Bertha Payne, 66–67, 76
New Orleans: civil rights movement in, 46, 186, 188, 260–61, 287; desegregation crisis in, 107, 112, 115–16, 119–20, 122, 222, 288n54
New South, 208, 239, 260
Niebuhr, Reinhold, 189–90
Nineteenth Amendment, 27, 58, 87, 234
Nixon, Arlette, 30
Nixon, E. D., 30, 37, 155
Noble, Elizabeth, 111
Nonviolence, 134–35, 139, 186, 189–93, 296n21; Student Nonviolent Coordinating Committee and, 179–80, 184
Nonviolent Action Group (NAG), 185–86
Northern Student Movement, 199, 214, 256
North Georgia Review, 94, 263
Now Is the Time, 97, 101, 139, 263, 292n15

Oakes, John, 222
Oakes, Rosalie, 208, 298n53
Odum, Howard, 258

Old South, 22–23, 219
Organizations Assisting Schools in September (OASIS), 115
Owen, Rebecca, 46, 298n53

Paine College (Augusta, Georgia), 186, 190, 193, 199, 265
Panel of American Women (PAW), 122–23, 299n61
Parchman Penitentiary, 186, 261
Parent-Teacher Association (PTA), 114, 117
Parks, Rosa, 155, 299n60
Parsons, Sara Mitchell, 15, 17–18, *174*, 304n52; autobiographical memoir of, 13, 53, 110, 238; biographical sketch of, 262; on gender and personal emancipation, 53, 106, 131–32, 236, 238, 240, 245
Partners for Progress, 125, 129
Paschall, Eliza, 92, 104, 218, 220–23, 241, 248; biographical sketch of, 262; and 1960s civil rights movement, 103–4, 110, 122, 288n53
Patch, Penny, 297n28
Paternalism, 7, 19, 21, 58, 66–70, 142, 193, 278n27
Patriarchy, 214–15, 233, 240, 245; challenge to, 96, 124, 165, 204, 218, 235; southern, 1, 8, 73–74, 23, 27, 35, 51–52, 56, 162–63, 249
Pauley, Frances, 16, 47, 86, *171*, 223, 245, 304n52; biographical sketch of, 262; and Georgia Council on Human Relations, 104, 109–10; and Help Our Public Education, 115, 117–19, 121; on lady activism, 129–31; and League of Women Voters, 87–88, 104–7, 110, 234; and 1960s civil rights movement, 122, 288n53, 289n55; on racial prejudice, 18–20; as role model, 111, 208
Pendergrast, Nan, 118, 122, 125–26, 129, *169*, *177*, 288n53, 289n60; biographical sketch of, 262–63
Pfister, James, 151
Phillips, U. B., 50
Poll tax, 57, 82, 87–90, 136, 141, 147, 234, 282n7

Powell, Faye, 28, *177*, 183, 186, 189, 193, 206–7, 296n19, 298n51; biographical sketch of, 263
Powell, Velma, 104, 114
President's Commission on the Status of Women, 304n46
President's Committee on Civil Rights (PCCR), 71, 90, 100, 131, 224, 264, 302n12
Price, Mary, 89
Progressive Party, 147, 156, 257

Race: racial etiquette, 1, 16, 29–30, 37, 43–44, 49–50, 95, 126, 186; racial guilt, 8, 39–41, 137, 139, 143–44, 146, 202, 226, 246–47, 251–54; racial oppression, 300n1, 304n52; racial prejudice, 16–22, 30, 42, 63, 67–68, 90, 93, 121–22, 141–43, 182, 190, 224, 247, 252–53; taboos, 35–39, 45–46, 66, 96, 109, 121, 166, 232, 235. *See also* Biracialism; Interracialism; Miscegenation
Rape, 29, 270n45; myth, 34–35, 41, 75, 77–78, 80, 245–49, 271nn55,58
Raper, Arthur, 75
Reagan, Ronald, 262
Reagon, Bernice Johnson, 215, 272n67
Redding, J. Saunders, 223
Reeb, James, 291n6
Report on the Economic Conditions of the South, 82, 86, 281n58
Republican Party, 57, 169, 294n45
Respectability, 2, 7, 73, 77–79, 84, 96, 112, 118–20, 131, 165
Richardson, Nancy, 298n53
Riley, Gwen, 123, 299n61
Riley, Negail, 123
Rilling, Paul, 117
Roberts, Augusta, 62, 64
Robinson, Reggie, 194
Robinson, Ruby Doris, 197, 275n106
Romaine, Anne Cooke, 196
Roosevelt, Eleanor, 81–82, 87, 89–90, 94, 280n55

Roosevelt, Franklin Delano, 81, 86, 281n58
Rusk, Dean, 221

Samuel, Irene, 130
Sarachild, Sarah Amatniek, 240, 242, 300n1
Sartre, Jean-Paul, 191
Save Our Schools (SOS), 115–17, 119–21, 125, 287n4, 288n45, 289n59
Save-the-schools movement, 112–23, 125–26, 288n52
Scarritt College (Nashville, Tennessee), 50, 61, 126, 184, 192–93, 264–65, 266, 269n32
Schutt, Jane, 286n26, 289n55
Scottsboro Case, 140, 245
Segregation: damages of, on blacks and whites, 14, 32, 40, 43–44, 48, 73, 138, 146, 161–62, 193, 201; as disease, 48, 73, 138, 146, 219–20, 274n92; laws, 6, 16–17, 64, 72, 102, 107, 121, 135, 191, 216; and southern culture, 6–8, 33, 37–38, 43, 142–43, 160, 225–26; and southern society, 14–15, 57, 146, 270n49, 275n1; as violation of democratic ideals, 84, 90, 95, 97, 108, 152, 156, 219–22
Sellers, Thomas Jerome, 19, 142
Selma, Alabama, 135, 222, 291nn5,6
Senate Internal Security Subcommittee (SISS), 108, 149–51
"Sex and Caste," 213–14, 258–59
Sexism, 213–16, 218, 233, 237, 240, 243–44, 300nn1,66, 304n52
Sherrod, Charles, 1
Shirah, Sam, 197
Sibley Commission, 287n42
Sisterhood, 73–74, 99, 103, 218, 233, 158–66, 279n38; and 1960s civil rights movement, 181, 204–16; and women's movement, 240, 301n1
Sit-in movement, 123, 135–36, 181–83; white women's participation in, 185–86, 188, 191, 199–200, 209, 256, 260–61, 263, 298n53
Smith, Elizabeth, 64
Smith, Fay, 102
Smith, Lillian, 13, 52, 81, 83, 157, *168*, 179, 219, 249, 253, 269n32; anti-Communism of, 90, 154, 292n15, 293n40; on Association of Southern Women for the Prevention of Lynching, 78, 80; biographical sketch of, 263; and *Brown* decision, 97, 101; friendships between other women and, 118, 163, 299n60; as moral radical, 95, 137–47, 283nn85,86; as role model, 206, 209, 212, 299n55; on segregationist culture, 8, 15–16, 30, 32–34, 42–44, 47–48, 93–95, 226–27; and southern liberals, 223, 292n24; and southern patriarchy, 24, 218, 235–36, 269–70n42, 283n85; on women, 93–94, 124, 126, 160, 162–63, 225
Snelling, Paula, 94, 235, 263
Social Gospel, 50, 62–67, 69, 277nn11,12
Southern Christian Leadership Conference (SCLC), 134–35, 151, 191, 210; white women's involvement with, 54, 122, 181, 184, 189, 193, 258, 263–64
Southern Commission on the Study on Lynching, 75
Southern Conference Educational Fund (SCEF), 135, 147–54, 223, 257, 265, 293n29, 304n47; Anne Braden's work with, 147–49, 152, *170*, 179, 196–97, 203, 209, 237, 240, 242, 255, 299n56; Communists, tolerance of, 149, 152, 154, 158, 293n40
Southern Conference for Human Welfare (SCHW), 82, 91, 151, 153, 281n60, 282n77; white women's involvement with, 87–89, 93, 106, 147–48, 257, 261, 265
Southern identity, 1–2, 4, 6, 19, 28–30, 50, 93, 217, 226–29, 239, 246; versus non-southern identity, 22, 79, 219–22, 224–25, 230–33
Southern liberalism, 67, 82, 95, 222–23
Southern liberals, 82, 91, 93, 98, 136, 283n86; white integrationist women's criticism of, 20, 95, 138–39, 144–46, 154, 220–21, 292n24
Southern Patriot, 148, 154, *170*, 209, 255–56, 299n56
Southern Project. *See* Southern Student Human Relations Project (SSHRP)

Southern Regional Council (SRC), 115, 117, 129, 135, 154, 282n78, 293n40; and Councils on Human Relations, 103–4, 158; white women's involvement with, 91–92, 100–101, 208, 222–23, 260, 264–65, 283n81

Southern Student Human Relations Project (SSHRP), 182–83, 186, 189, 195–96, 198, 207, 256

Southern Student Organizing Committee (SSOC), 196–200, 209, 240, 243, 256, 264, 297n35, 299n56

Southern Summer School for Women Workers in Industry, 64, 89, 277n18

Southern Wrongs to Civil Rights, From, 238, 262

Spearman, Alice. *See* Wright, Alice Norwood Spearman

Stanley, Thomas B., 113, 142

Stembridge, Jane, 47, 232; biographical sketch of, 263; and southern sisterhood, 205–6, 209, 275n103, 298nn48,49; and Student Nonviolent Coordinating Committee, 185, 189, 195, 203

Stevens, Thelma, 42, 90, 100, 109, 146, 278n27; biographical sketch of, 264; college experience of, 50, 269n32; as female leader, 73, 102, 111–12

Strauss, Lynne, 200

Student Christian Movement, 48, 51, 180, 183, 295n3

Student Nonviolent Coordinating Committee (SNCC), 295nn4,14, 297n35; Christianity and nonviolence in, 48, 188–92, 296n21; impact and meaning of, for white women, 201–3, 241, 249; older white women's support of, 122, 140, 157, 289n55; radicalism of, 38, 54, 135–36, 197, 223, 290n66; and sexism, 54–55, 213–16, 237, 275n106, 300n66; and Southern Conference Educational Fund, 148–49, 151; and southern sisterhood, 204–9, 299n56; white women's status and role in, 192–99, 232; young white women's involvement with, 179–88, 256, 258–59, 263–65

Students for a Democratic Society (SDS), 183–84, 197, 206, 214, 242, 256, 258; and SNCC, 191, 199, 296n21

Suasion, 58, 79, 90, 99, 109, 180, 224

Swanson, Gregory, 20, 35–36, 142

Talbert, Mary, 75
Talmadge, Eugene, 63
Talmadge, Herman, 105, 108
Tatum, Noreen, 102
Terry, Adolphine, 41–42, 89, 104, 127, *169*, 234; biographical sketch of, 264; and Women's Emergency Committee, 110–11, 114–15, 117–19, 229
Thoreau, Henry, 141, 191
Thrasher, Sue, 13, 46–48, 209–10, 236, 304–5n52; biographical sketch of, 264; civil rights movement, involvement with, 184, 190, 192–93, 196–98, 200–202; and women's movement, 241, 243, 245
Thurmond, Strom, 108, 284–85n10
Till, Emmett, 21, 245–46
Tillich, Paul, 189–90
Tilly, Dorothy, 47, 81, 93, 103, 146, 158, *167*, 279n32; biographical sketch of, 264; early work as churchwoman, 70–71, 73, 76, 279n32; federal government, work with, 89–90, 100, 302n12; and Fellowship of the Concerned, 100–102, 139, 285n13; as lady activist, 124, 126, 128–29, 131; and massive resistance, 108–9, 111–12; and South, 223–25; and Southern Regional Council, 91–92, 100–101
Tilly, Milton, 126
Tougaloo Southern Christian College, 185–87, 194, 199, 259, 261
Truman, Harry, 71, 90, 95, 131, 141, 147, 159, 264, 284n10

United Church Women (UCW), 48, 72–73, 99–104, 141, 108–9, 111, 127–29, 284n8; members of, 257, 261, 265, 266
United Confederate Veterans, 22
United Council of Church Women (UCCW), 72–73
United Daughters of the Confederacy, 22

University of North Carolina, 222, 274n97
University of Virginia, 35, 142
Urban League, 20, 93, 102, 107, 117, 122, 124, 262
U.S. Commission on Civil Rights, 143, 255

Vandiver, Ernest, 287n42
Virginia Commission on Public Education. *See* Gray Commission
Virginia Committee for Public Schools (VCPS), 112, 114, 117, 120, 286n35, 288n46, 289n59
Voting registration, 89, 135–36, *176*, 184, 187, 194–95
Voting Rights Act (1965), 4, 136

Wade, Andrew, 146, 152
Wade, Charlotte, 146
Wallace, Henry, 147, 156, 282n76
Wall Between, The, 146, 153, 209, 226, 236, 256
Wansley, Thomas, 246
Washington, Cynthia, 241, 301n1
Waveland retreat, 213–15, 275nn105,106
Webb, Elizabeth (Betty), 62–64
Wells, Ida B., 280n40
White Citizens' Councils, 97, 108–9, 111, 284n3
White Southern Student Project, 197
White supremacy: ideology of, 1, 12, 14, 19, 73, 77, 225, 229; and lynching, 34, 77, 164–65; restoration of, 17, 27, 30, 57; and white southern womanhood, 12–13, 22–23, 26–27, 29, 52, 56, 96, 159, 162, 164–65, 204, 236, 251, 272n59
White women: activism of, 4, 7–9, 74, 91–92, 116, 124–32, 159, 180–81, 190, 192, 203, 219, 233; networks of, 7, 9, 51, 59, 64, 73, 91–92, 112, 128, 133, 282–83n81; as oppressors, 31, 41, 68–69, 194–95, 251–54; relationships between black men and, 17, 33–38, 97, 245–48, 271nn55,58; relationships between black women and, 29–33, 38, 68, 102–3, 243–44, 270nn46,51; as victims, 8, 39, 78–79, 160–62, 226, 270n45; as victims and oppressors, 1, 9, 23, 34, 159, 217, 246–47, 252–53. *See also* Womanhood, white southern
Wilkins, Josephine, 91–93, 152, 158–59, 163, 223, 282–83nn81,82; biographical sketch of, 265; pre-*Brown* activism of, 85–87, 234, 282–83n81; and Southern Conference for Human Welfare, 83, 88–89, 148
Williams, Aubrey, 87, 149, 151–52
Williams, Frances, 63
Womanhood, white southern, 2, 12, 204; ideal and constraints of, 13, 25–27, 120, 163–64, 272n59; and interconnection of race, gender, and sex, 4, 8, 23, 53, 56, 73, 164, 244, 300n11, 304n52; lynching as defense of, 34, 75–80, 96, 165, 217, 239, 246, 271–72n58; marriage and, 25, 125–26, 205, 212; paradox of, 34, 131, 159, 217, 247, 252–54; redefinition of, after Reconstruction, 22–23, 29; re-appropriation of, by white women, 52–59, 130–33, 157–66, 210, 216, 235–39, 251–53. *See also* Ladyhood; Motherhood
Woman's Division of the Board of Missions of the Methodist Church (Woman's Division), 42, 48, 50, 59, 61, 73, 89–90, 100–102, 264, 278n27
Women. *See* Black women; Churchwomen; Jewish women; Methodist Women; White women
Women's Clubs, 76, 87, 103–4, 259, 265
Women's Division of the Democratic National Committee, 87, 234
Women's Emergency Committee to Open Our Schools (WEC), 104, 114–23, *169*, 182, 229, 264, 287nn40,41, 288nn45,46,50, 289n59; and lady activism, 125, 127, 130
Women's International League for Peace and Freedom, 141, 261, 265
Woods, Henry, 121
Woodward, C. Vann, 230–31
Woodward, Glenn, 230
Works Progress Administration, 85, 87, 265
World Conference on Women, 241
World War II, 38, 58, 82, 89–90, 94

Wright, Alice Norwood Spearman, 85, 87, 91; biographical sketch of, 265; as churchwoman, 65, 70, 73, 103–4, 278n20, 279n30; and 1960s civil rights movement, 122, 288n53; and South Carolina Council on Human Relations, 104, 283n82, 285n19
Wright, Skelly, 116

Young, Andrew, 195
Young, Louise, 50, 73, 76, 126; biographical sketch of, 265
Young Men's Christian Association, 295n3
Young Women's Christian Association (YWCA), 66–67, 85, 88–89, 96, 193, 210, 275n2; and antilynching movement, 76, 79; *Brown* decision, support of, 100, 102, 104, 107, 112, 117; female bonding in, 64, 74, 208, 298n53; individual members of, 256, 258–59, 261, 265–66; industrial branches, 64–65; racial progressivism of, 44, 48, 59–65, 71–73, 99, 185, 191, 275n2, 276nn3,4, 279n33, 302n19; southern branches, 276n8, 276–77n10; student branches, 51, 60–64, 72, 74, 135, 180, 183, 188, 228–29, 276n4, 295n3, 298n53

Zellner, Robert (Bob), 237, 303n37

ANNE STEFANI is professor of American studies at the University of Toulouse-Jean Jaurès, France. She is a specialist of the American South and southern history. After exploring the political and social dimensions of the segregationist system, she has focused on the intersection of gender and race in southern culture. Her research also has led her to study the civil rights movement extensively. She lives in France.

www.ingramcontent.com/pod-product-compliance
Lightning Source LLC
Chambersburg PA
CBHW031427160426
43195CB00010BB/640